South Asia
in the World

Syracuse University's South Asia Center has created a website called
Global South Asia (http://globalsouthasia.syr.edu/)
that augments the coverage in this book.

News from South Asia is regularly posted on the Facebook page South Asia SU.

—— **FOUNDATIONS IN GLOBAL STUDIES** ——

Series Editor: Valerie Tomaselli, MTM Publishing

The Regional Landscape

South Asia in the World: An Introduction
Editor: Susan Snow Wadley, Syracuse University

The Middle East in the World: An Introduction
Editor: Lucia Volk, San Francisco State University

South Asia
in the World

An Introduction

Edited by Susan Snow Wadley

M.E.Sharpe
Armonk, New York
London, England

The EuroSlavic fonts used to create this work are © 1986–2014 Payne Loving Trust.
EuroSlavic is available from Linguist's Software, Inc.,
www.linguistsoftware.com, P.O. Box 580, Edmonds, WA 98020-0580 USA
tel (425) 775-1130.

———— Maps by Joseph Stoll, Cartographer, Syracuse University ————

Library of Congress Cataloging-in-Publication Data

South Asia in the world : an introduction / editor Susan Snow Wadley ; contributors Sandeep Banerjee [and ten
others]
    pages cm.—(Foundations in global studies: the regional landscape)
Includes bibliographical references and index.
ISBN 978-0-7656-3966-0 (hardcover : alk. paper)—ISBN 978-0-7656-3967-7 (paperback : alk. paper)
1. South Asia—History. 2. South Asia—Social conditions. I. Wadley, Susan Snow, 1943–

DS340.S664 2014
954—dc23   2013021142

Printed in the United States of America

The paper used in this publication meets the minimum requirements of
American National Standard for Information Sciences
Permanence of Paper for Printed Library Materials,
ANSI Z 39.48-1984.

GP (c)   10   9   8   7   6   5   4   3   2   1
GP (p)   10   9   8   7   6   5   4   3   2   1

Contents

About This Book

South Asia in the World: An Introduction—the first book in the M.E. Sharpe series, Foundations in Global Studies: The Regional Landscape—provides a fresh, systematic, and comprehensive overview of South Asia. Comprising (in order of population size) India, Pakistan, Bangladesh, Afghanistan, Nepal, Sri Lanka, Bhutan, and the Maldives, the South Asia under consideration here is a diverse and complex region. The variations in its social, cultural, economic, and political life are explored within the context of the globalizing forces affecting all regions of the world.

In a simple strategy that all books in the series employ, this volume begins with foundational material (including chapters on history, language, and, in the case of South Asia, religion), moves to a discussion of globalization, and then focuses the investigation more specifically through the use of case studies. The set of case studies exposes readers to various disciplinary lenses that bring the region to life through subjects of high interest and importance to today's readers. Among others, these topics include sex trafficking in Nepal; ethnic conflict in Sri Lanka; drone warfare in the Pakistani-Afghani border region; and the history and cultural context of Bollywood.

In addition to her own contributions, editor Susan Snow Wadley, the Ford Maxwell Professor of South Asian Studies at Syracuse University, has assembled a team of specialists to contribute to the volume; nearly all are faculty, alumni, or current doctoral students of Syracuse's South Asia Program. The team represents the full range of disciplines brought to bear in the study of South Asia, including, among others, anthropology, communications and media, geography and the environment, geopolitics and international affairs, history, political economy, and sociology.

Resource boxes, an important feature of this book, are included to preserve currency and add utility. They offer links that point readers to sources—mostly online—on the topics discussed. The links, which include connections to timely data, reports on recent events, official sites, local and country-based media, and visual material, establish a rich archive of additional material for readers to draw on. The URLs included are known to be current as of March 1, 2013, and in the case of expired URLs, enough information has been provided for the reader to locate the same, or similarly useful, resources.

A special website, Global South Asia (http://globalsouthasia.syr.edu/), developed by Syracuse University's South Asia Center and under Wadley's direction, will also augment the reader's research capacity. The site includes additional graphics and other materials to complement several of the chapters in this book.

Outreach Activities for Teaching

The National Resource Centers for South Asia, funded by Title VI of the Higher Education Act of 1965, provide outreach activities for teaching at all levels. Most of the centers have film libraries, offer various workshops, provide school visits, and more. In this text, films marked with an asterisk (*) are available for the cost of return postage from the South Asia Center, Syracuse University.

As of 2013, the Title VI NRC South Asia centers are located at the following universities:

Columbia University, South Asia Institute	http://sai.columbia.edu/
Cornell University, Center for International Studies, South Asia Program	http://sap.einaudi.cornell.edu/
Syracuse University, Moynihan Institute, South Asia Center	http://www.maxwell.syr.edu/ moynihan/programs/sac/
University of California, Berkeley, Center for South Asia Studies	http://southasia.berkeley.edu/
University of Chicago, South Asia Language & Area Center (SALAC)	http://southasia.uchicago.edu/
University of Michigan, Center for South Asia Studies	http://www.ii.umich.edu/csas/
University of Pennsylvania, South Asia Center	http://www.southasiacenter.upenn. edu/
University of Texas at Austin, South Asia Institute	http://www.utexas.edu/cola/insts/ southasia/
University of Washington, South Asia Center	http://jsis.washington.edu/soasia/
University of Wisconsin, Center for South Asia	http://www.southasia.wisc.edu/

South Asia
in the World

1

Introducing South Asia

Susan Snow Wadley

South Asia is a region of contrasts, ranging from the world's tallest point, Mount Everest in Nepal, to the country with the lowest "high" point, the island nation of the Maldives (see topographical map). Located in the Indian Ocean off the southwest coast of India, the Maldives reaches only 8 feet (2.4 meters) above sea level at its highest point. South Asia has deserts in the northwest and heavy rain forests in the eastern regions. The climate ranges from extreme cold in the north to tropical in the south. Some areas face yearly droughts, while others have some of the world's heaviest rainfalls. In this age of global warming, the northern areas face the loss of snowmelt and glaciers, creating problems for agriculture and populations downstream. The islanders of the Maldives face the loss of their lands due to rising oceans. Two South Asian nations have a nuclear bomb, and two have Maoist insurgencies. The glitz and dance styles of Bollywood movies are now better known across the globe than the poverty of the region's rural farmers.

South Asia is composed of eight countries with a wide range of demographic features (Table 1.1). India is by far the most populous nation in the region. Indeed, it is the world's second-largest country by population, with 1.2 billion inhabitants, whereas the Maldives ranks as the 176th country by population, with not quite 400,000 inhabitants. Literacy ranges from almost 94 percent in the Maldives to barely 28 percent in Afghanistan. Afghanistan and Nepal are the poorest nations, based on gross domestic product (GDP) per capita. Both have suffered from recent wars and instability, and their mountainous terrains hinder everything from transport to education, making development initiatives difficult. The small nations of Bhutan and the Maldives are the most prosperous, the former because of its hydroelectric dams, and the latter due to tourism.

Climate and Monsoons

The South Asian climate is influenced by the yearly monsoons, the seasonal changes in winds and rain. The western, or summer, monsoon arrives in June, sometimes lasting through October. Coming from the south across the Indian Ocean and Arabian Sea, it flows across the western regions, around the tip of India, and along the coastline of the Bay of Bengal, eventually reaching the northern and central parts of the country. Newspapers in the region give daily reports on the position of the monsoons and the all-important rains. In the northeast regions, the monsoon has been known to dump more than 400 inches

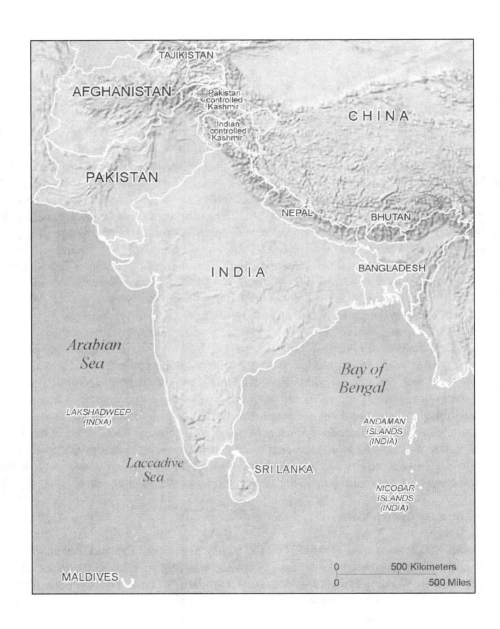

Table 1.1

Selected Demographic Factors, Countries of South Asia, Compared to the United States

Country	Population (2012)	Literacy (percent of total population)	Population under age 25 (percent of total)	Population growth rate (percent)
India	1,205,073,612	61.0	47.5	1.312
Pakistan	190,291,129	54.9	56.4	1.551
Bangladesh	161,083,804	56.8	52.4	1.579
Afghanistan	30,419,928	28.1	64.8	2.220
Nepal	29,890,686	60.3	56.0	1.768
Sri Lanka	21,481,334	91.2	40.2	.913
Bhutan	716,896	47.0	49.4	1.175
Maldives	394,451	93.8	46.1	−.127
United States	**313,847,465**	**99.0**	**33.8**	**.900**

Source: Compiled from the CIA *World Factbook*, https://www.cia.gov/library/publications/the-world-factbook/wfbExt/region_sas.html, accessed February 14, 2013.

(10,000 centimeters) of rain in a month, while some western desert regions often receive only 4 inches (10 centimeters) of rain a year. The southern regions receive their rainfall during the winter, or dry, monsoon, which is based on air flows coming across the Asian landmass and the Bay of Bengal. Over the bay, the winds pick up moisture, which provides the rainfall for Sri Lanka and southern India.

The monsoons and temperature changes produce three seasons, each about four months long, in most of South Asia: the hot, wet, and humid rainy season; the cold winters in the northern regions (New Delhi, the capital of India, reaches temperatures of 35 degrees Fahrenheit [1.67 C] in December and January, while Kabul and the Himalayas get snow); and a dry, very hot summer, with temperatures reaching daytime highs of 120 degrees Fahrenheit (49 C) in many regions. Farming also has three seasons: in the north there are the wet-season (July–October) crops of rice and corn; winter-season (November–February) crops of wheat, barley, and mustard seed; and hot-season (March–June) crops of melons and cucumbers. Most agriculture is still heavily dependent on the rains, though irrigation is important, especially since many of the new seeds used for wheat and other crops demand more water and chemical fertilizers than traditional seeds. Irrigation, however, produces other long-term effects. In particular, the water table in areas of heavy irrigation is falling significantly, requiring deeper wells to be dug and raising questions about the long-term sustainability of these irrigation and farming practices.

Population Diversity

The northern mountain barriers and the long seacoast have significantly influenced the history of South Asia. While there was trading between South Asia and the Middle East by 2500 BCE, as well as across the Bay of Bengal to Southeast Asia by 500 BCE, the most significant early human incursions came from across the mountains to the northwest. The

Traditional forms of irrigation included step wells, often built by local rulers as a social service for their subjects, such as this one in the Indian state of Rajasthan. Water was channeled into the well during the monsoon, and as it was used and evaporated over the ensuing months, the steps provided access to the water for those willing to climb down and then up again with their heavy pots. *(Photo by Victor Yu-Juei Tzen. Used by permission.)*

earliest human populations were those whose descendants now make up the so-called tribal populations of the area. They were followed by populations speaking Dravidian languages, whose descendants now live primarily in the southern portions of the subcontinent. By 2500 BCE there was an active literate civilization (whose script is yet to be deciphered), known as the Indus Valley Civilization, in the northwestern regions, with cities, trade via sea and overland routes to the Middle East, and agricultural surpluses.

As seen in Chapter 3, the passes through the mountains were also the routes taken by the Aryans and Alexander the Great in the period before the Common Era and by the various Muslim invaders after the ninth century CE. Only with oceangoing technologies of the Europeans in the sixteenth century were the coasts opened up to significant incursions from outsiders. Nevertheless, Jews and Christians as well as Arabs from East Africa and the Middle East reached the southwestern coasts long before the Europeans, bringing with them religious traditions still present in the subcontinent.

Approximately 31 percent of the world's Muslims live in South Asia, and 99 percent of the world's Hindus. Two countries, Sri Lanka and Bhutan, have majority Buddhist populations. Religious violence remains a major issue in several countries. In India, this takes the form of communal conflicts between Hindus and Muslims. In other countries, sectarian violence occurs, such as that prevalent in Pakistan between Sunni and Shia Muslims, and in Afghanistan between the Taliban and more moderate Muslims. Both Nepal and Sri Lanka recently emerged from long civil wars (in 2006 and 2009, respectively), with the Sri Lankan war fought between Tamil-speaking Hindus and Sinhalese-speaking Buddhists, while the Nepal war was a Maoist-led insurgency.

Except for two years of "Emergency Rule" in the 1970s, India has had an actively functioning democracy, with high voter turnouts in elections, since the nation won its independence in 1947. Other countries have faced invasions, as in Afghanistan; shifts between democratic and military rule, as in Pakistan and Bangladesh; and coups, as in the Maldives in 2012. Bhutan, long a monarchy, instituted democratic institutions beginning in 2007.

> For an interactive site with information on South Asia, including its geography, populations, economies, and more, see the online CIA publication *The World Factbook* (https://www.cia.gov/library/publications/the-world-factbook/wfbExt/region_sas.html).

Core Social Patterns

Most of South Asia shares several features of social structure, including a strong focus on hierarchy. Much of the region retains a system of patriarchy, with joint family structures and the resulting oppression of women, and often a feudal-like land system, with large landholdings and tenant farmers. The Hindu caste system is the most dominant form of hierarchy in the subcontinent, while the Muslim hierarchy is focused on where and how and when a person became a Muslim (with descendants of those who converted to Islam having the lowest status, and those claiming to be descended from the Prophet Muhammad having the highest). Many Dalits (formerly "untouchables") have sought to escape the caste system completely by converting to Buddhism, although the realities of daily life make this escape all but impossible.

Male dominance is pervasive in South Asia, although females in Hinduism are given powers as goddesses. The male gods in Hinduism are thought to be inert and powerless without their female consorts, who control the Shakti, or powers, of the universe. In the

Box 1.1

Female Heads of State in South Asia

Bangladesh	Kaleda Zia, 1991–1996, 2001–2006
	Sheikh Hasina Wazed, 1996–2001, 2009–
India	Indira Gandhi, 1966–1977, 1980–1984 (assassinated 1984)
Pakistan	Benazir Bhutto, 1988–1990, 1993–1996 (assassinated 2007)
Sri Lanka	Sirimavo Bandaranaika, 1960–1965, 1970–1979, 1994–2000
	Chandrik Bandaranaika Kumaratunga, 1994–2005 (first three months as prime minister, then as president)

human realm, Hindu brides are considered to be Lakshmi, the goddess of prosperity, so that any good—or bad—that comes to that family after the marriage is attributed to its women. In the 1970s, before the Emergency in India, Prime Minister Indira Gandhi was thought to be the somewhat benevolent goddess Durga, but after she invoked emergency powers in 1977, she was envisioned as the malevolent goddess Kali.

Islamic traditions allow polygamous marriages, but some protections are provided to women through the dowry system. Nevertheless, Muslim women face enormous discrimination in education and job opportunities, though significantly less than Muslim women in the Middle East. Pakistani women serve in the military and are members of Parliament; Benazir Bhutto twice served as the nation's prime minister (1988–1990 and 1993–1996). Bangladesh, India, Pakistan, and Sri Lanka have all had female heads of state.

The ideal structure for most families of any religion in South Asia is a joint family headed by the senior male, who with his wife rules over sons, their wives, and grandchildren. Although many women are clearly oppressed and often denied the educational opportunities enjoyed by men, individual women have always had power in some families and communities. Historically, land passed from father to sons, and only recently have laws been passed giving women rights to land. Variations occur, so that in one part of Kerala, in southern India, a matrilineal caste (the Nayars) has an inheritance system whereby land goes from mother to daughter, although the brother still is the most powerful figure in the household. Islam allows polygyny, although most men cannot afford more than one wife. In some Hindu communities in the Himalayan region, polyandry—having more than one husband—is the ideal form of marriage.

Rules regarding women's work also vary: some communities permit women to work in agriculture, while others, usually of the higher classes, forbid it. Growing rice requires

Box 1.2

Important Books and Films on Social and Economic Relations

No Shame for the Sun: Lives of Professional Pakistani Women, by Shahla Haeri (Syracuse, NY: Syracuse University Press, 2002), counters the prevalent view of women in South Asian Muslim communities.

The now classic film on joint families in South Asia is *Dadi's Family*,* directed by Michael Camerini and Rina Gill, and coproduced by Michael Camerini and James MacDonald (DER Films, 1981). It is available through the outreach centers of many university South Asia programs.

For a moving example of feudalism tied to hierarchy, see the short story "Paddy Seeds" by Mahasweta Devi in *Of Women, Outcastes, Peasants, and Rebels: A Selection of Bengali Short Stories*, edited and translated by Kalpana Bardhan (Berkeley: University of California Press, 1990).

For a film that captures the relationships between landlord and tenants, see *The Prince** (Life on the Edge Series 6, by TV/e, http://tve.org/films/the-prince/index.html), about a Pakistani landlord who seeks to help the peasants who work his land meet the United Nations Millennium Development Goals by obtaining a good water source, yet refusing to help to open the broken-down school belonging to the village.

Note: Films marked with an asterisk (*) are available from the South Asia Center, Syracuse University (http://www.maxwell.syr.edu/moynihan/programs/sac/).

more intensive labor than growing wheat, as paddy plants must be placed one by one in flooded rice fields. There is evidence that women in rice-growing areas have higher status vis-à-vis men than do women in wheat-growing areas. Evidence of this is seen in the skewed sex ratios across South Asia, with more women surviving to adulthood in the rice-growing areas than in the wheat-growing areas. (The sex ratio in India in 2011 was 914 females per 1,000 males, considerably lower than in most of the rest of the world, indicating that the mere survival of females is an issue. See case studies in Chapters 8 and 16.) Further complicating the picture, especially for rural areas, are rules for purdah, the practice of curtailing women's movements in both Hindu and Muslim upper-class rural and often urban families (see Chapter 8). In modern urban South Asia, many women continue to face conflicts surrounding work, as seen in Chapter 18 about the information technology (IT) industry in the southern city of Bangalore.

Literature and the Arts

Given a civilization that goes back close to 5,000 years, it is not surprising that South Asia has long traditions of art, music, and literature. From the figurines of the Indus Valley Civilization to the paintings of M.F. Husain (1915–2011) and the sitar music of Ravi Shankar (1920–2012), the arts in South Asia have offered much to the world. Many of these traditions are regional, as in the distinctions between northern and southern Indian

---

Box 1.3

Musical Styles Move East and West

While Indian middle class youth borrowed the styles of western rock music
in the 1960s, the Beatles added Indian musical styles to their repertoires
as well a concern for South Asian peoples; this led to the album "The
Concert for Bangladesh" at the time of the birth of the Bangladesh nation
in 1971 and the title song by George Harrison with strong Indian musical
overtones. In the 1990s, the British-born Indian rapper known as Apache
Indian created rap music with Indian themes connected to his heritage,
focusing on issues such as arranged marriages. More recently, Indian dance
styles borrowed from Bollywood films appear on shows such as *So You
Think You Can Dance.*

---

musical traditions or the *ghazals* (poems) of Afghanistan and Pakistan and the songs
of Rabindranath Tagore (1816–1941) in Bengal. The successive incursions into South
Asia brought new forms of art that became incorporated into local tradition, such as the
Gandhara Buddhas, which were heavily influenced by the Greek styles of Alexander the
Great; the brass band music borrowed from the British that accompanies most weddings
throughout the subcontinent; and the rock music of the Beatles and modern hip-hop that
influences both Bollywood film music and local pop bands. At the same time, South Asian
traditions have expanded the music and arts of the rest of the world, with George Harrison's "Bangladesh" and the Bollywood dances on modern American television shows
being just two examples.

Each of the many South Asian languages has developed its own literary traditions,
including Sanskrit religious verse and plays, Tamil devotional poems, Bengali love
lyrics and praise poems, and Hindi oral epics. Some were recorded thousands of years
ago, while others remain active oral traditions. Those who conquered various regions
of South Asia introduced new styles and new languages, so that the literature of the
Mughal court is often in Persian, though these are sometimes translations and rein-
terpretations of Sanskrit works. The British brought English and the literary style of
the novel, now one of the most prolific forms of writing in South Asia; South Asian
authors such as Salman Rushdie, Arundhati Roy, and Kiran Desai regularly contend
for the Booker Prize and other literary awards. One of the most famous modern literary
events, possibly the largest in the world, is the Jaipur Literature Festival held yearly in
the Rajasthan city of Jaipur.

The Challenges Ahead

As revealed in the case studies in Part Four, the challenges facing the South Asian subcontinent are many. While India remains the world's largest democracy, Sri Lanka is moving toward authoritarian rule. The conflict over Kashmir continues the tension between

Box 1.4

Examples of Literary Fiction

An accessible work by Salman Rushdie is *Haroun and the Sea of Stories* (London: Penguin, 1991), a novella about a young boy, Haroun, whose father loses his ability to tell stories because of the poisoning of the Ocean of Stories by the evil Khatam Shud, who wishes to end all storytelling forever. The work is a compelling tribute to the value of stories and storytelling.

An early novel, composed in Bengali in 1929, is *Pather Panchali (The Song of the Road)* by Bibhutibhushan Bandyopadhyay. The film version, directed by Satyajit Ray in 1955, became the best-known Indian-made film in the West in the 1960s. The film is available on YouTube (http://www.youtube.com/watch?v=IF7TlxUUFsA).

A more recent novel that provides a glimpse of the culture of southern India as well as its history is Padma Viswanathan's *The Toss of a Lemon* (Orlando, FL: Harcourt, 2008).

India and Pakistan, both nuclear powers, while the residents of the Kashmir Valley (the world's most militarized zone) remain victims of Indian occupation and frequent curfews and searches.

While some communities prosper, such as those working in the IT industry, tourism, or Bollywood, farmer suicides and debates about the use of genetically modified seeds have led many critics to worry about an agrarian crisis. Global warming will continue to present new challenges. For several countries, economic growth is strongly positive, though the gaps between rich and poor are significant.

In February 2013, the International Crisis Group issued a report, *Sri Lanka's Authoritarian Turn: The Need for International Action*, detailing the current situation in Sri Lanka. It can be found on the group's website (http://www.crisisgroup.org/en/regions/asia/south-asia/sri-lanka).

Poverty levels and the prospects for economic growth vary drastically across the region (Table 1.2). Afghanistan's projected growth rate is artificially inflated due to the infusion of foreign aid monies and foreign military expenditures through 2014. Bhutan benefits from its hydroelectric dams coming on line. Sri Lanka's robust growth rate is substantiated by the data on the growth of the industrial and service sectors and the remarkably low poverty rate of 8.9 percent, which is much lower than the U.S. rate of 15.1 percent. The industrial sectors of the United States and Sri Lanka are comparable, at 20.3 and 25.8 percent, respectively; but Sri Lanka retains a strong agricultural workforce

Table 1.2

Selected Economic Factors, South Asia–U.S. Comparison

Country	GDP per capita, in US$, est. for 2012	GDP increase, est. for 2012 (%)	Percent of labor force in agriculture	Percent of labor force in services	Percent of labor force in industry	Percent of population below the poverty line
India	3,900	5.4	53.0	28.0	19.0	29.8
Pakistan	2,900	3.7	45.1	34.2	20.7	22.3
Bangladesh	2,000	6.1	45.0	25.0	30.0	31.5
Afghanistan	1,000	11.0	78.6	15.7	5.7	36.0
Nepal	1,300	4.6	75.0	18.0	7.0	25.2
Sri Lanka	6,100	6.8	31.8	42.4	25.8	8.9
Bhutan	6,500	9.9	43.7	17.2	39.1	23.2
Maldives	8,700	3.5	11.0	65.0	23.0	16.0
United States	**49,800**	**2.2**	**0.7**	**79.1**	**20.3**	**15.1**

Source: Compiled from the CIA *World Factbook*, https://www.cia.gov/library/publications/the-world-factbook/wfbExt/region_sas.html, accessed February 14, 2013.

(31.8 percent), while the United States does not (0.7 percent). Both the United States and Sri Lanka have low birth rates of .9 percent, while the Maldives has a declining population, marked by out-migration (see Table 1.1). These economic factors both influence and are heavily influenced by health care, demographic changes, and urbanization.

Health Care

South Asia now has one of the best health-care systems in the world—for the wealthy. "Medical tourism" is common in Bangladesh, India, and Pakistan. Europeans, Asians, Australians, and Americans travel to South Asia seeking kidney transplants, heart surgery, and surrogate mothers to bear their children. Yet for South Asians themselves, medical care, though vastly improved in the past fifty years, as seen in declining child mortality rates and an increase in the average life span, faces new challenges, as well as the persistent concerns of malnutrition and maternal mortality. While polio is considered to be eradicated and smallpox no longer exists, tuberculosis and HIV/AIDS exist at rates second only to Africa. New drug-resistant forms of malaria are rampant. Dengue fever, also a mosquito-borne disease, hits both urban and rural populations. Yet the countries of the area spend barely 3 percent of GDP on health care, compared to 8.2 percent globally.

The documentary film *Made in India** (2011, http://www.madeinindiamovie.com/), directed by Rebecca Haimowitz and Vaishali Sinha, deals with surrogacy in India.

Steen Jenson's *Organs for Sale** (2004, http://filmakers.com/index.php?a=filmDetail&filmID=1295), deals with kidney transplants in Pakistan.

In Indian-administered Kashmir, the Indian military occupation makes the region the most militarized in the world. *(Photo by Chris Giamo. Used by permission.)*

With the neoliberal economic changes of the 1990s, along with structural adjustment policies imposed by the World Bank and International Monetary Fund, the responsibility for health care has shifted from primarily the public sector to private enterprise. With little previous government expenditure on health care and a further decrease after 1990, space was created for private investment once the economies of the region began to prosper. Now the middle and upper classes use private providers, while the poor use poorly funded public health-care systems. For example, approximately 185,000 women in the South Asian region die during childbirth every year. The presence of skilled professionals at childbirth ranges from 19 percent in Nepal to almost 50 percent in India. Given inadequate sanitation, lack of clean water, and a dearth of medical professionals, especially in the rural areas, South Asia (with the exception of Sri Lanka) provides its citizens with vastly inadequate health care.

For an overview of health issues, see *2010 Public Health in South Asia*, a report of the CSIS Global Health Policy Center (http://csis.org/files/publication/100715_Hate_PublicHealthSouthAsia_Web.pdf).

Demographic Transition and the Youth Bulge

The South Asian countries, with the exception of Afghanistan, have all begun what is termed the "demographic transition," a shift from high fertility and high mortality rates to low ones. The demographic transition is marked by an improvement in child survival followed by fertility decline. In the 1950s, the infant mortality rate (those who died before turning one year old) in South Asia was 160 per 1,000; in 2012 it was 60 per 1,000. Although the infant mortality rate in Afghanistan remains high, at 150 per 1,000, Sri Lanka is exceptionally low at 15 per 1,000 (as of 2012). This increase in children's health care has the unintended initial effect of creating a population explosion. Families with high fertility rates—resulting from the need for a woman to give birth to many children in order to have some survive to adulthood—suddenly find themselves with five to seven living children, instead of the three to five that were the norm before the transition. Because of this increase in the number of living children, and new aspirations such as the need for education (which has a high cost per child), fertility then declines.

However, when the children born before fertility rates decline reach adulthood, even if they practice birth control, their sheer numbers result in another population bulge. It is that second bulge that is propelling the youth population numbers in South Asia today, as seen in Table 1.1. Afghanistan and Nepal, along with Pakistan and Bangladesh, have a youth population (under age twenty-five) of more than 50 percent. None of these countries has either an educational system (see the literacy rates in Table 1.1) or an industrial sector equipped to handle this burgeoning youth population.

To explain population growth and its long-term effects, the University of Missouri offers an online course, "Introduction to the Humanized Earth" (http://online. missouri.edu/exec/data/courses/2342/public/lesson02/lesson02.aspx), which compares countries across the globe.

The website of the Population Reference Bureau also provides an easily understandable interactive article dealing with population, "From Population Pyramids to Pillars" (http://www.prb.org/Articles/2013/population-pyramids.aspx).

The U.S. Census Bureau provides an interactive website, the International Data Base (http://www.census.gov/population/international/data/idb/informationGateway.php), where users can compare population indices on various factors across the globe.

For more information on the effects of the youth bulge, see these two online essays:

- Justin Yifu Lin, "Youth Bulge: A Demographic Dividend or a Demographic Bomb in Developing Countries?" (http://blogs.worldbank.org/developmenttalk/ youth-bulge-a-demographic-dividend-or-a-demographic-bomb-in-developing-countries).
- Isabel Ortiz and Matthew Cummins, "When the Global Crisis and Youth Bulge Collide: Double the Jobs Trouble for Youth" (http://www.unicef.org/socialpolicy/ files/Global_Crisis_and_Youth_Bulge_-_FINAL.pdf).

The youth bulge has long-term social and economic consequences. If jobs are available and this young population gains employment, the youth bulge can lead to economic prosperity, as more income will be generated and reinvested in the economy. But most of those entering the workforce in South Asia and other developing countries are unable to find jobs, and the jobs that are available often pay poorly. In South Asia, 77 percent of those employed face vulnerable employment, comprising low-paying jobs, poor working conditions, and minimal workers' rights. Within households, the effects of unemployment are felt in hunger, child malnutrition, low educational levels, and often child abandonment (for one pattern, see Chapter 15 on sex trafficking in Nepal). Women and children are those most affected by poor health and hunger. Migrants and refugees are particularly vulnerable, facing difficulties related to both physical and mental health. It is estimated that 1.1 billion new workers will enter the world's workforce between 2012 and 2020. Hence, employment of the world's youth is perhaps the foremost problem facing all societies, especially those of South Asia.

Urbanization

Five of the twelve largest urban agglomerations are in South Asia: Mumbai, Delhi, and Kolkata in India, Dhaka in Bangladesh, and Karachi in Pakistan. India has fifty more cities with populations above 1 million, while Pakistan has three others and Bangladesh has two others. Dhaka, with a population of 14 million in 2009, is the fastest growing city in the world. Urban areas in India provide 65 percent of its gross national product (GNP). Karachi alone, with a population of 21 million, is estimated to provide 60 to 70 percent of Pakistan's national revenue. Urbanization is increasing across South Asia, bringing some pockets of prosperity and many issues of health, sanitation, and infrastructural development (Table 1.3).

Unfortunately, urban infrastructure and planning are often lacking, leading to a deteriorating urban environment across the subcontinent. Even in Bangalore, one of the centers of India's burgeoning IT industry (see Chapter 18), more than one-third of its residents live in slums. In Bangladesh, 5 million of Dhaka's residents lack access to public toilets. Dhaka's forty-seven public toilets are clearly inadequate. Millions, in Dhaka and across South Asia, are forced to defecate in public, using roadsides, empty fields, alleys, or drainage ditches, adding to the public health challenges.

Delhi provides an example of urbanization gone awry. Since the 1980s, the nearby rural community of Gurgaon, some 15 miles (24 kilometers) south of New Delhi, the national capital of India, has grown to be a satellite city of some 1.5 million residents, with a 70 percent growth rate since 2001. Land sells for astronomical sums, yet 50 percent of the residents live in slums. At the same time, Gurgaon has more than twenty-five malls selling products by companies such as Chanel and Louis Vuitton, as well as less pricey brands like Benetton, Urban Outfitters, and Nike. As Jim Yardley notes, "Gurgaon . . . would seem to have everything, except . . . a functioning citywide sewer or drainage system; reliable electricity or water; and public sidewalks, adequate parking, decent roads or any citywide system of public transportation" ("In India, Dynamism

Table 1.3

Urbanization in South Asia, 2010

	Urban population, 2010 (percent)	Urban annual growth rate, est. for 2010–2015 (percent)
Afghanistan	23	4.7
Bangladesh	28	3.1
Bhutan	35	3.1
India	30	2.4
Maldives	40	4.5
Nepal	19	4.7
Pakistan	36	3.1
Sri Lanka	14	1.1

Source: Compiled from the CIA *World Factbook*, https://www.cia.gov/library/publications/the-world-factbook/wfbExt/region_sas.html, accessed February 1, 2013.

Wrestles with Dysfunction," *New York Times*, June 8, 2011). Given Gurgaon's unreliable electricity and insufficient or failing infrastructure, large diesel generators provide electricity when the grid fails, while private bus companies transport workers to the city's industries and offices. Water scarcity persists, with private companies providing water via tanker trucks. Thus, private enterprise has filled the gaps left by inadequate government planning.

Searchlight South Asia (http://urbanpoverty.intellecap.com/), a monthly online magazine funded by the Rockefeller Foundation, provides insight into urban poverty trends in Bangladesh, India, Nepal, and Pakistan.

Summing Up

Urbanization, a burgeoning population, a youth bulge, and inadequate educational and health-care facilities: these are the challenges facing South Asia in the twenty-first century. Some of these needs are being addressed by the private and nongovernmental organization (NGO) sectors, but others demand government intervention and planning. Economic growth and a large middle class provide some balance to the problems still facing the region. Much of this growth is fueled by globalization, as seen in the case studies below.

Organization of This Book

The following chapter provides some background on the study of South Asia. The next group of chapters presents the basics: a brief history of South Asia followed by chapters on the region's languages and religions (emphasizing recent history and political conflicts).

The book then turns directly to modern South Asia, focusing extensively on issues surrounding globalization. An introduction to globalization is followed by eleven case studies representing a variety of disciplinary approaches. The cases were chosen to illustrate some of the current issues facing South Asia, introduce the best of recent scholarship, and, to the extent possible, highlight the countries that form the South Asian region. (While there are no cases related to Bhutan or the Maldives, these countries are discussed in other sections of this book.)

2

A Short History of South Asian Studies

SUSAN SNOW WADLEY

The study of South Asia by the West developed in conjunction with colonialism, although one of the first scholars to examine life in South Asia was the eleventh-century Persian scholar Abū Rayhān al-Bīrūnī, whose book *Tahqīq mā li-l-hind min maqūlah maqbūlah fī al-ʻaql aw mardhūlah* (Verifying All That the Indians Recount, the Reasonable and the Unreasonable) was a compendium of all that he knew about India from his travels there. Many consider it the first work of Indology, while others think of it as the first anthropology of India.

The first European writers about South Asia were missionaries and colonial administrators. The American missionary J.A. Dubois wrote *Description of the Character, Manners, and Customs of the People of India; and of Their Institutions, Religious and Civil* in 1817. In 1930 Americans William and Charlotte Wiser wrote *Behind Mud Walls*, a book on rural India that was still used in U.S. classrooms in the early twenty-first century. Further, William Wiser's 1936 master's thesis for Cornell University, *The Hindu Jajmani System*, continues to be read and to generate discussion as the first detailed examination of this complex system of Indian patronage. In addition, numerous colonial bureaucrats wrote about the regions in which they served. Their works include R.C. Temple's three-volume *Legends of the Punjab* and H.A. Rose's three-volume *Glossary of the Tribes and Castes of the Punjab and North-West Frontier Province.*

Not surprisingly, given the colonial desire to exert control over the native populations, an early focus was on languages. The Indian elite with whom most Europeans had the greatest contact directed Western attention to their religious language, Sanskrit, which was also the language in which many legal texts of the region were written. Europeans quickly became fascinated with Sanskrit, in part because they discovered its historical connections to Greek and Latin, which opened up the field of Indo-European studies. The German-born Max Müller, the most renowned of these early scholars of Sanskrit, translated many Hindu religious texts that became part of the fifty volumes of *Sacred Books of the East*, published between 1879 and 1910.

Since much of the South Asian region was under Muslim rule at the time that colonialism began, other scholars learned Persian, which was the language of the Mughal courts. But very quickly the need to understand vernacular languages became apparent, leading to the formation of Fort William College in Kolkata in 1800. British recruits were trained at the college in the languages of South Asia, both Sanskrit and Persian, but also the many vernaculars. Here, too, many of the first grammars of these vernaculars were compiled.

South Asian studies as an academic field in the United States began with Sanskrit at Yale University. Elihu Yale, the founder of the university, had worked for the East Indian

Company for three decades in the seventeenth century, developing a special affinity for South Asia. Harvard University started offering Sanskrit in 1872, and the University of Chicago started offering Sanskrit when it opened in 1892, though for many years there were seldom more than two students a year studying it.

Philology and religion dominated the teaching of topics related to South Asia until after World War II. Schools such as the University of Chicago barely maintained a Sanskrit curriculum, but studies of religion, especially training to support the spread of Christianity, were popular. Prior to World War II, Americans primarily went abroad as missionaries. In 1919, the University of Chicago had forty-nine graduates working in British India, most as missionaries (including William and Charlotte Wiser, mentioned above).

World War II spurred many academics in the United States to learn about other civilizations. The immediate effect was seen in name changes, such as the shift at Harvard University from the Department of Indic Philology to the Department of Sanskrit and Indian Studies in 1951. There was also a shift to teaching languages other than Sanskrit, as well as other disciplines. One of the early visionaries was William Norman Brown, who started a program called "India: A Program of Regional Studies" at the University of Pennsylvania in the immediate postwar period. Others also recognized the need for increased study of the non-Western world, including South Asia. The Carnegie Foundation, Rockefeller Foundation, and Ford Foundation were supporting innovative programs to study various world regions by the 1960s. One early result was the book *Village India*, edited by McKim Marriott and published in 1955. At the University of Chicago, a three-term sequence on Indian civilization was developed in the 1950s and continues today. At Columbia University, Ainslee Embree and colleagues provided a badly needed interdisciplinary reader, *Sources of Indian Tradition*, in several volumes.

By the late 1950s, in the midst of the Cold War, the U.S. government also realized the need for study of neglected parts of the world. In 1958, the National Defense Education Act funded language study for graduate students coming from a variety of disciplines. The major universities quickly added Bengali, Hindi, and Tamil to their offerings, with pockets of Telegu, Urdu, and other even less commonly taught languages. The Ford Foundation funding for doctoral studies began to include a "pre-field" course of language study, usually in England, where the languages of South Asia were regularly taught.

In 1961, William Norman Brown and colleagues founded the American Institute of Indian Studies, which continues to this day as the primary organization around which studies of India flow. Comparable organizations for Pakistan, Bangladesh, Afghanistan, Nepal, and Sri Lanka have developed more recently.

Institutes for the study of the various countries of South Asia include:

American Institute of Indian Studies (http://www.indiastudies.org/)
American Institute of Pakistan Studies (http://www.pakistanstudies-aips.org/)
American Institute of Bangladesh Studies (http://www.aibs.net/)
American Institute of Afghanistan Studies (http://www.bu.edu/aias/)
American Institute for Sri Lankan Studies (http://www.aisls.org/)
Association for Nepal and Himalayan Studies (http://anhs-himalaya.org/)

The 1960s saw more and more programs of South Asian studies open across the United States, aided by funding for a number of National Resource Centers (NRCs) at various U.S. universities, supported by the U.S. Department of Education under Title VI of the Higher Education Act of 1965. An additional shift that expanded South Asia studies from the major universities to other institutions was the development of study-abroad programs, mostly in India, beginning with the University of Wisconsin's Year-in-India Program in 1962, with funding for the initial years from the Carnegie Foundation. The relatively new Fulbright Program, which sent scholars abroad to study and to teach English, as well as the Peace Corps, which had a limited tenure in South Asia in the 1960s, also helped develop a base of young people interested in South Asia. (Contributors to this volume who were introduced to South Asia through such programs include Susan Snow Wadley, who was in the second year of the Wisconsin Program, and Karen McNamara, who was in the Peace Corps in Bangladesh.)

Currently, students can study the environment in the Himalayas, Tibetan religion and culture in Dharamsala, South Indian culture and gender in Madurai, and much more, through one of the numerous study abroad programs, many of which accept students from other colleges and universities. In addition, students can study languages at the South Asia Summer Language Institute at the University of Wisconsin. Those who have completed a beginner program can study in India through the American Institute of Indian Studies or in Bangladesh through the Critical Language Scholarship (CLS) Program. Funding for language study is available to U.S. citizens through the CLS program and also through the Boren Scholarship and Fellowship Programs.

> The following websites can be helpful in finding undergraduate study-abroad programs in South Asia:
>
> Boren Awards for International Study (http://www.borenawards.org)
> Critical Language Scholarship Program (http://www.clscholarship.org/)
> South Asia Summer Language Institute (http://sasli.wisc.edu/)
> Study Abroad (http://www.studyabroad.com)

Not surprisingly, the popularity of South Asian spirituality and music during the 1960s also helped develop scholarship in various fields, from music to religion to anthropology. During the 1970s and 1980s, while programs for undergraduates grew, wider interest in South Asia declined. The unfortunate political turmoil of the 1990s and first decades of the twenty-first century have created an upsurge in interest in South Asia, with universities and colleges adding courses on history, politics, and especially the Muslim regions of South Asia.

The early years of South Asian studies saw a focus on languages, religion, history, and society; today, more and more scholars are working in fields such as gender studies, media, economics, development, water management, and trade. Essential to any of these topics, however, is the interdisciplinary nature of the study of South Asia. As the case studies in this book demonstrate, especially those on the Federally Administered Tribal Areas (FATA) of Pakistan (Chapter 14) and the pharmaceutical industry in Bangladesh (Chapter 12), the disciplinary background of the author is muted because the topic itself demands an approach that takes into account history, international and local politics, economics, religion, culture, and social structures. Students seeking to explore South Asia can start at any of these entry points. The demands of their projects will lead them into the necessarily related fields.

3
_____

A Brief History of South Asia

_____

SANDEEP BANERJEE, WITH SUBHO BASU, STEPHEN CHRISTOPHER,
AND SUSAN SNOW WADLEY

As is the case with other parts of the world, the history of South Asia is a history of globalization. From its earliest times, visitors from over the mountains and across the seas often remained as residents. Numerous cultures and societies have crossed paths in the region since early humans migrated into South Asia 70,000 years ago. By 2500 BCE, the Indus Valley Civilization had trade links with the Middle East. Alexander the Great invaded in the third century BCE, bringing the Greek art forms seen in some Buddhist art. South Asia was a transit point on the Silk Road connecting western and eastern Asia, as well as a node in the expansion of imperial European empires. The perceived "spirituality" of South Asia influenced Western popular culture in the twentieth century. In the early twenty-first century, South Asia is the locus of international conflicts, both in the northwest in Afghanistan and Pakistan and in the northeast, in China and Myanmar. It also plays a critical role in international trade and commerce, eased by the widespread use of English and the presence of a well-educated middle class.

> For two excellent collections of maps of South Asia, see the University of Texas map collection (http://www.lib.utexas.edu/maps/india.html) and the Columbia University website (http://www.columbia.edu/itc/mealac/pritchett/00maplinks/index.html).

Early History and the Indus Valley Civilization

As revealed in recent archaeological investigation, *Homo sapiens* migrated into South Asia 70,000 to 50,000 years ago; some prehistoric sites in present-day Afghanistan are more than 50,000 years old. In Sri Lanka, the earliest record of human habitation can be traced back 34,000 years, to a site in Balagonda where Mesolithic hunter-gatherers lived in caves. In southern India, archaeologists estimate that the Neolithic era, marked by the introduction of farming and metal tools, had begun by 3000 BCE and lasted until about 1400 BCE.

South Asia's most ancient urban civilization developed around the Indus River and its tributaries in what is now Pakistan. The Greeks knew of the Indus, and they called the land beyond the river "India." Achaemenid rulers of Persia (c. 550–330 BCE) referred to the seven rivers of the Indus system as the Hepta Hindu (Sapta Sindhu in Sanskrit) river system. Now called the Indus Valley Civilization (IVC), it reached its height 2,500 years ago. Although archaeologists originally believed it to be an offshoot of Mesopotamian civilization, they revised their initial understanding of the IVC after a careful scrutiny of the evolution of agriculture and settlement patterns. During the Neolithic era, the expansions of farming allowed surpluses to develop, which led to the development of cities and trade. Archaeologists and historians now believe the IVC took shape over a period of 7,000 years, during which extensive agriculture, trade, and civic life developed.

The IVC developed between 2500 BCE and 1500 BCE, establishing itself around sites located in today's Pakistan (Mohenjo Daro, Harappa, and Ganeriwala) and India (Dholavira, Lothal, and Rakhigarhi). Marked by a rectangular grid of roads and granaries, as well as a great bath in Mohenjo Daro, these cities show a high level of social organization and well-developed civic amenities. Such objects as bricks of fixed size indicate a strong government.

For more on the Indus Valley Civilization, including slides of archaeological excavations, see the web page "Around the Indus in 90 Slides" (http://www.harappa.com/indus2/index.html), which chronicles the work of the researchers Jonathan Mark Kenoyer of the University of Wisconsin and Richard H. Meadow of Harvard University.

For more on the Indus Valley and its connections to Mesopotamia, see the lecture "Meluhha: The Indus Civilization and its Contacts with Mesopotamia," by Jonathan Mark Kenoyer, on YouTube (http://www.youtube.com/watch?v=8zcGLlLEbmI).

People from the IVC developed extensive skills in pottery, producing a variety of terracotta containers to store grains. A large number of seals used in official communications have also been unearthed, showing motifs such as the bull, the mother goddess, and boats. These seals point to the existence of a fertility cult and organized religious systems, as well as the development of maritime trade. The script on the seals indicates that at least some segment of the population was literate, although scholars have yet to decipher it. The IVC declined rapidly by 1500 BCE, owing to a combination of complex environmental factors.

Between 2000 and 1200 BCE, a branch of Indo-Europeans from central Asia settled in present-day Afghanistan. The new immigrants composed hymns of the Avesta, the principal text of Zoroastrianism, in the Ariana language from 1800 BCE. Zoroastrianism became the dominant religion of the Afghan region, with the city of Bactria, or Balkh, as its center. From 1500 BCE, another group of immigrants seeking pastures for their herds, called Aryans after their Indo-European language, penetrated further into the Indian subcontinent and settled down in the Punjab. Specialized bards preserved the religious hymns of different Aryan communities: over time, these hymns were collected into the *Rig Veda*, thought to be the earliest Hindu text.

Box 3.1

Hindu Gods

The primary Hindu gods are the *trimurti* (three forms) of the divine: Brahma, the Creator; Shiva, the Destroyer; and Vishnu, the Preserver. They, along with their consorts—Sarasvati, the Goddess of Knowledge; Parvati, or Shakti, the Goddess of Power; and Lakshmi, the Goddess of Prosperity or Wealth—are worshipped in all Hindu communities. Many other incarnations and forms of these deities are found in the villages and cities of India.

A priest worships the image of Durga, one of the consorts of the god Shiva, at a shrine in Ram Nagar, Bihar. *(Photo by Susan Snow Wadley)*

Agrarian settlement in South Asia led to the establishment of territorial units governed by clans, with leaders appointed from powerful lineages. As agriculture developed in these kingships, so did the fourfold social classification known as the *varna* system: highest was the priestly class of Brahmins, followed by the warrior class of Kshatriyas and then the Vaishyas, or merchants; at the lowest level were the serfs, called the Shudras. Later Aryan philosophy associated this social stratification with the notion of self-sacrifice of "cosmic man": the priest sprang from his mouth, the warrior from his arms, the Vaishya from his thigh, and the Shudra from his feet.

Many later Aryan philosophical writings are in the form of the *Upanishads*, dialogic texts that speculated about the creation of the world, its true nature, and the role of humans within it. The aim of life was *moksha*, the liberation from this cycle of birth and death. The Upanishads also emphasized the doctrine of *karma* (literally "to make" or "to do"), whereby one's actions determine one's position in society and in wider creation.

By 200 BCE, the two great Hindu epics, the *Ramayana* and *Mahabharata*, had been composed in Sanskrit (see also Chapter 5). The *Mahabharata* is the longest Sanskrit epic, roughly ten times the length of the *Iliad* and *Odyssey* combined. The *Mahabharata* tells the story of a dynastic struggle for the throne of Hastinapura, the kingdom ruled by the Kuru clan. The concluding battle produces complex conflicts of kinship and friendship, with instances of duty and family loyalty taking precedence over what is right (as well as the converse). The *Mahabharata* ends with the death of Krishna (an incarnation of Vishnu) and the ascent of the Pandava brothers to heaven.

The *Ramayana* remains an important religious and cultural touch point in contemporary India. When seventy-eight episodes of the *Ramayana* were broadcast on television in 1987–1988, the production drew over 100 million viewers. Nila Paley created a haunting animated version, *Sita Sings the Blues* (www.sitasingstheblues.com/watch.html). For teaching materials on the *Ramayana*, see the Syracuse University website (http://www.maxwell.syr.edu/moynihan/sac/The_Ramayana/).

The *Mahabharata* also contains the *Bhagavad Gita*, often referred to as the *Gita*, which narrates a conversation between the Pandava prince Arjuna and his charioteer, the god Krishna, on a variety of theological and philosophical issues. Krishna, through the course of the *Gita*, imparts knowledge about the path to devotion, the doctrine of selfless action, and the cycle of birth and death. Commentators see the text's setting on a battlefield as an allegory for the ethical and moral struggles of human life. Its call for selfless action inspired many leaders of the Indian independence movement, including Mohandas Gandhi, who referred to the *Gita* as his "spiritual dictionary."

The Expansion to the Gangetic Basin

Technological advances of farming, tools, and irrigation spread over time to the Ganges River basin in northern India, and the Gangetic basin was transformed from forest to fields. This led to the development of new kingdoms such as Kosala, Kashi, Videha, and later Magadha. Advances in irrigation once again led to agricultural surpluses that could support urban populations, and new cities began to develop. The new centers that emerged with the eastward expansion of Aryan culture drew upon the cultural resources, such as beliefs in powerful goddesses, of earlier Neolithic settlements and of non-Aryan immigrants from the neighboring regions of central Asia, the Middle East, and the eastern Mediterranean region as far as Greece. The intermingling of these cultures gradually led to the evolution of classical India.

Box 3.2

Gandhara: A Westward Connection

Gandhara was an ancient kingdom along the Silk Road, in present-day Pakistan and Afghanistan. The region, situated where it was, became a point of confluence for Greco-Roman art and Buddhist imagery, and many of the statues built from the first to the fifth centuries CE reflect the fusion of Indian and Western artistic styles. To view the Greco-Roman influence in Gandhara's art, see "The Art of Gandhara" at the Asia Society's website (http://sites. asiasociety.org/gandhara/exhibit-sections/classical-connections).

Religions such as Jainism and Buddhism also evolved in these regions as a protest against the Vedic sacrificial cults presided over by Brahmin priests (see Chapter 5).

The Greek ruler Alexander invaded northwestern India in 330 BCE. Though the Greek army emerged victorious in battle, the war-weary soldiers revolted in 326 BCE. Under pressure from his army, Alexander retreated, and he died on his way back to Greece. Nonetheless, Alexander's invasion opened up new routes of trade and commerce and led to an explosive growth in economic activities in the subcontinent.

Magadha, located on the eastern fringe of the Gangetic basin around the city of Pataliputra, near modern Patna, gradually became a powerful kingdom. Control over the Gangetic waterways yielded new revenues from trade, while elephants captured from nearby forests and trained for military purposes provided an advantage on battlefields. The location of iron mines in the nearby areas also worked to the kingdom's advantage. The new concept of *chaturanga*, or four-limbed army, comprising infantry, cavalry, chariots, and war elephants, now became characteristic of South Asian warfare. It also gave birth to the game of chess. Magadha came under the control of the Mauryan Empire, and Chandragupta Maurya's experienced army brought the entire Gangetic valley under its control.

Around 300 BCE, the Greek ambassador Megasthenes attended the court of Chandragupta. His account of the Mauryan court survives as a fragment called *Indica*. Megasthenes refers to Indians worshipping Dionysus (Shiva) and Hercules (Krishna). In addition to describing the Himalayas and the island of Sri Lanka, the *Indica* also describes a sevenfold social stratification system, a prosperous peasantry, a crime-free society, and a benevolent criminal justice system. Also written at this time was the *Arthashastra* by Chandragupta's minister Kautilya. The *Arthashastra* is a treatise on the art of government, not unlike Machiavelli's *The Prince*. Still influential today, it notes that the ideal king should be wellborn, energetic, and intelligent, and it describes six different constituents of the state: ministers, forts, treasury, army, a circle of allies, and country. Emphasizing the king's complete control over the system of governance, the *Arthashastra* prescribes espionage as a desirable and necessary aspect of governance.

The Magadhan Empire reached the height of its influence during the reign of Ashoka

Box 3.3

The Grand Trunk Road

For more than 2,000 years, the Grand Trunk Road has connected the eastern and western parts of South Asia, from Bangladesh all the way to Kabul, Afghanistan, covering some 1,600 miles. Rudyard Kipling, a British colonial writer, described the Grand Trunk Road as "such a river of life as nowhere else exists in the world."

(304–232 BCE), Chandragupta's grandson, who became a Buddhist. Ashoka is known through his rock inscriptions, the Ashokan edicts, which are found in the territory stretching from near Jalalabad in present-day Afghanistan in the northwest to Karnataka in southern India and to Assam in eastern India. Though the edicts reflect a Buddhist moralizing tone, they also aim to bolster the existing social order by exhorting people to obey their teachers and parents as well as to be kind to their slaves and servants. Such exhortations reflected a desire to extend monarchical control over populations scattered over a wide imperial territory.

However, such vast territories were not administered by a centralized state apparatus. Historians estimate nearly four different territorial centers located in the far northwest, in central India, in the south, and in the southeast. These areas were connected by a complex network of roadways, and the most important of these is now called the Grand Trunk Road. The locations of Ashokan edicts throughout this network indicate the emperor's attempt to announce his authority to all the traders passing along these roads.

Ashoka himself represented a complex model of an emperor. After a bloody campaign against Kalinga, he apparently experienced a spiritual crisis and embraced Buddhism. He was also a globalizing figure who used the maritime trade networks to send emissaries to extend the message of Buddhism, which spread to Sri Lanka, Burma (Myanmar), and eastern and western Asia. The combination of trade and the exportation of religion placed ancient India under Ashoka at the heart of a pan-Asian network of ideas and commerce.

In ancient Sri Lanka, the kingdom of Anuradhapura flourished from the time of Ashoka and was crucial to the rise of Theravada Buddhism. The kingdom was ruled during Ashoka's time by Devanampiya Tissa, a Sinhalese king of the Maurya clan, and it is believed his grandson defeated a Chola invasion from southern India and established a unified administration over Sri Lanka.

Within a few years of Ashoka's death, the Mauryan Empire ended. The ensuing period witnessed fragmentation of political power and the rise of nomadic states expanding from central Asia. Other kingdoms such as the Chera, Pandya, and Chola emerged in southern India. Also during this period, fishermen from southern India reached the islands of the modern Maldives and settled there. Eventually, the Maldives were ruled by a Chola king. The Tamil Chola dynasty came to rule most of southern India, including Sri Lanka. The

Cholas were powerful warriors and crafty politicians, establishing diplomatic relations as far away as China and Malaysia. Chola rulers patronized the arts, establishing temples and monumental statues.

Over time, South Asia, extending from Afghanistan in the northwest to the deepest part of peninsular India, came together through cultural interaction and shared religious devotional culture. Within the core South Asian region, forms of kingship, religion, poetry, drama, and science gradually developed and were reproduced for many generations. The durability and reproducibility of cultural forms across time and space are often described as hallmarks of classical India.

The classical Indian tradition reached its height under the Gupta dynasty (c. 320–550 CE). Later Gupta conquests under Vikramaditya extended the Gupta Empire to almost the entire expanse of South Asia. The Gupta kings presided over a vast arrangement of institutions, from trade guilds and artisanal production centers to temples that enjoyed a substantial degree of autonomy. Brahmins enjoyed tax-free land grants from the monarchs and ran educational centers. The Gupta monarchs were bound by the code of *rajdharma*, literally the "righteous rule of the king," whereby they were obliged to protect these self-governing institutions. *Rajdharma* also demanded that kings be brave, but bravery had to be combined with spirituality and adherence to a moral code defined by membership in the Kshatriya (warrior) *varna*. Rama, hero of the *Ramayana*, is the epitome of *rajdharma*. *Rajdharma* remains a model for righteous political leadership even today, when modern politicians might be accused of failing to follow it in various disputes. Trade and commerce with Southeast Asia flourished under the Gupta monarchy. Gupta rule also saw the restoration of Brahminical power and the development of a devotional religion centering on Shiva and Vishnu.

The Gupta monarchs claimed the title of *Chakravartin*, a metaphorical term implying that they constituted the wheels of law rolling through the land and were the ideal rulers. Though Gupta rulers built up an impressive military presence and satellite states, the empire suffered from the massive invasion of Huns from central Asia. Gradually, many smaller central Asian rulers in the western regions transformed themselves into Rajputs, thought to be Kshatriyas, or the warrior group in Hinduism, and joined the Brahminical religious system. The classical pattern established by Guptas in the form of *rajdharma* and the aesthetics of governance soon spread throughout Southeast Asia and established a pattern of high culture that is often referred to as the Sanskrit cosmopolis.

The Beginning of the Medieval Period

The decline of Gupta rule led to the gradual disappearance of the political unity of South Asia. The region of modern Bhutan, heavily influenced by Tibet, converted to Buddhism in the seventh century CE. At the same time, Islam began to penetrate from the west. In Afghanistan, a Shahi dynasty ruled part of Kabul valley. Between 606 and 647 CE, Harsha, the king of Kannauj, established his sway over the Indo-Gangetic plain, but after his death his empire also disintegrated. Buddhist Pala rulers established their dominion over Bengal, while in peninsular India, Chalukyas, Pandyas, and Cholas predominated.

Box 3.4

The Essence of Bhakti

This poem by Basavaṇṇa, translated from Kannada by A.K. Ramanujan in *Speaking of Śiva* (New York: Penguin, 1973, 19), captures the essence of bhakti.

The Temple and the Body

The rich
shall make temples for *Śiva*.
What shall I,
a poor man,
do?

My legs are pillars,
the body the shrine,
the head a cupola
of gold.

Listen, O Lord of the meeting rivers,
things standing shall fall,
but the moving ever shall stay.

Basavaṇṇa 820

Nearly forty dynasties left their records in South Asia between the seventh and eleventh centuries.

The new era was also marked by the triumph of Vedic Brahminical traditions over various other non-Vedic traditions, such as Buddhism. In the eighth century, Shankara, a Hindu monk from present-day Kerala, established Vedanta, a form of Hindu philosophy based on the texts known as the *Upanishads*, which express the primary theological ideas embodied in Hinduism as the dominant religious tradition in the subcontinent. However, the dominance of Brahmin authority led to a religious movement known as bhakti, whose emphasis on devotion to a personal god eliminated the need for priests as intermediaries to god as well as eliminated the need for worship that had to be led by priests in temples.

Bhakti also gave rise to vernacular devotional literature across South Asia. The spread of bhakti can be traced through the spread of these new religious traditions, from Tamil in the south to Bengali in the east and ultimately to dialects of Hindi in the north. Versions of the *Ramayana* were a primary form of transmitting bhakti, as were many poetic traditions. With roots in southern India in the tenth century, bhakti was fully entrenched in the north as well by the seventeenth century. Today, bhakti is the primary form of religious devotion in Hinduism.

The peninsular kingdoms became centers of maritime trade in this era, exporting religion along with trade goods. Pandya kings accumulated their wealth through interna-

Statues of the god Krishna as a baby are lined up in a market ready to be dressed and taken home for worship. These are a prime manifestation of bhakti in modern India, where the daily bathing and dressing of images is a clear mark of devotion. *(Photo by Susan Snow Wadley)*

tional commerce, and their maritime presence is noted in Latin sources. They imported Chinese silk and porcelain from Southeast Asia and then reexported them to the eastern Mediterranean world. Peninsular kingdoms also exported black pepper, sandalwood, and textiles. Trade links between South Asia and the Arabian Peninsula, the Mediterranean world, and East Africa expanded rapidly. Arab, Jewish, African, Armenian, and Indian merchants transformed the Arabian Sea into a busy center of sea trade.

Flourishing agriculture and commodity production, as well as expanding networks of trade, attracted new invaders from central Asian regions. These invaders brought Islam, which came to Afghanistan around 642 CE, when Arab armies conquered the city of Herat. By 870, the region was under the sway of Islamic rulers. The most prominent Islamic ruler, Mahmud of Ghazni, made repeated incursions into India. Islam also came to India initially with Muslim (and Jewish) merchants who were engaged in trade in the Malabar region of India's west coast. As Muslim armies moved into central Asia and converted Turkish nomadic pastoralists to Islam, local Buddhists from central Asia to Afghanistan, as well as in the Maldives, were gradually converted to Islam. At the same time, the southern portions of the Silk Road were expanding overland trade in the region and connecting South Asia to central and eastern Asia.

The travelogue/ethnography-cum-novel *In an Antique Land* by Amitav Ghosh (New York: Vintage, 1994) captures the story of the trade by Jews and Arabs between Egypt and the Malabar coast.

Politically, the Delhi sultanate began with central Asian invaders and collapsed with the invasion of Timur in 1398. In 1206, the Mamluk sultans conquered Delhi and concentrated on establishing the supremacy of the sultan over the land. The sultanate slowly lost its viability as a political system as it experimented with diverse economic and fiscal systems. Timur, the famous central Asian ruler also known as Tamerlane, first incorporated Afghanistan into his empire and then invaded Delhi in 1398, putting an end to the Delhi sultanate.

Conversion to Islam occurred primarily at the edges of the Delhi sultanate—in Bengal and Punjab—and was aided by the tax-free land grants to Sufi saints, who brought new agricultural knowledge into a land where people were not under the sway of organized religion. Sufi religious practices emphasized religious devotion, performance of miracles, and the collective singing of devotional songs, features familiar from bhakti.

In the south, the Vijayanagara Empire flourished in the dry regions of the peninsula. The kings ran a cosmopolitan empire through their trade connections with Portuguese sailors, who supplied them with horses and perhaps small firearms. They employed a largely Muslim Turkish artillery and donned the dress of Muslim monarchs, but in political practice they claimed divine status. As devotees of Lord Virupaksha, they ruled their kingdom with the assistance of Brahmin governors and Nayak warriors, revealing the syncretic nature of the Indian political system, where central Asian Muslims were accepted as Indian kings and where Indian Hindu kings adopted the Perso-Arabic culture.

The Mughal Era

In 1501, Babur, a descendant of Timur and Genghis Khan and the ruler of Samarkand (in present-day Uzbekistan), was exiled from his native city. He slowly moved into South Asia, first establishing his base in Kabul. When trouble erupted among members of the ruling Afghan Lodhi dynasty in Delhi, he invaded India and conquered Delhi in 1526. He passed away before consolidating his regime and lies buried in Kabul. His son Humayun eventually regained control over Delhi; but it was Humayun's son Akbar who consolidated the Mughal regime, which continued to grow for the next 150 years. Mughal rule connected the disparate ethnic groups in the Indo-Gangetic heartland, transforming South Asia into a unified space.

The success of Mughal rule lay in the institutional structure consolidated by Akbar and his associates. Following the structure of the Delhi sultanate, Akbar built up a military-bureaucratic system based on meritocracy. His military was divided into ranks of *mansabdars*, who held their rank based on the number of soldiers they supplied to the imperial army. The lowest-ranking *mansabdars* were assigned the responsibility of maintaining ten soldiers, while the highest-ranking officers commanded 10,000 soldiers. The Mughal administration also gave some *mansabdars* land grants called *jagirs*, from which they collected revenue for the administration. These officers, called *jagirdars*, were not hereditary owners of the land and could be transferred from one place to another. They received a salary from the revenues they collected and were provided with financial support to maintain the soldiers under their command.

Below the *jagirdars* existed a hereditary class of revenue collectors attached to the land, known as *zamindars*. Mughal *jagirdars* often farmed out the right to collect revenues to the highest bidder from among the *zamindars*. Thus the Mughal state depended on vast layers of intermediaries who negotiated the flow of revenue from the villages to

Box 3.5

Babur and His Successors

Babur (1483–1530), a descendant of Genghis Khan, was the first Mughal emperor of India. He had many successors, notably including Humayun (1508–1556), considered the ideal man on account of his peacefulness and wisdom; Akbar (1542–1605), who was famous for his liberal attitude toward the many religions of India; Shah Jahan (1592–1666), who built the Taj Mahal; and Aurangzeb (1618–1707), who greatly expanded Mughal rule through military conquest.

the imperial coffers. This tiered system of administration created overall control over the imperial bureaucracy, which emphasized dependence on the emperor. When the British ruled India, they recognized the land grants made by the Mughals in many parts of India as hereditary. In the 1950s, some states of independent India enacted Zamindari Abolition Acts to return the lands held by the large zamindars to the peasants who actually farmed them.

While the military bureaucracy remained the backbone of the state, Akbar expanded the base by recruiting the support of Hindu Rajput warriors. The emperor, who married into ruling Rajput families, appointed them to the highest positions within the Mughal administration. This tied the Rajput clans to the imperial administration. Akbar also removed the discriminatory pilgrim taxes on non-Muslim subjects. Though he was a devout Muslim, his policies broadened the base of the state and provided the state with legitimacy to bridge religious differences.

The Mughals also asserted their presence in the cultural sphere through the promotion of classical music and dance. Mughal emperors commissioned a number of forts, palaces, mausoleums, mosques, and gardens. Architecturally, Mughal forts announced the formidable might of the rulers, but their mausoleums expressed the height of aesthetic creativity in Indo-Islamic traditions. The Taj Mahal, built under the order of Akbar's grandson Shah Jahan, is one the finest examples of Mughal architecture.

Mughal India experienced the gradual integration of South Asia with the global economy. Portuguese trade with India began in 1499 when a sea route was discovered linking Europe and Asia. The export of Indian textiles and silk to the European market generated widespread interest in India among various emerging European mercantile economies. Trade with these European powers—including the Dutch, English, and, later, French—expanded, bringing Spanish silver bullion from South America to buy Indian goods. India gained a massive trade advantage vis-à-vis Europe, facilitated by sophisticated banking networks spreading from port towns to the interior. These bankers financed the operations of European merchant companies through loans, and they also extended loans to the Mughal state and its successors.

The expanding trade networks in the Indian Ocean region attracted Arab, Chinese, Ar-

The Taj Mahal (built between 1632 and 1653) is the mausoleum for Mumtaz Mahal, the third wife of Emperor Shah Jahan. He had planned to build his own mausoleum in black marble across the river from the Taj, but he was deposed and jailed by his son Aurangzeb *(Photo by Susan Snow Wadley)*

menian, and Jewish traders to Indian markets. They also linked Indian internal trade with central Asian markets. The trade and demands of Mughal aristocracy for specialized food transformed the nature of agriculture, and specialized orchards and farms came into being, leading to the spread and commercialization of agriculture. Delicacies such as apricots and nuts grown in the Kabul region of Afghanistan reached Delhi homes. Despite these impressive successes, the Mughal state remained an institutionalized military-bureaucratic state whose existence depended on constant expansive wars. It was the military success that impressed the vast layers of intermediaries to remain loyal to the imperial court.

Aurangzeb, one of the most powerful and able Mughal emperors, attempted to expand the empire into Assam, in the northeast of India, but he failed because the local terrain made it impossible for the Mughal cavalry to march against Assam's rulers. Aurangzeb then sought to consolidate his rule in southern India. He successfully undermined local kingdoms but faced resistance from Maratha landed elites, led by Shivaji, in the area that is now Maharashtra. The Maratha wars left the Mughal state bankrupt. The failure of the state to expand the frontier and its defeat at the hands of the rather ignoble Marathas signaled to the military bureaucrats the weakness of the emperor. Despite acknowledging the Mughals as the supreme rulers of South Asia, these regional leaders soon became quasi-independent in their provinces.

Between the sixteenth and eighteenth centuries, parts of Afghanistan were ruled by different imperial elites. The Khanate of Bukhara extended its control over northern Afghanistan, while western Afghanistan was under the Safavid dynasty. The Mughals extended their control over the east, particularly the Kandahar region. With the decline of Mughal influence, Shia Safavids extended their sway over all of Afghanistan, but a rebellion brought southwestern Afghanistan under the sway of Pashtun-speaking rulers. The Persian general Nadir Shah defeated the Afghans and made his way through Afghanistan into the heart of India. He captured the city of Delhi in 1739 and massacred the local population, heralding the end of Mughal rule in India.

The Rise of the British East India Company

With the growth of global exploration in the 1400s, the first Europeans reached South Asia by sea, marking a new phase of globalization. In 1498, the Portuguese explorer Vasco da Gama reached the Indian port of Calicut. The Portuguese entered Sri Lanka in 1505, and they set up a permanent base in India by 1510. The profit earned by the Portuguese from their Asian trade attracted the attention of other European seafaring kingdoms, which issued charters of monopoly trade to their respective East India companies (EICs). While the Dutch and the English EICs were privately owned joint-stock companies, the French EIC was a government-run company. These companies competed with each other to gain access to Indian products, which were sold in European markets. In 1600, Elizabeth I of England granted the British EIC the charter for monopoly trade with India. In 1618, King James I sent Sir Thomas Roe to the court of the Mughal emperor Jahangir, who gave Roe permission to set up a warehouse at Surat.

The British EIC faced rivalry from the Dutch EIC, and both companies, following the Portuguese, established ports and forts in the coastal areas of India. Seeing the success of the Dutch and the English, the French set up their EIC in 1664. While European EICs built up their port cities on India's sprawling coastlines, the Mughal Empire steadily declined after the death of Aurangzeb in 1707. In the twilight of Mughal rule, the Marathas emerged as a dominant power in India. The Maratha territory passed over to Shivaji's grandson Shahuji. Between 1740 and 1761, a powerful Maratha confederacy controlled a vast area of the Indian subcontinent. The Marathas, like the Mughals, followed a pragmatic policy of compromise with diverse communities.

The French EIC established a protectorate in southern India, but it was defeated by British EIC troops under Robert Clive, and Bengal became the new flash point. As Bengal faced repeated Maratha attacks, Siraj-ud-Daulah, the young ruler of Bengal, tightened his grip over the administration and sought to mobilize new resources. When the British began fortifying at Calcutta, a furious Siraj attacked Fort William and devastated it. After the British forces under Clive regained Calcutta, they plotted the overthrow of Siraj. In 1757, at the Battle of Plassey, British troops defeated Siraj's forces by bribing his commander, Mir Zafar, who stood aloof from the fighting. Clive's victory in Bengal paved the way for the rise of the British East India Company in South Asia.

Over the next 100 years, the British consolidated their position in South Asia. The other contenders for power, the Marathas and the Afghans, fought against each other at Panipat in 1761. In South India the most formidable challenge to the British EIC came from Tipu Sultan, who was defeated by the British in 1799. In 1805, the British victory over the Maratha chieftains clearly established Britain's supremacy in the Indian subcontinent. The Punjab region came under British control after the British defeated the Sikhs in 1849.

The Move Toward Empire

The rise of the British East India Company occurred just as the British Empire lost its American colonies. The British EIC government was a bureaucratic machine headed by a governor-general who ran the administration from Calcutta. In the initial stages, British officials in India often emulated the lifestyles of the Indian nobles of the Mughal state, learned Indian languages, participated in Indian festivities, and kept Indian mistresses. As the company became more powerful, these customs were frowned upon, and gradually a structured bureaucratic corps was created.

Warren Hastings, the first governor-general, was succeeded by Charles Cornwallis, who promulgated a new civil and criminal code. Cornwallis was of the opinion that Indians or Europeans of mixed origin did not have the ability of British-born officials, and he reduced them permanently to subordinate positions. In 1793, Cornwallis also instituted the Permanent Settlement in Bengal, which gave tenure-holding landlords (zamindars) property rights over land, ignoring the rights of other cultivators. In return, the zamindars had to pay a fixed annual tax to the British. Defaulting zamindars would have their estates auctioned off. (In other regions, different land arrangements were made.)

The most significant change under the British EIC was in trade. Since the Gupta period, India had been not only a prominent hub of Eurasian trade but also an exporter of textiles, spices, opium, and indigo, while at the same time it imported silver bullion. This process was accelerated in the Mughal period, and India witnessed the development of pockets of protocapitalistic society. Between 1780 and 1860, India became an exporter of raw materials such as cotton and an importer of finished industrial products like textiles. However, the protective tariffs introduced by the British government in the early nineteenth century hit Indian exports. The introduction of cheap cotton textiles in the wake of industrial development in Britain especially damaged the export of Indian goods.

In 1813 the British parliament rescinded the East India Company's monopoly charter of trade, allowing private British traders to invest in the Indian market. Despite the retreat of the British EIC from directly managing Indian trade, the position of Indian traders and producers did not improve. British agents established control over the lucrative trade between Europe, India, and China; from 1842, with the defeat of the Chinese by the British, such trade was conducted directly by the British agencies.

After consolidating their positions, the British debated how to govern India. In the initial stage, most officials agreed that India should be governed according to its customs. Known as the Orientalists, these scholar-administrators built institutions dedicated to preserving Persian, Arabic, and Sanskrit. The East India Company also excluded British missionaries from its territories in fear of Indian reactions. In the nineteenth century, there was a shift toward English education. Evangelist Christians and utilitarian philosophers argued that Indian society could be transformed through the introduction of the English language and rational European laws. The British politician Thomas Babington Macaulay argued for the development of English-educated Indian intermediaries who would be "brown" in appearance but English in taste and manners.

Many Indians were seeking a Western education to understand the culture of their new

---

Box 3.6

A Rare Practice

Sati (or *suttee*), from the Sanskrit word *sat*, meaning "truth," is the practice, more common in Rajasthan and Gujarat, whereby a Hindu wife will immolate herself on her husband's funeral pyre. The immolated woman (called a sati) is then thought to become a goddess. Sati shrines are worshipped throughout the region. Some say that a sati in one's family removes all sins for seven generations. Extremely rare by the late twentieth century, sati is still thought to occur under pressure from the husband's family, but any instances of the practice lead to massive protest from women's movements.

---

masters and to find employment in the new administration. In response, Hindu College was established in Calcutta in 1818. In 1854, the government recommended mass education for Indians, and it introduced state-funded elementary and higher education institutions. These institutions served the high-caste, wealthy Hindu families but were ill equipped to provide mass education. Indeed, mass literacy was never the goal of the colonial state.

The Indian Response to the East India Company

Bengal, where the British EIC administration was established by the middle of the eighteenth century, exhibited diverse reactions to the regime. Rammohan Roy, a key figure in the Indo-British cultural encounter, was an advocate of European modernity and syncretic monotheistic Hinduism that combined Vedanta and Sufi traditions. A versatile scholar and reformer, Roy's efforts led to a reformist Hindu association, the Brahmo Samaj. Roy was also an avid proponent of the abolition of *sati*, the custom of burning a widow on the funeral pyre of her husband. Roy's support for social reforms emboldened the colonial administration to initiate the Abolition of Sati Act of 1829, despite protests from conservative Hindus. Roy, the first public intellectual of India, became a pioneering figure in the cause of modernizing India.

Another social movement in Calcutta emerged around the figure of Henry Derozio, a professor of English at Hindu College. Derozio espoused rationalist philosophy, and his questioning pedagogy inspired a new social movement called the Young Bengal. The iconoclastic nature of the Young Bengal movement drew criticism from influential segments of both Hindu and British society, and Derozio lost his job. The Sanskrit scholar Ishwar Chandra Vidyasagar propagated women's education and advocated remarriage for widows. He also wrote a primer for Bengali that remains an introductory text for the language in elementary schools. Though this intellectual ferment was limited to the high-caste, upper-class Hindu Bengalis of Calcutta, this movement marked the beginning of the formation of a powerful civil society in the city based on liberal bourgeois values.

Indian soldiers employed by the British East India Company were discontented with the low pay and archaic promotion rules of the company. For instance, Indian soldiers

JUSTICE.

A print by Sir John Tenniel showing British restoration of imperial power after the 1857 Indian uprising. *(Wikimedia Commons, http://commons.wikimedia.org/wiki/File:JusticeTenniel1857Punch.jpg)*

with twenty-five years of service did not have the rank and pay of newly recruited British officers. Soldiers serving outside the Indian subcontinent enjoyed a special allowance, but in 1856 a new clause denied such provisions to new recruits. In 1856, the company took administrative control of the area of Awadh in central India, and many soldiers from this region feared that the British would raise taxes. Increasing missionary activity further alienated the soldiers, who feared that the government would introduce a mass conversion drive. When the government introduced new Enfield rifles with paper-wrapped cartridges that had to be bitten off before pouring the gunpowder down the barrel, rumors circulated that the cartridges were smeared with cow and pork fat, a deliberate ploy of the government to insult Hindu and Muslim sentiments. Many battalions refused to use the new cartridges.

In May 1857, soldiers incensed by the imprisonment of their comrades for refusing to use the Enfield cartridges revolted and released their colleagues. They killed several British officers and marched to Delhi, where they restored the old Mughal king, Bahadur

Shah Zafar, to the throne of India. The king was a reluctant leader, but the soldiers used his position as the legitimate ruler of India to rally Indian aristocrats. Soon the revolt, termed the "Sepoy Mutiny" by the British and the "First War of Independence" by the Indians, spread across northern India.

The great rebellion actually ended British control over a substantial part of India. Yet despite its magnitude, the rebellion did not move beyond the core territories of northern India because of the lack of coordination among rebel leaders and the absence of strategic planning. By mobilizing troops from Punjab who were untouched by the uprising, the British suppressed the rebellion by 1858. The rebellion ended the administration of the British East India Company, and India came under the direct rule of the British crown.

British Crown Rule in India

The new British administration regarded its Indian territories as a unitary state where the British enjoyed complete sovereignty. The supreme authority was vested in the secretary of state for India, appointed by the British parliament, and its representative in India, the viceroy. In 1857, Queen Victoria promised to treat Indians as equal subjects, but Indians were nonetheless systematically excluded from the higher levels of power and were recruited only into lower administrative positions.

As Indian agriculture was integrated into the global circuit of trade, the government did little to protect the interests of peasants. Devastating famines swept through the provinces, followed by epidemics. The average age of Indians in the late nineteenth century through the first decades of the twentieth century remained in the mid-twenties.

> Famines during British colonial rule (1765–1947) killed millions of Indians. Mike Davis's *Late-Victorian Holocausts: El Niño Famines and the Making of the Third World* (New York: Verso, 2001) examines the massive famines in British India in the nineteenth century.

Indian political associations developed during the late nineteenth century, dominated by emerging professionals and the industrialist class. By the 1870s, different regional associations sought an all-India platform, which took concrete shape in 1885, when leaders of regional associations, along with the retired British civil service officer Allan Octavian Hume, founded the Indian National Congress (INC). Despite its presumptive title, the INC represented high-caste Hindus and wealthy Parsi men from professional, trading, and large landholding backgrounds. The INC began by passing resolutions demanding that the British government hold Indian civil service exams simultaneously in India and Britain. The INC aimed for the Indianization of the civil service and the protection of nascent Indian industries. It was also concerned about the plight of the farmers and famines, but it did not take up issues that would attract the government's hostility. The moderate INC left a lasting legacy. In particular, Dadabhai Naoroji developed the doctrine of "economic nationalism." Along with Romesh Chunder Dutt, a former Indian civil service officer, he argued against the "un-British" nature of British rule that was systematically impoverishing India. Despite its elitism, the INC became the most important political platform for Indians in British India.

The late nineteenth century saw a range of social movements. Most notably, women professionals and writers offered systematic critiques of Hindu society. Pandita Ramabai, a Sanskrit scholar, wrote *The High Caste Hindu Woman*, in which she criticized Hindu customs that devalued the position of women in society. In Bengal, women of the aristocratic Tagore family took to writing, composing music, and formulating nationalist theories. The Bengali writer Begum Roquia Sakhawat Hussain advocated the abolition of gender disparity and established a school for girls in Calcutta. Social movements against caste discrimination also gained momentum. In Maharashtra, Jyotiba Phule opened schools for women and set up an organization to promote social equity and stop caste-based discrimination. In Kerala, Narayana Guru, a Hindu religious reformer born in the Ezhava community, preached a message of universal brotherhood.

The late nineteenth century was also a period of Hindu revivalism. Reformist movements such as the Arya Samaj, established by Dayananda Saraswati, promoted the removal of the caste system and the education of women, while forbidding pilgrimages, temple offerings, idol worship, and early marriages. Social reforms opened up opportunities for marginal communities to assert their presence in society while also inspiring a new sense of Hindu assertiveness that created conditions for Hindu-Muslim confrontation.

Colonial India had the largest Muslim population in the world. New educational movements started among Muslim elites in northern India, the heartland of the erstwhile Mughal Empire. In 1866, Maulana Qasim Nanotvi and Maulana Rashid Gangohi established the Darul Uloom theological seminary at Deoband, which became an important center of Islamic learning in the subcontinent. Another reformer, Sir Syed Ahmad Khan, an official in the EIC, argued for cooperation between former Mughal elites and the British. He also reinterpreted Muslim culture and practices in the light of rationalism and scientific discoveries and founded the Mohammedan Anglo-Oriental College (later Aligarh Muslim University) in Aligarh in 1875.

In Bengal, Hindu revivalism informed the writings of novelists such as Bankim Chandra Chattopadhyay. Chattopadhyay's hymn "Vande Mataram," from his novel *Anandamath*, imagines the Indian landscape as a mother and a mother goddess, a potent image in India today.

Various social protests in Bengal eventually led the British to believe that their administrative offices would be safer in Delhi, and the capital of British India was shifted from Calcutta to Delhi in 1911. Planned by the noted architects Edwin Lutyens and Herbert Baker, New Delhi was built on the site of many previous Indian capitals, going back to 1000 BCE. Its spacious landscape stands in sharp contrast to the old city surrounding the Mughal Red Fort. It was finally completed in 1931.

Mass nationalism became the most critical feature of Indian politics after World War I. The British war against the Ottomans alienated pan-Islamist politicians. The curtailing of civil liberties, even after the war, antagonized moderate Indian nationalists. Although the

---

Box 3.7

Key Terms for Understanding Gandhi's Nonviolent Movement

ahimsa. Literally, "without violence"; this is a key concept in Gandhian thought.

satyagraha. Literally, "truth force" (also used by Nelson Mandela and Martin Luther King Jr.); it is thought to arm the user with moral power. The power of ahimsa and satyagraha together should prevail against those who would be violent.

swaraj. Independence.

khadi. Handwoven cloth, used to protest foreign clothes and foreign cloth, and hence to promote self-reliance.

swadeshi. Literally, "of one's own country"; that is, a boycott of all foreign goods; the buying and wearing only of that which came from India.

charkha. The tabletop spinning wheel used by Gandhi to spin the thread for handwoven cotton (khadi). It became an icon of self-reliance in colonial India and a symbol of Indian independence.

Harijan. Children (*jan*) of God (Hari), a term Gandhi used for the untouchable castes.

Readers should note the Hindu origins of these terms, often mentioned in critiques of Gandhi's ability to reach across religious groups.

Government of India Act of 1919 gave some control over certain ministries, such as health and agriculture, to ministers answerable to provincial legislatures, the British retained control of foreign affairs, defense, and communications, leaving many Indian politicians displeased with progress toward independence. Moreover, Indian peasants had to bear the burden of wartime dislocation in the Indian economy. While the Indian peasantry suffered due to the wartime economic shortages, Indian industries made phenomenal profits during World War I, because the British cities of Lancashire and Manchester could not export their products to India. These many events created a space for leadership, which was filled by Mohandas Gandhi.

The Rise of Gandhi

Mohandas Gandhi, born in Gujarat in 1869, made his presence felt in Indian politics during the early decades of the twentieth century. In 1915, Gandhi returned to India from South Africa, where he had been involved in the civil rights struggle for the Indian population there.

As Gandhi emerged as the leader of the Indian National Congress (INC), the viceroy invited him to a war conference in Delhi in 1918. Gandhi's campaign to recruit troops brought into question his consistency on *ahimsa* (nonviolence). Gandhi also launched an agitation in Bihar. The British landlords were forcing farmers to grow indigo, a cash crop, and sell it to them at a fixed price. Pursuing a strategy of nonviolent protest, Gandhi won concessions from the authorities.

In 1919 Gandhi decided to broaden his base among British Indian Muslims. The Khilafat movement, a worldwide protest by Muslims against the status of the caliph in the collapsing Ottoman Empire, provided an opportunity. Gandhi became a prominent spokesman for the movement and attracted substantial Muslim support. Gandhi's success made him India's first national leader with a multicultural base and helped him rise within the Congress ranks.

On April 13, 1919, a group of Hindus, Sikhs, and Muslims, defying a British prohibition, gathered at Jallianwala Bagh (Garden) in Amritsar to celebrate the festival of Baisakhi. The garden was surrounded on all sides by houses and buildings and had only a few narrow entrances. Enraged that crowds had gathered, Brigadier-General Reginald Dyer blocked the main exits and ordered his troops to open fire at the densest sections of the crowd (including women and children). In addition to those shot, many died in stampedes at the narrow gates or by jumping into the solitary well on the compound. The British put the casualties at 379 dead and 1,100 wounded, while the INC estimated that about 1,000 people had been killed.

Rabindranath Tagore, the Nobel laureate for literature in 1913, renounced the knighthood given him in 1915 in protest against the massacre. Gandhi and the INC called for immediate action against Dyer. The government set up the Hunter Commission to investigate the event. In his deposition, Dyer claimed his objective was not to disperse the meeting but to punish the Indians for disobedience. The Viceroy's Executive Council decided that although Dyer had acted in a callous and brutal way, he could not be prosecuted because of political reasons. He was relieved of his command, but faced no other consequences for his actions.

In December 1921 Gandhi was invested with executive authority by the INC. Under him, the INC was reorganized, a new constitution was drafted, and the organization's stated goal became *swaraj* (independence). Gandhi expanded his platform of ahimsa to include *swadeshi*—the boycott of foreign-made, especially British, goods. He also advocated that Indians wear *khadi* (homespun cloth) instead of British-made textiles, and he encouraged Indians to spend time each day spinning khadi in support of the independence movement.

With the INC behind him, Gandhi continued the Non-Cooperation Movement begun in 1920, which aimed for a nonviolent resistance to British rule in India. Protesters refused to buy British goods, used handicrafts, and picketed liquor shops. Gandhi also urged people to boycott British educational institutions and law courts, to resign from government jobs, and to give up British titles and honors. Gandhi's ideal of ahimsa and his ability to rally thousands of people for Indian independence were first seen on a large scale during this period, and the success of the movement took the British by surprise. In March 1922, Gandhi was arrested for sedition and sentenced to six years in jail.

Box 3.8

B.R. Ambedkar and the Indian Constitution

B.R. Ambedkar (1891–1956), who was to become the primary author of the Indian constitution in 1949, was an untouchable from Baroda in Gujarat who received degrees from Columbia University and the London School of Economics. He worked continuously for the welfare of the untouchables throughout his life, converting to Buddhism in 1954 in order to challenge the Hindu hierarchy that he felt kept his people suppressed. Many also think that Gandhi's use of the term "Harijan" continued the oppression of the Dalits, as it did nothing to change their roles or status.

For a convincing portrayal of Ambedar and his interactions with Gandhi, see Jabbar Patel's film *Dr. Babasaheb Ambedkar* (2000).

With Gandhi in jail, other movements filled the political vacuum. The Communists held their first Indian congress in 1926. The All India Trade Union Congress (AITUC), established in 1920, began organizing industrial workers in Bombay (Mumbai). General strikes took place in the Bombay cotton textile industry in 1928 and in the Calcutta (Kolkata) jute industry in 1929. Alarmed by the Communist organizing of workers, the British arrested labor leaders and imprisoned them.

In 1927, the British government formed a commission for administrative reforms under John Simon. Called the Simon Commission, its membership did not include any Indians. The commission was thronged by protesters who greeted the members with black flags. During protests in Lahore, the police beat the nationalist leader Lala Lajpat Rai, who died a few weeks later. Following the Simon Commission's recommendations, the Government of India Act of 1935 established representative government at the provincial level, with the first provincial elections held in 1937. It was in this election that the Federally Administered Tribal Area of Pakistan, under the leadership of the Khudai Khidmatgar, went against the Muslim League and supported Gandhi's nonviolence movement and the INC (see also Chapter 14).

In 1930, Gandhi and the INC launched the civil disobedience movement, which began with the Dandi Salt March. Making salt was a monopoly of the government, which also levied significant taxes on this everyday commodity. With several of his followers, Gandhi marched 241 miles (388 kilometers) from his Sabarmati ashram to Dandi, a village on the west coast of India. There Gandhi launched a protest against the salt law by making salt himself. Gandhi's actions were a direct challenge to the British government.

All of India was affected by the civil disobedience movement. Strikes paralyzed general life; government schools, colleges, and offices were boycotted; foreign goods were burned in bonfires; and people stopped paying taxes. The government headed by Viceroy Irwin decided to negotiate with Gandhi, and the Gandhi-Irwin Pact was signed in 1931. The British freed all political prisoners in return for the suspension of the civil disobedience movement. Gandhi was also invited to the Round Table Conference in London, but the conference was a disappointment to him because there was no discussion on the transfer of power. Viceroy Lord Willingdon, Irwin's successor, took a hard line against nationalism, and Gandhi was again arrested.

In 1932 the government granted minority communities in India—such as Muslims, Sikhs, and Dalits (literally, "the oppressed," previously known as untouchables, and called Harijan, or "Children of God," by Gandhi)—separate electorates under the new constitution, known as the Communal Award. Gandhi protested the separate award for Dalits, which led to a conflict with B.R. Ambedkar, a Dalit political leader.

Religious Conflict, World War, and India's Independence

From 1915 onward, Hindus organized themselves into a separate organization called the Hindu Mahasabha, whose chief ideologue was the former nationalist revolutionary Vinayak Damodar Savarkar. While the Hindu Mahasabha attracted those who were disappointed by the absence of direct Hindu overtones in the nationalist movement, it did not gain much popularity initially because it opposed the INC-led Civil Disobedience Movement. In 1925, Keshav Hedgewar established the Rashtriya Swayamsevak Sangh (RSS), a right-wing, paramilitary, Hindu nationalist group. The RSS sought to energize Hindu nationalism through organized drills, and it advocated Hindu nationalist education through its schools and charities. Its leaders claimed that only those who deemed India a holy motherland should be considered Indians, and its leaders praised Adolf Hitler's policy toward the Jews, believing (as did Hitler) in the idea of purity of race and culture, and hence in a pure homeland.

From the mid-1920s, riots between Hindus and Muslims heightened tensions between these communities, and Muslim support for the Indian National Congress waned. The INC claimed that it adequately represented the Indian nation and that religion was not the basis of nationality. By the 1930s, however, the Muslim League was being led by Mohammed Ali Jinnah, a longtime INC leader. In a fourteen-point program, he argued that the future Indian constitution should be federal in nature, granting power to the provinces, and he claimed that the INC represented a Hindu Raj. The INC favored a centralized government in independent India, with federal characteristics. Unable to gain much support until the start of World War II, Jinnah claimed that Islam was threatened in India under the rule of the "Hindu" INC. In 1939, the British viceroy declared war on Germany on behalf of India without consulting the elected INC provincial ministries. The INC ministries resigned in protest.

At the annual conference of the Muslim League in 1940, Jinnah declared that India was composed of two nations, Hindus and Muslims, and demanded autonomous independent dominions in Muslim majority areas of British India. This demand transformed the Muslim League from a minority pressure group to a national political body seeking national independence for the Muslim majority provinces. The vague spatial notion of Pakistan became the basis of the Muslim League's negotiation with the British government and the INC.

While the Japanese attacks on Pearl Harbor on December 7, 1941, drew the United

---

Box 3.9

Bose, Indian Independence, and World War II

During World War II, the Bengali Subhas Chandra Bose, angry at the slow movement toward Indian independence, joined the Axis forces, especially the Japanese in Burma, and created the Indian National Army, which fought on the side of the Japanese against the British. Bose's legacy of violent struggle against British rule strongly contrasts with Gandhi's principles of satyagraha. Hailed now as a hero, Bose is thought to have died in a plane crash near the end of the war.

States into World War II in the Allied camp, Japan was gaining ground against British forces in Asia. By 1942, Japan had occupied Burma (Myanmar) on India's eastern border. In August 1942, the INC, fearing an imminent Japanese attack, announced the Quit India movement, demanding immediate British withdrawal from India. Though the British arrested INC leaders, the movement shook the British Indian government.

At the end of World War II, Britain's Labor Party made it clear that it would negotiate an exit from Britain's Indian empire. The new government held elections to provincial legislatures and the Central Legislative Assembly, hoping to pave the way for creating a constituent assembly for India. In 1946, the Muslim League won in Bengal and Punjab, defeating regional parties, which sealed the case for the eventual creation of Pakistan. In March 1946, the British government sent a cabinet mission to negotiate with the INC and the Muslim League. The Muslim League declared it would accept separate groupings of Muslim and Hindu provinces, with power belonging to the states. The INC opposed the idea of parity and state rights, and the Muslim League rejected the INC demand for a unitary government with federal characteristics.

In February 1947, Prime Minister Clement Atlee announced that Britain would withdraw from India by June 1948. The situation in India was tense not simply because of sectarian political propaganda, but also because of the British colonial government's administrative lapses during the war. Nearly 4.3 million Indians had died during famines in the middle of the war because the British government did nothing to manage food shortages. In the wake of the Muslim League's call for "direct action," Hindu-Muslim riots broke out in Calcutta during August 1946, leaving 6,000 people dead.

Amid this crisis, the British government appointed Lord Mountbatten as viceroy of India in March 1947, with the directive of leaving India without damaging British power and prestige. Mountbatten proposed that India be divided along religious lines. This meant the partition of Punjab with its Hindus, Muslims, and Sikhs, as well as Bengal, which was home to Muslims and Hindus. The INC and the Muslim League accepted this proposal, and the British government appointed Sir Cyril Radcliffe to demarcate the boundaries of India. The Radcliffe Line was announced on August 17, 1947, two days after India and Pakistan were granted independence.

The partition of British India led to a complete breakdown of law and order in Punjab and the adjoining areas. Nearly 16 million people crossed the border as refugees, and another million died in the ensuing riots. India and Pakistan thus gained independence amid violence and bloodshed. Gandhi made a final attempt to bring peace by traveling to East Bengal villages to restore communal harmony. Muslim villagers resented his presence and criticized him for his failure to save Muslim lives. He then traveled to Calcutta, where his fast in September 1947 restored calm. This was a significant instance of Gandhi using fasting, a practice that he had followed for years, as a political tool to press for his demands. Moving to Delhi, he tried to help both Muslim and Hindu refugees and was critical of the Indian government for failing to protect Muslim lives. On January 30, 1948, Gandhi was shot dead while walking to a platform from which he was to address a prayer meeting. The assassin, Nathuram Godse, a Hindu nationalist with links to the Hindu Mahasabha, held Gandhi guilty of favoring Pakistan and opposed his doctrine of ahimsa. Godse and another conspirator were tried and executed in 1949.

The Postcolonial World of South Asia

Partition created the nations of India and Pakistan, and independence was later given to Sri Lanka and the Maldives (Afghanistan, Nepal, and Bhutan were never under direct colonial control). As a result, the history of South Asia began to diverge. Pakistan became more Islamic (and ultimately two separate countries after the Bangladesh Liberation War), and India slowly moved from a secular socialist state to one divided by religion and participating in neoliberal economic practices. Afghanistan endured more than thirty years of war, with invasions by both the Soviets and the United States. Sri Lanka and Nepal both survived long-term civil wars, while the Maldives, whose highest spot is some 8 feet (2.4 meters) above sea level, now faces the loss of land due to global warming. Bhutan has become democratic while slowly easing restrictions on global communications amid fighting to retain its Buddhist heritage. The post-1947 histories of these now separate nations are detailed below.

Republic of India

After independence, India faced a massive crisis, with millions of Hindu refugees pouring in from Pakistan. Punjab experienced a massive population exchange, while Bengal witnessed waves of refugee influx. The India-Pakistan relationship was shaped by further crises as a result of conflicts over Kashmir and Hyderabad.

It is estimated that 1 million people died during the chaos of the Partition of India in 1947. There was unprecedented violence and sexual assault against women—approximately 100,000 women were raped or kidnapped. *The Other Side of Silence: Voices from the Partition of India*, by Urvashi Butalia (Durham, NC: Duke University Press, 2000), explores how the traumas of Partition linger in contemporary India.

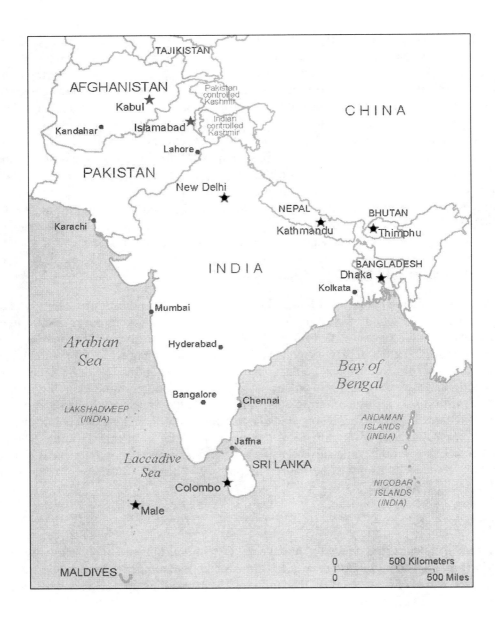

Kashmir was one of the largest princely states in British India, with a diverse population of Muslims, Buddhists, and Hindus. It was a Muslim majority state ruled by a Hindu
monarch, and local Muslim leaders were divided about the future of the state, with many
preferring independence or an autonomous status within India. The Kashmiri king wanted
to remain independent, while Pakistan claimed Kashmir because of its Muslim majority.
In 1948, after Kashmir was invaded by Pakistan, the king appealed to Jawaharlal Nehru,
India's Prime Minister, who agreed to help only if Kashmir joined India. India and Kash-

mir then signed the Instrument of Accession, and the Indian army moved into Kashmir. Nehru soon went to the United Nations demanding a plebiscite, provided both armies withdrew from Kashmir. This never happened, and Kashmir was unofficially partitioned, with both armies guarding the ceasefire line.

Separatist violence and police and army brutality in Kashmir have killed thousands of people. Indian-administered Kashmir is the most militarized zone in the world. Since 1947, there have been three major wars between India and Pakistan over the disputed region. The documentary film *In Shopian,** produced and directed by Chris Giamo (Fogtooth Media 2011), outlines the history of this conflict zone.

In Hyderabad, in central India, a Muslim monarch ruled a region of mostly Hindus. After outbreaks of communal violence in neighboring states in 1947, large numbers of Muslims flocked to the state. The local ruler—called the nizam—declared independence, despite his kingdom being surrounded by India. The INC adopted a cautious policy, but the situation took a new turn when Communists leading a peasant movement in the Telengana region seized land from the local landlords and redistributed it among the peasantry. Ultimately, India sent troops to Hyderabad and ended the nizam's rule. The Communist peasant insurgents were suppressed, and the movement retreated in the face of repression.

Since the late nineteenth century, Indian nationalists had been demanding a gradual transfer of political power to the emerging Western-educated elites who could act as partners in the British Indian administration. In the post–World War I era, the rise of mass nationalism further expanded the process of democratization of both the state apparatus and civil society. Throughout the interwar period, successive constitutional reforms extended voting rights to different segments of the population and slowly made various components of the political system accountable to the public. After independence, the Indian Communists demanded universal adult suffrage and a secular, democratic system. Nehru agreed with this, though he remained extremely critical of Communists. The result was the emergence of the Indian democracy, considered the largest in the contemporary world.

Elections in India constitute the dynamic core of the existing political system. This is evident from the increasingly high turnout of rural voters and the concomitant changes in political elite formations. As a wide range of rural social groups were drawn to ballot boxes, the formerly cloistered circle of elite, upper-caste politicians started losing its control over the political levers of society. With the gradual elimination of the hold of Anglicized upper-caste elites, many "traditional" political establishments with national constituencies experienced a steady decline in their support base. Since 2000, even the INC, the premier political party in postcolonial India, has experienced irreversible erosion in its popularity. Similarly, the motley collection of Socialist groups, which had once constituted the main opposition to the Congress, also suffered a rapid political demise. In comparison, the regional elites drawn from mainly intermediate caste groups in various

Every empty wall becomes space for election propaganda, as seen in this 2006 mural painted by the Indian National Congress in the state of Kerala. *(Wikimedia Commons, http://commons.wikimedia.org/ wiki/File:Kerala2006_%289%29.JPG#filehistory)*

regions came to dominate the political center stage in India. This social transformation paved the way for the regionalization of the Indian political system.

The ascendancy of intermediate caste groups and regional elites can be attributed to the growing political hold of the agrarian bourgeoisie. The abolition of intermediary tenure holdings and land reforms in the 1950s and 1970s benefited those landlords who supervised the cultivation process directly. This agrarian bourgeoisie, often called "bullock capitalists," increasingly vaunted their political muscle in the rural areas and established their dominance over the poor. Under the pressure of the commercialization of agriculture, the relationship between agricultural laborers and the emerging rich peasants was broken. In such circumstances, elections tended to create a situation of political competitiveness. The rural poor remained divided along diverse caste lines, lacking a common social network that would allow them to confront the new masters of rural society. Rich peasants, drawn from intermediary caste groups, constituted a far more consolidated support base for political parties. The recent assertion of Dalits, the most visibly oppressed rural social group, in the Indian political system has added yet another dimension to caste politics. Given the weakness of class mobilizations in most parts of India, caste constitutes a template for new sociopolitical arrangements among the relatively deprived social groups to articulate their ambitions.

Another aspect of Indian electoral politics is the assertion of political supremacy by Hindu fundamentalists. The rise of the Rashtriya Swayamsevak Sangh (RSS), leading to the establishment of the Bharatiya Janata Party (BJP) government in New Delhi in 1998, has been generally ascribed to the decline of centrist political formations such as the INC. The INC leadership found itself in a deep crisis in the mid-1960s. Droughts, wars with

China and Pakistan, and the pressure of the United States in the form of restricted loans had compelled the INC to look to increase agricultural productivity. A technical solution was found in the so-called Green Revolution, based on Western-led projects comprising new improved seeds and the heavy use of fertilizers and irrigation, which vastly increased the yields of rice and wheat. The INC failed to appreciate that such technological innovation needed a social base to succeed, however. This failure resulted in a steady erosion of the political fortunes of the Congress Party, dramatically exposed by its first major electoral debacle in the 1967 elections.

A solution to the INC's political crisis came in the form of the populist authoritarianism of Indira Gandhi, daughter of Jawaharlal Nehru, who employed radical rhetoric to initiate structural adjustments for sustaining the Green Revolution. The political price for such radical pretensions was paid in the form of a dynastic democracy, deinstitutionalization of the INC party structure, and the silencing of political dissent. A centralized party operating through a centralized bureaucracy and the adoption of radical hyperboles such as "Garibi Hatao" ("Remove Poverty") became the salient features of this new style of INC politics.

The INC failed to stem the tide of socioeconomic resentment among different segments of the population. Indira Gandhi could initially sustain her populist base because of the sheer inefficiency of the fragile non-Communist opposition to her rule. The Emergency in 1975, which involved the suspension of elections and civil liberties, gave the government complete power, including the ability to arrest anyone without trial. This led to a growing opposition stemming from regional elites and a pan-Indian democratic movement organized by Jay Prakash Narayan. When the political and civil liberties were restored, and elections held in 1977, Gandhi lost, paving the way for the first non-INC government in independent India.

To recover its lost power, throughout the 1980s, the INC embraced a softer version of Hindutva (Hinduness), which had been championed by the RSS since before independence. This was ironic, as Indira Gandhi had inserted the word "secularism" into the preamble to the country's constitution. The INC failed utterly in this new attempt to fraternize with fundamentalist forces, which rose in power as a direct result—most notably in the form of the BJP, which championed the idea of India as a Hindu country. The RSS and its sister organizations were able to use the ideas of stability and Hindu nationalism for political gain much more than the INC. Moreover, as Dalit and Other Backward Class (OBC) social groups formulated an independent strategy of pursuing their interests, the panic-stricken upper castes in northern India deserted the sinking INC boat and joined the BJP.

A crucial economic factor in this political realignment came in the form of the changing priorities of global capitalism. After the death of Rajiv Gandhi—the son of Indira Gandhi and Indian prime minister from 1984 to 1989—in a suicide bombing in 1991, the INC came back to power. In 1991, the INC government, under P.V. Narasimha Rao, submitted to the force of globalization and adopted a policy of economic liberalization. The dynamic interaction between global capitalism and the changing social configurations in India informed and influenced the processes of political realignment in India.

India is perhaps the only nascent democratic state in South Asia where ruling parties

Box 3.10

Militant Communism in India

There are various militant Communist groups in India. Usually referred to
as Maoists due to their commitment to Mao Zedong's version of Marxism,
they are also called Naxalites, from the village called Naxalbari in West
Bengal that was the site of a Communist-led uprising in 1967. The Indian
government considers the almost 100,000 Maoists in India to be terrorists.
While Maoists support the uplift of marginalized tribes, castes, and oppressed agriculturalists, their usually violent means are largely denounced
by the Indian state.

or coalitions have repeatedly lost elections both at national and provincial levels. This
certainly testifies to an increasing political consciousness of the Indian electorate. Moreover, the Left Front governments in West Bengal, Kerala, and Tripura have successfully
experimented with alternative styles of governance within the national polity to amelio-
rate the conditions of the rural and urban poor. It would be inappropriate, however, to
presume that the rise of new social groups to power, and the regionalization of politics,
will end institutionalized social deprivation. However, radical potentials for democratic
transformations are clearly visible in the twists and turns of Indian electoral politics.

In the late 1990s, a change in the political environment of India took place as Hindu
nationalists gained political power in India and in certain states. In 2002, a vicious pogrom
in Gujarat that targeted Muslim minorities was believed by many to have been orchestrated
by the BJP government in power. Members of the civil society, intellectuals, and sections
of the media criticized the Gujarat chief minister, Narendra Modi, and his BJP provincial
government for failing to stop the violence. In 2004, the BJP government was voted out
of power, and the INC, allied with the parliamentary Left, acquired a majority in parliament. They passed several legislative measures to address the needs of the rural poor.
But the increasing liberalization policies of the government made income disparity more
visible. India now faces a serious threat from a Maoist insurrection among the poorest
segment of the Indian population, the inhabitants of mineral-rich regions of central and
south central India. In 2006, Prime Minister Manmohan Singh identified the Maoists as
the greatest threat to India's democracy.

Aside from the country's political struggles, many people in India have prospered in
the last twenty years, with an annual gross national product (GNP) growth rate of 6.1
percent in 2011. Yet almost half of India's children are below average in weight. Poverty
is ever-present for many. Contrasts are enormous—for example, India is increasingly a
site for medical tourism, with people from neighboring countries as well as Europe, Japan,
and the Americas seeking heart or kidney transplants and other medical interventions,
while only one-quarter of the population has easy access to clean drinking water. Many
of these anomalies are explored in the case studies below.

For images of popular culture in South Asia, see the website Tasveer Ghar: A House of Pictures (http://www.tasveerghar.net/).

Islamic Republic of Pakistan

Pakistan was carved out of Britain's Indian empire along with India in 1947 and was bifurcated geographically into West Pakistan and East Pakistan (which would later become Bangladesh). Its postindependence history has been characterized by periods of military rule, political instability, and conflicts with neighboring India. In 1947–1948, Partition led to the massive migration of some 8 million refugees from what became India, transforming cities such as Karachi, where many of the *muhajirs* (Indian Urdu-speaking migrants) settled, as well as Punjab. Then, in the 1980s, the Soviet invasion of neighboring Afghanistan led to another massive migration, with some 3 million Afghani refugees settling primarily in the North-West Frontier Province. The country continues to face challenging problems, including terrorism, poverty, illiteracy, and corruption.

At independence, Pakistan had no viable organization to sustain the political structure of the new nation. Unlike the INC, which had an enduring presence in the politics of British India, the Muslim League was a patchy body with practically no organizational presence. After 1947, the Muslim League fell back on regional political networks among locally powerful landed magnates who were not subject to any rigorous party control. The tenuous political hold of the Muslim League leader Mohammed Ali Jinnah and the central government over local politics was further complicated by the ethnic diversity of the country and by its geographical splintering, with West Pakistan separated from East Pakistan (later Bangladesh) by thousands of miles of Indian territory.

The lack of effective party machinery within the Muslim League was countered by the centralized military-bureaucracy structure. Inevitably, whenever the generally fractious politicians agreed on the adoption of a constitution to govern the country, the military-bureaucracy complex stepped in to assume political power. The preeminence of this military-bureaucratic grouping was sustained by the U.S.-led Western bloc, which sought to use Pakistan as a South Asian outpost in the Cold War. Pakistan's Western patrons felt that, given the brittle state of the country's economy, a depoliticized military regime would facilitate economic growth in neoclassical terms, with little regard for social equity.

Under Mohammad Ayub Khan (1958–1968), Pakistan underwent economic growth, with an unprecedented rise in GNP and per capita income. The industrial sector grew substantially, as did the agriculture sector, due to the adoption of Green Revolution technology. Pro-Western foreign policies also meant that Pakistan received a liberal dose of foreign aid. Nevertheless, Ayub Khan's economic boom brought little benefit to the masses, instead deepening class polarization. Industrialization accrued benefits primarily to twenty-two families who exercised control over most of the industrial, insurance, and banking sectors.

Pakistan's investment in education was among the lowest in Asia. Wages of industrial workers also steadily declined. Small traders were ruined by the government's preference for large industrial companies and big businesses. Inflation eroded the income of students and minor government employees. The agrarian policies of the Ayub Khan regime also undermined the economic position of poor peasants. Land reforms in 1959 proved to be cosmetic, and the introduction of new production technologies led to a shrinkage of employment opportunities in rural areas. This intensified class polarization was accompanied by regional economic imbalances within the country, especially between its western and eastern wings.

Pakistan's failure in its war over Kashmir with India in 1965 further incited a massive upsurge against the military junta. At this time Zulfiqar Ali Bhutto stormed onto the stage with a new political agenda. The son of a wealthy landlord, Bhutto had served in Ayub Khan's ministry since 1958. Yet he became a vocal opponent of the Soviet-sponsored Tashkent Declaration that ended the 1965 war with India, accusing Ayub Khan of a total sellout. Bhutto resigned from the cabinet in 1966 to form his own political party, the Pakistan People's Party (PPP). Buoyed by a responsive political constituency, Bhutto decided to contest the presidential election against Ayub Khan, who responded to his subordinate's rebellion by putting Bhutto in prison. This further exalted Bhutto's political position, however, and upon his release, Bhutto developed the doctrine of Islamic socialism, promising social justice to the underprivileged.

While other political parties failed to offer any clear social or economic program, the PPP advocated the nationalization of banks, as well as investments in heavy industries, communications, and the energy sectors. The party also pledged to end military dictatorship, feudalism, and monopoly capitalism, and it promised to establish a "truly" democratic state. Further, Bhutto adopted a sharp nationalist stance against India. Using radical socioeconomic rhetoric coupled with jingoism, the PPP mobilized the urban and rural poor in a series of agitations against the military regime. In the 1970 elections, the PPP secured a comfortable majority of seats in the western wing of the country.

While Bhutto secured the elections in the western wing of Pakistan, the increasingly uncomfortable populations in East Bengal sought an end to West Pakistani industrial and political dominance, as well as the imposition of Urdu as the official language. Numerically dominant, the East Pakistanis supported the Awami League of Sheikh Mujibur Rahman and gained a majority in the national assembly. This unnerved the military bureaucratic oligarchy, which retaliated with a civil war in East Pakistan that led to another war with India in 1971, resulting in the emergence of the independent nation-state of Bangladesh.

Bhutto's failure to prevent the secession of Bangladesh and establish a democratic polity in Pakistan was due to the power of the landed aristocracy within the PPP ranks. During the 1970 election, Bhutto made deals with feudal lords, many of whom joined the new party in the hope of establishing a presence in the industrial sector of the country. They became PPP leaders and had few radical inclinations. The dominance of propertied elites within the PPP also prevented Bhutto from implementing "social-democratic" reforms. Land reforms in 1972 were again cosmetic. Bhutto's promise to improve the economic plight of industrial labor also remained a false hope. Soon after assuming power, Bhutto marginalized the radical section of the PPP that had mobilized working-class support for such change.

The bifurcation of Pakistan also dealt a severe blow to the country's developmental process. The loss of East Pakistan implied a reduction in national income, a decrease in export earnings, and the loss of part of the domestic market. Pakistan now needed to import the tea and jute that had come from the eastern part of the country. West Pakistan now had to bear the entire defense budget. Finally, haunted by the fear of India and needing to placate the army, Bhutto spent more than 50 percent of the national budget on the defense establishment.

The abject failure of Bhutto to implement his electoral promises compelled him to undermine the democratic aspects of the state apparatus. This proved disastrous for both himself and Pakistan. When he called for an election in March 1977, the opposition groups closed ranks against Bhutto and formed the Pakistan National Alliance. Alarmed by this alliance, Bhutto rigged the election, which instantly caused a massive political agitation under the leadership of the urban middle classes who had earlier helped Bhutto come to power. The army intervened. Bhutto was tried, condemned, and hanged, and General Zia-ul-Haq, the head of the Pakistani military establishment, came to power.

Zia-ul-Haq's regime was a blending of military dictatorship and theocracy. Islam had certainly played a pivotal role in the creation of Pakistan, but it had not been used so nakedly to bolster a dictatorship. Early rulers had even dropped Islam from the formal nomenclature of the Pakistani state. Religious fundamentalist groups also tended to remain confined to the political fringe. Haq institutionalized Islam in Pakistani politics, distorting the largely tolerant nature of local political culture. Eventually, his death in a plane crash in 1988 opened new opportunities for experimenting with formal democracy in the country.

A 2010 documentary *Bhutto*, on the life and death of Benazir Bhutto, the prime minister of Pakistan (1988–1990, 1993–1996), is available on the website Top Documentary Films (http://topdocumentaryfilms.com/bhutto/).

Pakistan witnessed another democratic wave in 1988 when Benazir Bhutto (the eldest daughter of Zulfiqar Ali Bhutto) led the PPP to victory against the Muslim League factions led by the Zia-ul-Haq protégé Nawaz Sharif. Her brief reign as Prime Minister ended when Sharif was elected to power in 1990, serving as Prime Minister until 1993. In 1993 the PPP returned to power, with Benazir Bhutto again as Prime Minister, before being dismissed by the President in 1996. The ML under Nawaz Sharif won the 1997 elections. In 1999 the Pakistani army compelled Sharif to conduct nuclear tests in retaliation against India's. That year the Pakistani army also fought a limited war in Kashmir with India. In 1999, Pervez Musharraf, the Pakistani military chief, captured power through a coup.

Despite growing public anger, Musharraf remained in power for nearly nine years. He aggressively supported separatists in Indian Administered Kashmir while assuming the role of a reformist, pro-Western administrator. He initially armed the Taliban, but under U.S. pressure after the terrorist attacks in the United States on September 11, 2001, he took military action against them. Initially an ardent champion of a military solution to the Kashmir question, he later supported dialogue for peace, motivated by a need for international legitimacy for his rule. Finally, popular pressure compelled him to hold elections in 2008. The leader of the PPP, Benazir Bhutto, was assassinated under mysterious circumstances while campaigning. Her death paved the way for the government headed by Bhutto's husband, Asif Ali Zardari. In 2013, general elections returned the Muslim League to power, with Nawaz Sharif becoming Prime Minister for a five-year term. This administration remains weak, and Pakistan appears to be sliding into chaos, with a section of the army, and army-sponsored Islamic organizations, favoring the establishment of an Islamic regime.

People's Republic of Bangladesh

The present-day borders of Bangladesh were established during the British partition of Bengal in 1947, when the region became East Pakistan, part of the newly formed nation of Pakistan. Due to political exclusion, ethnic and linguistic discrimination, and economic neglect by the politically dominant western wing, popular agitation grew and gave rise to a nationalist movement, leading to the declaration of independence and the Bangladesh Liberation War in 1971. In the aftermath of war and independence, the new state endured poverty, famine, political turmoil, and military coups. The restoration of democracy in 1991 has been followed by relative calm and economic progress.

Bangladesh is a unitary secular parliamentary republic, with an elected parliament called the Jatiyo Sangshad. It is the world's eighth most populous country and has one of the highest population densities in the world. Though the Bengalis form the vast majority of its population, Bangladesh is also home to various indigenous peoples in its northern and southeastern districts.

During the 1970 general election in Pakistan, Mujibur Rahman, head of the Bengali political party the Awami League, inspired millions of Bengalis in East Pakistan with his passionate speeches. Affectionately called Banga Bandhu (friend of Bengal) and commonly called Sheikh Mujib, he became a symbol of the liberation struggle of Bangladesh. His return to Dhaka from a jail in Pakistan at the end of the civil war was celebrated by unprecedented crowds. Yet four years later, when junior army officers assassinated him, there were few mourners.

There are several reasons for the rapid erosion of Mujib's popularity. He could not arrest the economic decline in postliberation Bangladesh that culminated in the famine of 1974. He also failed to curtail the lawlessness that swept across the country after liberation. His distrust of the army further contributed to the growing anarchy. Corruption became rampant, and many corrupt officials were allegedly Mujib's immediate family members.

Frustrated by factional rivalries within the Awami League, Mujib increasingly concentrated political power in his own hands. A sizable section of the Bangladeshi population felt betrayed by a person who had promised them democracy but established a new form of autocracy. A corollary of this process was the transfer of political power to the military that made the Bangladeshis experience dictatorship for nearly two decades.

Mujib's failures reflect a much wider insufficiency of the Awami League as a political organization. Although the Awami League adopted a socialist rhetoric, it remained an organization dominated by rich farmers, traders, and the salaried middle classes. Since most prominent Awami League leaders worked from outside Bangladesh throughout the civil war, the party could not develop adequate networks to harness the political and economic transformation unleashed by the war. Bangladesh had been radicalized by the Bangladesh Liberation War, and the people expected a radical redistribution of social and economic resources, as well as fundamental reforms of the political system.

One crucial task for the AL leadership was the revitalization of Bangladesh's war-ravaged economy. The disruption of traditional economic ties with erstwhile West Pakistan forced Bangladesh to locate new sources for raw cotton and oil seeds. The withdrawal of the Pakistani bourgeoisie from the insurance, banking, and manufacturing sectors created a severe shortage of skilled labor. The devastating cyclone of 1970 also had a severe impact on agricultural production. Further, Bangladesh had to resettle the nearly 10 million refugees who had fled to India during the Bangladesh Liberation War and later returned.

The Awami League came to represent an intermediate regime, where rich peasants, petty traders, and low-income salaried professionals exercised domination over the state structure. Indeed, the Awami League government did not adversely affect mercantile interests, nor did it initiate any drastic land reforms. The Mujib regime became overtly dependent on international capital and foreign aid to augment the supply capital, which again acted as a restraint on the pursuit of a socialist restructuring program. Mujib followed his economic policies by introducing one-party rule. Realizing Mujib's political vulnerability, a group of military officers organized a coup that led to his assassination, and that of his entire family except one daughter, in August 1975.

Vice President Khandaker Mushtaq Ahmed was sworn in as president, with most of Mujib's cabinet intact. Two army uprisings in November 1975 led to the declaration of a national emergency to restore order and calm, and the country came under temporary martial law, with three service chiefs serving as deputies to the new president, Justice Abu Sayem, who also became the chief martial law administrator.

Lieutenant General Ziaur Rahman (Zia) became president in 1977 after a plebiscite to gain popular legitimacy for the military government. Zia restored the old East Pakistani ruling elites to political power in independent Bangladesh. He founded the Bangladesh Nationalist Party (BNP) and redefined Bangladeshi nationalism in Islamic terms to distinguish it from the larger Bengali identity, of which the Hindus are also a part. Zia emulated Ayub Khan by encouraging the army to penetrate civil and political organizations. Zia's rule ended when he was assassinated by elements of the military in 1981.

Zia's death was followed by a presidential election in 1982, which the BNP candidate Abdus Sattar won with military support. Later that same year, Hussain Mohammed Ershad, another military leader, removed Sattar from power in a bloodless coup and became the president of Bangladesh. Ershad emulated Zia by establishing his own party and rigging elections. He also developed a new patronage structure to sustain the prominence of the military within the civil institutions. Ershad's control was not absolute, however, and he faced constant opposition from major political formations: the BNP led by Khaleda Zia, Zia's widow, and the Awami League under the leadership of Sheikh Hasina, Mujib's surviving daughter.

In the face of popular protests, Ershad's regime collapsed in 1990. In the parliamentary elections that followed, Begum Khaleda Zia's BNP was swept into power. However, the next elections, in 1996, were in favor of the Awami League. Democracy did not bring political stability to Bangladesh, as the two main political parties promoted cronyism, with no fundamental reforms at the grassroots level. The BNP came back to power in 2001 with the help of Islamist parties, which almost took control of the administration. The Awami League staged a civilian revolt of sorts in 2007 and the army stepped in again to stabilize the situation. In December 2008 the army oversaw elections that saw the return of the Awami League to power.

Despite the political upheavals since independence from Pakistan, Bangladesh has also prospered, slowly raising its rank in the Legatum Prosperity Index, with a growth rate of 6 to 7 percent for a number of years preceding 2013. With a growing market-based economy, foreign exchange earnings from migrant laborers in the Middle East, a burgeoning service economy, and self-sufficiency in rice, Bangladesh has also benefited from a decrease in its population growth rate to 1.6 percent, down from a high of 3.3 percent in 1967, and with a steady decline since the late 1970s.

Federal Democratic Republic of Nepal

A monarchy throughout most of its history, Nepal was ruled by the Shah dynasty of kings from 1768, when Prithvi Narayan Shah unified its many small kingdoms. However, a decade-long civil war begun in the mid-1990s involving the Communist Party of Nepal (Maoist) and several weeks of mass protests by all major political parties led to the "twelve-point agreement" of November 2005. The ensuing elections for the constituent assembly in May 2008 overwhelmingly favored the abolition of the monarchy and the establishment of a federal, multiparty, representative democratic republic.

In many ways, the contemporary political structure of Nepal evolved through interacting with Indian social reform movements and nationalist politics. Beginning in 1846, the British Indian government supported the kin-based, authoritarian political rule of the hereditary prime ministers of Nepal known as Ranas. At the same time, Indian nationalist political movements and leaders inspired political opposition to Rana rule. Efforts to create a modern political organization culminated in the establishment of the Nepal Congress in 1947 at Calcutta, in neighboring India. After independence, the Indian government provided open assistance to the Nepal Congress to organize political movements to establish a democratic system of governance in Nepal.

The Rana rule led to the creation of a parasitic, rent-receiving class of landowners that was divorced from the production process, thus reducing the capacity of the state to gather revenue. The upshot of this arrangement was a skewed pattern of landholding whereby a minority owned most of the land in the country. Any proposal for land reforms in Nepal encountered royal displeasure, however. Still, popular discontent and the British withdrawal from India in 1947 made Rana rule increasingly untenable. In 1950, the political situation had deteriorated so far that the personal safety of the royals was in doubt. Open revolt ensued, and by the end of the year the Ranas agreed to a co-alition government under King Tribhuvan in which they shared power equally with the Nepal Congress. By the end of the year, the Ranas were maneuvered out and Nepal had a democratic government under a constitutional monarch. In 1955 King Tribhuvan died and was succeeded by his son, Mahendra.

When the elected prime minister, B.P. Koirala, proposed the nationalization of land resources and the abolition of tenure without compensation, King Mahendra and other landed interests became nervous. In December 1960, the king suspended the constitution and dissolved the Nepal Congress ministry. The royal action provoked a popular unrest that disrupted public life throughout 1961. The king complained of the Indian hand in fomenting disorder, but fortuitously for him, the Sino-Indian War of 1962 compelled India to pressure the Nepal Congress to suspend its rebellion.

In 1962, King Mahendra introduced a new constitution to institutionalize the royal hold on the country's political structure. The new constitution envisaged a four-tier political structure involving local government bodies with limited power, known as *panchayats*: at the lowest level were village assemblies (gram sabhas) that elected members to the district and regional panchayats. At the uppermost tier was an apex body called the National Panchayat. Representatives to village assemblies were to be directly elected by the local population, the district and regional-level units were to be constituted by members of village and town panchayats, and the National Panchayat was to be formed through a complex voting system whereby diverse professional organizations, class-based unions, and members of zonal panchayats were to send their representatives. This arrangement also banned political parties; elections to panchayats were designed on a non-party basis. The National Panchayat of about ninety members could not criticize the royal government, debate the principles of partyless democracy, introduce budgetary bills without royal approval, or enact bills without approval of the king. Mahendra was supreme commander of the armed forces, appointed (and had the power to remove) members of the Supreme Court, appointed the Public Service Commission to oversee the civil service, and could change any judicial decision or amend the constitution at any time.

By replacing parliamentary democracy with the *panchayati* system, the Nepalese monarchy attempted to preserve and freeze the sociopolitical system of the country within a carefully stipulated hierarchical political order. The crown feared that in a diverse, multi-ethnic society like Nepal, democratic political dynamism would inevitably undermine the existing social structure and economic organization of the country. In 1972, Mahendra's son Birendra succeeded him as king.

There was severe opposition to the panchayati system, but the most crucial obstacle to political mobilization was the political difference between the Nepal Congress and the Communists. While a substantial number of Communists were united against the

Pashupatinath Temple in Kathmandu, Nepal, is a site closely associated with the monarchy and high caste elites. *(Photo by Luca Galuzzi, http://www.galuzzi.it)*

panchayati system, the Nepal Congress refused to cooperate with them. This crippled political opposition to the king, and in a 1984 referendum the Nepalese people rejected a proposal to return to a multiparty democracy. During the 1980s, the ideological difference between the various Communist parties and the Nepal Congress was considerably influenced by their conflicting perceptions of Indo-Nepalese ties. While the Nepal Congress maintained close ties with India, the Communist Party of Nepal (Unified Marxist-Leninist) (CPN-UML) advocated a more critical scrutiny of the 1950 Indo-Nepal Treaty of Peace and Friendship, which remains the cornerstone of bilateral ties between the two neighbors.

The Nepal Congress increasingly proved to be a faction-ridden body, several of its leading personalities having been old panchayati figures. Even in terms of policies, it did not envisage a radical reform of society and the economy. In contrast, the Communists appeared more dynamic and committed to a radical social reorganization. In the closely contested second general election of 1994, the CPN-UML captured eighty-eight seats, while the Nepal Congress won eighty-three seats. A Supreme Court judgment prevented the elected prime minister from the CPN-UML, Manmohan Adhikari, from holding elections to obtain a fresh mandate. This led to a political stalemate, against the backdrop of which the Maoists of Nepal declared a "people's war," or armed rebellion. In 2001, the immediate royal family was shot dead by Crown Prince Dipendra for not allowing his marriage to the girl of his choice. Gyanendra, the assassinated king's brother, ascended the Nepali throne and hardened his stand against the Maoist insurgency.

Box 3.11

Maoism in Nepal

Maoism is a major political force in Nepal. The Unified Communist Party of Nepal (Maoist) was founded in 1994. In 1996, the Maoist party launched a civil war that pitted Maoist fighters against the Nepali government and lasted until 2006. From 2008 to 2009, the Maoist party became the dominant party and led by coalition. Currently, the party is named the Unified Communist Party of Nepal (Maoist).

Gyanendra's position prompted popular uprisings, and the king was forced to reinstate the parliament in 2006. In an election to the constituent assembly in April 2008, Maoists secured a simple majority. In May of the same year, the newly elected parliament ended 240 years of monarchy, making Nepal a republic. The constituent assembly, however, failed to produce a constitution. Nepal witnessed the appointment of five prime ministers in six years following the formation of the constituent assembly. The country has yet to draft a formal constitution.

Although Nepal is somewhat politically stable, the country faces serious economic and social issues, with unemployment as high as 46 percent and literacy at barely 60 percent. Agriculture employs some 76 percent of the population. The physical terrain continues to make education and development problematic: the popularity of trekking for tourists speaks to the difficulty of movement for residents, with more than one-third living a two-hour walk from an all-season road. While tourism could be a growth industry, the country's political instability has hampered its growth, though GDP was expected to reach 5 percent in 2012.

Islamic Republic of Afghanistan

The political history of the modern state of Afghanistan begins in 1709, when the Hotaki dynasty was established in Kandahar followed by Ahmad Shah Durrani's rise to power in 1747. In the nineteenth century, Afghanistan became a buffer state between the British and Russian empires, which were locked in a strategic and diplomatic rivalry termed the "Great Game." Following the 1919 Anglo-Afghan War, King Amanullah began a European-style modernization of the country that included literacy campaigns and education for women, modeled on measures in Turkey.

Both the conservative clerics from rural areas and the local chiefs felt that Amanullah was violating Islamic traditions, and a revolt by different local communities led by Habibullah Kalakani soon removed him from power. Amanullah's cousin Nadir Khan then defeated Kalakani, executed him, and assumed the throne. Khan was assassinated by a student and succeeded by his son, Zahir Shah, who was only nineteen. Zahir had many mentors among his uncles and cousins, who acted as his prime ministers. Though

Zahir wanted to democratize the country, he retracted in the face of unrest. Afghanistan was ruled by a cautious group of royal advisers with a cosmopolitan outlook, who were keenly aware of their inability to mold the rural society. In 1964, Zahir introduced a constitution and tolerated the growth of a left-wing, pro-Soviet Communist party known as the People's Democratic Party of Afghanistan (PDPA).

During this period, Kabul became a cosmopolitan city with a thriving university enrolling both male and female students, as well as a significant foreign population. Western goods were readily available, and the first Marks and Spencer store in Central Asia opened there. In this sense, the capital was markedly at odds with the rural countryside, where education was almost completely lacking, for both males and females, and most people survived on meager and inefficient landholdings.

In 1972–1973 the slow and steady move toward a quasi-democratic political system was abandoned when Prince Daud, known to be pro-Soviet, captured political power in a bloodless coup. He transformed Afghanistan into a republic, but his measures failed to stabilize the economy. Prince Daud's government arrested PDPA leaders and killed Mir Akbar Khyber, a prominent Afghan Communist. The PDPA, with connections in the army, staged a coup in April 1978. The new Afghan regime was headed by Nur Muhammad Taraki, who moved aggressively toward socialist land reforms, a declaration of women's rights, and even a ban on women wearing head coverings and men having beards. He promoted a secular education system to replace traditional religious education. The new regime faced opposition from conservative mullahs, and it brutally suppressed opposition from religious groups. But the PDPA was faction-ridden, and Taraki was killed by the chief of the military, Hafizullah Amin. Amin's takeover of Afghanistan was backed by Soviet forces. In the face of Communist persecution, religion became a rallying issue for an ethnically divided population.

As this was during the Cold War, the U.S. administrations of presidents Jimmy Carter and Ronald Reagan extended military support to the refugees and the opposition. Zia-ul-Haq, the Pakistani military dictator, conducted military resistance with U.S. support through his secret service organization, the Inter-Services Intelligence. Saudi Arabia also funded the *mujahideen*, or holy warriors. Divided into several groups, the mujahideen were not a very cohesive force, but generous U.S. and Saudi assistance enabled them to inflict massive casualties on Soviet forces. The civil war saw the death of nearly 600,000 Afghans, and another 6 million Afghans took shelter in Pakistan and Iran. Soviet forces withdrew in 1988–1989, but the PDPA-led Afghan government under Mohammad Najibullah held on to power until 1992, when the mujahideen took over Kabul.

Seeking to extend its influence in Afghanistan and Central Asia, Pakistan engineered peace among the Afghan mujahideen. The new government was undermined by the Islamic militant Gulbuddin Hekmatyar, supported by Pakistan. Afghanistan witnessed intense civil war during this period, and different warlords divided the country. In the midst of this turmoil, Mullah Omar, who had been educated in a Pakistani madrassa, launched a new military-political formation called the Taliban in 1994. He captured many Afghan cities and received liberal assistance from Pakistan. The Taliban seized Kabul in September 1996 and founded the Islamic Republic of Afghanistan. Meanwhile, the Tajik leader Ahmad Shah Massoud and the Uzbek warlord Abdul Rashid Dostum formed a united front, the Northern Alliance, to defeat the Taliban.

The Taliban slowly and steadily captured much of Afghan territory. They also began killing members of the Hazara communities who were Shia Muslims. This heightened tensions between the Taliban (a Sunni Muslim formation) and Iran, a Shia Muslim state. Iran sent troops to its Afghan border after Iranian diplomats were killed in Mazar-i-Sharif in northern Afghanistan. Supported by Pakistani soldiers and the Islamist Saudi exile Osama bin Laden, the Taliban started a process of Islamization that curbed the influence of local leaders. This generated deep resentment against the Taliban and its foreign supporters for its cruel massacres of ethnic minorities in a multiethnic society. The curbing of women's rights, forced seclusion and public flogging of women, dramatic burning of films, and blasting of the giant Buddha statues with howitzer guns and dynamite at Bamiyan made the Taliban an international pariah. Massoud expressed his hope for a democratic Afghanistan run on the basis of consultation and consensus, but he was assassinated by suicide bombers posing as journalists. Soon after the terrorist attacks on U.S. soil on September 11, 2001, the United States declared war on the Taliban and dislodged them from power. The United States also compelled the Pakistani establishment to fight against its former protégés, the Taliban.

The United States eventually committed to removing its troops from the country by 2014, leaving the country under the charge of a coalition government under President Hamid Karzai. However, three decades of war have made Afghanistan one the most dangerous countries in the world, as well as the largest producer of refugees and asylum seekers. While the international community is rebuilding war-torn Afghanistan, terrorist groups such as the Haqqani Network and Hezb-i-Islami are actively involved in a nationwide Taliban-led insurgency, which includes hundreds of assassinations and suicide attacks.

Meanwhile, across the country, schools have opened, or reopened; literacy rates are rapidly expanding; and access to health care has vastly improved. While health conditions are still deplorable, with a life expectancy of forty-nine years and one in ten children dying before the age of five, some 60 percent of the population is within two hours of a health clinic. The disability rate is also high, due in part to the landmines that still pocket the countryside. Literacy is about 28 percent, with female literacy rates around 10 percent. Yet almost 100,000 students are now attending universities, and some 7 million children are in school.

Afghanistan has vast deposits of oil and natural gas, as well as huge amounts of lithium, copper, gold, coal, iron ore, and other minerals. China, the United States, Pakistan, and India all seek to exploit these natural resources. In recent years, India and China have received rights to excavate several mineral deposits in Afghanistan.

Democratic Socialist Republic of Sri Lanka

Sri Lanka, formerly Ceylon, is a diverse country with many religions, ethnicities, and languages. The Sinhalese people are the majority; ethnic minorities include Tamils, Muslim

Box 3.12

A Land-Water Bridge from India to Sri Lanka

Adam's Bridge, also known as Rama's Bridge, is a series of interconnecting limestone shoals that probably connected India and Sri Lanka in a previous ecological epoch. Some of the connecting sandbars are so shallow that a person can stand, making nautical navigation difficult. Such a natural land bridge was first mentioned in the Ramayana, when Hanuman and his monkey clan constructed a bridge to Lanka in order to rescue Sita from Ravana, the demon-king. Some Hindus still believe that Adam's Bridge is in fact the historical bridge used by Rama to rescue his wife. In 2007, a Sri Lankan tourism development firm began advertising the bridge as a pilgrimage place for devout Hindus following the Ramayana Trail. There is a gap between popular religious and scholarly opinion on the bridge, however, and most historians and geologists strongly disagree with the Rama thesis.

Moors, Burghers, Kaffirs, Malays, and the aboriginal Vedda people. Sri Lanka has a rich Buddhist heritage, though its recent history has been marred by a thirty-year civil war between Tamil insurgents and the Lankan state, which ended in the latter's victory in 2009 (see Chapter 13). The civil war developed from the fear of ethnic marginalization of the Sinhalese against the background of historic privileges enjoyed by Hindu Tamils because of their close connection with the British administration. The nationalist movement in Sri Lanka, though divided between moderate constitutionalists and radical proindependence forces, cooperated with the British during World War II and gained British support for independence after the war.

The Sri Lankan nationalist Don Senanayake, founder of the United National Party (UNP), negotiated with the British to gain dominion status for the country in 1948. The politics of Sri Lanka were dominated by the failure to negotiate the national question involving the Sinhalese as well as Hindu and Muslim Tamils. The failure to resolve this issue was reflected in the declaration of Sinhala as the only national language in 1956 and an anti-Tamil pogrom in 1958 in Colombo.

In April 1971, the Marxist group Janatha Vimukthi Peramuna (JVP) launched an insurrection against the Sri Lanka Freedom Party (SLFP) government led by Sirimavo Bandaranaike. The government suppressed the revolt in the south ruthlessly. In 1977, the UNP returned to power under the leadership of Junius Jayewardene. The new government sought to address the Tamil question through constitutional measures.

This period also saw the rise of the Liberation Tigers of Tamil Eelam (LTTE), also known as the Tamil Tigers, who sought a separate homeland for Lankan Tamils. The LTTE attacked government forces and undermined the peace process. Meanwhile, the government passed the Prevention of Terrorism Act of 1978, leading to the suppression of civil liberties in Tamil areas. This situation led to a civil war between Tamil and Sinhala communities in 1983. The Indian government sent members of its army to Sri Lanka, but they were completely defeated by the LTTE. The LTTE also assassinated the Indian politician and INC leader Rajiv Gandhi in 1991 in a suicide bombing. The civil war continued until 2009, when LTTE was militarily defeated. This defeat was made possible by the new international climate against terrorist militancy and Indian toleration of the Sri Lankan army operation. During the conflict both the LTTE and the Sri Lankan army violated the human rights of ordinary people, including both Tamils and Sinhalese.

Sri Lanka is the second most prosperous country in South Asia, with its GDP growing 11 percent in 2011. The poverty rate has been cut in half since 2005, to 7.6 percent, while unemployment is a mere 4.9 percent. With a literacy rate of 92 percent and computer literacy at 35 percent, Sri Lanka is well positioned for modern commerce and industrialization.

Republic of the Maldives

The Republic of the Maldives gained full independence from its protectorate status under the British in 1965. For three years, the country was ruled by the previous sultan, Muhammad Fareed Didi. In 1968, the electorate voted for a republic, and Ibrahim Nasir became the nation's first president.

The 1970s were mixed, both politically and economically. Tourism began in earnest, eventually coming to dominate the local economy. At the same time, the British closed their airbase at Gan. Ultimately, Nasir escaped to Singapore with millions of dollars from the treasury. In 1978, Maumoon Abdul Gayoom was elected president, and he served for six consecutive terms. This period ushered in stability as well as an economic boom, based largely on tourism. There were several coup attempts throughout the 1980s; the attempted coup in 1988 was countered with Indian naval intervention.

The 2004 tsunami across much of South and Southeast Asia caused huge devastation to this low-lying island nation, with damages estimated at some US$400 million, or 62 percent of GDP. Currently, the region faces a serious threat from global warming. In 2008, the government of President Mohamed Nasheed announced the creation of a sovereign relief fund to aid citizens in buying property in other parts of the world if sea levels rose and inundated their lands.

President Nasheed's government was also controversial—beset with constitutional conflicts and accused of lack of transparency. He himself had spent years, including more than twenty jail sentences, fighting against what he viewed as the corruption of President Gayoom. But Nasheed was ousted in a coup in 2012 and replaced by his vice president, Mohammed Waheed Hassan. As of the middle of 2013, the constitution has been suspended and no new elections have been held.

The primary issue in the Maldives is actually its geography, with the highest point of land on its more than 1,900 islands a mere 8 feet (2.4 meters) above sea level. The population of approximately 300,000 is scattered across the islands, with the population of the capital, Malé, only 62,000. The country has a 99 percent literacy rate and life expectancy of seventy-two years, making it the most prosperous South Asian nation. At the same time, it has an illegal immigrant population, drawn from other South Asian countries, of some 33,000. Finally, it allows only Islam to be practiced as a religion, and it is considered one of the most religiously restrictive countries in the world.

Kingdom of Bhutan

In contrast to the Maldives, Bhutan is a land-locked nation, with a population of some 600,000. It has purposely remained isolated, with a ban on television and the Internet lifted only in 1999.

Bhutan's modern history begins in 1907, when a group of elites recognized Ugyen Wangchuck as the hereditary king of the country. In 1953, King Jigme Dorji Wangchuck initiated a legislative assembly to bring some democratic representation to the country. Democracy in the form of a constitutional monarchy finally arrived in 2008, after the fourth king abdicated his throne in favor of his son, the crown prince Jigme Khesar Namgyel Wangchuck, who was crowned in an elaborate coronation ceremony in 2008, after the first democratic elections were held. Elections in 2013 led to the surprise victory of the People's Democratic Party against the ruling Bhutan Peace and Prosperity Party that had won the first election with the support of the monarchy in 2008.

Since the turn of the twenty-first century, Bhutan has had the world's fastest-growing economy, due to the Tala Hydroelectric Project, which is producing power only for India. Nevertheless, 80 percent of the population lives on subsistence agriculture, with minimal industry and little infrastructure. Roads are few and railways nonexistent, making any move toward industrialization difficult.

Bhutan does have an ongoing territorial dispute with its neighbor China, with the Chinese starting to build roads and bridges in the disputed area beginning in 2005. From 1947 until 2007, an Indo-Bhutanese treaty gave India control over Bhutan's foreign affairs. A new treaty put that authority in the hands of the Bhutanese.

References and Further Research

Barfield, Thomas. 2012. *Afghanistan: A Political and Cultural History*. Princeton, NJ: Princeton University Press.

Bose, Sugata, and Ayesha Jalal. 2011. *Modern South Asia: History, Culture, Political Economy*. 3rd ed. New York: Routledge.

Dalrymple, William. 2003. *City of Djinns: A Year in Delhi*. New York: Penguin.

Forbes, Geraldine. 2007. *Women in Modern India*. Cambridge: Cambridge University Press.

Guha, Ramchandra. 2008. *India After Gandhi: The History of the World's Largest Democracy*. New York: HarperPerennial.

Holt, John Clifford. 2011. *The Sri Lanka Reader: History, Culture, Politics*. Durham, NC: Duke University Press.

Kenoyer, Mark, and Kimberley Heuston. 2005. *The Ancient South Asian World*. New York: Oxford University Press.

Khan, Yasmin. 2008. *The Great Partition: The Making of India and Pakistan*. New Haven, CT: Yale University Press.

Metcalf, Barbara D., and Thomas R. Metcalf. 2012. *A Concise History of Modern India*. 3rd ed. Cambridge: Cambridge University Press.

Nehru, Jawaharlal. 2004. *The Discovery of India*. 2nd ed. New Delhi: APH.

Oldenburg, Philip. 2010. *India, Pakistan, and Democracy: Solving the Puzzle of Divergent Paths*. New York: Routledge.

Possehl, Gregory L. 2003. *The Indus Civilization: A Contemporary Perspective*. Walnut Creek, CA: AltaMira Press.

Talbot, Ian. 2010. *Pakistan: A Modern History*. 2nd ed. New York: Palgrave Macmillan.

van Schendel, Willem. 2009. *A History of Bangladesh*. Cambridge: Cambridge University Press.

Whelpton, John. 2005. *A History of Nepal*. Cambridge: Cambridge University Press.

Wickramasinghe, Nira. 2006. *Sri Lanka in the Modern Age: A History of Contested Identities*. Honolulu: University of Hawaii Press.

Wolpert, Stanley. 2010. *India and Pakistan: Continued Conflict or Cooperation?* Berkeley: University of California Press.

Zavos, John. 2000. *The Emergence of Hindu Nationalism in India*. New Delhi: Oxford University Press.

4

Language in South Asia

SUSAN SNOW WADLEY

Twenty-two constitutionally recognized languages in eighteen different scripts, with two official languages (Hindi and English)—this is the most basic summary of the languages of India. Without doubt, the language situation in South Asia is complex. For example, Pakistan has two official languages, with one, Urdu, spoken as a native language by less than 10 percent (16 million) of the population, and the other, English, spoken primarily as a second language by only 11 percent (18 million). While languages in South Asia have been written for more than three millennia, some, such as minority Tibeto-Burman languages in Nepal, still have no writing system. One language common to Pakistan and India, Punjabi, is written in three different scripts, Perso-Arabic, Devanagari, and Gurmukhi, depending primarily on the religion of the speaker (Muslim, Hindu, or Sikh, respectively). Moving across the subcontinent, there are more than 1,000 "languages" and dialects, representing four distinct language families. To begin to understand this complexity requires careful attention to history, politics, religion, and everyday social life.

Linguists group languages into "families," based primarily on common phonological features (sounds), morphology (words), and syntax (grammar), as well as known historical connections. The largest precolonial language family in South Asia is Indo-European, brought to the subcontinent by the Aryan pastoralists in the second millennium BCE. Languages from the Indo-Iranian branch of the family are spoken in Afghanistan, Pakistan, India, Nepal, Bangladesh, Sri Lanka, and the Maldives. Next is Dravidian, representing languages spoken primarily in southern India today, but also found in small pockets in Pakistan, Nepal, Sri Lanka, and Bangladesh, and quite probably related to the undeciphered language of the Harappa civilization. A third language family, Austroasiatic, is represented primarily by the tribal languages of central India. The fourth, Tibeto-Burman, is represented by languages spoken in Pakistan, India, Nepal, Bhutan, and Bangladesh, but especially in the northeastern regions of India and Bangladesh and in northern Nepal. Bhutan's national language, Dzongkha, is also of Tibeto-Burman origin.

The Indo-European languages and related dialects (Bengali, Dari, Hindi, Gujarati, Sindhi, etc.) and the Dravidian languages (Tamil, Kannada, Malayalam, and Telugu) all have substantial and ancient literary traditions, as do some Tibeto-Burman languages. For more on the literary history of South Asia, see Pollock (2003).

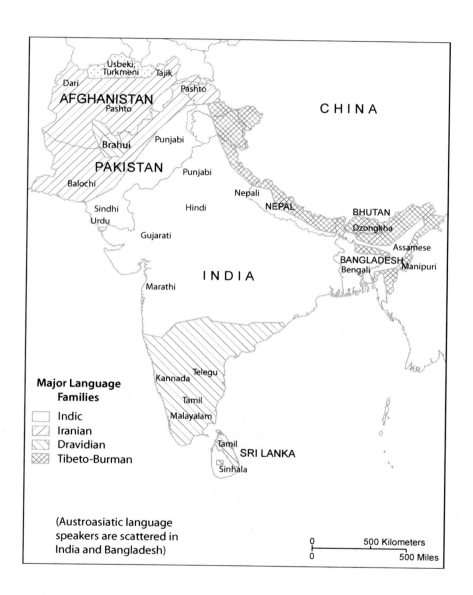

Usbeki,
Turkmeni   Tajik
Dari
          Pashto
AFGHANISTAN
          Pashto   CHINA
                    Punjabi
     Brahui
     PAKISTAN
                    Punjabi
Balochi
                              Nepali
     Sindhi   Hindi   NEPAL   BHUTAN
     Urdu   Dzongkha
                    Gujarati   Assamese
                                             BANGLADESH Manipuri
                    INDIA   Bengali
          Marathi

                                   Telegu
                         Kannada
**Major Language
Families**
          Indic   Tamil
          Iranian Malayalam
          Dravidian
          Tibeto-Burman   Tamil
                         SRI LANKA
                         Sinhala

(Austroasiatic language
speakers are scattered in
India and Bangladesh)

0   500 Kilometers
0   500 Miles

Table 4.1

Language Families of South Asia

	Number of languages	Number of speakers (millions)
Indo-European	110	1,000
Dravidian	35	250
Austroasiatic	25	12
Tibeto-Burman	150	11

Source: Adapted from Asher 2008, 33.

The Indo-European language family has three major points of contact with South Asia: the Indic language of the Aryan tribesmen who came into South Asia by 1500 BCE and whose religious dialect, Sanskrit, was the language of the Rig Veda and other early religious texts; Persian, the Iranian language of the Mughal courts and the Indian elite from the 1500s CE on; and English, the language of British colonial rule. Each of these three—Sanskrit, Persian, and English—has functioned as an elite language in South Asia in a diglossic situation. Diglossia refers to a situation where two or more languages are widely spoken within the same society, with each fulfilling certain functions not common to the other language or languages. Sanskrit was the ritual and religious language of Aryans. It remains the ritual and religious language for all Hindus, although many local and regional religious traditions exist in other languages and dialects. Since knowledge of Sanskrit was allowed only for elite males, lower-caste individuals and women all spoke a Prakrit language (literally a more "natural" language) that was also the native/mother tongue, or the language of the home, of everyone. An elite male, therefore, would speak Sanskrit in religious and other legal situations and a Prakrit language in the market, with his servants, and with his family. Likewise, Pali, the language of Theravada Buddhist texts and rituals, was also in a diglossic relationship to the Prakrits, one dialect of which, Sinhalese, became the dominant language of the Buddhist majority living in Sri Lanka. Other Prakrit dialects evolved into the North Indian Indo-European languages, such as Hindi, Bengali, Oriya, and so on.

Persian was brought to South Asia by various Muslim invaders. Today, Dari, the language spoken in western Afghanistan, is closely related to the modern Persian, known as Farsi, of Iran. Persian was well established as the language of the Mughal courts by 1500. In some areas, such as Kashmir, it became so entrenched as the language of the courts and intellectual elite that Hindu religious texts were composed in it, according to Braj B. Kachru (2008), as well as written in the Perso-Arabic script. At the same time, Persian was Indianized and eventually contributed substantially to the development of Urdu, the "Muslim" language that derives from the Hindustani of northern India, while Hindi became the "Hindu" language with the same origins. Today, Urdu and Hindi are interchangeable as an everyday spoken language, but with different writing systems—Perso-Arabic for Urdu and Devanagari for Hindi—and different religious vocabularies.

Although the first Europeans to colonize South Asia were the Portuguese, subsequent British dominance led to the ascendance of English as the colonial language of schools and courts and eventually to its status as the second official language of India and Pakistan. At least as important as the colonial rulers were the missionaries who sought to replace native languages in schooling. The "Minute on Indian Education," a memo introduced into the British Parliament in 1835 by Thomas Macaulay, advanced the cause of English. Macaulay, though he knew no Sanskrit or Arabic, had only contempt for the knowledge of the East. As he noted in his Minute, "It seems to be admitted on all sides, that the intellectual improvement of those classes of the people who have the means of pursuing higher studies can at present be effected only by means of some language not vernacular amongst them." His mission, then, was to create "a class of persons, Indians in blood and colour, but English in taste, in opinions, in morals and intellect."

Thomas Macaulay's 1835 "Minute on Indian Education" can be found on Fordham University's Modern History Sourcebook site (http://www.fordham.edu/halsall/mod/1833macaulay-india.asp).

Education in English was also highly gendered, with women lagging far behind men in acquiring proficiency in this new powerful and prestigious language. But as schools for native women opened—such as the Poona Native Girls' High School, founded in 1884—English came to be additionally charged with "being modern," according to Shefali Chandra, the author of *The Sexual Life of English* (2012), and a wife's knowledge of English became essential to the new form of companionate marriage being encouraged among elite Indians.

Ironically, English ultimately served to unite Indians across the boundaries of their many regional languages. It was the English-educated elite, such as Mohandas Gandhi, Jawaharlal Nehru, and Mohammed Ali Jinnah, who came together to dislodge the English colonists. Yet English continues to have a significant position in commerce and education in every South Asian country. There are more speakers of English in South Asia than in the core English-speaking world (the United Kingdom, Ireland, the United States, Australia, and New Zealand). While English has enormous influence on South Asia, Indian languages also made contributions to the English spoken in Western countries. Probably the best-known word of Indian origin is *pajama*, used in South Asia to designate the starched white shirt and baggy pants of the politician or dressed-up male, but in the United States and England to designate nighttime wear.

Complicating the language landscape in South Asia are differences in script. There are eighteen scripts in use in India alone, plus the Roman script of English. The Maldives has its own version, Thaana, of the Perso-Arabic script used in Urdu and Pashto. While the scripts are primarily phonological, with a single character representing a sound (though sometimes with alterations to mark vowels), the combinations of characters create some problems in writing and more when creating computer fonts.

To better understand the scripts of South Asia, as well as South Asian languages in general, see the website Languages and Scripts of India (http://www.cs.colostate.edu/~malaiya/scripts.html).

For information on issues related to computer fonts and South Asian scripts, see the website Acharya: Multilingual Computing for Literacy and Education (http://acharya.iitm.ac.in/about.html).

South Asian Sociolinguistics

Language is intimately tied to culture—in fact, it is a core part of culture—and understanding how language is used in conversation and interpersonal interactions can give enormous insight into cultural forms. Further, language use helps to create, and then often mirrors, social structures. Hence, some understanding of language use clarifies many issues involving languages in South Asia.

Dialect and *language* are both terms that have no strict meanings based on the internal structures of any given linguistic system. Rather, these terms are social constructions, in that they represent societal attitudes toward whatever form of speech is being studied. Thus the multitude of dialects found in South Asia are "dialects" only in that they are not taught in schools, there is no standard form, and they are spoken within a relatively limited region. If society gave one dialect recognition and prestige, defined the grammatical system, and named a standard form, as happened with Black English in the United States in the 1960s, then that dialect might now be defined as a "language."

In the Indian state of Goa, the debate over the local language, Konkani, illustrates this process. The first step was to get Konkani recognized as a distinct language, separate from Marathi, the language of the surrounding state of Maharashtra. In 1975, on the basis of its linguistic structure and the abundance of literature in Konkani, the Sahitya Academy (the National Academy of Letters) recognized Konkani as a distinct language. In 1987, the Goa Legislative Assembly declared Konkani the official language of the state of Goa. Finally, in 1992, the Indian government passed a constitutional amendment that listed Konkani as a national language in the Eighth Schedule of the Constitution of India. Konkani is now one of the languages represented on rupee notes.

Since the 1960s, scholars have recognized that languages in South Asia can vary even within one village. Indeed, there are village-level dialects: some groups within a single village use different phonological, morphological, and semantic systems that differentiate one group from another. Most of these differences are related to class or caste, or both. With relatively little everyday communication linking high and low castes, especially in communities where untouchability was practiced and low castes lived in separate neighborhoods, caste-based dialects formed. And since caste and class have been intimately linked, especially in rural areas, these also mark class. Using these dialects then designated one as a member of a high or low caste, reinforcing the social meaning of

---

Box 4.1

Continuing Debates Regarding Konkani

Currently there is a new debate about which script to use in writing and teaching Konkani in schools, as it is written in five different scripts, each associated with a caste, religion, or ethnic group of the region. The Brahmin elites support writing it in Nagari, the script used for Sanskrit, Hindi, and Marathi, while the Catholics and those with large diasporic constituents support using the Roman script. Muslim communities advocate the Perso-Arabic script used for Urdu. For more on this controversy, see http://www.epw.in/web-exclusives/konkani-script-controversy.html.

---

the dialect. A.K. Ramanujan, in his "Structure of Variation: A Study of Caste Dialect" (1968, 469) demonstrated this process for the South Indian language of Tamil. Focusing on food terms, Ramanujan showed that high-caste Brahminical speech used a term for undrinkable water (*taṇṇī*) that was the general term for water, including drinking water, used by the low castes. The implied insult of a high-caste person using a term that means undrinkable—when to the low-caste person the same word means drinkable—is clear. In a comparable way, a Hindi-speaking villager detailed the uses of the three versions of the name Paras Ram (also the name of a deity): Pasu, for the low-caste and poor man; Paras, for the average man; and Paras Ram, for the respected person. To call a high-caste rich man "Pasu" would then be an enormous insult.

South Asian languages have numerous other ways of showing respect or disrespect, which is not surprising in this highly hierarchical society. The second-person pronoun "you" usually has three or more forms: in Hindi, *tu*, between intimates (husband and wife); *tum*, to those of lower status than oneself; and *āp*, for those of higher status or for whom respect is mandated. Speakers can thus manipulate respect and insult by their choice of the second-person pronoun. Verbs carry a similar array of politeness, such as the following: "Get out" (*bahār jāo*), "you go out" (*bahār jānā*), and "please go out" (*bahar jāīye*). In northern India, respect demands that a woman does not use her husband's name or that of any affinal (related by marriage) male elder, so when referring to or addressing her husband, a wife must use a convention such as "father of X."

Another example of language use related to societal norms involves the first-person pronoun "I," which is avoided in many situations; the more inclusive "we," even if referring rather specifically to oneself, is preferred. The use of "we" reflects the importance the society places on community over individuality. In another grammatical convention also tied to concepts of self and individuality, one does not claim certain states of being for oneself; rather they "happen" to oneself or are attached to oneself. Hunger is one of these states. As an Indian student explained, to say "I am hungry" (*main bhūkhī hūn*) in Hindi infuriates her mother, who sees her as being singular and selfish—and modern. An acceptable phrase would be "hunger is upon me (or attached to me)" (*mujhe bhūkh hai*), while even more preferable would be "hunger is upon us" (*ham ko bhūkh lagtī hai*).

Table 4.2

Adult Literacy Rates in South Asia, 2005–2008

Country	Percent literate
Afghanistan	NA
Bangladesh	59
Bhutan	53
India	63
Maldives	98
Nepal	58
Pakistan	54
Sri Lanka	91

Source: United Nations Children's Fund, Regional Office for South Asia, 2011 *South Asia Data Pocketbook,* http://www.unicef.org/rosa/Final_Booklet__29_March%283%29.pdf.

Language and Education

Any discussion of language demands attention to educational policies vis-à-vis language, especially in the complicated settings of South Asia. Literacy rates vary drastically from country to country and even from state to state within a country (Table 4.2).

With the spread of education in the nineteenth and twentieth centuries, standard regional languages became more widespread. Schooling demanded grammars and dictionaries and a focus on the "right" way to speak. The language in which literacy is achieved, therefore, is crucial. India, with its complex language situation, including numerous languages from four different language families with long literary histories, faced the biggest challenge. Yet even the Maldives and Bangladesh, with their much more homogeneous societies, declared official or national languages and made decisions about the role of English in education.

After independence, India ultimately chose what is known as the "three-language formula" for education. This strategy, developed by educational commissions in the 1950s, was recommended by the National Commission for Education and later incorporated into national education policies. In essence, according to the *Report of the Education Commission, 1964–66,* the formula states that teaching after the primary grades should be done in:

1. the mother tongue or the regional language;
2. the official language of the Union [of Indian states] or the associate official language of the Union as long as it exists; and
3. a modern Indian or foreign language not covered under (1) and (2) and other than that used as the medium of instruction. (Ministry of Education 1966, 192)

Hence all schoolchildren should be learning two languages by grade six, including their regional or mother tongue and either Hindi or English, since both are official languages of India.

Recognizing the importance of English, the report continues:

> Even after the regional languages become media of higher education in the universities, a working knowledge of English will be a valuable asset for all students and a reasonable proficiency in the language will be necessary for those who proceed to the university. (Ministry of Education 1966, 192)

With more than 850,000 primary schools and nearly 50,000 secondary schools in India, close to 90 percent follow the formula, teaching at least two languages by middle school (grades six through eight), with increasing numbers (13 percent) teaching English as a first language from the primary grades on.

> For a thorough review of the current functioning of the three-language formula, including state-by-state practices, see the report by the British Council titled "Dreams and Realities: Developing Countries and the English Language" (http://www. teachingenglish.org.uk/sites/teacheng/files/Z413%20EDB%20Section04_0.pdf).

Hence, at the secondary level, the Hindi-speaking regions would teach English and one South Indian language or Sanskrit. In non–Hindi-speaking regions, a regional language would be taught, along with (ideally) English and Hindi. No provision was made for teaching in an area's native language, which is often a dialect of a regional language—a dialect that can be vastly different from the standardized regional language. For example, in the village of Karimpur (see Chapter 8), the local dialect differs from the Standard Hindi taught in school. Hence, in Standard Hindi, the phrase for "he said" is *unhone kahā*, while in the village dialect, it is *bine kāī*. Karimpur children, especially those with uneducated parents, usually have no knowledge of Standard Hindi, and they learn to read at the same time that they learn a new language. Nowadays, however, some do know a bit of Standard Hindi or a market version of it, due to increased levels of contact with the media and urban areas. In addition, parents may have some education, although the female literacy rate in Karimpur is still below 50 percent. Critically, the native language in Karimpur remains the village dialect.

Yet even as regional-language instruction expands, English is increasingly demanded. Schools in India (and throughout the subcontinent) generally designate their medium of instruction in attracting students. Hence in the northern Hindi-speaking regions, schools are either Hindi-medium or English-medium schools, meaning that the core educational subjects are taught either in Hindi or English. Elsewhere, the regional language (Tamil, Bengali, Marathi, etc.) would be the medium of instruction, if not English. Currently, the demand for English-medium education is enormous. The privately run English-medium school in Karimpur opened in the early 1990s and has grown continuously ever since, despite the fact that fees for the lower grades—minimal at two dollars a month—are not affordable for many families.

Not surprisingly, there is enormous variability in the quality of education generally and in English-language education specifically. The downside of the three-language formula and the demand for English is that there is a vast divide between those who know English well and those who do not. Students from lower-class families and rural areas, who are also likely to be lower-caste, have far fewer opportunities to gain strong English skills. Usually, the regional-language schools are public and free, whereas the English-medium schools are private, and the better the school, the more expensive it is. Most Christian schools are English-medium, and all the elite schools are English-medium. Hence educational achievement in English is class-based in India. For the situation in Pakistan, see the works of Tariq Rahman (1996, 2004, 2009). Many upper-class and upper-middle-class South Asians are now more fluent in English than in their native tongue, especially in reading and writing.

The 2000 film *Doon School Chronicles*, directed and produced by David Mac-Dougall, explores the lifestyle and culture of what many consider India's most prestigious boy's school. Information on the film is available online (http://www. roninfilms.com.au/feature/526/doon-school-chronicles.html).

In a problematic anomaly, India's Central Universities—the most prestigious and well-funded in the country—all teach only in English, yet students who attended school in their regional language can take the admittance tests in their regional language. Admission is based on score and caste status, and students from the "scheduled castes and tribes" are admitted with lower scores than are those whose caste status is deemed high(er). Therefore, a significant portion of students is enrolled whose English is not sufficient for real success. Although remedial English-language courses are offered, these too lack consistency and quality. With lack of English-language ability added to the cultural, social, and economic differences already separating students who gained admission with scores based on regional-language tests, these students are unable to take full advantage of the opportunities that they have earned, as noted by Iswari Pandey in *Global English, Remedial English* (2013).

Related to education is English language employment, especially in the burgeoning call center business in both India and Pakistan, but also in the outsourcing of advertising, medical transcription, individual tutoring, and other Internet-based jobs. Although some native language call centers exist, most are for the foreign English-speaking market. Using employees who usually have a master's degree, the call centers demand English proficiency. Potential employees often spend weeks honing their English skills, according to Tariq Rahman, including their accents, their vocabulary, and their cultural knowledge, so they can become the "Raymond" who speaks with the foreign customer without divulging that they are actually working in Lahore, Mumbai, or Bangalore. The website for the Integra Call Center (http://www.integracallcenter.com/call-center.html), one large outsourcing company, states that its agents are "100 percent University educated" and speak "fluent English" with a "neutral accent." Without a doubt, South Asia's large English-speaking population has given India an advantage in the global workforce.

The Politics of Language Policies

For any new nation, or even older ones, language policies are often fraught with controversy and conflict. Choosing an official language is a highly contentious political act. While language might not be considered part of human genetics (contrary to some European thinking from the 1700s through World War II), language can be thought of as a "primordial sentiment," defined by the eminent twentieth-century anthropologist Clifford Geertz (1963) as

> a feeling of a corporate sentiment of oneness which makes those who are charged with it feel that they are kith and kin. This feeling is a double-edged feeling. It is at once a feeling of "consciousness of kind" which, on the one hand, binds together those who have it so strongly that it overrides all differences arising out of economic conflicts or social gradations and, on the other, severs them from those who are not of their kind. It is a longing not to belong to any other group.

As a primordial sentiment, language in South Asia—serving as a key marker of ethnic communities—sometimes separates and sometimes unites citizens. Of course, each speech community wants to retain its linguistic and its ethnic identity.

In South Asia, each country has faced different challenges with regard to language policies and politics. For instance, India chose a route of multilingualism and the recognition of diversity, whereas Pakistan and Nepal sought to deny such multiplicity by imposing one language on all linguistic and ethnic groups. Below is a brief survey of the language policies of the countries in the region.

India

In 1948, Jawaharlal Nehru, soon to be the first prime minister of an independent India, was appointed to the Linguistic Province Committee. As India was forced eventually to move toward state boundaries defined by language, he noted, "Some of the ablest men in the country came before us and confidently and emphatically stated that language in this country stood for and represented culture, race, history, individuality, and finally a sub-nation" (quoted in Harrison 1956).

At the levels of both the states and the nation, India faced problematic choices at this crucial juncture in its history. It had more than fourteen languages with significant populations and long literary histories, and each community wanted its language recognized. However, the Indian states in 1950 were not organized along linguistic lines. Two questions needed to be answered: What would the language of the nation be, and should there be a reorganization of the states on linguistic lines?

No one language could adequately represent India, but Hindi, in its various dialects, was spoken across the northern states and had the largest representation—about 35 percent of the population. Choosing a route that did not impose one language on all, the Constitution of 1950 proclaimed Hindi the national language, with English an official language until 1965, by which time it was thought that the 65 percent of the population who did not know Hindi would have had the opportunity to learn it. Instead, the 1960s were a time of extreme language agitation, as the southern states revolted against the imposition of Hindi. In 1963, Nehru was able to obtain passage of the Official Languages Act, which made English and Hindi both official languages, with each state allowed to name its own state official language. With India now the country with the largest English-speaking population in the world—a critical factor in its considerable economic development in the past decades—this political compromise appears to have paid off.

In the 1950s the states were reorganized, mostly along linguistic (and thus cultural) lines. That process has continued, with new states recognized in the northeast in 2008. The Constitution of India, Schedule 8, also recognizes what are now termed "national languages," currently numbering twenty-two.

Language politics is still contentious in India, however. The northeastern state of Assam provides one example. In this state, language is embroiled in a dispute about minority rights, illegal immigrants, and ethnicity. Over the past decades, thousands of illegal Nepalis and Bangladeshis have moved into the territory of what is now the state of Assam. Due to the huge numbers of migrants, the Assamese are rapidly moving toward minority status in their homeland. The process started with the British colonialists who first built tea plantations in Assam and then administered the area with Bengali officials. In 1831, Bengali was declared the official language of Assam, becoming the language of government and schools. Only in 1873 was Assamese recognized as a separate language. Throughout the twentieth century, Bengali Muslims immigrated into Assam, a flow that continued well after 1947. After Assamese was declared the official language of the state in 1960, the many tribal groups feared for their own cultural survival. As a result, Assam was eventually split into five states: Assam, Nagaland, Meghalaya, Arunachal Pradesh, and Mizoram. Assam itself thus became a much smaller state than it was before. Today, the Assamese language is an important symbol of ethnicity and, like the ethnic languages of the surrounding states, a rallying cry for those who seek to displace the immigrants.

Nepal and Pakistan

Whereas India chose a path that recognized linguistic and cultural diversity, both Pakistan and Nepal sought to make a statement about nation and nationalism through language policies that ignored linguistic minorities (or, in the case of Pakistan, majorities).

In 1947, Pakistan had five regional languages: Punjabi, Sindhi, Balochi, Pashto (or Pakhtun), and Bengali. Bengali speakers constituted the language of the majority (56 percent) in unified Pakistan, but the government selected Urdu, a language that is widely associated with northern Indian Muslim culture, as the official language. Mohammed Ali Jinnah, the Pakistani leader, made this choice clear when speaking in Dhaka, East Pakistan, in March 1948: "Let me make it very clear to you that the state language of Pakistan is going to be Urdu and no other language. Anyone who tries to mislead you is really the enemy of Pakistan. Without one state language, no nation can remain tied up solidly together and function" (Islam 1978, 144).

At that time, Urdu was spoken by a mere 7 percent of the Pakistani population. Brought into Pakistan from the Lucknow region of what is now northern India, it was primarily the language of Muslim refugees who fled India at the time of Partition. Even today, Urdu is the native tongue of less than 10 percent of the population. But to the leaders of the new nation, Urdu represented "Islam," in contrast to the other languages, most of which were spoken by significant Hindu populations, either in Pakistan or India. Urdu thus became a symbol of the "Islamic Republic of Pakistan." Differences about language contributed to the ultimate breakup of Pakistan, as East Pakistan (the modern Bangladesh) united around language as well as political and economic discrimination in the 1971 civil war.

Even today, language issues cause considerable tension in Pakistan, although Urdu is taught to all schoolchildren. Punjabi is now also written in a Perso-Arabic script, although Punjabi speakers in Indian Punjab use a script based on Devanagari, and Sikhs use Gurmukhi. Various separation movements call the imposition of Urdu a symbol of discrimination, advocating instead the use of Sindhi, Balochi, or Pashto. Like Nepal until the 1990s, Pakistan has chosen to deny the diversity of its peoples and their cultures and languages, rather than celebrating this diversity and its history.

> An eloquent call for recognition of Pakistan's diversity is found in a blog post by the respected journalist Aamir Raz Soomro, titled "Pakistan Should Mind All of Its Languages!" (http://blogs.tribune.com.pk/story/6179/pakistan-should-mind-all-of-its-languages/).

Nepal similarly aimed to unite its nation through language. With its mountainous terrain and hidden valleys, where communication is difficult, Nepal encompasses a multitude of minority ethnic groups and languages. As of the 2001 census, ninety-two separate languages are recognized (Yadav 2007, 3), and according to the 2007 Interim Constitution, all are "national" languages. This recognition is recent, however.

Through 1990, under the panchayat and previous regimes, Nepal had an ideological goal of "one language, one dress, one country." Nepali, spoken by some 48 percent of the population, enjoyed the status of "official language" and was the only language taught in government schools. The goal was to eliminate all other languages, to create a "one-language" state. This dominance of one language led to the marginalization and impoverishment of the many minority languages. Only recently, with the restoration of democracy in 1990, have linguistic minorities been able to value and acknowledge their mother tongues, many of which are still unwritten. Since 1990, the Nepalese constitution has allowed for education in the mother tongue (1991 Constitution of Nepal, Part 1, Article 18.2; Interim Constitution of Nepal, Part 3, Article 17), but the lack of writing systems and textbooks makes such education highly problematic. Demands for the creation of states based on smaller minority languages became the most crucial issue in Nepali politics, leading to the dissolution of the constituent assembly in May 2012.

Not surprisingly, the lowest literacy rates are found in the non-Nepali speaking communities (Yadav 2007, 14). Nepal is a prime example of a country that recognizes linguistic diversity as valuable to society, not something to be eradicated. But in Nepal, as across

South Asia, minority languages, especially when they remain unwritten and are spoken by very small communities, remain threatened.

Afghanistan

Afghanistan recognizes two official languages, Pashto and Dari. Pashto, also widely spoken in Pakistan, is the primary language of many in government and of the Taliban. Dari, closely related to the Farsi spoken in Iran, is spoken in the western parts of the country and in some areas in Kabul; it is also the first language of Tajiks and the Hazara people of central Afghanistan. Article 16 of the 2004 Afghan constitution recognizes that the Turkic group of languages, including Uzbek and Turkmen, should be regarded as official languages in those regions where the majority of the population speaks them.

Sri Lanka

In Sri Lanka, the tension between Tamil speakers of the north and east and Sinhala speakers led to a long civil war between Hindu Tamil-speaking advocates of a separate state and the Buddhist Sinhalese majority. The Sinhalese-speaking population had a significant majority (74 percent), while the Tamil speakers (18 percent) held a large and disproportionate share of government and service jobs. Some consider language the trigger point that led to the war, as it was the imposition of Sinhalese on university education that angered the Tamils in the 1960s and 1970s.

Prior to independence from the British, a joint movement for *svabhasa*, or "native" languages, pressed for both Tamil and Sinhalese to be named official languages. But as ethnic politics grew more contentious after independence, Sinhalese was declared the official language of Sri Lanka in 1956. Only in 1987 was Tamil declared an official language. In the early 1970s, new rules for admission to universities further exacerbated the tensions, as Sinhalese students were given preference and were given seats based on lower scores on the entrance exams. Prior to 1970, Tamils had secured through merit 35 percent of the seats in engineering and science courses: by 1974, they were given only 7 percent of the available seats. The new preference given to Sinlalese students triggered a massive protest (see Chapter 13). Now that the civil war is concluded (as of 2009), language discrimination continues, despite constitutional mandates that Tamil be used in all government documents. As Sasanka Perera noted in a 2011 address titled "Reflections on Issues of Language in Sri Lanka," additional language issues remain, such as schooling and contact with the government, including police forces that lack the knowledge of Tamil needed to interact with the populations that they serve.

Bangladesh, Bhutan, and Maldives

Since separation from Pakistan, Bangladesh has followed a Bangla-only policy, ignoring the fraction (2 percent) of its population (mostly in the hill regions) that speaks ethno-minority languages. Despite this approach, minimal political issues surround language policy. About 3 percent of the population, mostly urban, also speaks English, and the best universities are English-medium.

The two small countries of Bhutan and the Maldives face different language concerns. In the Maldives, the official language of its 350,000 residents is Dhivehi, an Indo-European language related to Sinhalese and now heavily influenced by Arabic. Dialects are spoken on the various islands, but no contention exists around language.

Bhutan has followed a single-language policy, with the Tibeto-Burman language of Dzongkha as the official language, although English is widely used in education. The imposition of a dress code and the Dzongkha-only language policy met resistance from the Nepali-speaking people in the southern regions of Bhutan, who were then evicted from their homes. Since the 1990s, more than 100,000 Nepali-speaking Bhutanese have been living in the refugee camps of eastern Nepal. Since 2008, some of these refugees have relocated to third countries, with a majority of them in the United States.

Summary

South Asia presents a complicated language picture, not only in the numbers of languages with different roots and literary traditions, but also in the role that language plays in the politics of each nation. While India has made the greatest attempt to support minority groups and linguistic diversity, Pakistan and Bhutan are notable for denying minority language rights, as was Nepal until recently. The common thread throughout is the use of the English as a prestigious language, a move that has contributed to the economic development of the region as a whole.

References and Further Research

Andersen, Walter K. 2011. "Ethnicity and Politics in South Asia." *Saisphere* 2011–2012. Published by the Paul H. Nitze School of Advanced International Studies, Johns Hopkins University. http://media.sais-jhu.edu/saisphere2011/article/ethnicity-and-politics-south-asia.

Asher, Ronald E. 2008. "Language in Historical Context." In *Language in South Asia*, edited by Braj B. Kachru, Yamuna Kachru, and S.N. Sridhar, 31–48. Cambridge and New York: Cambridge University Press.

Chandra, Shefali. 2012. *The Sexual Life of English: Languages of Caste and Desire in Colonial India*. Durham, NC: Duke University Press.

Geertz, Clifford. 1963. "The Integrative Revolution: Primordial Sentiments and Politics in the New States." In *Old Societies and New States: The Quest for Modernity in Asia and Africa*, edited by Clifford Geertz, 105–157. New York: Free Press of Glencoe. http://faculty.washington.edu/charles/562_f2011/Week%2010/Geertz%20The%20Integrative%20Revolution.pdf.

Gosselink, Robert G. 1994. "Minority Rights and Ethnic Conflict in Assam, India." *Boston College Third World Law Journal* 14: 83–118. http://lawdigitalcommons.bc.edu/cgi/viewcontent.cgi?article=1267&context=twlj.

Harrison, S. 1996. "The Challenge to Indian Nationalism." *Foreign Affairs* 34: 620–636.

Islam, Rafiqul. 1978. "The Bengali Language Movement and the Emergence of Bangladesh."
In *Language and Civilization Change in South Asia*, edited by Clarence Maloney, 142–152.
Contributions to Asian Studies, 11. The Hague: Brill.

Kachru, Braj B. 2008. "Introduction: Languages, Contexts, and Constructs." In *Language in
South Asia*, edited by Braj B. Kachru, Yamuna Kachru, and S.N. Sridhar, 1–28. Cambridge
and New York: Cambridge University Press.

Kachru, Braj B., Yamuna Kachru, and S.N. Sridhar, eds. 2008. *Language in South Asia*.
Cambridge and New York: Cambridge University Press.

King, Robert D. 2008. "Language Politics and Conflicts in South Asia." In *Language in South
Asia*, edited by Braj B. Kachru, Yamuna Kachru, and S.N. Sridhar, 311–324. Cambridge
and New York: Cambridge University Press.

Meganathan, Ramanujam. 2011. "Language Policy in Education and the Role of English in
India: From Library Language to Language of Empowerment." In *Dreams and Realities:
Developing Countries and the English Language*, edited by Hywel Coleman. Teaching
English, Paper 4. London: British Council. http://www.teachingenglish.org.uk/sites/
teacheng/files/Z413%20EDB%20Section04_0.pdf.

Ministry of Education. 1966. *Report of the Education Commission, 1964–66*. New Delhi:
Government of India, Ministry of Education.

Pandey, Iswari. 2013. *Global English, Remedial English: Caste, Class, Nation*. New York:
Routledge.

Perera, Sasanka. 2011. "Reflections on Issues of Language in Sri Lanka: Power, Exclusion
and Inclusion." Keynote address delivered at Language and Social Cohesion: 9th International Language and Development Conference, Colombo, October 17, 2011, co-organized
by the Ministry of National Languages and Social Integration, Ministry of Education,
GIZ, AusAID, and British Council. *Groundviews: Journalism for Citizens*, October 24.
http://groundviews.org/2011/10/24/reflections-on-issues-of-language-in-sri-lanka-power-
exclusion-and-inclusion/.

Pollock, Sheldon, ed. 2003. *Literary Cultures in History: Reconstructions from South Asia*.
Berkeley: University of California Press.

Rahman, Tariq. 1996. *Language and Politics in Pakistan*. Karachi: Oxford University
Press.

Rahman, Tariq. 2004. *Denizens of Alien Worlds: A Study of Education, Inequality and Polarization in Pakistan*. Karachi: Oxford University Press.

Rahman, Tariq. 2009. "Language Ideology, Identity and the Commodification of Language
in the Call Centers of Pakistan." *Language in Society* 38: 233–258.

Ramanujan, A.K. 1968. "The Structure of Variation: A Study in Caste Dialects." In *Structure
and Change in Indian Society*, edited by Milton B. Singer and Bernard S. Cohn, 461–475.
Chicago: Aldine.

World Bank. *The Root Causes of the Ethnic Conflict in Sri Lanka*. http://siteresources.world-
bank.org/INTSRILANKA/Resources/App1.pdf, accessed March 28, 2013.

Yadav, Yogendra P. 2007. "Linguistic Diversity in Nepal: Perspectives on Language Policy."
Paper presented at a seminar on Constitution and Diversity in Nepal, organized by the
Centre for Nepal and Asian Studies, Trivandrum University, in collaboration with MIDEA
and ESP-Nepal, Kathmandu, Nepal, August 22–24, 2007. http://www.unibielefeld.de/
midea/pdf/Yogendra.pdf.

5

Religion in South Asia

SUSAN SNOW WADLEY

Religion is inescapable when thinking about South Asia. A person must swear allegiance to Sunni Islam to be a citizen of the Maldives. Two South Asian countries have a religious affiliation in their official name (the Islamic Republic of Pakistan and the Islamic Republic of Afghanistan). Political parties tied to Islam are widely popular in both these countries, while a civil war based partially on religious differences (Buddhist and Hindu) was waged for more than thirty years in Sri Lanka (see Chapter 13). Both India and Nepal have major political parties based on their members' Hindu identities, and until recently the Nepali monarchy claimed to be the custodian of Hindu identity, in contrast to the secularism dominant in India. In northern India, Sikhs have sought autonomy for more than thirty years. At the same time, along with Sri Lanka, Bhutan is largely Buddhist, Nepal has a significant Buddhist population, and Buddhism has had a resurgence in India as former untouchables have renounced caste-based Hinduism for the equality of Buddhism.

Jainism is also found in the region, especially in India's northwestern states of Gujarat and Rajasthan, while Kerala, on India's southwest coast, has long been home to both Christian and Jewish communities. While the region was under colonial rule, missionaries spread Christianity more widely, especially in what is now India's northeast. Adding in a mix of Parsis, especially in Mumbai, and tribal religions through India's midsection as well as in the border regions of Afghanistan and Pakistan, makes South Asia one of the world's most religiously diverse areas.

Religion in South Asia is a result of centuries of commingling of traditions, a process that continues today. The numerous incursions into South Asia—whether it was the Aryans around 2000–1500 BCE, Alexander the Great in the fourth century BCE, Jews by the Common Era, Muslim merchants and rulers from 750 CE on, or Christian colonists after 1500 CE—have all contributed to the enormous diversity of religious practice found in South Asia. Each of the major religions is found in a multitude of forms, making any simple statements of core tenets difficult, given the internal variety found in each tradition.

Moreover, no distinct lines exist between any of these religious traditions as practiced— to quote a Sufi poet, "you can't draw a line in water." In Kerala, the Hindu goddess Lakshmi is considered the sister of the Christian Saint George. In Gujarat, Muslim Ismaili songs (*ginas*) have resonances of Hindu religious songs. In Ajmer, India, persons of all religious traditions worship at the *dargah* (a shrine built over the grave of a revered religious figure) of the Sufi saint Moinuddin Chishti, himself a member of the Chishti order that began in Herat, Afghanistan, in the twelfth century CE. The guardian saint of the small,

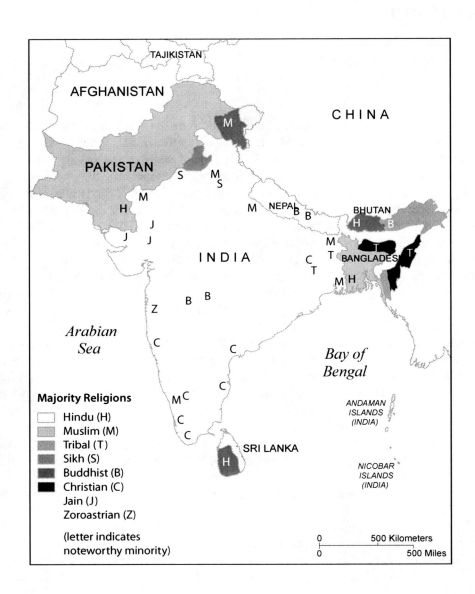

mostly Hindu village of Karimpur (see Chapter 8) is a Muslim, Khan Bahadur. Regularly worshipped by all, both Hindu and Muslim, on Thursdays, Khan Bahadur is thought to both protect the village and solve problems surrounding such things as marriage, births, school examinations, and various court cases. Near the southern tip of India, the Christian Shrine of Our Lady of Vailankanni (also known as Our Lady of Good Health) receives some 2 million visitors a year, representing numerous religious traditions.

> One of the most famous Muslim religious sites in South Asia is Dargah Ajmer, the *dargah* of Moinuddin Chishti, where millions of people, from all faiths, come to worship yearly (http://www.dargahajmer.com/a_about.htm).

This brief chapter on religions in South Asia first sketches the core history of each religious tradition in the region and then briefly notes the key religious issues and conflicts facing each of the South Asian countries. No attempt is made to explain the tenets and beliefs of these religious traditions, as those materials are readily available elsewhere (see Clothey 2006 and Lopez 1995 for more detailed treatments of religion in the region).

History of Religions in South Asia

Hinduism

Hinduism itself is a relatively new "tradition," as it is mostly a creation of colonial rulers from the eighteenth century onward. In order to better rule, the British consolidated various religious beliefs and traditions with different core texts and philosophical tenets into the broad category that they termed Hinduism. Based on the word *Sindhu*, for the region of the Indus River in what is now Pakistan, Hinduism has neither a "great book" nor a founding figure. There are no religious institutions that set religious boundaries or standards of behavior. Muslims were the first to use the word *Hindu* for the non-Muslim inhabitants of South Asia, and the British used the term *Hinduism* to refer to those practices and beliefs that did not fall within the framework of Islam, Christianity, or other named religions. According to Donald S. Lopez Jr., a professor in the Department of Asian Languages and Cultures at the University of Michigan, elite Indians, anxious to adopt religious approaches and concepts comparable to those of Europe, adopted the term as well, and it is now a pan-Indian term of identification.

Most commentators cite the Vedas, composed in the religious language of Sanskrit by the Aryan herdsmen who moved into South Asia shortly after the Harappa civilization collapsed around 1900 BCE, as the core of modern Hinduism. With Sanskritic texts recited by the Brahmin priests, Vedic Hinduism is heavily dependent upon ritual actions prescribed to maintain the stability of the world. Most Hindu life cycle rituals—such as naming ceremonies, marriages, and funerals—are based on Vedic rituals in which offerings are made through the Vedic god Agni, the intermediary between humans and gods.

The modern *havan* ceremony, or fire ritual, marks any ritual as having Vedic origins, even when performed in conjunction with more modern elements.

Hinduism is also marked by the *varna* system, a hierarchy related to the modern caste system that is inscribed in the Vedic hymn of the first man, Purusha. As described in the Rig Veda, as the world was created, the Brahmins, or priests, sprang from Purusha's head; the Kshatriyas, or warriors, came from his arms; the Vaishyas, or merchants, came from his thighs; and the Shudras, or serfs, came from his feet. (Outside of this organization of the four *varnas* are the former untouchables, who are often derisively referred to as the *panchmas*, or the fifth one.) The first three hierarchically ranked groups are the "twice-born," those whose males have a right to the sacred thread ceremony and to study the Vedic scriptures. As in the modern caste system, intermarriage between these groups is prohibited. Most modern castes claim membership in one of the four *varnas* as a way of marking adherence to a prestige system that is wider than the local village. While the concept of caste is outlawed by the Indian constitution, caste continues to play a key role in Indian politics at both the national and local levels, with most political parties associated in the minds of the public with one or another caste group. Further, local village politics and power struggles are still based on caste blocs. The lower castes have gained ground politically, however, and the state of Uttar Pradesh recently elected a former untouchable woman as its chief minister.

> Two videos that present different views on caste are *Caste at Birth** (1991), written and directed by Mira Hamermesh, and *This Is a Music: Reclaiming an Untouchable Drum** (2011), directed by Zoe Sherinian. The former examines a variety of settings where caste is important, including medical schools, elite colleges, temples, and slums in Mumbai, as well as caste violence in villages in rural Bihar. The latter examines the ways in which music has been used to raise the consciousness, if not the actual status, of an untouchable community of outcaste drummers in Tamil Nadu.

While modern writers emphasize the potential oneness of Hindu deities in a supreme, monotheistic God, this concept is partly due to the comparison of Hinduism with Christianity, Islam, and Sikhism. Most Hindus believe in many deities, each having his or her role to play in daily, weekly, monthly, or yearly ritual cycles. Many Hindus also have a relationship with one or more chosen deities: this relationship is marked by *bhakti*, a sense of devotion and love for that deity, a love that is thought to be returned from the god to humans. Bhakti developed as a concept in South India around the tenth century CE, partially in response to the rigidity of the Brahmin-dominated Hinduism of the time, especially the necessity of using a priest as an intermediary in all ritual action. Bhakti, individual devotion to one's chosen deity, allowed anyone to worship any time at any place. Priests and temples were not needed. While temples certainly still play a role in modern Hinduism, most Hindus also worship their chosen deity at home shrines, often daily.

Popular Hinduism is an amalgamation of Sanskritic and textual traditions, to which access was denied to the general populace until the twentieth century, along with regional and local variants of stories, gods, goddesses, and rituals, often handed down orally. One feature of popular Hinduism is devotion to ascetics and living gurus or gurumatas (guru mothers). Many of these cults also feature belief in the powers of yoga, so that the ancient Indian spiritual and healing practices of yoga and the newly recognized ascetic figures are merged into a form of Hinduism popular both in South Asia and abroad, accessible to both those born Hindu and the spiritual "seekers" of the West. Nowadays, one can perform rituals in temples (by paying a priest), listen to lectures from a guru, and practice yoga via television or the Internet.

One of the most important temple sites in India is the Tirumala Tirupati Devasthanam, home to Lord Venkateswara, at Tiruati in Andhra Pradesh, and one of the richest religious organizations in the world (http://www.tirumala.org). See also Joyce Burkhalter Flueckiger's *When the World Becomes Female: Guises of a South Indian Goddess* (Bloomington: Indiana University Press, 2013) for more information.

Many of the tenets of Hinduism are portrayed in an easily understood narrative form in Hinduism's two great epics, the Mahabharata and the Ramayana. The Ramayana, in particular, with its god-king Rama as hero and his wife Sita as the epitome of the perfect Hindu wife, remains extremely popular in a vast variety of forms—comic books, television serials, movies, and numerous tellings in oral and written texts over the past 2,000 years (see Richman 1991). The god Rama has become the figure around which Hindu conservative religious parties unite, in part because Rama's supposed birthplace was covered by a Muslim mosque, the Babri Masjid, during the early years of Muslim rule in north India. Tearing down the Babri Masjid in the town of Ayodhya was the central political statement by the religious right (Hindutva) in the early 1990s.

The South Asia Center at Syracuse University has an extensive website with a variety of lessons plans and other information on the Ramayana (http://www.maxwell.syr.edu/moynihan/sac/The_Ramayana/).

Jainism and Buddhism

Jainism and Buddhism are both heterodox religious movements that arose in response to social issues of the sixth century BCE. In part, they were responses to the dominance of Brahminical ritual, both its costs and its elevation of the Brahmin priesthood. Both also originated in the royal courts, perhaps in part because under the Vedic system of Hinduism then dominant, even kings were subject to priestly ritual powers. Jainism remained purely a South Asian phenomenon, while Buddhism reached across most of Asia.

The proclaimed founders of both Jainism and Buddhism—Mahavira and Gautama (or Siddharta, the Buddha) respectively—are believed to have been of noble birth and to have renounced wealth in their search for the truth. Both became ascetics, renouncers, and both appealed to groups who sought their own liberation without the mediation of the Brahmin priesthood. Both also emphasized social egalitarianism, in direct opposition to the hierarchy that is so central to Hinduism. Jainism—according to Fred W. Clothey, in his *Religion in India: A Historical Introduction*—is thought to have appealed especially to women, merchants, and traders, while Buddhism drew more from the lower classes, although with many wealthy patrons. Both were venerated monastic orders.

Buddhism quickly gained precedence and spread throughout India and eastern and southeastern Asia, with two main branches: Mahayana (The Great Vehicle), which was dominant in Tibet and East Asia; and Theravada (School of the Elders), dominant in Sri Lanka and Southeast Asia. (Early Buddhists came down the eastern coast of India and settled in Sri Lanka in the fifth century BCE, bringing with them the Indo-European dialect that became Sinhalese.) Buddhism, despite its origins in what is now India, had mostly disappeared from India by the thirteenth century (though it flourished in Nepal and Sri Lanka), while Jainism continued as a major religious tradition in western India, particularly among the trader and merchant castes, where it flourishes today. In 1956, Dr. B.R. Ambedkar, an untouchable who was independent India's first law minister and a key writer of the Indian constitution, converted to Buddhism as a statement of his belief in the equality of all people. Some 5 million former untouchables, now called Dalits ("the oppressed"), have since followed his lead.

The PBS documentary on the Buddha is an excellent introduction (http://video. pbs.org/video/1461557530/).

Islam

Islam has been in constant tension with Hindu practices since it was brought to South Asia during the eighth century CE by Arab incursions into the region from Central Asia and through mercantile contacts along the west coast, from Sindh to Kerala. With a ban on idolatry, a belief in one god (the unknowable Allah), and a single holy book (the Koran, or Qur'an) that is the source of revelation of God's intentions for humankind, the clash seems inevitable. Critically, since Islam is a religion of conversion, many rulers—some harsh, others not—sought converts among conquered populations. Since Islam bans idols, some conquerors defaced the images in Hindu temples, while others destroyed Hindu temples, especially in the north, where their rule was dominant. Recent historical interpretations claim that because temples are centers of power and custodians of wealth, Muslim rulers often raided the temples for such secular reasons as displaying power and wealth. Others,

Box 5.1

Muslim Religious Sites

While the mosque is considered to be the key space for the Muslim community for their daily ritual prayer, in fact there are many different kinds of structures where Muslims come together for prayers including the famous khanaqahs of the Sufis; the variety of saints' tombs, such as the dargah of Chishti in Ajmer; and places of pilgrimage, most notably the Ka'ba in Mecca. Many of these religious sites are tied to a specific community's ethnic and sectarian identity. For example, the Shia Ismailis congregate for prayer in their Jamat Khanas that are purposely built for a variety of social and administrative activities. Whereas any Muslim may attend a mosque, the jamat khana is restricted to those who accept Muhammad's cousin and son-in-law Ali and his direct descendants as their living Imam and spiritual guide.

such as the Mughal emperor Akbar (1542–1605), sought to find a common ground among religions. Akbar gave Hindus positions of responsibility in his government, and he built the Ibadat Khana at Fatehpur Sikri, his new capital (in the present-day northern state of Uttar Pradesh, India), as a site for religious discussions, although these were so contentious they were eventually canceled. Akbar himself was devoted to Moinuddin Chishti, whom he considered his spiritual preceptor, and twice he traveled from Agra to Ajmer (226 miles [364 kilometers]) on foot to demonstrate his devotion to the saint.

While Sunni Islam dominates in South Asia, there are significant populations of Shias, Ismailis, and Sufis. The split between Sunnis and Shias goes back to the eighth century CE, with a dispute about the Prophet Muhammad's designated successor. Some thought that Ali, the Prophet's nephew, was the proper spiritual and political leader of the community, while others favored Abu Bakr, a convert to the faith, as the one best suited to lead. These two groups fought for power. Eventually, Ali's son Husain was assassinated in 680 CE in Karbala, an event still mourned today by Shias during the month of Muharram. Several generations later, another dispute around spiritual succession led to the Ismaili-Shia split. For conservative Sunnis, both the Shias and the Ismailis are not true Muslims. The Ismailis are particularly condemned because they do not practice the Five Pillars of Islam and do not worship in a *masjid* (mosque) but in a ritual space called a *jamat khana.*

Yet in the tenth through the twelfth centuries, the Ismailis ruled the Fatimid Empire, controlling most of North Africa, Syria, and Palestine. Nowadays, pockets of Ismailis dot the landscape of Afghanistan, Pakistan, and India. Through their spiritual leader, the Aga Khan, they also contribute extensively to development activities in the region, including rebuilding heritage sites such as Humayan's Tomb in New Delhi and building hospitals in Pakistan.

Much of the strife over who is or is not a Muslim is related to the Ahmadiyya order, founded by Mirza Ghulam Ahmad in 1889. Claiming that he himself was the Messiah, he attracted followers in South and Southeast Asia as well as Africa. Some 4 million Ahmadiyyas are found in Pakistan, with about 1 million more in India and less than 200,000 in Bangladesh. Both Sunni and Shia Muslims claim that the Ahmadis are not Muslim.

Equally important to modern-day practice in South Asia are the Sufi orders. Drawing on a mystical tradition, Sufis speak of a "jihad of the heart," rather than a "jihad of the sword." Those who were master teachers, called *pirs*, often became recognized as saints to whom numerous miracles are attributed. Their *dargahs*, or tombs, such as that of Moinuddin Chishti, have become major pilgrimage sites.

The Indian Mutiny, also called the Sepoy Mutiny, was seen by the British as an uprising that sought to reinstate Mughal (Muslim) rule in India, which put Islam into some political jeopardy. Moreover, Hindus moved more rapidly into the new educational institutions created by British colonial rule and Hindu elites, especially those from high castes, and soon became the educated class. Those who led the movement for independence were largely Hindu. Gandhi himself relied heavily on Hindu ideas and terminology as he motivated the Indian populace. At the same time, the Indian independence movement advocated the creation of a secular state, but the Muslim elite worried that they would be ill-treated in an Indian nation dominated by Hindus.

Educated Muslims eventually started a movement for a separate Muslim state, resulting in the creation of Pakistan and India as separate entities in 1947. While India's constitution proclaimed it a secular state, Muslims in Pakistan consciously moved toward an Islamic state. When Bangladesh was eventually carved out of Pakistan in 1972, the religious diversity of Pakistan was severely reduced, as most of the Hindus who had remained in Pakistan were located in Bangladeshi territory (Bangladesh still remains 10 percent Hindu). Pakistan's history reflects increasing adherence to Islamic principles and increasing intolerance for difference, both within Islam and without.

Christianity

Christianity in South Asia began with the arrival of Syrian Christians and other heterodox Christian communities on the southwest coast in the first centuries of Christianity. Local legends claim that the apostle Saint Thomas arrived in 42 CE and died in South India. European colonialists, starting with Vasco da Gama in 1498, brought a second influx of Christianity to South Asia, although in a multitude of varieties ranging from Portuguese Roman Catholics to Baptists and Mennonites from North America. Christian missionaries gained a firm foothold in India's northeast in the nineteenth century as England's rule became more imperialistic and missionaries from Europe and North America were given rights to open schools and churches in different parts of the subcontinent. The result was a patchwork of Christian denominations with an overlay of Roman Catholicism, except in Kerala in southwestern India, where Syrian Christians and Catholics dominate. Eventually much of Protestant North India (Methodist, Congregational, Anglican, Presbyterian, Reformed) was brought under one umbrella in the Church of North India, with a comparable Church of South India. Other prominent denominations include Baptist, Lutheran, and the Church of Brethren (Mennonite). Overall, 73 percent of the Christians in India are Roman Catholic. Christian schools are often among the best in any locale, and many elite Indians have gone to either "convent" schools or those run by Protestant denominations.

Sikhism

Unlike Islam and Christianity, which were imported into India and then transformed, Sikhism is best thought of as a syncretic religion, one built out of a combination of Islam and Hinduism. Guru Nanak (1469–1539), the founder of Sikhism, was born a Hindu but had many contacts with Islam. His religion combined elements of the belief in one god, but one who is accessible in ways comparable to those found in Sufism and the Hindu practice of bhakti. Humans should be submissive to God, who should also be celebrated and relished. Later Sikh gurus emphasized the equality of all humans, symbolized by the *langur*, or common kitchen, where all would eat and anyone could cook. With scriptures collected into the Adi Granth, the Golden Temple established as the spiritual site of Sikhism, and a distinctive set of rituals based on comparable Hindu ones, Sikhism was well established by 1600. Eventually, the Sikhs and the Mughals battled over the Land of the Five Rivers (Punjab), losing only to British dominance in 1849.

The main Sikh political party in India, the Shiromani Akali Dal, is integrally tied to the management of Sikh temples, which the British had attempted to control through the 1920s. The temple committees, elected by ordinary Sikh devotees, are organized in a hierarchical fashion, with the supreme body controlling the main Sikh *gurdwara*, the Golden Temple, in Amritsar. The association of the Punjabi language with Sikhs, who use a distinct script called Gurumukhi, gives a regional basis for Sikh nationalism.

Judaism

Judaism was imported into South Asia prior to the Common Era, and it developed, especially in Kerala, through the next century. Now known as Cochin Jews, the descendants of these early Jewish settlers have almost all departed for either Israel or the West. In addition, there exists a small indigenous community in western India, called Bene Israeli, who practiced a particular version of Judaism for nearly 2,000 years. Located in the current state of Maharashtra, the Bene Israel were barely recognizable as Jewish when "discovered" by Europeans in the 1700s. They too have mostly departed from India.

Parsi (Zoroastrianism)

Rising in the modern area of Iran in the seventh century BCE, Zoroastrians believe in the powers of fire, including sun and moonlight. With prayers offered to the sun daily and the moon thirteen times a month, Zoroastrians believe in a core ethical life: good ethics lead to immortality in paradise. One should avoid greed, arrogance, and vengeance, and instead be charitable, work hard, and seek wisdom. With the coming of Islam to Persia in the seventh century CE, Parsis, as Zoroastrians are now called, began moving into the area of modern Gujarat, and they eventually became an important force in modern Mumbai. Believing that a dead body would contaminate the earth, their funeral rituals involve placing the dead in "Towers of Silence" to be eaten by birds of prey.

Religion in Modern South Asian Countries

These religious traditions play an important role in South Asia today, in both social life and politics. Each South Asian country confronts key issues that have their roots in religious traditions.

> An important resource on the current situation in every country is the U.S. Department of State's *2010 International Religious Freedom Report* (http://www.state.gov/j/drl/rls/irf/2010_5/index.htm).

Afghanistan

The constitution of Afghanistan declares that Islam is the "religion of the state" and that "no law can be contrary to the beliefs and provisions of the sacred religion of Islam." With some 80 percent of the population Sunni and 19 percent Shia, only 1 percent is non-Muslim. In order to protect the Shia minority, the Shia Personal Status Law was put into effect in 2009. Found primarily in certain tribal groups around the country, the Shia, including Ismailis, are scattered in pockets across the country, especially in the northern and central regions. Significant numbers of Sufis are also present, with shrines such as the Chishti near Herat attracting large numbers of visitors. Given that the Taliban are Sunni and follow a highly conservative version of Hanafi Islam as taught at the Darul Uloom (institute of higher religious education) at Deoband in northern India, religious strife remains an issue in modern Afghanistan.

Bangladesh

Bangladesh, with 90 percent of the population Muslim and 9 percent Hindu, is constitutionally a secular nation, following a ruling of the Bangladesh Supreme Court in 2010. Yet religious strife does exist, especially since those belonging to the minority religions tend to be at the lower end of the socioeconomic scale, and thus have few political options to redress wrongs. Nevertheless, the government provides protection for all religious holidays. Bangladesh has a small population of Ahmadiyya Muslims (some 100,000 in the Dhaka region alone), who are frequently subject to minor attacks from mainstream Muslims. The hill regions to the north and east have more minority religious groups, Buddhist and Christian, and are most prone to religious strife. Theravada Buddhists in the Chittagong Hills fought the Bangladesh government until a peace treaty was signed in 1997. Critically, Sharia law is not imposed on any population.

Bhutan

The Bhutanese constitution respects the rights of all religions while declaring Mahayana Buddhism as the country's "spiritual heritage." Conversion and proselytizing are prohibited. However, in recent years the Nepali Hindu immigrants in the south have been heavily discriminated against, and many have been forced to leave.

India

After independence in 1947, India sought to be a secular nation, and religious freedom is proclaimed in the Indian constitution. Current figures (2013) show that India is 80.5 percent Hindu, 13.4 percent Muslim, 2.3 percent Christian, and 1.9 percent Sikh. According to the Pew Forum for Religion and Public Life (2011), India is the world's third-largest Muslim country, behind Indonesia and Pakistan. Only the northern state of Jammu and Kashmir has a Muslim majority, however, although there are significant Muslim populations across all the northern states and in Andhra Pradesh. The northeastern states have Christian majorities (Mizoram is 87 percent Christian, Meghalaya is 70 percent Christian, and Nagaland is 90 percent Christian). Only Punjab has a majority Sikh population. Buddhism is most prominent in Maharashtra due to the Ambedkar-led conversion movement of former untouchables, now called Dalits, in that state. Since the late 1950s, some 150,000 Tibetan Buddhists have fled to India as a result of the Chinese occupation of Tibet; they are scattered in refugee centers and monasteries in both northern and southern India. The Dalai Lama's government-in-exile, the Central Tibetan Administration, is located in Dharamsala in the northern state of Himachal Pradesh.

Religious parties played a relatively minor role from independence through the early 1970s, although Hindu nationalists have increasingly sought public attention. A loose coalition of several dozen Hindu conservative parties, known as the Sangh Parivar, or Hindutva, dominates this movement. One of the parties is the Rashtriya Swayamsevak Sangh (RSS), a paramilitary right-wing Hindu organization, one of whose members, Nathuram Godse, assassinated Mahatma Gandhi in 1948. Since the demolition of the Babri Masjid (the mosque built over the possible birthplace of the god Rama) in 1992, Hindu-Muslim riots have broken out repeatedly, while the 2002 Gujarat riots, causing thousands of deaths, are often attributed to the actions—or inactions—of Narendra Modi, the chief minister of the Bharatiya Janata Party (BJP). From 1998 to 2004, the BJP, with RSS support, ruled India, and disputes about its right-wing Hindu message continue to dominate Indian politics.

A compelling film on the trauma imposed by the Indian military in the Kashmir region, including purported violence against women and youth, is *In Shopian* (2011), produced and directed by Chris Giamo.

Box 5.2

**Pakistan-India, Muslim-Hindu
Conflict Over Kashmir**

The conflict over Kashmir represents a flashpoint for religion in the region. With a majority Muslim population (and the emigration of most Hindus to other parts of India), Kashmir has been disputed since Indian independence. At that time it was ruled by a Hindu maharaja, but since 1947 it has been a disputed state, with portions ruled by India, Pakistan, and China.

In 1947, when the Maharaja Hari Singh did not immediately cede his territory, which was 77 percent Muslim, to Pakistan, the Pakistanis sent in a small irregular force to compel him to do so. Instead, he sought the help of Lord Mountbatten, the governor-general of India, who agreed to help only on the condition that the maharaja cede the territory to India, which he did. Pakistan retained the area it had already controlled, while China clipped off a portion on its border. Although Jawaharlal Nehru, then prime minister of India, sought a United Nations mandate on Indian-occupied Kashmir to determine its status as an independent, Indian, or Pakistani state, successive Indian governments have not allowed that vote, and Kashmir still remains a trigger point between Pakistan and India. Scholars working in the area suggest that most Kashmiris in the Indian-occupied territory seek independence. Meanwhile, Indian-occupied Kashmir is the most militarized territory in the world, as India keeps about 500,000 troops there in order to control the independence movement, with one Indian soldier for every ten to seventeen Kashmiris.

In addition to the conflict in Kashmir (see Box 5.2), the other major controversy surrounding religion in India is conversion, especially conversion to Christianity. In 2008, there were numerous attacks on Christians and Christian places of worship, due to the perception that missionaries were attracting followers. Foreign missionaries have been banned since 1975, although one European mission Internet site claims that 1,000 missionaries are currently using various strategies to gain entrance to India. In fact, most missionary activity in India is now in the hands of Indian natives. Mission activity was most prominent in the northeast, where the combination of Christianity and modern education led to a breakdown in traditional structures of control and opened a space for the insurgencies that emerged against Indian rule in the period since independence.

The Maldives

The smallest country in South Asia in terms of land mass, as well as population, the Maldives has a Muslim population of 98.4 percent, and Sunni Islam is the official state religion. In the last few years, tourism has driven the country's economic growth, causing conflict in its governing institutions over policies related to serving alcohol at the island country's resorts. Beyond this issue, religion has stirred no serious unrest in the country.

Nepal

Religious issues in Nepal are in part related to the Maoist insurgency that gained ascendance in 2008, at which time the interim constitution named Nepal a "secular state" in contrast to the "Hindu Kingdom" of the former monarchy. Of the country's 30 million people, some 80 percent are Hindu, 9 percent are Buddhist, and 4 percent are Muslim, while the remaining religions, including Christianity, each represent 1 to 3 percent of the population. Proselytizing is prohibited. Those facing the greatest discrimination are Tibetan Buddhists, with some refugees being forcefully returned to Chinese-controlled Tibet. Aside from the inequities of the caste system, still dominant in the majority Hindu population despite being constitutionally banned, there is relatively little religious strife in Nepal.

Pakistan

Like Afghanistan, Pakistan is an Islamic state, with Islam proclaimed as the state religion. In fact, Pakistan has become increasingly Islamic over the sixty-plus years of its independence. The constitution states that "subject to law, public order, and morality, every citizen shall have the right to profess, practice, and propagate his religion," but as Sharia law is increasingly imposed by the Sunni majority and the courts become more Islamic in nature, religious freedom is minimal. Christians, Ahmadis, and Shias have all faced recent discrimination, harassment, and violence, which the government does little to prevent. Religious congregations have been attacked, and violence against Sufis and Shias is frequent.

Perhaps the most contentious and extreme form of governmental control comes in the form of the Pakistani blasphemy laws, which are used by the government to enforce Islam and to attack religious minorities. Freedom of speech and expression, including the press, is "subject to any reasonable restrictions imposed by law in the interest of the glory of Islam," according to the constitution. Yet in 1982, under the leadership of General Muhammad Zia-ul-Haq, Section 295(b) of the Pakistan Penal Code made blasphemy against the Koran punishable by life imprisonment, while in 1986, Section 295(c) made blasphemy against the Prophet Muhammad punishable by death. In June 2012, the leading Pakistani arts college, the National College of Arts in Lahore, was forced to close when charges were brought that its recently released journal promoted homosexuality and defamed Islam. Earlier that month, one person was killed and nineteen injured when a group of Muslims near Quetta charged that a mentally retarded man had burned several pages of the Koran and attacked the police station where he was held. In May 2012, a pastor at a Christian church was accused of blasphemy when he compared the Koran with the Bible. Leading politicians have also been attacked on the blasphemy issue. In January 2012, the governor of the state of Punjab, Salman Taseer, was assassinated when he spoke out in favor of repealing parts of the blasphemy laws. Earlier, in 2010, Shahbaz Bhatti, the federal minister for minorities, who had sought repeal of the blasphemy laws, was also assassinated. To this day, the blasphemy laws continue to restrict the freedom of religion in Pakistan.

The Ahmadis are the focus of numerous regulations that seek to constrain their religious freedoms. In 1974, the constitution of Pakistan declared that the Ahmadis were not Muslim and had no right to declare themselves Muslim. Sections 298(b) and 298(c) of the Penal Code further targeted the Ahmadi population, making it illegal for them to call themselves or their beliefs Muslim. National identity cards, which mandate that one declare one's religious identity, are required in order to vote (see Chapter 11). This ordinance is particularly aimed at the Ahmadis, because if one declares oneself a Muslim, one must swear belief in the Prophet Muhammad as the final prophet. Because of this restriction and in order to hide their religious identities, Ahmadis, who believe that their founder, Mirza Ghulam Ahmad, was the Messiah, do not vote.

Another regulation is especially problematic: in 1979 the Hudood Ordinance, also instituted under President Zia, mandated Sharia law, especially in cases of rape or adultery, despite Article 23 of Pakistan's constitution, which guarantees each citizen equal rights regardless of gender. Thousands of women were incarcerated under this ordinance before it was partially amended by President Pervez Musharraf, in the 2006 Protection of Women Act, leading to the release from prison of some 7,000 women who had been convicted of having sex outside of marriage, either through acts of rape or adultery. Evidence suggests that many were jailed due to local-level political disputes between men, in which women became the pawns of men in Pakistan's patriarchal society.

Finally, the conflict over Kashmir between Pakistan and India involves issues of Muslim and Hindu identity and religious strife (see Chapter 3).

Sri Lanka

Sri Lanka was the site of a twenty-six-year war between the ruling government, made up of members of the Buddhist Sinhalese majority, which comprises 70 percent of the population, and the Liberation Tigers of Tamil Eelam (LTTE), a group of Hindu Tamils eventually proscribed as a terrorist group by the United States, EU, India and twenty-nine other countries. Within Sri Lanka, the Tamils are a minority group that makes up 15 percent of the population. Despite this conflict, which officially ended with the defeat of the LTTE in 2009 at the hands of the government's military, religious friction per se is rather limited in Sri Lanka. Indeed, the war was largely focused on ethnicity rather than religion. Nevertheless, moves against religious minorities occurred on both sides, with the LTTE expelling tens of thousands of Muslims from the areas in the north and Jaffna that it controlled, while the government forces committed human rights abuses at places of worship. Muslims make up 7 percent of the population, and Christians, largely Roman Catholic, make up 8 percent. As some observers, such as Dennis B. McGilvray (2008), have indicated, Muslims, Hindus, and Buddhists largely lived in peaceful coexistence before and after the conflict.

No More Tears Sister: Anatomy of Hope and Betrayal (2006), directed by Helene Klodawsky, is an insightful film on the Sri Lankan conflict. It portrays the effects of the war on one Tamil family.

References and Further Research

BBC. 2009. "Religions: Sunni and Shi'a." http://www.bbc.co.uk/religion/religions/islam/subdivisions/sunnishia_1.shtml.

Bhaumik, Subir. 2007. *Insurgencies in India's Northeast: Conflict, Co-option and Change.* East-West Center Working Papers, no. 10. Washington, DC: East-West Center. http://scholarspace.manoa.hawaii.edu/bitstream/handle/10125/3540/EWCWwp010.pdf?sequence=1.

Clothey, Fred W. 2006. *Religion in India: A Historical Introduction.* New York: Routledge.

Dempsey, Corinne G. 2001. *Kerala Christian Sainthood: Collisions of Culture and Worldview in South India.* New York: Oxford University Press.

Flueckiger, Joyce Burkhalter. 2013. *When the World Becomes Female: Guises of a South Indian Goddess.* Bloomington: Indiana University Press.

Hirst, Jacqueline Suthren, and John Zavos. 2011. *Religious Traditions in Modern South Asia.* New York: Routledge.

International Crisis Group. 2003. *Kashmir: Learning from the Past.* ICG Asia Report no. 70. Islamabad: International Crisis Group. http://www.crisisgroup.org/en/regions/asia/south-asia/kashmir/070-kashmir-learning-from-the-past.aspx.

Kassam, Tazim. 1995. *Songs of Wisdom and Circles of Dance: Hymns of the Satpanth Ismāʿīlī Muslim Saint, Pir Shams.* McGill Studies in the History of Religions. Albany: State University of New York Press.

Lau, Martin. 2007. "Twenty-five Years of the Hudood Ordinances: A Review." *Washington and Lee Law Review* 64, no. 4: 1291–1314. http://law.wlu.edu/deptimages/Law%20Review/64-4Lau.pdf.

Lopez, Donald S., Jr. 1995. *Religions of India in Practice.* Princeton, NJ: Princeton University Press.

McGilvray, Dennis B. 2008. *Crucible of Conflict: Tamil and Muslim Society on the East Coast of Sri Lanka.* Durham, NC: Duke University Press.

Moon, Vasant. 2000. *Growing Up Untouchable in India.* Translated by Gail Omvedt. Introduction by Eleanor Zeillot. Lanham, MD: Rowman & Littlefield.

Pew Forum on Religion & Public Life. 2011. *The Future of the Global Muslim Population.* http://www.pewforum.org/The-Future-of-the-Global-Muslim-Population.aspx.

Richman, Paula. 1991. *Many Rāmāyanas: The Diversity of a Narrative Tradition in South Asia.* Berkeley: University of California Press.

Films

Films marked with an asterisk are available through the South Asia Center at Syracuse University (http://www.maxwell.syr.edu/moynihan/programs/sac/), as noted in Part One of this book. The directors and producers are cited when available.

Wages of Action: Religion in a Hindu Village. * 1979. Produced by David Thompson. Madison: Center for South Asia, University of Wisconsin. This film explores everyday religious practices in the village of Soyepur, near Banaras. The film observes, among other practices, young men praying to Lord Hanuman before a wrestling match, a grandmother offering water to a sacred *tulsi* plant, a Brahmin priest conducting a *satyanarayan puja* a ritual conducted partially in Sanskrit, a low-caste religious specialist known as an *ojha* exorcising spirits from the ill, and a Soyepur couple making a one-day pilgrimage to a shrine by the Ganges River.

I Am a Sufi, I Am a Muslim.* 1994. Written and directed by Dirk Dumon. Belgian Radio and Television. This program introduces Sufism, a branch of Islam. Ranging from India and Pakistan to Turkey and Macedonia, the film explores how Sufism is practiced in various parts of the world today.

In Shopian.* 2011. Produced and directed by Christopher Giamo. Fogtooth Media. A discussion of the abuses faced by the Kashmiri populations in Indian-occupied Kashmir in 2010, when two women were allegedly raped and murdered by members of the Indian army.

No More Tears Sister: Anatomy of Hope and Betrayal. 2005. Produced by Pierre Lapointe. Written and directed by Helene Klodawsky. Ottawa, ON: National Film Board of Canada. An insightful telling of the Sri Lankan conflict from the viewpoint of one family affected by the war.

Raam Ke Naam (In the Name of God).* 1992. Directed by Anand Patwardhan. A portrayal of the Bharatiya Janata Party's suspicious moves during the Babri Mosque demolition in December 1992, this documentary explores the ethics of the Hindutva movement and its effects on Indian society.

This Is a Music: Reclaiming an Untouchable Drum.* 2011. Directed by Zoe Sherinian. This ethnomusicological documentary focuses on the psychological and economic transformation of a group of untouchable drummers from a village in Tamil Nadu, South India. Through rarely filmed folk performances and the experience of an American ethnomusicologist who comes to study with them, nine drummers are shown trying to eke out a living while negotiating ongoing discrimination in their village.

6

Globalization in South Asia

SUSAN SNOW WADLEY

Globalization is the primary thread that links the various aspects of South Asia considered here, including its history and current issues. With its various meanings and a wide range of supporters and detractors, *globalization* refers to a process of increasing interconnectedness of peoples across the earth. Critically, this process goes back much further than the latter part of the twentieth century, when the term entered the lexicon and gained currency; many scholars consider the first globalization to be the migration of humans out of Africa.

Historical Background

Looking at all the phases of globalization requires a shift away from the Eurocentric focus that dominates current thinking about it. Around 500 CE, the Middle East was the site of the integration of the Euro-Asian economy. This process shifted to South and East Asia after 1100 CE, especially with the introductions of new technologies and the importance of the Silk Road and the trade associated with it. It was only after 1500 that Europe became a primary site of globalization, with the Euro-Atlantic economy dominating from 1800 through World War II, when the formerly colonized states gained their independence. In some ways, the world was more unified in the late 1800s than it is now, according to some observers, notably Jan Nederveen Pieterse (2009), because Western countries controlled as much as 96 percent of the earth's surface at that time. That unification was primarily territorial, however, based on trade and with cultural encounters of enormous significance. The globalization of the late twentieth century and the early twenty-first century is less about territorial control and more about economic and cultural control. Moreover, the speed of modern communications has made twenty-first-century globalization vastly different in tone from its nineteenth-century counterpart.

Over time, advances in technology increased the rate by which humans could travel and exchange ideas. This speeding up of communications, travel, and exchange marks the modern era of globalization. By the 1960s, satellites provided instant communication across the globe, while air travel made the movements of peoples increasingly easy. These advances contributed significantly to new forms of finance flows and the workings of the world's economies, in addition to the transfer of ideas and the opening of imaginations. This increasing connectedness led to the popularization of the term *globalization* in the latter part of the twentieth century, and it is this speeding up and intensification of flows

---

Box 6.1

The Globe in History

Essential to the idea of globalization is the idea of the earth as a globe, a three-dimensional sphere. This concept dates back to ancient Greek astronomers, but it apparently died out in Europe during the Middle Ages. The oldest depiction of this globe in the modern sense dates back to 1492, when Martin Behaim of Nuremburg created his *Erdapfel*, or "earth apple." Since the Erdapfel preceded the return of Columbus from the Americas, it featured a huge swath of ocean between Europe and Asia.

---

of trade, investment, finances, migration, and culture that is implied in the current use of the term.

An excellent introduction to the history of globalization is found on the website of the Yale Center for the Study of Globalization (http://www.ycsg.yale.edu/).

For more on the modern concept of globalization, see the Global Transformations website (http://www.polity.co.uk/global/).

Types of Globalization

Globalization is not one thing. Scholars frequently talk about economic globalization, political globalization, and cultural globalization. *Economic globalization* refers to changes in economies—including markets, products, producers, and financing—such as the activities of the World Bank and the International Monetary Fund (IMF). The World Bank and IMF were especially important in South Asia during the financial crises of the 1980s and 1990s. For example, when India faced a shortage of foreign exchange in the 1990s, the IMF linked financial aid to the restructuring of the country's economy. India devalued its currency, adopted market-driven economic policies, and moved away from the state-controlled planned economic model that it had followed since gaining independence in 1947. These shifts succeeded in opening India's economy, making it one of the world's fastest-growing economies in the twenty-first century. By 2007, India's growth rate of 9 percent was second only to China's. More recently, in 2012, Bangladesh received a $987 million loan from the IMF to ease balance-of-payment pressures and declining foreign reserves.

Political globalization refers to the ways in which nation-states are formed and linked. Especially important are new forms of power relations, the relative insignificance of the boundaries of nation-states, and the growth of international regulatory agencies such as the World Health Organization and the World Trade Organization. Politically, the United Nations plays a key role in globalization, and even the most powerful countries must

---

Box 6.2

Global Economic Institutions

The World Bank, founded in 1944, states on its website (http://www.world-bank.org) that "poverty reduction through an inclusive and sustainable globalization remains the overarching goal of our work." The World Bank primarily provides low-interest loans and other support for projects ranging from education to agriculture to urban transport. With its headquarters in Washington, DC, it has more than 9,000 employees worldwide.

The International Monetary Fund "promotes international monetary co-operation and exchange rate stability, facilitates the balanced growth of international trade, and provides resources to help members in balance of payments difficulties or to assist with poverty reduction" (http://www.imf.org/external/about/overview.htm).

---

resort to it, as the United States did when it sought world approval for the 2003 invasion of Iraq. Many scholars also attribute to globalization the increasing role of civil society organizations, the nongovernmental organizations (NGOs), both local and transnational, which play such a large part in contemporary social advocacy movements, such as UNICEF and local organizations fighting AIDS. Many believe that NGOs are taking on roles that nation-states have abdicated, especially with regard to the social sector. Further, the role of nation-states is changing, giving rise to regional organizations, such as the European Union, that have enormous power, as demonstrated in the 2012 Greek financial crisis. The movement of citizens across the globe also demands new forms of "belonging" to a nation. For example, the Tamil Tigers (see Chapter 13) could not have waged war in Sri Lanka for more than twenty-five years without the financial and moral support of the Tamil diaspora.

Cultural globalization refers to such diverse phenomena as the spread of mass media and the instant transfer of news from one region to another, thereby significantly magnifying their impact. News reports of the December 2012 rape and murder of a woman in New Delhi, India, for instance, reached American households via local newspapers, television shows such as *Today*, and numerous online sources. Cultural globalization also refers to the personal connectedness created by social media. For example, an anthropologist in Syracuse, New York, can get daily news via Facebook from the community in rural India where she has done research. Cultural globalization also includes the spread of ideas, such as ideas of justice and human rights that compel rural artists to paint about the rights of women or the poor. It also includes efforts by the advertising industry and various corporations to sell new consumer goods to populations across the globe. The growth of the cultural supermarket, whereby communities and societies can pick and choose among new ideas and products, is an important aspect of cultural globalization. Further, in an interesting local twist on globalization, communities choose ideas and goods from the

Box 6.3

Diaspora: A Global Phenomenon

Diaspora is a term commonly used to refer to the dispersal of humans from a homeland across the globe. Hence the Tamil diaspora refers to the spread of Tamil-speaking peoples from Sri Lanka and southern India to countries such as Sweden, Canada, and the United States.

A shop in a traditional marketplace in the district town of Mainpuri, India. *(Photo by Susan Snow Wadley)*

global supermarket and then repackage them to fit their own needs. Since many people in South Asia live on wages earned and paid daily, for example, it is more common in much of the region to buy shampoo in a foil packet that contains enough for one wash than to buy a bottle with enough shampoo for many weeks; and if there is no income that day, cheap soap can always be used to wash hair.

Many aspects of globalization cross these artificial categories. For example, multi-national corporations are the central producers and distributors of cultural products, so that Pepsi is now found spread across the globe, from the plateaus of Tibet to the plains of rural India. The spread of products such as Pepsi or Coca-Cola, or even the Barbie doll, has aspects of both economic and cultural globalization, since these multinational companies are introducing new products that might change, in the case of Pepsi, food consumption and diets, while Barbie carries the Western value of thinness, which is contrary to traditional ideas of femininity held by many cultures. Sometimes these multinational ventures become embroiled in political disputes as well. An attempt by Walmart to enter the Indian market, for example, led to mass political protests because people across India feared the loss of the local markets and small shops that dot their landscape.

The increasing flow of humans from one area to another, such as South Asian males laboring in the Middle East, also demonstrates these various kinds of globalization. Economic globalization is seen due to the need for labor caused by the economic prosperity that has come with the oil boom in countries like Qatar and Saudi Arabia. Political globalization occurs as these laborers become embroiled in Middle East politics (e.g., those caught in Kuwait during the first Iraq War who were airlifted home), as well as policies put in place by the home country to protect their emigrants from abuse by middlemen or in the host country. Finally, cultural globalization takes place as the migrants are introduced to new ideas, new forms of social behavior, and new consumer goods that fill the baggage claim areas at South Asian airports upon their return.

The Value of Globalization

The value of globalization is often contested. Some critics argue, for example, that globalization has increased violence across the globe. The global arms trade has intensified as new technologies, including nuclear capabilities, have spread much more rapidly than previous innovations, such as gunpowder, while cyber warfare, international terrorism, ecoterrorism, and transnational organized crime increase the security threats to states. Indeed, both India and Pakistan became nuclear states in the 1990s. Sex trafficking—from Nepal to India, and from the South Asian region to other regions—is part of a worldwide network of organized crime that targets women and children. Climate change, caused by the burning of fossil fuels, especially in developed countries, is leading to global warming that will affect all humans, though several scholars argue that the poor will suffer the most. Many Indians rue the cultural changes that have lead Indian girls to wear jeans, while at the same time women's literacy continues to increase, leading to changes in the age of marriage, family relationships, and women's status more generally. While many feminists and others applaud these advances for women, many males, especially, are threatened by them and respond with violence—whether in the West or in South Asia.

Scholars and the public alike differ on whether globalization is good or bad, as well as what its impact is. Americans are frequently told that "outsourcing" is taking away American jobs, so that a Ford automobile factory in Mexico hurts Detroit. Yet, as noted above, Indians fear Walmart and its potential threat to their small shopkeepers. Some scholars argue that globalization lowers labor standards as well as product quality, despite the enormous success of Japanese car manufacturers in the late twentieth century—which ultimately forced American manufacturers to produce their own high-quality cars. Scholars and the general population alike often believe that globalization destroys the environment. Factories built in countries without environmental standards or legal sanctions certainly can do this, as they have done for generations in the United States, where pollution from factories and inadequate sewer systems, both in the past and today, is rampant. Residents of the EU and India are particularly vocal about their fear that the global spread of genetically modified

A Kolkata grocery store, with a wide range of products elaborately displayed. *(Photo by Susan Snow Wadley)*

seeds will have far-reaching effects on humans, livestock, and the land, even though genetically modified wheat, with its fourfold increases in yield, led to the Green Revolution in South Asia and brought many farmers out of poverty in the 1960s and 1970s.

> For an introduction to the highly controversial issues of genetically modified foodstuffs, see the website Food Dialogues (http://www.fooddialogues.com/). In addition, the United Nations report *International Trade in GMOs and GM Products: National and Multilateral Legal Frameworks* (http://unctad.org/en/docs/itcdtab30_en.pdf) deals with international trade issues concerning genetically modified organisms.

These debates are related to various myths about globalization. First, globalization and the interconnectedness of humans across the globe is not a precursor to utopian peace. Rather, the Internet and modern media are just as likely to spread hatred, misinformation, and a lack of understanding of other people's positions on everything from religion to divorce to economic policies. With anyone able to create a web page on any topic, the Internet is filled with misinformation and often divisive opinions. For example, many websites discussing Islam claim that the Ismailis—Shia Muslims who founded the Fatimid Caliphate that controlled most of North Africa, including Egypt, from the Red Sea to the Atlantic Ocean during the tenth and eleventh centuries—are not in fact Muslims. This claim, spread by modern media, is fundamental to the ongoing sectarian violence in Pakistan.

Second, while globalization sometimes appears to widen the gap between rich and poor, it has in fact helped countries in South Asia, Latin America, and the Far East to gain prosperity, send more children to school, and increase their gross national product. What has remained, and in some cases increased, is the gap *within* countries between rich and poor. For example, the United States has higher inequality between rich and poor than any South Asia country, despite ranking fourth in the world on the Human Development Index (HDI), which measures issues related to education, health, and income. Sri Lanka ranks highest of the South Asian countries on the HDI, but also it has the highest income inequality in South Asia.

For more comparisons across the region and the world, see the map of "International Human Development Indicators" prepared by the United Nations (http:// hdr.undp.org/en/data/map/) and the *2013 Human Development Report* (http:// hdr.undp.org/en/reports/global/hdr2013/).

Homogenization or Hybridity?

The global forces of modern capitalism are often criticized for their power to create a homogeneous world order, one that will erode the local cultures with which it comes into contact. Although global linkages move ideas and traditions between the First World and the Third World and back, the consumer culture and cultural norms of the Western (Euro-American) world have tended to dominate this cross-fertilization. But to believe in the all-consuming power of global forces is to deny any power and agency to local cultural traditions and to the people who enact and live those traditions. It is to deny people's abilities to accommodate, to resist, or to reject the ideals, symbols, practices, and goods emerging from the cultural and material "supermarket" of globalization. As numerous scholars have pointed out, localization involves multiple, divergent interpretations of what is "global." Rather, facets of a global culture provide new materials with which peoples can forge new identities and new traditions.

One popular term that captures the idea of homogenization is *McDonaldization*, which refers to the fear that corporations and consumer outlets such as the fast-food chain will impose Western culture across the globe. The reality is more complex, however, and speaks to what is meant by localization. First, in countries like Russia, China, and India, McDonald's is too expensive for the poor; instead, it attracts the upper-middle and upper classes. Spending one or two days' wages for a burger is not viable for most people in these countries. Second, the food on offer changes in these countries. McDonald's in India does not offer beef, for example. The Maharaja Mac, replacing the Big Mac, is made with chicken, while the restaurants also offer a McVeggie, a burger made with *paneer*, an Indian cheese and a Chicken Tikka Burger. Moreover, in the North Indian state of Punjab, near the Golden Temple, which is the most sacred site for Sikhs, McDonald's is building its first all-vegetarian outlet. In Pakistan, with its Muslim ban on pork, the breakfast sandwich is made with chicken sausage. Finally, researchers in various parts of Asia have shown that eating at McDonald's is not a "fast" food excursion, as customers stay, on average, three to five times longer than customers in the United States. It is also quite common for a trip to McDonald's to be a relatively expensive date. And lastly, fast-food chains, with their emphasis on cleanliness and access, have altered the restroom culture of most of Asia.

> Pizza Hut, Subway, McDonald's, Kentucky Fried Chicken, Taco Bell, and other fast-food restaurants are all found in South Asia. An Internet search for any of these outlets, plus a country name, will reveal the adaptations that they have made for South Asian customers. (Bangladesh does not have McDonald's, but it does have other international fast-food outlets.)

The transformations of McDonald's in Asia are a clear reflection of hybridity, the mixing of elements from two different sources into a new form. Related to ideas of acculturation, localization, and mixing, hybridity does not favor the forms of one group over another. Both acculturation and localization imply that the "lower" adapts to the "higher" group. The idea of "acculturation" usually refers to a situation in which two social groups meet in the same space, such as when immigrants arrive in a new land. The immigrants, as part of the lower-ranked group, are expected to adopt the habits of the higher-ranked group (acculturate to the more powerful group's norms and language), rather than acknowledging that both change. Localization is somewhat similar, in that the local, thought inferior to the global, adopts the global idea. Hybridity also emphasizes the mixing and lack of strict boundaries and hence argues against the ethos of order and neat separation that are so much a part of modernity.

Hybridity thus recognizes that the processes of globalization and localization are not all unidirectional, and it does not assume that one group is superior. This is especially important because not all the ideas and products and finances move from north to south. A prime example, again, is food. In Britain, the popular sausage roll, a quick snack sold in bakeries, pubs, and shops across the country, is now commonly a chicken tikka (or tandoori) sausage roll; that is, the British sausage is replaced with spicy Indian chicken.

Another instance of hybridity with South Asia roots is yoga, now taught widely across the United States, including in elementary school classrooms and jails. Losing most if not all of its connection to Hindu spirituality in many places where it is taught, yoga is a "new" exercise and sport of modern America. For example, this is how the nonprofit organization USA Yoga describes its function: "USA Yoga is a non-profit organization formed for the purpose of developing and promoting Yoga Asana (yoga postures) as a sport," and it advertises regional and national championships for the "sport of yoga" (http://www.usayoga.org). In the competitions, contestants have a given time period in which to assume a certain number of yoga-based postures, which are then judged for "grace" as well as the contestants' ability to assume the pose. No mention is made of yoga's spiritual roots. The practices in place today in organizations such as USA Yoga are actually as rooted in the international physical culture movement as they are in Indian spiritual practices. USA Yoga also seeks to gain Olympic status in the future. In this case, Western sport and Hindu spiritual practice have united in a new hybrid form that keeps key elements of the physical exercise but eliminates the cultural underpinnings. The teaching of yoga across the globe varies widely, with some focusing on the spiritual base and other solely on the exercises.

See the website of the South Asia Center at Syracuse University, Global South Asia (http://globalsouthasia.syr.edu/), for an additional case study on the globalization of yoga.

For the efforts by some conservative Christians to ban yoga in various U.S. communities and sites, see the October 2012 article "California Parents Protest Teaching of Yoga in School" by Eli Epstein, on the website of the *International Business Times* (http://www.ibtimes.com/) and the judge's decision to allow it to be taught, claiming that it was stripped of all religious and cultural terms as taught at this school (http://search.proquest.com.libezproxy2.syr.edu/docview/1372854295).

The chicken tikka sausage roll, the Maharaja Mac, and the yoga taught in the American university all represent the idea of hybridity, of ongoing mixing, whether of social rules, values, foods, dress, or ways of engaging in finance. Hybridization requires a new mixing, a separation from old ways and a redevelopment of unique new forms. There is a crossing over, a mixing of ethnicities, political forms, beliefs (as in religious syncretism), and cultural traits (as in the saying, "Muslim in the daytime, disco in the evening").

This hybridity is not new, just as globalization is not new. Over the centuries, the local has been constantly influenced by ideas and products from outside, whether from the next village, town, tribe, or country. One lesson is that there is no true "local"—or at least there has not been for most of the world's populations for many centuries—forcing us thus to examine the negotiations that people in any given locale have been making with different lifeways, or with the global, for many years. While we can and should seek to understand the local, we must recognize that any local phenomenon is a product of negotiation and paradox, and it is these combinations that provide insight into the concerns driving human actors. Equally important, however, is recognizing that any form of "local" is marked by class divisions that present critical alternatives of choice, and hence identities, whether chosen from the local bazaar or the global supermarket.

The various types of globalization and the processes underlying them discussed in this chapter are explored in greater depth through the case studies that follow in Part Four.

References and Further Research

Barfield, Thomas. 2010. *Afghanistan: A Cultural and Political History*. Princeton, NJ: Princeton University Press.

Boo, Katherine. 2012. *Behind the Beautiful Forevers: Life, Death, and Hope in a Mumbai Undercity*. New York: Random House.

Cohen, Stephen P., ed. 2011. *The Future of Pakistan*. Washington, DC: Brookings Institution Press.

Deb, Siddhartha. 2012. *The Beautiful and the Damned: Life in the New India*. New York: Penguin.

Einsiedel, Sebastian von, David M. Malone, and Suman Pradhan, eds. 2012. *Nepal in Transition: From People's War to Fragile Peace*. Cambridge: Cambridge University Press.

Ferguson, Yale H., and Richard W. Mansbach. 2012. *Globalization: The Return of Borders to a Borderless World?* New York: Routledge.

Gardener, Katy. 2012. *Discordant Development: Global Capitalism and the Struggle for Connection in Bangladesh*. London: Pluto.

Gupta, Dipankar. 2009. *The Caged Phoenix: Can India Fly?* Washington, DC: Woodrow Wilson Center Press.

Pieterse, Jan Nederveen. 2009. *Globalization and Culture: Global Mélange*. 2nd ed. Lanham, MD: Rowman & Littlefield.

Sernau, Scott. 2012. *Global Problems: The Search for Equity, Peace, and Sustainability*. 3rd ed. New York: Pearson.

Shaikh, Farzana. 2009. *Making Sense of Pakistan*. New York: Columbia University Press.

Turner, Bryan S., and Habibul Haque Khondker. 2010. *Globalization East and West*. Los Angeles: SAGE.

Films

Bom: One Day Ahead of Democracy. 2011. Directed by Amlan Datta. PVR Director's Rare. The film chronicles the impact of modernization on a pre-Aryan community speaking a near-extinct language, Kanashi, and living in a remote mountain village called Malana in Himachal Pradesh.

Char . . . The No-Man's Island. 2012. Directed by Sourav Sarangi. Documents the illegal smuggling of rice across the Bangladesh-India border by a fourteen-year-old boy who often has to stay on the uninhabited island of Char, patrolled by both Indian and Bangladeshi border guards.

Made in India.* 2010. Produced and directed by Rebecca Haimowitz and Vaishali Sinha. This provocative film follows a couple from Texas as they seek a surrogate mother in Mumbai, India.

My Migrant Soul. 2003. Directed by Yasmine Kabir. This documentary details the life of a young Bangladeshi who seeks to escape the poverty of his native land and becomes an illegal migrant to Malaysia.

The Story of India. 2007. Written and presented by Michael Wood. A six-part BBC documentary (broadcast by PBS in the United States) that documents the history of the Indian subcontinent.

The World Before Her. 2012. Written and directed by Nishu Pahuja. This full-length documentary contrasts the Miss India contest in Mumbai with a training camp for girls run by a militant fundamental group in rural India.

7

Introduction to the Case Studies

SUSAN SNOW WADLEY

The case studies presented in this volume cover a wide range of subjects intended to explore some of the critical forces at work in the region and are representative of the globalizing processes shaping contemporary South Asia. Examples include economic, political, and cultural forms of globalization in the countries of Bangladesh, India, Pakistan, Nepal, and Sri Lanka.

Additional case studies, including ones on Afghanistan, on yoga, and on Indian-occupied Kashmir, can be found on the Syracuse University website Global South Asia (http://globalsouthasia.syr.edu/).

For up-to-date news on South Asia, friend the Facebook page South Asia SU.

The first case study, by the anthropologist Susan Snow Wadley, looks at change in the rural community known as Karimpur in northern India, where Wadley has done research periodically since the 1960s. She sets the stage for understanding modern South Asia, where more than 70 percent of the population continues to live in rural areas. As shown in Karimpur, change is everywhere, whether in age of marriage, education, migration to urban areas, or the importance of genetically modified seeds in increasing crop yields and lowering the levels of poverty. Nevertheless, much remains the same, especially in aspects of social life such as arranged marriages, purdah rules for women, conflicts between castes, and significant class differences. Issues facing all the countries of South Asia are also noted, including the pressures of population increases, the lack of appropriate education, and unemployment.

Shifting to Madurai in southern India, the anthropologist Nicole Wilson explores how urbanization and middle-class status change marriage practices for people in the community, while they also retain key components of traditional practices. In this middle-class community, new values of slimness and education are imposed on brides, and grooms are expected to have "the right education" and jobs that demand technical skills. New financial expectations make arranging a marriage challenging: the bride's family seeks the most financially stable groom, and the groom's family seeks a bride with the right dowry. The Internet plays a crucial role in these modern arranged marriages. In this case study, for example, the potential bride, in Madurai, and groom, in Bahrain, meet via Skype. Facebook is then used to send a modern wedding invitation. Because guests of different castes will attend the wedding itself, other wedding invitations include descriptions of the Brahmin rituals with which the lower-caste guests might not be familiar.

Two very different case studies examine the role of local and international nongovernmental organizations (NGOs) in South Asia. Looking at issues of the commons and forestry management in rural Rajasthan, India, the geographer Mitul Baruah examines how new ideas about the roles of indigenous peoples and the management of the forests that have been a primary source of their traditional livelihoods are being implemented with the help of a transnational NGO. Until recently, the regulations for forestry use in India were based on the policies of the British colonialists, carried over to independent India. The primary goal of these colonial policies was to deny access to the forests to "save" them from the incursions of humans. More recently, consideration of the rights of tribal peoples has led the Indian government to rethink its forest management practices. NGOs, such as the Foundation for Ecological Security, studied here, have obtained funding to act as intermediaries between local communities and the government, especially its forestry department. The role of NGOs in civil society is amply demonstrated, as is the government's addressing, due to international pressures, the rights of local communities. Most important, though, is the return of basic forest management to the local community, in line with revisions in understanding forestry management that are global. As the photos illustrate, returning the forests to the control of their users works: as a community, the people of Gogunda, Rajasthan, have created policies to protect their forests so that they can continue to benefit from them.

NGOs also play a key role in the lives of transgendered men, or *khwaja sira*, in Pakistan, as seen in Faris Khan's examination. Here the traditional *guru-chela* relationship found in cities like Karachi is being challenged by new modes of belonging, as evidenced by organizations devoted to the prevention of HIV/AIDS. Khan also illustrates the shift by NGOs to community-based organizations, such as those working in Karachi. Here again, as with forestry management, we see an important shift to putting responsibility in the hands of the users. Further, new forms of identity (especially "gay") are challenging the traditional understandings of being a khwaja sira.

Turning to Bangladesh, the medical anthropologist Karen McNamara uses an economic lens to demonstrate how traditional herbal medicines and the pharmaceutical industry are jointly affected by the roles of international organizations, particularly, in this case, the World Trade Organization and the World Health Organization. Pressured by these international agencies, the Bangladeshi state has established new laws pertaining to the production and quality of traditional medicines, despite their connection to medical systems like Ayurveda and Unani that are thousands of years old. By meeting these new regulations, companies in Bangladesh are able to enter the global marketplace, selling ancient cures to modern citizens. Here old and new are juxtaposed, with old remedies packaged in new ways and subjected to new controls, yet still being used across the globe to cure human ills.

Both Sri Lanka and the FATA region of Pakistan bring our attention to questions of governmentality, religious and ethnic conflict, and the role of diaspora populations as well as international organizations. The political scientist Robert Oberst uses his thirty years of work in Sri Lanka to examine the recently ended Tamil liberation movement there. As he notes, this war was rooted in British colonial policies and disputes over ethnicity, language, and education that erupted after independence in 1948. Denied by the Sinhalese majority the educational prerogatives that they had under the British and finding their economic prosperity in peril, the Tamils aimed to create a Tamil nation, Ealam, in the north and east of the island. Under the leadership of Prabhakaran and the Liberation Tigers of Tamil Eelam (or Tamil Tigers), the Sri Lankan conflict was heavily financed by Tamils who had emigrated out of the Tamil regions of Sri Lanka, both before and after the conflict escalated in the mid-1980s. In order to fight the Sri Lanka army, the Tamil Tigers relied heavily on new modes of communication as well as the vast increase in the global arms trade that has accompanied globalization.

The Federally Administered Tribal Areas (FATA) of Pakistan has never been under state control, and even today the region exists outside of the legal authority of the constitution of Pakistan. The historian Subho Basu and the anthropologist Susan Wadley analyze the FATA region's special status as a buffer area between contesting great powers (in the nineteenth century, the British and Russians; in the twentieth century, the Americans and Russians). Most critical, however, is the extralegal status of this mountainous region, contributing to both military interventions and drone attacks. Its ambiguous legal status has also contributed to Pakistan's lack of development efforts and other interventions that might have precluded the Taliban insurgencies currently based there.

Women are the focus of two very different case studies, although the role of NGOs is essential in both. In Nepal, as discussed by the social psychologist Mary Crawford, the ease of communication and travel, as well as greater disparities in income and increased poverty, have made young women even more vulnerable to sex trafficking than they were in the past. The desire for more income, factory jobs, and an attractive mate all entice young women to leave with traffickers for the city, where they are sold into brothels and often transported to Mumbai or other parts of India. NGOs such as Shakti Samuha and Maiti Nepal work to bring girls back to their homeland, though rehabilitation and reentry into Nepalese society are difficult.

As shown by Susan Snow Wadley, trained in folklore and gender studies, the female painters of Mithila art, on the India side of the Nepal border, are able to use their traditional art form to speak out on the kinds of injustices that women face in both India and Nepal. Here, too, support from an international NGO, the Ethnic Arts Foundation, is currently fundamental to their ability to get training and find global markets for their art. But without the efforts of the Indian government in the 1960s, this art form may well have remained on mud walls and not found the markets and attention that it now receives around the world. Nowadays, modern communications play their part, allowing the young women painters to know of and paint about injustices in their country and across the globe.

Globalization has brought significant changes to several industries in South Asia. Two cases studies are included here: one on the transformations within the Bollywood film industry over the past century, and one on the more recent development in cities like Bangalore of high-technology companies tied to computers, the Internet, and other global connections.

Tula Goenka, a professor of documentary filmmaking who was trained in Bollywood and the United States as a film editor, examines the history of Bollywood filmmaking since its inception in the first decade of the twentieth century. Changes in government regulations, such as the easing of the Censor Board rules regarding the representation of sexuality and the opening of the Indian economy forced by the International Monetary Fund, have affected Bollywood and its films. Here culture and economics unite in creating the new style of Bollywood film so popular across the globe.

The geographer Sanjukta Mukherjee takes us to the high-technology centers of the South Indian city of Bangalore, where she explores the changing landscape of the city. High-tech industrial zones and gated communities have transformed the region, while also making sharper the distinctions between rich and poor. Women working in high-tech fields face particular challenges, ranging from physical safety to negotiating their dual roles as wives and employees in demanding professions. The modern Bangalore is without doubt a product of globalization, of finance, of communications, and of cultural transformations. It is a fitting symbol with which to end our exploration of globalizing South Asia.

8

Social Change in Rural India
A Village Study

SUSAN SNOW WADLEY

Girls in jeans, cell phones everywhere, televisions blaring: this is modern rural India. Along with India's cities, the country's rural communities are changing, due to the urban employment of many residents, increased levels of education, higher ages at marriage, lower fertility rates, changing roles of women, and increased use of the products of global markets. Representative of the odd twists of change is the fact that 50 percent of Indian households now have a cell phone but no toilet facilities.

Understanding key factors of social change in rural India is fundamental to understanding South Asia today. With some 70 percent of India's population of 1.2 billion still living in several hundred thousand villages in rural areas, rural communities continue to form the core of the Indian nation. In these rural communities lie both the strengths and the potential weaknesses of the nation, as the benefits of a modern India are unevenly distributed and accessed, both in individual communities and across communities.

In this case study, I focus on social change in the village known as Karimpur, with the goal of laying a framework for further explorations of modern South Asia. Certainly the best studied "village" in South Asia, Karimpur has been the focus of social science research since the 1920s, when William Wiser—a Presbyterian missionary and agricultural specialist who would go on to obtain a PhD in rural sociology from Cornell University—first sought to understand the lifeways and farming practices of its rural residents in order to better focus his work with Indian farmers. He and his wife, Charlotte Wiser, continued to live and work with and to write about Karimpur residents through the 1960s (see Wiser and Wiser 2000).

In the late 1960s, I began doing my doctoral research in Karimpur, and I have continued my connection to the village ever since (see my 1994 book, *Struggling with Destiny in Karimpur, 1925–1984*). This chapter is based on my more than forty years of work in Karimpur, as well as the work of the Wisers. During that time, I have lived in Karimpur for more than three years, and I have visited almost yearly for the past twenty-five years, sometimes for a week, sometimes for six weeks. When there, I live with a family, sharing their house (and helping to rebuild it), enduring the lack of electricity, the monsoon rains, the all-too-present mosquitoes, while loving what was once the only latrine in the village. I have close friendships with many of the people in the village and nowadays look forward to the once a month e-mails with news of my friends and more recently Facebook posts.

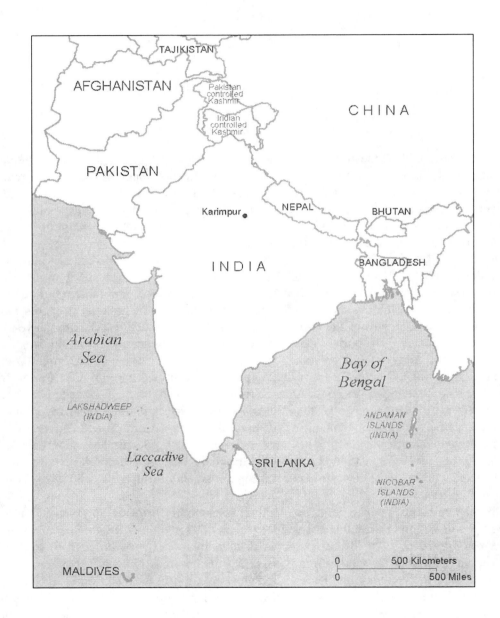

In the 1920s, the Wisers had a car they used to travel to the village. *(Photographer unknown)*

Box 8.1

Methodologies Used in This Case Study

Anthropology as a discipline relies on a variety of methods, ranging from "participant observation," implying that one often lives with and interacts daily with one's consultants, to survey questionnaires that might include standard demographic data, household consumer goods, maternity histories, land and land use patterns, and more. This chapter, based on more than forty years of research in one community, uses participant observation, extensive interviews, and census data from 1967, 1974, 1984, and 2010, as well as year-long stays in 1967–1969, 1973–1974, and 1983–1984, followed by regular visits of one to six weeks in the years since 1984. Additional data was provided by census data compiled by the Wisers in 1925. Insights developed were then compared against district, state, and national data collected by a variety of scholars.

In the late 1960s, Charlotte Wiser produced a filmstrip on Karimpur. That filmstrip, now adapted to a web page that includes updates from the last forty years, provides a visual of the changes discussed here (http://sites.maxwell.syr.edu/karimpur/).

See also the SU website for this book.

The mud walls that form the living quarters of the village can be seen in this image, as can the government tube well. *(Photo by Susan Snow Wadley)*

Background

Although this case study looks at only one village, Karimpur is representative of much of northern India. It is located in the state of Uttar Pradesh, sometimes referred to as the Hindi-speaking heartland of India, about 150 miles (240 kilometers) southeast of New Delhi and some 9 miles (16 kilometers) from Mainpuri, the nearby district town with a population of some 100,000. It is four hours' driving time east from Agra, the site of the Taj Mahal, traveling first on India's new National Highway 2 and then on a back road for the final two hours. You know you have reached Karimpur when a hillock rises out of the flat alluvial plain known as the Ganga-Yamuna Doab, a term indicating the rich farmlands lying between India's two major northern rivers, the Ganges and the Yamuna. The now fully earth-covered ruin of an old eighteenth-century fort, the Karimpur *khera*, is the only hill within miles. Topped by the shrine of the village guardian saint, a Muslim known as Khan Bahadur, the *khera* clearly demarcates one's arrival in Karimpur.

Box 8.2

The Use of Pseudonyms

The village name Karimpur is in fact a pseudonym, as are almost all the names of individuals found in both the Wisers's writing and my own writings. Through the late twentieth century, anthropologists and sociologists thought that their research consultants should be protected from the gaze and interference of others, and they therefore gave both communities and individuals pseudonyms. I have retained the names given by the Wisers for purposes of continuity.

When the Wisers first came to Karimpur in the 1920s, they termed it the village "behind mud walls," because from the road, one could see only mud walls, unmarked by even a window, as openings were an invitation to robbery and uninvited visitors. Gates faced the village lanes, and windows opened onto walled courtyards. Now, however, it could also be termed the village "behind brick walls," for although many mud walls remain, new houses are being built everywhere, with piles of bricks scattered in every empty space. The development has resulted, in large part, from the remittances of men working in Delhi, Mumbai, and other cities throughout northern India.

Before looking at Karimpur specifically, understanding a bit about the state of Uttar Pradesh, in which Karimpur is located, is helpful. Uttar Pradesh has a population of more than 200 million (if it was a country, it would be the fifth largest in the world, behind China, the United States, Indonesia, and Brazil). While massive in population, Uttar Pradesh is one of the least affluent of India's states, with a low urbanization ratio (22.3 percent) and 73 percent of the population earning a living from agriculture. Following economic liberalization in the early 1990s, India's economy has grown threefold or more, from a gross domestic product of $460 billion in 2000 to $1.72 trillion in 2010. Uttar Pradesh has lagged behind, however, ranking in the bottom three of India's states on most human development indices. Approximately 35 percent of its people live at or below the poverty line ($0.60 per day), and the birth rate is the highest in India; life expectancy is barely sixty years.

Nevertheless, Karimpur's residents are clearly better off than they were forty years ago. Most have access to clean drinking water through government-installed pumps. The Green Revolution, which introduced new seeds and crops into India in the late 1960s and 1970s, increased crop yields 200 to 400 percent. Most of the land is now irrigated, allowing for three crops a year. The local shops sell shampoos and good soap, replacing the yellow bar soap used in the 1960s for clothes, bodies, and hair alike. Many homes have electricity, although the supply remains erratic, and about 30 percent own a television. Whereas bicycles were a highly desired luxury item in the 1960s, a motor scooter is now the preferred vehicle, though only big landowners or those with sons in well-paying urban jobs can afford one. A couple of families own a truck or jeep. Some of the village

Table 8.1

Basic Facts in Karimpur's Demographic History

	1925	1984	2010
Total population	754	2,048	3,349
Number of families	161	327	509
Average family size	4.7	6.3	6.0
Adult sex ratio (F/1,000 M)	866	814	848
Juvenile sex ratio (F/1,000 M)	900	790	879

Source: Karimpur census data collected by Edward Wiser (1925) and Susan Snow Wadley (1984, 2010).

lanes are paved with bricks. Income from sons or brothers working in Delhi or other cities gives many residents enough cash to add a brick room or two to their mud-walled houses, and sometimes even a bathing cubicle for the women. Ten percent of the houses have a latrine. Very rarely, the people in the village can afford fruits to supplement their diet of whole-grain breads, rice, lentils, and vegetables, and only rarely can the 50 percent who are not vegetarian afford meat. The major expense facing all families is weddings, which families finance for their daughters. Often, this expense leaves a family in debt for years to come, as a daughter's dowry and marriage costs may equal a year's income or more. Yet despite this increased standard of living, the majority of Karimpur residents barely feed themselves and their families, and the better-off families have very few luxury items, not even a car.

Families and Family Life

In 1925, Karimpur had a mere 161 households, with a total population of 754 (Table 8.1). By 1984, the population had grown to 2,048 in 327 households, and by 2010 it was 3,349 people in 509 households.

Types of Households

Defining what is meant by a household in Karimpur challenges Western assumptions about family and family organization. To Karimpur's residents, a household typically means those (married couples and their children) who live together as one economic unit and share a cooking hearth. If this unit comprises a father and mother, their married sons, and the sons' wives and children, it is termed a *joint family*. A single married couple living with their unmarried children is called a *nuclear family*. A nuclear family with some other relative (uncle, aunt, widowed parent, unmarried adult sibling) is termed a *supplemented nuclear family* or a *stem family*. A household without a married couple is a *subnuclear family*.

In a landowning joint family, the land is shared equally by all the males of the oldest generation; such a family may comprise two elderly brothers, their wives, and all their married sons and grandchildren. Other resources are also shared—and maintaining the equal treatment of all the sons and their families is a major job of the male head of the household and his wife. Equally important is religious unity. Rituals with goals such as household prosperity are done for the whole unit, not for individual married couples.

According to the Sanskrit texts that prescribe model Hindu living, joint families are the ideal family structure. That the joint family is the model for many is true, as it demonstrates economic well-being, political strength, and control of one's women and sons. As one well-off Brahmin male from Karimpur said, "One straw from a broom cannot sweep" (Wadley 1994, 59), referring to the idea that a family has no economic or political power without the strength of several adult males. But while the joint family was and is the ideal family structure for many Indians, both urban and rural, the ideal is rarely borne out in people's lives. In fact, the reality of early death—life expectancy in India in the early twentieth century was a scant twenty years, and in Uttar Pradesh it is still only sixty years—made achieving a joint family almost impossible.

Indeed, joint families have not dominated in Karimpur for nearly 100 years: 15.5 percent of families were joint families in 1925, 27.8 percent were joint families in 1984, and 31 percent were joint families in 2010. Moreover, based on the modernization models of the 1960s, Western social scientists argued that the joint family would disappear with the modernization of the Third World. Interestingly, however, data from Karimpur suggest the opposite, as a greater percentage of residents live in joint families now than at any time in the twentieth century (as seen in the percentages noted above). A further complexity in the analysis of family structure is that even when a segment of the family, often a married couple and their children, lives for much of the year in Delhi or some other city, the family is still considered a joint family, with members stating that there has been no separation, either ritual or economic. Like many in modern India, Karimpur's residents are redefining the family unit, as well as what being a "joint" family means.

Houses and Their Social Structures

Whether made of mud or brick, the layout of the houses in Karimpur has been largely unchanged since the 1920s. In wealthy families, a veranda, possibly with a room off it, faces the village lane. Cattle—water buffaloes, bullocks, and cows—are tied in open areas near the veranda. This is the domain of the men, who will sleep on the verandas in the hot season, resting on their cots, and often smoking hookahs, when not working. The men's room may contain the television, if the family owns one. Since electricity is highly erratic, a TV set is as much for show as for watching. Beyond the veranda is the domain of the women. Here the primary space is an open courtyard, with a low wall surrounding a cooking area consisting of a clay hearth, with cow dung and wood for fuel, built into one corner. Nowadays a hand pump, or even a latrine and bathing area, may occupy another corner. Surrounding the courtyard are rooms for sleeping and storage. Most eating takes place in the courtyard, and it is here that both humans and animals sleep, with humans shifting to inner rooms during the rains or when temperatures turn cold.

A couple of families that have returned to Karimpur after living in urban areas for many

A woman washes dishes while her husband's brother bathes at the hand pump. *(Photo by Susan Snow Wadley)*

years have brought a new model of house structure with them, with the major change being a brick kitchen area in the house itself, rather than using the walled-off area of the courtyard for cooking. These kitchens, where the fuel is propane gas instead of cow dung and wood, have built-in shelves, and cooking is done standing at the gas stove, not squatting on the ground. These houses also have a latrine and bathing area incorporated into the original design.

Poor families often lack an enclosed courtyard, so that their one room may be off a veranda that also holds the cooking area. If possible, however, the poor seek a tiny courtyard for women, in order to observe the rules for purdah, which require women to be secluded or protected from interaction with men of a particular stature or age.

Purdah

As in much of rural northern India, both Hindu and Muslim women in Karimpur practice purdah. In Karimpur, only women married into the village practice purdah, and, conversely, daughters of the village practice purdah only in their husbands' villages. Hindu women cover their faces with the end of their sari before all men older than or senior to their husbands. They also cover their face when rituals or other events demand that they show respect to their mothers-in-law or other older women; hence, all younger women cover their faces at an all-women's songfest in order to show respect to the older women present. As a woman ages, the demands for purdah decrease, though only the very old drop it completely. Muslim women in Karimpur also cover their faces with their sari or shawl, though a few now use the enveloping burqa when outside their homes. Aside from face covering, though, purdah also implies the seclusion of women in their courtyards, so that the village lanes are primarily spaces belonging to men and children.

Poor women cannot keep purdah so easily, because they lack the courtyards and other spaces that belong primarily to women. Furthermore, they must often work in the households of richer families, perhaps washing pots or collecting clothes to be washed, distributing flowers for rituals, or carrying water. Hence, poor women have greater freedom of movement, and their work serves to keep the richer women in purdah.

All the married women in Karimpur come from some other village or town, as these north Indian communities practice village exogamy, or marriage outside of the woman's natal village. Leaving her natal family at marriage is one of the most traumatic events for a woman, as she is usually married into a family of strangers, often miles away from her parents. One of the primary goals of education for women, beginning some forty years ago, was the ability "to write a letter home" so that a woman could call upon her family if mistreated in her husband's household. Today she might have access to a cell phone for emergency needs. Moreover, higher-caste and better-educated women can now move by bus and other means to nearby towns or to visit relatives. Women without education have fewer opportunities and less support for this independent movement outside of the village.

Caste

Social change in Karimpur is closely tied to the traditional caste-based village social structure. The key marker of social identity in Karimpur, as it is in most of India outside of the urban elite, is caste. Currently, Karimpur has a total of twenty-three caste groups. An exact ranking is impossible to arrive at, because local opinion varies about which caste is exactly higher or lower than another.

In understanding caste in India, it helps to recognize that the native Hindi term for caste, *jāti*, is related etymologically to the Latin term *genus*. *Genus*, used to demarcate different kinds (species) of life in Western biological taxonomies, marks different kinds of beings. Likewise, the Hindu jātis demarcate different kinds of beings, beings that should not, according to prevailing belief systems, intermarry. Members of these different jātis are also born with different levels of bodily purity, and traditionally the different jātis were associated with different occupations. Jāti, or caste, is not the same as the *varna* system that, dating to 1000 BCE or earlier, is also used to define Hindu hierarchy. Varna is a term meaning "color." The four varnas are Brahmin (priests), Kshatriya (warriors), Vaishya (merchants), and Shudra (workers). The untouchables fall outside this schema. Most jātis claim a connection to one of the varnas, which can serve as a way of claiming a higher status.

In reality, purity levels are closely connected to economic standing, and the actual "on the ground" rankings of caste groups shift from village to village, depending on local economics. The rankings also change over time, and today they are often contested by lower-ranked groups seeking greater societal recognition. Nevertheless, a person is born into his or her parent's jāti and cannot change it. An individual is almost always required to marry someone from the same jāti. In addition, each jāti is associated with a particular occupation (carpenter, goldsmith, oil presser, water carrier, priest, etc.), although the majority may never have practiced that occupation. Until the 1990s, most men in Karimpur were farmers or farm laborers, regardless of their designated caste occupation.

Caste and Food

One of the primary transactions that mark status in India is the giving and taking of food; that is, giving food to someone marks a higher status than receiving food. Castes in rural India are often ranked by who can take or give food to another caste. The taking of food is a clear mark of the superiority of the giving group, and who can and cannot take food from someone else is highly contested. The distinction between *kaccā* (raw, unfried) foods and *pakkā* (fried in ghee, or clarified butter) foods is key to these food transactions. *Kaccā* foods are thought to easily transmit the purity or pollution of the giver (who has touched these foods and therefore contaminated them with her or his bodily substance). *Pakkā* foods protected by the purifying qualities of the cow—the most highly ranked and purest object in the material world—are less contaminated by the touch of the giver and hence more easily shared across caste and other hierarchical boundaries. For example, a son-in-law cannot take *kaccā* foods from his wife's family, as in northern India the groom's family is almost always thought to be of a higher rank than the bride's family. The Brahmins almost never take food cooked by another caste. The Brahmins may sometimes take *pakkā* foods from the houses of non-Brahmins, but only if the cook is also a Brahmin. Likewise, those who are sometimes still thought to be untouchable take food from most other castes, even accepting their leftovers, the least prestigious food in Karimpur.

While these rules still largely hold in Karimpur, the increased mobility to urban areas has led to some changes. More men and children, especially, are willing to eat in roadside tea shops or even urban restaurants, where the castes of the cooks and servers are unknown. This situation is different in southern India, where one can find restaurants labeled "Brahmin," designating the caste of the cooks. Upper-caste Brahmin women are now as rigid as in the past, however, taking only bottled drinks when on the road and carrying their own food. If they migrate to Delhi or elsewhere, they socialize with women of their caste and, when possible, with those from the same original geographic area.

A Profile of Four Different Castes

Patterns of social change in Karimpur vary most significantly by caste. An examination of four different caste (jāti) groups will illustrate these patterns. First are the Brahmins, whose traditional assigned occupation was as priests for life cycle rituals, but who in Karimpur were the traditional landlords and leaders of the community. Second are the Kachis, a middle-ranking group of small landholders and sharecroppers who were assigned the role of farmers or vegetable growers. Third are the Kahars, or traditional water carriers, who were often landless sharecroppers. Fourth are the Dhanuks, one of the untouchable caste groups in Karimpur. The Dhanuks were formerly midwives, as well as leaf-plate makers who primarily worked as landless laborers.

Each jāti has a perceived level of bodily purity that, combined with its economic standing in its local community, places it in a local hierarchy. In Karimpur, the Brahmins (priests) are not only the highest group by occupation—as they communicate with the gods and goddesses of the Hindu pantheon, conduct most marriage and birth ceremonies, and have the highest perceived bodily purity—but also they are the major landowners. The Brahmins have cultural traditions, both ritual and social, that are not shared with other castes. For example, Brahmins have believed in educating their sons, and to a lesser extent their daughters, for generations. Nowadays their children marry at later ages than most other caste groups. Certain rituals, like Karvācauth, a ritual seeking the husband's longevity, are mandatory, while others, like Janamāsthamī, celebrating the birth of the god Krishna, are minimally celebrated by the Brahmins in contrast to the elaborate Janamāsthamī celebrations of the Kayastha (accountant) caste. Brahmins are strict vegetarians, and many families do not even allow onions, thought to be "hot," to be added to their food. By contrast, the Kayasthas, also landowners and well educated, are meat eaters.

Not far below the Brahmins is the Kachi caste, traditionally vegetable growers or farmers. In Karimpur, they were the second most numerous caste group through the 1980s, and they are now the largest caste. While many owned small plots of land, they also served as sharecroppers for the Brahmin landlords, providing the seeds, fertilizer, and other inputs—including labor—for planting and harvesting a field and receiving 50 percent of the resulting crop, with the rest going to the landlord. While certainly not educated at the levels of the Brahmins, the Kachis became more educated than most other lower-caste groups. They also engaged in other societal changes, such as out-migration from the village, more quickly than most other lower-caste groups.

The third group considered here is the Kahars, the traditional water carriers. Their job in the *jajmani* system of patron-client relationships was to carry water from the open wells that dotted the lanes of Karimpur. Higher-caste women would not have been permitted to leave their courtyards to get water, so the men and women of the Kahar community provided it to their patron families. The Kahar women also helped their patrons with cooking chores, such as grinding grain on a grinding stone, making bread dough, or preparing vegetables. Though they were low-caste, they were not untouchable and were therefore allowed in the women's courtyards. But they could not do the actual cooking, a task that could not cross caste lines. In addition, the Kahar men often worked as sharecroppers or day laborers for their patron families.

At the other end of the hierarchy, the Dhanuk, or midwife caste, is one of the two lowest-ranking caste groups in Karimpur. Even today they are not allowed into the courtyards of higher-caste families unless those spaces are already polluted by childbirth or illness. Starting in the 1970s, however, some fought for education, though none have gone beyond twelfth class. Unlike the untouchable sweeper caste, previously known as Bhangis but now called Valmiks after one of India's renowned sages, the Dhanuk caste members are no longer strictly untouchable, although they are still banned from high-caste homes, and their children must eat the noon lunch provided by the primary school on a nearby hill-

This Muslim family migrated to Delhi and is now part of the urban middle class. *(Photo by Susan Snow Wadley)*

ock, separate from the higher-caste students. Forty years ago the members of the Dhanuk caste attended almost all Karimpur births, but only one Dhanuk woman currently works as a midwife, the others having given up this role due to political pressure to resist this low-status occupation and especially the pollution associated with childbirth.

Over the eighty-five or so years for which accurate census and other records for Karimpur are available, these four castes groups have had very different patterns of social change. Eleven percent of the Brahmins have moved out permanently, while another 9 percent are temporary migrants (making up 12 percent of the temporary migrants for Karimpur as a whole), in part due to their ability to use their higher levels of education to obtain jobs. Other castes have used connections through relatives to find jobs, whether in factories, as security guards, as masons, or most commonly as day laborers. Some migrants have done well and have been able to build houses of several stories on the fringes of Delhi. Others have only one room for a family of four or five in a concrete building, and some live in urban slums.

Changing Demographic Patterns

One change that the village itself considers very important, due to the typically high turnout for elections in India, is population increase (Tables 8.1 and 8.2). Elections are fiercely contested, often based on caste identities, so that the groups with the most voters tend to have success at the polls. In Karimpur's most recent election for a village headman—a

Table 8.2

Population and Migration of Selected Castes in Karimpur, 1925–2010

Caste	1925 Population	1984 Population	2010 Population*	Number of temporary migrants, 2010	Number of permanent out-migrants, 2010
Brahmin (priest)	188	443	532	39	82
Kachi (farmer)	152	415	701	57	51
Kahar (water carrier)	83	236	497	35	38
Dhanuk (midwife)	25	167	400	47	35

*Not including permanent residents or temporary migrants.
Source: Karimpur census data collected by Edward Wiser (1925) and Susan Snow Wadley (1984, 2010).

position of great local power—the Brahmin candidate won, not because of greater numbers of voters but because the Brahmin community allied behind one candidate, whereas the lower castes split their votes among several candidates. Out of some 2,500 votes cast (the voting district includes some hamlets not considered part of Karimpur itself), the Brahmin candidate won by twenty-five votes. In 2010, the Dhanuk men, angry at the outcome, started a fight with their Brahmin neighbors, throwing bricks and using sticks as weapons. This led to a week-long police presence while tempers cooled. (See Roy 2012 for a similar tale of caste in politics in villages in West Bengal.)

Through the mid-1980s, the rates of population increase across caste groups were not significantly different, but the advent of birth control programs and higher levels of education contributed to significant change over the following decades. Quickly adopting various forms of contraception, the Brahmins had a population increase of only 16.7 percent from 1984 to 2010, while the Kachis increased 40.6 percent, the Kahars 52.5 percent, and the Dhanuk caste 58.3 percent. These figures correlate with the 2010 figures on the juvenile (under sixteen) population: 27 percent of the Brahmins are under the age of sixteen, while the Kachis, Kahars, and Dhanuks have juvenile rates of 40, 41, and 43 percent, respectively. This enormous growth of the juvenile population with minimal literacy and job skills presents a problem for the future of Karimpur and India, especially due to the low levels of education and vast unemployment, even for young people who are educated.

Information on population in India and related issues can be found on the website of the Population Reference Bureau. See the 2011 article by Carl Haub and O.P. Sharma titled "India Releases Latest Census Results, Showing Population Catching Up to China" (http://www.prb.org/Articles/2011/india-census-results.aspx), which includes a link to a table with census figures for all of India (http://www.prb.org/pdf11/india-population-2001–2011.pdf).

The Karimpur figures align with the 2011 Census of India, which shows the overall population growth since 2001 to be 17.64 percent. This increase has been very unevenly distributed across social groups and regions, however. India as a whole has undergone what is commonly known as the "demographic transition," referring to a shift from high fertility and high death rates to low fertility and low death rates. Improvements in health care along with better wages and sanitation, beginning in the late 1950s, began to have an effect, and the average life expectancy at birth went from about twenty-two in the 1920s to almost sixty-five in 2009 (but only sixty in Uttar Pradesh).

Related to the overall fertility rates are the sex ratios of India and Karimpur. Sex ratio, as commonly reported for India, refers to the number of living females per 1,000 living males. Across the globe, this ratio favors females over males, but in South and East Asia, including India, males outnumber females. The most recent Indian census shows a child (0–6 years) sex ratio of 914 females per 1,000 males. In Karimpur, the juvenile (0–15 years) sex ratio rose from 790 in 1984 to 879 in 2010, while the adult sex ratio went from 814 in 1984 to 848 in 2010 (see Table 8.1). Access to medical care and the increased incomes from the Green Revolution have no doubt contributed to this positive shift in Karimpur's sex ratios, although there remains a significant female deficit.

> The World Bank's Data site (http://data.worldbank.org/country/india) provides detailed country information on India, as well as comparative data on the South Asia region.

The increasing adoption of birth control is one of the major factors in these demographic changes. When a community values education and removes its children from the child labor force (even if just farming or herding cattle), it faces the dual costs of lost income from child labor and the costs associated with education. These factors drive a shift toward the use of birth control, but in Karimpur this shift is very uneven.

Education

While several changes and innovations have led to educational development since the Wisers began their study of Karimpur, the village lags in many markers of education. In the 1920s, Karimpur's sole school offered only first and second grades. In the 1940s, an elementary school was built in the village for grades 1–5. Only in the mid-1960s was a middle school (grades 6–8) built in Karimpur; and only then did girls begin attending school past the fifth grade. The high school (grades 9–10) was still in the district town of Mainpuri, 9 miles (16 kilometers) away. In the 1920s, the few men who went to high school resided in Mainpuri. By the 1960s, however, residence in town was less important, because bicycles and better bus service made daily commutes possible. Students going beyond high school could choose an intercollege (grades 11–12) or BA colleges (grades 13–15). But high school was still not an option for girls. Not much had changed by 1984.

A class in the Karimpur government school. *(Photo by Susan Snow Wadley)*

In that year, only a few girls joined their brothers on the commute to high school and intercollege in Mainpuri. None had a BA or higher degree.

By the mid-1990s, there was road and bus service from Karimpur to Bichwan, a small town on a major highway 2 to 3 miles (4–5 kilometers) away. Bichwan became a prime locale for high school and intercollege students. Since many older students were also needed for household labor, the shorter travel times encouraged staying in school.

Equally important, one of the Brahmin men returned to live in Karimpur after working as a schoolteacher in nearby Rajasthan, and he opened a private school that emphasized English from pre–K on. The teaching was of higher quality with supervision of both attendance and the actual teaching, and any family who could afford it sent their children to Rajender's school, which quickly grew to twelve grades. Meanwhile, with less supervision and the lack of enforcement of attendance policies, the teachers in the government primary school had irregular attendance, and often one teacher had to try to teach all five classes, totaling well over 100 students. One benefit, however, was that, in order to encourage attendance as well as poverty relief, the government started providing free lunches to children enrolled in the government primary school.

Despite these improvements in educational opportunity, literacy remains low in Karimpur, with a female literacy rate (six years and older) of 46 percent and a male literacy rate of 62.5 percent. The four caste groups being considered have vastly different rates (Table 8.3), ranging from 88 percent Brahmin literacy to 51 percent for the Dhanuks. Overall, there are sixty-nine men and thirty-two women with a BA or MA degree (excluding those who are permanent out-migrants) living in Karimpur. The majority of these are Brahmin—thirty-two

Table 8.3

Percent Literate by Selected Castes in Karimpur, 2010 (above age five)

Caste	Total	Male	Female
Brahmin (priest)	88.1	88.5	86.4
Kachi (farmer)	64.9	75.1	53.3
Kahar (water carrier)	53.5	61.0	44.0
Dhanuk (midwife)	51.0	59.0	41.0

Source: Karimpur census data collected by Susan Snow Wadley, 2010.

Brahmin men and nineteen Brahmin women have a BA or MA degree. In contrast, there are only five Kahar women over the age of thirty (out of a population of fifty-seven) with any education, and there are no Dhanuk women over thirty with any education.

Marriage in Karimpur

Karimpur has seen a steady rise in the age of marriage for females since the 1960s, though many are still "illegal," since the bride is often younger than the legal age of eighteen. In 1925, almost all Karimpur girls were married by age twelve, with almost 50 percent married by age ten. By 1984, the majority was married at sixteen, with only one girl married before the age of thirteen. By 2010, while at least three girls were married by age thirteen, more than 50 percent were married only when they were eighteen or older. Seven, all but one a Brahmin, remained unmarried in their late twenties. These older unmarried women were also well educated: three had MA degrees, and one was employed as a schoolteacher.

In order to understand the implications of "age of marriage" in Karimpur, understanding the ritual of marriage, and its implications, is important. With very minor exceptions, marriages are all arranged, with the bride and groom having little or no say about what is planned (see Chapter 9). Marriage in northern India has traditionally been a three-stage ritual, with the "marriage" ceremony (*shādī*) being stage one. After a marriage ceremony in the girl's house, the girl was taken to the boy's home for a few days, although the marriage was not consummated (in fact, it was thought highly immoral for a girl to return pregnant from her husband's house after this first visit). Only when the girl reached puberty, between the ages of fourteen and sixteen, was she sent back to her husband's house for the consummation ceremony (*gaunā*), which was typically three or four years after the marriage ceremony. This second visit was typically about a month in length. After she returned once again to her parents' house, for perhaps six months or a year, the girl would then go to her husband's house a third time (termed *ronā*, literally "to cry"), which marked her more or less permanent residence in her husband's household. A few young brides, whose husbands' families lacked needed female labor, resided in their husbands' households at an early age, though these relationships were almost never consummated until the girl reached puberty.

A Brahmin bride and her groom in 2003. *(Photo by Susan Snow Wadley)*

Nowadays, with girls marrying at or well past puberty, the ritual cycle is condensed. Most often the ceremony and consummation are combined. Not only are the girls older, and thus thought ready for sexual relations, but having a separate consummation ceremony is very expensive. In 1994, the fourteen-year-old daughter of one of the village washermen was getting married, and a point of contention between mother and father was whether to combine the ceremonies. Her father argued strongly that they should do the two ceremonies as one, while her mother, arguing for the mental well-being of her young daughter, wanted them separated by at least a few months. With the age of marriage continuing the increase, today many brides have only the actual marriage ceremony.

New Consumer Patterns

Karimpur is now tightly connected to the global market place, with consumer goods—such as hair oils, shampoos, dish soap, and toothpaste—readily available at small shops in the village and at the bazaar in the nearby district town, where ready-made clothes have largely replaced the work of the village tailors, and stylish hair ornaments, shawls, pots and dishes, and modern foodstuffs (biscuits, jams, bread, etc.) are found. Increased incomes from the Green Revolution as well as remittances from urban migrants have led to vastly increased expenditures on everything from cosmetics and clothing to gas stoves and tractors. Now residents can buy a tank of propane gas from a distributor in Karimpur itself, an indication of the extent to which propane has moved into rural areas. Television is found throughout the village, though limited by both the number of TV sets and the availability of electricity, with frequent short- and long-term outages.

One visible sign of a new modernity is the clothing of both males and females. Whereas girls would wear saris at ages as young as ten or twelve into the 1960s, now they adopt saris only at marriage, wearing Western-style dresses until puberty and then the increasingly common "Panjabi suit" until marriage. A form of clothing originally worn in the Panjab region of what is now India and Pakistan, the Panjabi suit is a baggy pant (*silwar*) with a long loose tunic top (the *kamiz*). This suit provides coverage of the legs lacking in a western style dress, but does not have the implication of sexuality that a sari does, with its increasing association with marriage.

> The SU web page contains a previously published article by the author devoted solely to the question of changing clothing styles for women in Karimpur.

In addition, girls sometimes wear jeans, though this is not common in rural areas. Further, modern saris are not the hand-loomed cottons of the 1960s, but are instead made of nylon or synthetics that do not require pressing, hold their colors much longer, and wear out slowly. Boys and young men never wear the dhoti of their grandfathers' generation, preferring the Western-style pants and shirts shown in advertisements and Bollywood movies.

Dowries for marriage, especially for brides marrying grooms from urban areas, are likely to include a small refrigerator, perhaps a washing machine and a motor scooter, and the sofa set so desired by the upwardly mobile. Dowries remain the biggest expense facing Karimpur residents, costing the equivalent of at least a year's income for many families. Marriages are always arranged within the same caste. For educated Brahmins, seeking an educated and employed groom is costly. If the bride-to-be is employed, finding a family that will continue to let her work raises additional barriers (see Chapter 9).

Communication has also changed, with 50 percent of Indian households owning a cell phone. Dependence on mail for communication to relatives, whether the migrant in Delhi or the sister married into a village miles away, has been replaced by phones. A few Karimpur residents know how to use a computer at an Internet café, and now a few own one and can use the Internet in the village itself through wireless connections. Television brings world news directly to about one-third of the village homes. Without a doubt, Karimpur residents, in varying degrees, are now participating in the global cultural supermarket, albeit adapting new goods and technologies to meet their own needs and desires.

Conclusion

Karimpur shares with most of the South Asia—and the world—a new interconnectedness, whether via new forms of communication, urban migration, or education. Yet like much of rural India, it still faces enormous problems, including a youth "bulge" that portends future unemployment; increasing disparities in wealth related to education and employment; challenges of female equality, including mere survival, marriage, and edu-

Here a young girl wears a frock, the two unmarried girls wear Panjabi suits, and their married sister wears a sari. *(Photo by Susan Snow Wadley)*

cation; and an increased demand for consumer goods of varying kinds—a demand that the rewards of the Green Revolution and increased urban employment have been able to meet, although economic pressures are likely to increase as large numbers of juveniles reach working age. Although the details of these pressures differ from village to village, region to region, and country to country, they are shared around the globe.

References and Further Research

Dev, S. Mahendra, and M. Venkatanarayana. 2011. *Youth Employment and Unemployment in India*. Mumbai: Indira Gandhi Institute of Development Research. http://www.igidr.ac.in/pdf/publication/WP-2011-009.pdf.

Doron, Assa and Robin Jeffery. 2013. *The Great Indian Phone Book: How the Cheap Cell Phone Changes Business, Politics, and Daily Life*. Cambridge, MA: Harvard University Press.

Indian Child. 2010. *Life Expectancy and Mortality in India*. http://www.indianchild.com/life_expectany_mortality_india.htm.

International Institute for Population Sciences. 2010. *Education and Transition to Work Among Youth in Andhra Pradesh. Youth in India: Situation and Needs, Policy Brief* 27. Mumbai: International Institute for Population Sciences. http://www.popcouncil.org/pdfs/2010PGY_YouthInIndiaBrief27.pdf.

Jeffrey, Craig, Patricia Jeffery, and Roger Jeffery. 2008. *Degrees Without Freedom? Education, Masculinities, and Unemployment in North India*. Stanford, CA: Stanford University Press.

Lukose, Ritty A. 2009. *Liberalization's Children: Gender, Youth and Consumer Citizenship in Globalizing India*. Durham, NC: Duke University Press.

Mines, Diane P. 2009. *Caste in India.* Ann Arbor, MI: Association for Asian Studies.

Mines, Diane P., and Sarah E. Lamb. 2010. *Everyday Life in South Asia.* 2nd ed. Bloomington: Indiana University Press.

Roy, Dayabati. 2012. "Caste and Power: An Ethnography in West Bengal, India." *Modern Asian Studies* 46, no. 4: 947–974.

Wadley, Susan Snow. 1994. *Struggling with Destiny in Karimpur, 1925–1984.* Berkeley: University of California Press (Indian Edition, New Delhi: SAGE, 1996).

———. 2008. "Clothing the Female Body: Education, Social Change and Fashion in Rural North India." In *Wife, Mother, Widow: Exploring Women's Lives in Northern India.* New Delhi: Chronicle Books.

Wiser, William H., and Charlotte V. Wiser. 2000. *Behind Mud Walls: Seventy Five Years in a North Indian Village.* Updated and expanded edition. With new chapters by Susan Snow Wadley, and a foreword by David G. Mandelbaum. Berkeley: University of California Press.

Films

*Caste at Birth.** 1990. Produced and directed by Mira Hamermesh. New York: Filmmakers Library. This film focused on continuing issues of caste, looking at elite schools and slum dwellers in Mumbai as well as the continuing caste violence in rural Bihar.

*Dadi and Her Family.** 1981. Directed by Michael Camerini and Rina Gill. Watertown, MA: Documentary Educational Resources. Now a classic, this film clearly demonstrates issues of living in joint families, including gender roles, husband-wife relationships, and relationships between a mother-in-law and her daughters-in-law.

*Wages of Action: Religion in a Hindu Village.** 1979. Produced by David Thompson. BBC Open University, in collaboration with the University of Wisconsin Center for South Asia. This film explores everyday religious practices in the village of Soyepur, near Banaras. The film observes, among other practices, young men praying to Lord Hanuman before a wrestling match, a grandmother offering water to a sacred *tulsi* plant, a Brahmin priest conducting a *satyanarayan puja* a ritual conducted partially in Sanskrit, a low-caste religious specialist known as an *ojha* exorcising spirits from the ill, and a Soyepur couple making a one-day pilgrimage to a shrine by the Ganges River.

9

Arranging a Marriage in Middle-Class Southern India

NICOLE A. WILSON

A boy and girl meet for the first time via Skype. They nervously laugh and joke, most likely having very little previous interaction with unknown members of the opposite sex. This awkward conversation will determine the final verdict concerning a marriage between this boy and girl, a modern assessment of compatibility in a cultural context where, traditionally, arranged marriage has been performed between relative strangers. These circumstances describe a common scenario in contemporary urban South Asia. In negotiating between traditional ideas of marriage and global representations of love and status, a new generation of urban middle-class South Asians is altering the ways in which social relationships are created and maintained.

This is nowhere truer than in Tamil Nadu, the fifth-largest state in India and one of the most urbanized segments of the subcontinent. Listed as one of the top six states with respect to urban growth, Tamil Nadu saw its urban population expand by 42.4 percent between 1991 and 2001. By comparison, the national average for the same time period was 31.2 percent (Government of Tamil Nadu 2011, 536). While rapidly urbanizing, Tamil Nadu is also considered by many Indians to be the heart of the "religious south," home to a plethora of Hindu pilgrimage sites, and its capital city, Chennai (formerly Madras), is often described as less cosmopolitan than other major Indian cities, such as New Delhi, Mumbai, and Kolkata. This contrast between Tamil Nadu's fast-paced urbanization, with its associated valuation of modern goods and bourgeoning culture of consumption, and the state's local positioning as a more traditional and conservative locale makes Tamil Nadu an ideal site to study processes of social change in modern South Asia.

Additional materials for this case study, including photographs and video material of marriage practices and rituals, are available on Syracuse University's South Asia Center's website Global South Asia (http://globalsouthasia.syr.edu/). This chapter refers to the website in specific sections with "see SU's website" in the text.

In this chapter, I use the example of marriage arrangement in Tamil Nadu to describe some of the social changes occurring among India's urban middle classes, a socioeconomic

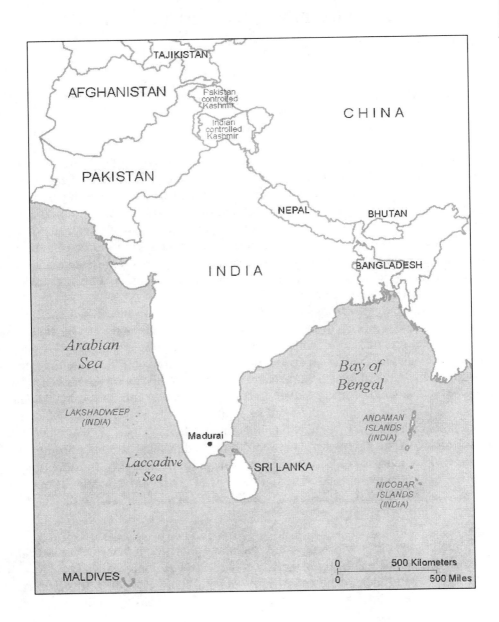

A stand selling materials for temple worship in the Meenashki Amman Temple in Madurai. *(Photo by Nicole A. Wilson)*

segment that is projected to become three-quarters of the country's urban population by 2025 (Beinhocker, Farrell, and Zainulbhai 2007). These modifications to South Asian marriage practices have been inspired by global interconnectedness, and they provide examples of how understandings of tradition and modernity collide in the important life event of a nuanced Tamil arranged marriage. Similar to many other studies of specific social practices, this in-depth investigation of marriage arrangement in southern India allows for an instructive approach to social change and its relationship with global influences, showing how the two interact with local understandings of consumption, moral conduct, and social status-building.

One of the most productive ways to approach studies of culture and social change is to participate in the culture that one is observing. Often used by anthropologists such as myself, the participant-observation method positions the researcher at the heart of cultural action, privileging that researcher with informed interpretations of cultural practices and opportunities for building rapport with informants. For this study of marriage arrangement, I lived with and participated in the daily life of a middle-class Tamil Brahmin family. My intimate connection to this family was formulated over a period of five years, during which I honed my Tamil language skills and, in the end, developed such close relationships with family members and their friends that I was given unique access to the intricacies of arranging a marriage in middle-class India.

This case study examines contemporary arranged marriage practices, from the intricate details of matchmaking to the culmination of the marriage itself. The location is a city in Tamil Nadu called Madurai, considered by many an important hub of Tamil culture and language and home to some 1.8 million urban residents in 2011 (Government of Tamil Nadu 2011, 4). In my five years of visiting and/or living in the city between 2006 and 2011, Madurai changed dramatically, with the growth of the middle class, as well as its identity markers, at the heart of this change. In addition to a significant middle-class population, Madurai is also home to many caste communities, and these affiliations continue to affect interpersonal interactions in the city, as well as variations in marriage practices. A primary distinction to be made here is between Brahmins, considered the highest caste, and non-Brahmins. In the following discussion, I include depictions of marriage arrangement practices from both Brahmins and non-Brahmins, with middle-classness as a main unifying factor among my interlocutors. But first, a brief description of the history of the Indian economy is provided, as this history is directly tied to the formation and maintenance of the country's current socioeconomic class divisions and respective perceptions of status and behavior. Early marriage practices in the region are then reviewed, so as to illuminate the changes that are occurring in contemporary South Asia.

The Liberalization of the Indian Economy

Up until 1991, India was segregated from much of the world in terms of trade and other forms of interconnectedness. This period in Indian economic history was based on an idea of India as a self-sufficient social and political body, one that did not need or value foreign investment and trade to inspire its economic success and growth. Due to this economic plan, as well as a dependency on Nehruvian socialist ideals, "by the end of the 80s [India was] the most regulated and protected, closed, subsidy-ridden, inefficient and corrupt major industrial economy outside of eastern Europe," and "by 1991, the Indian economy was virtually bankrupt" (Stern 2003, 12). Inspired by the coming of Rajiv Gandhi's government and a national fiscal crisis in 1991, a new era in Indian history was born. This period was formulated on the liberalization of the country's economy and the global interconnectedness and influence that was to spring from it. Today, India is one of the fastest-growing countries in the world, and its middle classes have been the primary segments of society that have grown and benefited from India's economic liberalization. In addition, Indian perceptions of the world, social status, morality, and consumption have been irrevocably altered and constitute a major foundation for popular opinion and public influence. This extends to perceptions of marriage and its manifestations in modern India. In order to appreciate the social change partially inspired by this economic revolution, one must first consider what are locally known to be "traditional" marriage practices of the past.

Arranged Marriages in South Asia: The Past

Arranged marriages are one of the most well-known social conventions when people around the globe think of South Asian culture. Indeed, arranged marriage has a long history in the region, but that need not imply that the practice has remained the same over decades. Older generations of women in Madurai note that their parents made all the decisions about their marriage. If their parents wanted to marry them to a relative (see below), they might have been at least slightly familiar with their future husband, but if their family practiced clan exogamy, or marriage to a nonrelative, they most likely would not have seen their husband until their wedding day.

While this is not completely unheard-of in contemporary Madurai and the broader region of South Asia, there also exists a nuanced type of arranged marriage that is becoming increasingly popular around the world, especially among the middle classes. Called "companionate marriage," this form encourages contact between the potential bride and groom to ensure that the couple is compatible, a concern that was only previously addressed through a less personal assessment of horoscopes.

In addition to preventing the bride and groom from knowing each other, arranged marriages have traditionally emphasized the virginity of the bride. More common in previous generations, the assurance of virginal purity at marriage was obtained through the practice of child marriage, with consummation occurring after the girl reached puberty. The older generation of women with whom I spoke were all married at the age of fifteen or sixteen, suggesting that by the 1950s, the cultural demand for child marriage was already changing. However, unlike today's middle-class urban women, once they attained puberty, they were no longer allowed to attend school for fear that their chastity could be called into question. Hence, many of these women were taken out of school at the onset of menstruation and their parents immediately took the necessary steps to arrange their marriage. I discussed this life event with Uma, a sixty-seven-year-old Tamil Brahmin woman:

Uma: The three of us [siblings] went there [to school]. Our father wouldn't let us go anywhere but there [school]. . . . Because if girls went out a lot their reputation would go bad. If they said she was going from here to there, afterwards people wouldn't want to marry her. Then, I passed 10th (standard/grade). Up until 10th I had not matured [menstruation hadn't started]. At 10th I became mature. As soon as my periods started, I stopped going to school.
NW: Really?!
Uma: I could not go. I stopped going to school.
NW: Who told you [that you could not go to school]?
Uma: Our mother . . . our mother and father. Immediately I stopped studying and they looked for [a match] for marriage. They started looking for a bridegroom. I couldn't go to school. They said I couldn't go. I was sad. I cried. I didn't want to work [do housework] or go anywhere. I was sad.

In addition to the rules of arranged marriage that pervade the South Asian region, the state of Tamil Nadu, as well as some neighboring states, has its own particular traditional marriage practices and ideals that should be considered when speaking of changes in marriage practices and wider social transformations in modern South Asia. Three of

Photo of Uma Amma, at age 16, with her new husband, T.S. Sankaran, September 1959. *(Original photographer unknown. Photo of photo by Nicole A. Wilson)*

these practices and ideals are Dravidian kinship, dowry and bride-price, and auspicious womanhood.

Dravidian Kinship

Residents of Tamil Nadu speak Tamil, one of five southern Indian Dravidian languages. The Dravidian linguistic group is often associated with a specific Dravidian culture, which traditionally encourages a girl's endogamous caste marriage with her cross-cousin (the child of one's mother's brother or father's sister) or her mother's brother. This distinct kinship pattern is referred to by scholars of South Asia as "Dravidian kinship" and is thought to afford southern Indian women more control in their marital relationships via their access to affinal support, in contrast to their northern Indian counterparts. The latter traditionally practice clan and village exogamy, or marriage outside of both their clan and natal villages (see Chapter 8), and hence lack affinal allies in their marital home. However, the Dravidian kinship pattern has never been the only model for marriage arrangement in southern India, and marriage between nonrelatives is becoming increasingly common in contemporary Tamil Nadu. The choice of whether or not to follow a Dravidian kinship pattern translates into variations in matchmaking practices.

Dowry and Bride-Price

Dowry and bride-price are common facets of marriage in many parts of the world. The former refers to the goods that are brought into a marriage by a bride, while the latter denotes items presented by the bridegroom to the bride and her family. In contemporary middle-class Tamil Nadu, the bride-price, or *paricam*, is most often presented at the betrothal ceremony, usually in the form of a sari and jewelry.

In contrast, dowry is more extravagant and exists in two forms. One form, *varataṭcaṇai*, describes the hard currency given by the bride's family at the time of marriage. The second form is called *cīr* or *cītanam* and constitutes everything from gold, pots, and washing machines to fruit and packaged biscuits. If the couple follows a Dravidian kinship pattern, dowry and bride-price reinforce an already existent blood-bond between the families of the bride and bridegroom. If not, dowry and bride-price are given to cement the union between the bride's and bridegroom's kin. In both scenarios, these gifts advertise wealth and social status, a fact discussed later in the chapter.

Auspicious Womanhood

When considering arranged marriage and the changes it is undergoing in South Asia, it is crucial to note cultural conceptions of womanhood and gender roles, topics that undergird how marriage has been and continues to be perceived and performed. As in other states in India, the idea of a proper, good, and auspicious wife is encapsulated by the term *cumaṅkali*. This designation is commonly used among middle-class women in Madurai to denote a prized life stage that should be not only attained, but maintained. In order to be a *cumaṅkali*, one must be a married woman with a living husband. Hence, the term itself places a high social value on the practice of marriage. A *cumaṅkali* is responsible for assuring the auspiciousness of her family by making daily ritual offerings (*puja*) in the home and participating in other rituals at Hindu temples in order to maintain social status. She also holds a special position at social functions and is given a high amount of respect due to her married state.

Modernity and Marriage in South India

The practices of Dravidian kinship, the presentation of a dowry or bride-price, and the cultural valuation of the auspicious married woman continue to affect how marriages are arranged and performed among today's middle classes in southern India. However, modern middle-class marriage in the region has also been transformed in significant ways, with many changes instigated by a burgeoning middle-class preoccupation with social mobility and socioeconomic status, but also inspired by the simple reality of increased global interconnectedness.

Matchmaking

The first step in modern middle-class Tamil marriage arrangement is the overwhelming task of matchmaking. Historically, many women and men were not involved in the selec-

---

Box 9.1

Blemishes in Horoscopes

A blemish in a horoscope occurs when the stars are negatively aligned during a person's birth (culturally determined what is negative here) and this misalignment will cause problems in the future of the person. For example, a certain misalignment might indicate that a girl will become a widow early in her life. If the boy with whom she is being matched also has this same misalignment, then they often cancel each other out in both horoscopes and neither bride nor bridegroom will have an issue of early widowhood any longer. Other blemishes do not indicate such concrete outcomes and are simply just inauspicious.

---

tion of their own mate, but today potential partners are often in contact, in some cases using Skype. In addition, Dravidian kinship practices were much more common in the past, negating the necessity for in-depth matchmaking altogether, since the match was often between cross-cousins or a girl and her uncle. Today, due to the lessening popularity of marriage between relations, often inspired by Western medical discourses about genetic defects, matchmaking has surfaced as an intricate and time-consuming cultural practice.

Modern matchmaking entails a complex analysis of horoscopes, socioeconomic status, social capital, and outward appearance. The search for a suitable match among middle-class Tamils begins by weeding through hundreds of profiles and corresponding horoscopes. First and foremost, the bride and groom must be of the same caste. After this, birth stars must be analyzed for compatibility and the existence of blemishes, or *tōṣaṅkaḷ*. If a blemish is present in a person's horoscope, the family must determine whether its existence can be rectified. For example, a blemish in one horoscope might be canceled out by a comparable one in the other.

Once caste and astrological categories have been scrutinized, details about the potential bride or bridegroom's age, education, employment, salary, and physical appearance are assessed. Mala, one of the women interviewed for this study, was asked what she desired when looking for a match for her son in 2002. She replied:

> Number one was astrology. The girl should be a good height with good color. Both have to be educated. My son-in-law (also) had to be educated because if he only studied until 10th, what would he do? Both have to have graduated. Color . . . but we can compromise. Astrology is main.

In addition to astrological and educational qualifications, Mala's description of her ideal daughter-in-law also communicates social valuation of light-colored skin, an important factor among women and men of previous generations as well. Sundaradevi, a sixty-seven-year-old woman living in Madurai, described her concern about skin color in the search for her marriage partner:

First they wanted to marry me to my mother's brother and I thought it was going to happen and that was what everyone thought. But then he asked for a big dowry and my parents had many children and they said "How can we give one daughter a big dowry? What will we do about the other daughters?" So my parents said they didn't want the marriage. They found another bridegroom and I cried and said I wouldn't do it. I said he was too dark and wouldn't do it and I didn't like it. I cried for a whole day. Then my father's younger brother scolded me, "Your father and I are both dark. This is how it is. You are thinking you can get another bridegroom?" So then I was silent.

Today, skin color remains a common concern. Marriage advertisements often include descriptions of brides and bridegrooms as either "wheatish" or "fair." In addition, photos placed on websites or mailed to prospective brides' and bridegrooms' families are often airbrushed to create the illusion that the potential match has lighter skin than is actually the case.

The website Tamil Matrimony (www.tamilmatrimony.com) is commonly used by Tamils for marriage arrangement. One usually pays a fee to post a profile and to have access to other profiles and contact information listed on the website. There are also matrimony websites that cater to specific castes, such as the Brahmin-only website Chennai Sai Sankara Matrimonials (http://ssmatri.net/setup/index.html).

Age Gap

In the previous middle-class Tamil generation, the bridegroom to be matched was at least ten years older than his potential bride. Today, however, the age difference is much smaller. The catalyst for this change surfaces in an examination of the relationship between more institutionalized forms of marriage alliance and Tamil middle-class identity construction. In contemporary Tamil Nadu, members of the urban middle class encourage a two-child maximum in family planning. This is a consequence of many factors, but an important one is the sophistication and status accorded to the smaller family, in part because such a family can afford higher education for its children and greater luxuries via surplus income. In conjunction with the promotion of a smaller family are the greater employment and educational opportunities afforded to women, which often delay the commencement of this smaller family. Nevertheless, even a small age difference between the bride and bridegroom is still preferred, as it maintains South Asian patriarchal social structures.

Language, Employment, and Education

Specific key words and phrases are used during the matchmaking process. These terms and phrases communicate particular cultural meanings and symbols to the parties involved in arranging the marriage. This nuanced language of matchmaking reflects an interpretation of arranged marriage commensurate with the fast-paced globalized and modernized world. For example, the English word *broad-minded* is used to describe a potential bridegroom. This term indicates that a bridegroom has most likely traveled outside of India and is familiar with Western culture. Indeed, in an attempt to arrange my own marriage while I was carrying out research in Madurai, one Brahmin interlocutor described the "broad-minded" bridegroom that she had chosen for me by saying that he lived in London and would allow me, as his wife, to eat chicken and wear T-shirts. Crucially, broad-mindedness is a more acceptable quality for a bridegroom than a bride. The desirability of a middle-class Tamil girl is often dependent on the balance between her knowledge of tradition and her hopefully limited exposure to the immodest actions of Western women.

The ever-popular acronyms in South Asian culture also reflect social and temporal changes in matchmaking practices. It is common for families engaged in the matchmaking process to weigh the participation of the potential bridegroom or bride in an MNC, or "multinational corporation"; BPO, or "business process outsourcing"; or "BITS," an indication that the boy or girl has studied at the Birla Institute of Technology and Science. While there is little question that a bridegroom who works for an MNC or who studied at BITS has desired characteristics, participation in a BPO is much more contested. A middle-class bridegroom working at an outsourcing center is probably making a sufficient salary, but aligning with him in marriage is not likely to fulfill the promise of socioeconomic hypergamy, or "marrying up," aspired to by the family of the bride. A middle-class potential bride working in a BPO is even more questionable. Regardless of whether the girl has actually worked overnight shifts at an outsourcing location, it is assumed that she has. Working overnight automatically calls into question her reputation (read virginity), due to her location in a mixed-gender environment at all hours of the night. The selection of a girl who works or has worked at a BPO requires additional investigation to be assured of her purity and respectability, qualities also important in arranged marriages of the past. Here, the value of moral integrity is elevated above the material possessions that could be acquired via the additional salary of the potential bride.

In the past, jobs associated with the Indian government were highly valued due to the guarantee of a pension, as well as their historical association with higher caste status and the formation of the early Indian middle class during the British Raj. With the pervasiveness of wealth acquired through MNC employment in modern India, one might assume that the traditional high status accorded to a "government job" has diminished; however, this is not the case. Today, Tamilians are well aware that salaries are elevated in MNC positions, but they still place "government jobs" in a valued category. Conversely, working in "business," especially for Brahmins who are hunting for a match, implies less stability and an association with lower castes, whose livelihoods traditionally depended on small and unstable roadside businesses that required the labor of the family's women. Occasionally, proof of a successful business, such as the existence of a factory or the employment of several workers outside of the family, is enough to allow a family to overlook historical associations with financial instability and lower social status groups.

Dowry

Dowry is a contentious issue in India, as it is banned by the government but increasingly important in marriage negotiations, even in southern India. Among certain castes in Tamil Nadu, print and online wedding advertisements state outright that a dowry is not

Dowry items arranged for viewing, November 2010. *(Photo by Nicole A. Wilson)*

required. In reality, the parents of the bridegroom often demand certain items during the alliance process, such as motorbikes, king-size mattresses, and washing machines, but they avoid labeling these articles as part of a "dowry." The formal dowry is then understood as the array of fruits and sweets that are presented during the betrothal ceremony (see SU's website, "Global South Asia"). Publicly stating that dowry items are not desired presents these middle-class individuals as moral and virtuous, qualities that are coveted in future in-laws.

However, this philosophy of outwardly rejecting a dowry is not shared by everyone in the middle class. Only certain castes use the denial of a dowry as a method of communicating their moral middle-class status. Other castes use the dowry (and the bride-price) as a mode of conspicuous consumption, publicizing their material wealth and exhibiting rooms of dowry items, which wedding guests are requested to view before the ceremonies begin.

The "Girl-Viewing"

The details appearing in matrimonial advertisements are not immediately taken as fact. Issues of dowry, location of employment, and level of "broad-mindedness," among other factors, must then be assessed face to face at the matchmaking event known as the "girl-viewing," or *peṇ pārkka*. This social encounter includes the parents of both the potential bride and bridegroom, as well as the extended family of the bride. The girl-viewing is the setting in which first impressions are made between the potential bride's and bridegroom's families. Before the event, there might be pictures included in an envelope containing a horoscope, but a real sense of the possessions and lifestyle of each family is not known until this first actual meeting.

One particular "girl-viewing" I witnessed, that of my friend Radhika, exemplifies how middle-class socioeconomic status and consumption are implicated in this cultural tradition. Radhika's family had spent the entire previous day scrubbing the house from top to bottom in order to prepare for their honored guests. They had seen a picture of the possible groom's home and were already feeling inadequate about the appearance of their home and its contents. As they sat waiting for the potential groom's parents to arrive, Radhika, the potential bride, privately expressed her anxiety about the looming event and her uncertain future, saying she would soon be a *māṭṭupoṇṇu*, or daughter-in-law.

Upon reaching the home, the boy's mother and father were seated and offered snacks and coffee by Radhika. After this, the men proceeded to discuss their social networks and people they might know in common, while the women shared embroidery patterns and spoke of their participation in pilgrimages and other Hindu temple activities. The potential bridegroom's mother was the only woman seated on the raised sofa, while the female members of Radhika's family sat below her to show deference and respect.

This "viewing" of Radhika served as a venue for elaborate gift giving, which was meant to augment the status of each family. Radhika's family gave their visitors a tray filled with fruit and small Hindu god statues. In return, they received fruit, and Radhika personally received dress materials, which was an attempt to establish the guests' identity as upper-middle-class. Within two days, Radhika's family received a letter from their recent callers stating that there was "no match." When Radhika's mother was asked why she thought the match was declined, she replied that her family had fewer amenities, or luxuries (*vacatikaḷ*), compared to the boy's family. In this case, "amenities" and "luxuries" referred to items such as a drinking water filter, a car, an iPod, and a microwave. According to Radhika's mother, the lack of these material articles had outweighed the family's religious orthodoxy and higher-caste subsect status, qualities that can socially translate to moral integrity.

Matchmaking Compromises

Radhika went through five or six girl-viewings (ranging from fifteen minutes to two hours) before an alliance was finally settled. In the end, a bridegroom was found for her through a social connection of her father. It was only later revealed that Radhika had initially been assessed for her bridegroom's cousin, whose family had decided she was not a desirable match due to her weight. Although culturally deemed a little heavy, Radhika also had qualities which made her attractive to potential suitors: she was from the highest subsect of Saivite Brahmins; her skin was relatively light and free of blemishes; and she had a bachelor's degree in computer science, which is considered just the right amount of education for a woman. (Too little education is perceived as damning to the groom's social capital, and too much education is thought to encourage the neglect of household duties and child care.) Radhika's bridegroom, Senthil, also had desirable qualities: his upper-middle-class family owned a successful textile business and all the material goods obtained through that success; he had a master's degree in engineering and was working abroad in Bahrain at the time of the arrangement; and he spoke fluent English. What made it difficult to settle a marriage for Senthil was his skin color. According to anyone that was consulted, Senthil was extremely dark-skinned, a factor that negated some of his more attractive qualities.

True to the findings of C.J. Fuller and Haripriya Narasimhan (2008) with respect to "companionate marriage" among Tamil Nadu's middle classes, the final decision regarding the marriage settlement and compatibility had to be made by Radhika and Senthil themselves, no matter what their relatives thought about appearances and other characteristics. In the end, Radhika and Senthil made their decision to marry after a nearly forty-minute conversation over Skype, with Radhika secluded in a room in her small house in Madurai, India, and Senthil in an Internet café cubicle in Manama, Bahrain.

The marriage of Radhika and Senthil was based first on their approval of each other and only then on their families' mutual negation of undesirable qualities (plumpness and dark skin). Having gone through several girl-viewings without finding a match, Radhika's relatives had begun to fear that her weight was a more serious factor than they had anticipated, and they recognized that a compromise was in order. The dark pigment of Senthil's skin, however, would remain a concern, as the potentially dark appearance of Radhika's offspring could inspire difficulties in future matchmaking pursuits.

Wedding Preparations

Once a marriage alliance is set through a successful girl-viewing, the costs of wedding preparation increase at a rapid rate. According to some caste prescriptions, two separate betrothal ceremonies are held, one several months before the wedding, as well as one at the time of the wedding, requiring two separate rentals of the wedding hall. For both occasions, these halls have to be decorated to the hilt, including huge billboards announcing the event. Food has to be provided for all the guests, and higher status is often communicated via the presentation of food in the form of a buffet, which is seen as inherently Western and modern. In addition, the main stage has to be lavishly decorated so that group photos taken during the reception can be admired later, in both the wedding video and the wedding album.

Billboard outside the wedding hall announcing the marriage of Radhika and Senthil in Madurai, September 2010. *(Photo by Nicole A. Wilson)*

The decorated stage at a middle-class betrothal in Madurai, September 2011. *(Photo by Nicole A. Wilson)*

Traditional "mañcaḷ (yellow) invitation" given to relatives and close friends, December 2009. *(Photo by Nicole A. Wilson)*

Wedding Invitations as Communication of Status

Wedding preparations in modern Tamil Nadu also entail attention to what, at first, might be perceived as a relatively minimal matrimonial detail: the design and dispersal of invitations. Indeed, wedding invitations are a crucial means of communicating one's social status to one's guests. In previous generations, people of upper- and middle-class standing may have been able to convey their status through the dispersal of one rather simple invitation, but today's Tamil middle classes use at least two types of wedding invitations, which are produced and dispersed according to the social distinction of invited guests. The first type is less concerned with the communication of status, as it is printed for family members and close friends, people who are already privy to the family's financial circumstances and hence do not need to be convinced that the family is of a high socioeconomic and social station. These invitations are usually printed in Tamil and include no more than four colors, which reduces cost. The invitations are referred to as "*mañcaḷ* invitations," as they are traditionally printed on glossy yellow (*mañcaḷ*) paper. The moniker of "*mañcaḷ* invitation" also corresponds to the South Asian belief in the auspiciousness of turmeric (also called *mañcaḷ* in Tamil). For example, Tamil women have for centuries washed their faces with yellow turmeric powder, which is believed to improve their complexion and contains purifying qualities that also are necessary to maintain the appearance of a proper, traditional Tamil woman. Turmeric also connects to

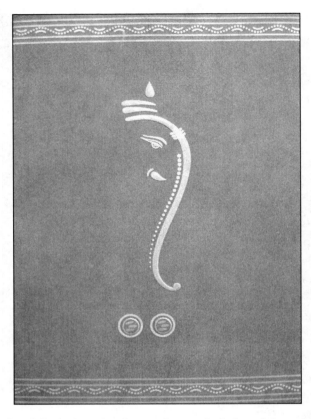

Front cover of a cardstock invitation, showing an abstract depiction of the god Ganesh, April 2009. *(Photo by Nicole A. Wilson)*

the auspicious appearance of a *cumaṅkali*, in that the necklace symbolizing her married status (*tāli*) is rubbed with turmeric in order to highlight its bright yellow appearance and overtly express her marital status in public.

Although the *mañcaḷ* invitations are thought to be better suited for close family members and friends, they also include some status-communicating elements. For one, most modern wedding invitations include a list of family members that will be joined together through the union of the couple. In an inconspicuous demonstration of social status, the academic degrees and professions of these family members are often listed next to their names. In some cases, the foreign locations of relatives will also be listed, as connections with cultures outside of India lend social distinction to an entire family.

In contrast to the *mañcaḷ* invitations, invited guests who are not as familiar with the family or are of higher socioeconomic and social status (e.g., the bride's father's boss) receive an embossed invitation on cardstock. While similar to *mañcaḷ* invitations in the listing of degrees and foreign locations of family members, this cardstock invitation also communicates status in other ways. First, the cardstock invitation is printed in English and contains abstract representations of gods, goddesses, and "Indian culture." Due to

A Brahmin wedding invitation explaining caste-specific marriage practices in English, February 2010. These invitations have become increasingly popular among Brahmins in Tamil Nadu. *(Photo by Nicole A. Wilson)*

these differences, cardstock invitations tend to resemble something similar to a Western wedding invitation, employing creative and innovative aspects to convey an association with modern culture and its associated lifestyle. In giving these cardstock invitations to specific guests, the parents of the bride or groom conspicuously display the social status that is demonstrated by the knowledge and use of this modernity.

In addition to communicating a middle-class family's familiarity with modernity, cardstock invitations are also used to highlight the family's caste affiliation and its unique culture. This is best exemplified in the now relatively common Brahmin wed-

Facebook wedding invitation, July 2012. The message portion inviting guests states, "We, Praveena and Rajkumar, welcome you to be a part of our life's new beginning."

ding invitation, which explains caste-specific wedding rituals in detail. This invitation is divided into three sections, with each ritual description written in English, accompanied by a color drawing of the caste custom being described. This newly popular invitation is an artifact of social change, for in the past, people who were unfamiliar with Brahmin marriages (i.e., non-Brahmins) were not usually welcome at Brahmin functions due to the threat of caste pollution. In modern India, however, contemporary urban neighborhoods are occupied by a multitude of castes, diluting strict caste segregation. This fact, as well as an increasing appreciation for middle-class values over particular caste values in terms of community-building, has lessened the threat of caste pollution and inspired intermingling at most marriages. Moreover, like the general cardstock invitations, the sheer cost of producing this lavish type of invitation implies a change in the perceived use of the marriage invitation as a mode of demonstrating status among the Indian middle classes, a body of people that seems to place an increasing social value on consumption and displays of wealth.

Perhaps the most recent nuanced wedding invitation is one posted on the globally pervasive website Facebook. Unlike other types of wedding invitations, the Facebook invitation does not follow any status-communication formula, such as the use of a yellow background or creatively embossed representations of Hindu gods and goddesses, as the mere use of the World Wide Web is indicative of high educational qualifications and global interconnectedness, characteristics that carry with them a particular upwardly mobile social status. The Facebook invitation also takes the concept of "companionate marriage" further, in that the middle-class bride and bridegroom have not only privately talked and consented to the marriage but are also now mutually inviting guests to their marriage via the Internet, demonstrating their freedom from parental surveillance.

Facebook now constitutes the cutting edge of status communication in wedding preparations. It remains to be seen how this practice will filter through and be influenced by the wider social changes occurring in South Asia. While the region continues to change socially, economically, and politically, increasing its connection to an ever-developing global culture, one cultural practice has remained influential in the lives of every Indian: marriage. This case study presents this enduring quality and the significance of marriage in the social lives of modern middle-class South Asians. Yet, like any cultural practice, marriage is not immune to the impacts of either organic local change or global stimuli.

Conclusion

Like many of the other case studies in this volume, this chapter depicts a changing South Asia, complete with rapidly increasing global interconnectedness and negotiations between tradition and modernity. While many aspects of South Asian culture may still seem unfamiliar and inapplicable in the daily lives of most Americans, the changes that it is undergoing will induce significant future consequences for the global community. By sheer numbers alone, this shift is evident. With a general population growth rate estimated at 17.64 percent between 2001 and 2011, according to the Census of India (compare the United States, at 4.5 percent), the country is projected to establish itself as the world's fifth-largest consumer market within the next two decades, with its middle classes forming a major section of this market (Beinhocker, Farrell, and Zainubhai 2007). The effects of this kind of growth are twofold. On the one hand, economic growth has been linked to lowering poverty rates; on the other hand, it also has the potential to accentuate social divisions and create wider gaps between segments of society. By observing and investigating the social changes that are occurring in India, one gains insight into how modern socioeconomic class identities are created and performed within a populace that constitutes 17 percent of the world's total population (Burke 2011).

References and Further Research

Banerjee, Manjistha, Steven Martin, and Sonalde Desai. 2008. *Is Education Associated with a Transition Towards Autonomy in Partner Choice? A Case Study of India.* Indian Human Development Survey Working Paper no. 8. New Delhi: National Council of Applied Economic Research. http://ihds.umd.edu/IHDS_papers/PartnerChoice.pdf.

Beinhocker, Eric D., Diana Farrell, and Adil Zanulbhai. 2007. "Tracking the Growth of India's Middle Class." *McKinsey Quarterly* 3: 51–61.

Burke, Jason. 2011. "Census Reveals That 17% of the World Is Indian." *The Guardian,* March 31. http://www.guardian.co.uk/world/2011/mar/31/census-17-percent-world-indian.

Census of India. 2011. "Census 2011: Provisional Population Totals." New Delhi: Office of the Registrar General and Census Commissioner. http://www.slideshare.net/indiacurrentaffairs/provisional-2011-census-report.

————. 2011. "Provisional Population Totals, Rural-Urban Distribution, Tamil Nadu, Series 34." Paper 2, Volume 1. New Delhi: Government of India. http://www.censusindia.gov. in/2011-prov-results/paper2/data_files/tamilnadu/Tamil%20Nadu_PPT2_Volume1_2011. pdf.

Dickey, Sara. 2000. "Permeable Homes: Domestic Service, Household Spaces, and the Vulnerability of Class Boundaries in Urban India." *American Ethnologist* 27, no. 2: 462–489.

————. 2012. "The Pleasures and Anxieties of Being in the Middle: Emerging Middle-Class Identities in Urban South India." *Modern Asian Studies* 46, no. 3: 559–599.

Donner, Henrike. 2008. *Domestic Goddesses: Maternity, Globalization and Middle-Class Identity in Contemporary India.* Aldershot, UK, and Burlington, VT: Ashgate.

Fuller, C.J., and Haripriya Narasimhan. 2008. "Companionate Marriage in India: The Changing Marriage System in a Middle-Class Brahman Subcaste." *Journal of the Royal Anthropological Institute* 14, no. 4: 736–754.

Government of Tamil Nadu, Department of Economics and Statistics. 2011. "Select Socio Economic Indicators of All States and India." In *Statistical Handbook of Tamil Nadu.* Chennai, India: Government of Tamil Nadu. http://www.tn.gov.in/deptst/.

Hancock, Mary. 1999. *Womanhood in the Making: Domestic Ritual and Public Culture in Urban South India.* Boulder, CO: Westview Press.

Hirsch, Jennifer, and Holly Wardlow. 2006. *Modern Loves: The Anthropology of Romantic Courtship and Companionate Marriage.* Ann Arbor: University of Michigan Press.

Kapadia, Karin. 1995. *Siva and Her Sisters: Gender, Caste, and Class in Rural South India.* Boulder, CO: Westview Press.

Nishimura, Yuko. 1998. *Gender, Kinship, and Property Rights: Nagarattar Womanhood in South India.* Delhi and New York: Oxford University Press.

Reynolds, Holly Baker. 1980. "The Auspicious Married Woman." In *The Powers of Tamil Women,* edited by Susan Snow Wadley, 35–60. Syracuse, NY: Maxwell School of Citizenship and Public Affairs, Syracuse University.

Stern, Robert. 2003. *Changing India: Bourgeois Revolution on the Subcontinent.* 2nd ed. New York: Cambridge University Press.

Trautmann, Thomas. 1981. *Dravidian Kinship.* Cambridge: Cambridge University Press.

Films

The Great Indian Marriage Bazaar. 2011. Directed by Ruchika Muchhala. Singapore: Caldecott Productions and NHK. Filmmaker Ruchika is put on the spot by her family in "mission son-in-law" and captures the ensuing events here.

Modern Brides. * 1985. Directed by Happy Luchsinger. Madison, WI: Luchsinger Productions in collaboration with University of Wisconsin Center for South Asian Studies. Though dated, much of this film remains true for those in middle and lower middle classes, including the searches for an astrological reading of the horoscopes.

Monsoon Wedding. 2002. Directed by Mira Nair. Delhi, India: Mirabai Productions, in association with Key Films, Pandora Films, and Paradis Films. A Bollywood film, this portrayal of an upper-middle class urban wedding is a classic.

10

Forest Management in Rajasthan
Tribal Groups, NGOs, and the State

MITUL BARUAH

Common property resources, also known as the "commons," constitute a significant part of rural livelihoods in the Global South, and their ecological significance is critical. In recent years, however, the commons have come under serious threat worldwide due to the increased privatization and subsequent transformations of these resources. The conservation of the commons, therefore, requires serious and urgent attention. This case study on joint forest management in the northwestern state of Rajasthan in India explains the critical role of the commons in the rural Indian context, as well as the role of local communities in conserving these resources. Unlike the rest of the state, forest constitutes a dominant land use in southern Rajasthan, and the rural communities in these areas actively participate in the conservation of the forests through different institutional arrangements. Drawing on two examples from the Gogunda administrative block of Udaipur district, this case study shows that effective collaborations among local communities, nongovernmental organizations (NGOs), and the state Forest Department (FD) can lead to successful forest management.

The history of scientific forest management in India dates back to the mid-nineteenth century, when the British colonial government established the Imperial Forest Department to extract timber from the forests and bring large tracts of forestlands under government control. Subsequent forest policies, which continued until the late 1980s, were driven primarily by the objective of maximizing timber yield and forest revenues. The local people's rights to forest resources were curtailed, resulting in popular discontent as well as large-scale degradation of the forests. As a result, the National Forest Policy of 1988 was enacted by the government to reverse the revenue-oriented forest policies and include local people in the protection and management of forests. This policy laid the foundation of the joint forest management (JFM) program, which was formally initiated by the central government on June 1, 1990. The JFM program is an attempt to forge partnerships with the rural users of forest resources in order to regenerate degraded forestlands and promote decentralized governance of the forests. NGOs also can be a "facilitating agency" in JFM. This means that the NGOs can provide financial, technical, and institutional support to the village forest protection and management committees, just as the state forest departments do. Overall, JFM established the legal frameworks for community participation in forest governance, and it enhanced the institutional robustness of this governance by

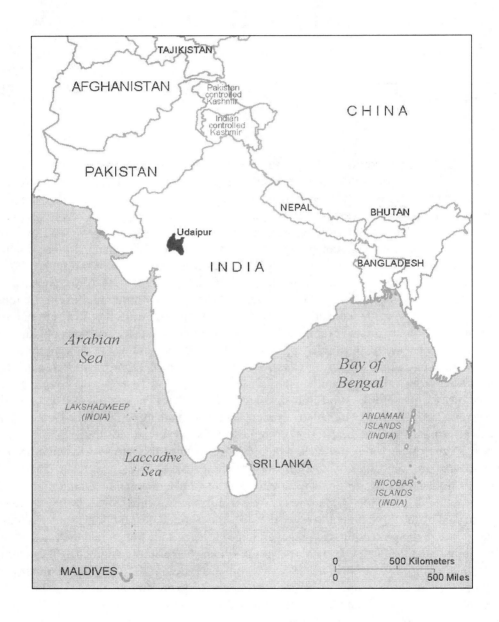

Box 10.1

Acronyms Used in the Case Study

CPR: common-pool resource, also referred to as common-property
          resource
FD: Forest Department (state level)
FES: Foundation for Ecological Security
FRA: Forest Rights Act (2006)
JFM: joint forest management
NGO: nongovernmental organization
NRM: natural resource management
VFPMC: village forest protection and management committee

---

enabling the role of multiple actors, including local communities, NGOs, donors, and the Gram Panchayats (elected institutions for decentralized rural governance). However, JFM has been criticized for its several policy loopholes and implementation flaws (see Lele 2000 and Nayak and Berkes 2008). The focus of this case study, nonetheless, is on the opportunities that JFM provides for community participation in and local benefits of forest management.

Drawing on ethnographic fieldwork conducted over several years in two JFM institutions and on the analysis of governmental, NGO, and community-level documents, I make the following arguments: (1) the role of local communities and their traditional resource-management practices are central for successful forest management; (2) the success of JFM requires strong coordination among communities, NGOs, and the state Forest Department; (3) effective governance of the commons (in this case, forests) involves intervention at various levels so as to enhance rural livelihoods and develop overall natural resources; and (4) JFM can help in effective implementation of the Forest Rights Act (FRA), which is a step ahead of JFM in that it ensures the "rights" of rural forest users over their forestlands. The next section provides a brief overview of JFM, with special reference to Rajasthan. This is followed by a detailed discussion of the two cases.

Joint Forestry Management (JFM), with a Particular Focus on Rajasthan

Since the early 1990s, JFM has emerged as a dominant practice in forest management across India. Currently, more than 100,000 JFM committees protect about 54.36 million acres (22 million hectares) of forestlands in India, which is about 28 percent of the country's total forestlands, involving about 23 million people living within the periphery of the forest areas (Government of India 2011). Although JFM rules and procedures vary from one state to another, there are some common features, including the following:

1. Government resolutions are passed specifying membership rules, roles, and duties of the state Forest Department and the community, and forest benefits to be shared between both.
2. JFM committees—known variously as forest protection committees, village forest protection and management committees (VFPMCs), or Van Suraksha Samitis—are constituted among the forest users, and roles and responsibilities are assigned to these committees.
3. Active involvement of village communities in the protection and management of the forests is promoted.
4. JFM committees prepare their microplans through participatory rural appraisal.
5. Wherever possible, NGOs are involved in JFM processes.
6. Developmental activities, also known as "entry-point" activities, are undertaken outside the forestland to gain the trust of the communities and strengthen local livelihoods.

> The Rajasthan State Forest Department website (http:// www.rajforest.nic.in) is a good source of information about all aspects of the state's forests.

JFM in Rajasthan has made significant progress since it began in 1991. By March 2007, according to the Rajasthan Forest Department, 4,882 VFPMCs managed about 1,927,000 acres (780,000 hectares) of forestlands, which is 24 percent of the state's total forestland. However, given that forestland constitutes only 9.5 percent of the total geographical area of Rajasthan, the overall area under JFM is limited. Moreover, the geography of JFM within the state is uneven, since only the southern districts, namely Udaipur, Chittaurgarh, Banswara, and Dungarpur, have sizable forestlands in the state—hence their prominence in JFM. The limited availability of forestland and its large-scale degradation increase the significance of JFM for forest-dependent communities in the state. By integrating traditional resource management practices into JFM, communities in southern Rajasthan hybridize JFM and create locally appropriate institutional arrangements, as observed in the cases discussed below.

JFM and the Experiences of Tribal Communities in Udaipur

Located on the south of the Aravali mountain range, Udaipur is a district enriched with natural resources, including forests, wildlife, river systems, lakes, and several precious minerals. According to the Foundation for Ecological Security (FES), 28 percent of the total land in the district is forestland, which accounts for 20 percent of the total forest cover of the state. The district is also a mosaic of various ethnic communities—including Rajputs, Dangi-Patels, Brahmins, Bhils, Garasias, Meghwals, and many others—with diverse sociocultural practices, such as different marriage and death ceremonies, religious practices, food habits, and festivals. Much like the rest of the state, Udaipur suffers from

---

Box 10.2

The Importance of Tribal Groups in Rajasthan's JFM Efforts

While Rajputs and Brahmins are caste groups, most of the people relying on forests belong to groups identified as tribal (such as the Bhils or Garasias). Indian tribal groups have religious practices only vaguely connected to Hinduism, live in fairly remote areas, and are often heavily dependent on forests. They are also usually among the poorest and least educated of Indian social groups.

---

several ongoing ecological crises, including deforestation, groundwater depletion, low and erratic rainfall, and excessive mining, all with serious socioeconomic implications. As a step toward reversing deforestation, JFM, then, has ecological and socioeconomic relevance for the district as a whole.

More data on land use in Rajasthan can be found at the website of the Foundation for Ecological Security (www.fes.org.in).

The two village forest protection and management committees examined here are those of Chitravas and Karech in the northwest of Udaipur district. Both VFPMCs were organized in 2002 under the initiative of an NGO called the Foundation for Ecological Security, which provided financial and technical assistance to the two VFPMCs through 2012. Table 10.1 provides a brief profile of the two VFPMCs.

Located adjacent to each other, the two VFPMCs share similar socioecological characteristics. Both are parts of the Aravali mountain range; the forests have similar diversity; both VFPMCs are on the periphery of a wildlife sanctuary (recently designated a national park); the ethnic composition in both VFPMCs is the same; and the livelihood practices in

Table 10.1

A Brief Profile of Two VFPMCs

Name	Year of constitution	Forestland under JFM (hectares)	Membership (households)	Type of community
Chitravas	2002	276	485	Garasia and Bhil-Gameti
Karech	2002	339	255	Garasia and Bhil-Gameti

Source: Compiled by Nicole A. Wilson.

Box 10.3

Methodologies Involved in This Case Study

The ethnographic fieldwork for this case study consisted of participant observation with the two VFPMCs and the Foundation for Ecological Security; semistructured and open-ended interviews with government officials, members of FES, and community representatives; and focus-group interviews with community members. Additionally, various documents of the VFPMCs, FES, and Rajasthan Forest Department were analyzed for more in-depth understanding. Theoretically, the study combines the literature on the commons with political ecological scholarship. I draw heavily on Ostrom's (1990) theoretical framework on common-pool resource management (see Table 10.2). However, as a geographer, I find that a political ecological approach on environmental governance helps in critical examination of the role of multiple actors in the management of the forests.

---

both consist of a mix of rain-fed agriculture, dependence on commons, livestock rearing, and wage labor. Despite degradation, the forest provides the communities with resources, including timber and several other forest products.

The design principles of common-pool resource (CPR) institutions outlined by Ostrom (1990) highlight conditions that account for the success of community institutions in sustaining a forest or other CPR through generations. Depending upon the type of the resource and the specific sociohistorical context of a community, some of the design principles may be more applicable than others, and some may not apply at all. However, a strong CPR institution generally adheres to most of the principles and adapts them to the local contexts. The following section elaborates some of the important institutional mechanisms of the two VFPMCs.

Defining Boundaries of the Forest and Its Users

First and foremost, JFM requires a clear demarcation of the forest boundary, which can then be fenced. The measures commonly undertaken for establishing forest boundaries include conducting a physical survey of the forestland, verifying the boundaries with FD maps, resolving "encroachment" (which refers to illegal occupation of forestland by someone either for cultivation or residence), and fencing the forest with stone or other locally available materials.

Both the Chitravas and Karech VFPMCs settled their respective forest boundaries in innovative ways. Encroachment was a common feature in both, making it a challenging task to demarcate the actual forest boundaries. Most of these encroachments were *nazari qabzas* (claims based on sight possession) for future use, without physically occupying the land. In other words, the land use of the forestland under *nazari qabza* remained as forest. After having deliberated in several village assemblies (*aam-sabhas*), both VFPMCs

Table 10.2

Design Principles Illustrated by Long-Enduring Common-Pool Resource Institutions

Principle	Explanation
1. Clearly defined boundaries	Individuals or households with rights to withdraw resource units from the common-pool resource and the boundaries of the common-pool resource itself are clearly defined.
2. Congruence	a. The distribution of benefits from appropriation rules is roughly proportionate to the costs imposed by provision rules. b. Appropriation rules restricting time, place, technology and/or quantity of resource units are related to local conditions.
3. Collective-choice arrangements	Most individuals affected by operational rules can participate in modifying operational rules.
4. Monitoring	Monitors, who actively audit common-pool resource conditions and user behavior, are accountable to the users and/or are the users themselves.
5. Graduated sanctions	Users who violate operational rules are likely to receive graduated sanctions (depending on the seriousness and context of the offence) from other users, from officials accountable to these users, or from both.
6. Conflict-resolution mechanisms	Users and their officials have rapid access to low-cost, local arenas to resolve conflict among users or between users and officials.
7. Minimal recognition of rights to organize	The rights of users to devise their own institutions are not challenged by external governmental authorities.

For common-pool resources that are part of larger systems:

8. Nested enterprises	Appropriation, provision, monitoring, enforcement, conflict resolution, and governance activities are organized in multiple layers of nested enterprises.

Source: Ostrom 1999, 7; see also Ostrom 1990, 90, for a detailed discussion of the design principles.

resolved this issue peacefully as everyone possessing a *nazari qabza* agreed to surrender it for the purpose of JFM. This did not mean, however, that the forest boundaries in these villages matched perfectly with the maps, as some of the lands on the fringes were occupied years ago, by rich and poor alike, and were converted to residential or agricultural use. In an astute move, the communities decided to go ahead with fencing the available lands, since they did not want to risk losing more lands by delaying the JFM processes while trying to get the encroached lands back (a goal that they recognized as futile). In their respective village assemblies, both communities came to a consensus on the encroachment issue and demarcated the forest boundaries for protection.

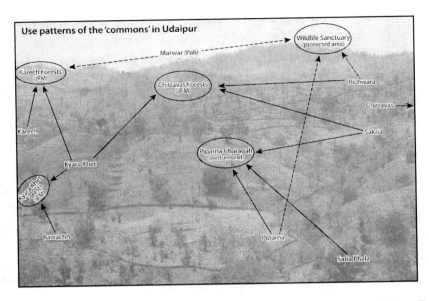

A depiction of the complex resource-use practices in the area under the Chitravas Village Forest Protection Management Committee (the dotted lines symbolize secondary or seasonal dependence on a resource). *(Photo by Mitul Baruah)*

With regards to VFPMC membership, the Rajasthan state JFM rules specify that a VFPMC member has to be an adult residing within the "revenue boundary" (an administrative demarcation of land in India for the purpose of revenue collection by the government) of the village or hamlet to which the forest belongs. According to Nandini Sundar, the author of "Unpacking the 'Joint' in Joint Forest Management" (2000), the communities that the JFM policy assumes are, then, products of the government rules and procedures, lacking any other traditional attribute of communities. However, the two VFPMCs challenged such narrow notions of community or membership, and they redefined these concepts by successfully hybridizing the JFM rules with traditional resource-use practices.

Traditionally, rural communities belonging to different "hamlets" and "villages" (hereafter "habitation") in the study region used multiple sites of common lands—forest or pasture—in order to meet their multiple needs. Thus, *user boundaries* of common lands in the region also transgressed different administrative boundaries. As such, the Chitravas forestland was used by communities belonging to the habitations of Sakria, Chitravas, Kyara Khet, and Richwara, whereas the forestland of Karech was used by people belonging to Karech, Kyara Khet, and a few habitations in the neighboring Marwar region. At the same time, these communities also used other forests and pasturelands (*charagah*) as primary or secondary sources of their livelihoods. Such complex resource-use patterns posed organizational challenges to the VFPMCs, but with the support of FES and dedicated community leaders, both the VFPMCs were able to overcome these challenges. In fact, they turned them into opportunities. Let us look at the Chitravas VFPMC.

A VFPMC was constituted in Chitravas in the early 1990s under the initiative of the Forest Department. It remained nonfunctional, and the forestland continued to be used as an "open-access" resource until 2002. As per the JFM guidelines of Rajasthan, the Forest Department included only the people of Chitravas in the VFMPC, since Chitravas was the "revenue village" to which the forestland belonged. Thus, when the FES initiated JFM activities in the village in August 2002, the FD officials suggested a revival of the existing VFPMC instead of constituting a new one. Accordingly, on August 26, 2002, a village assembly was held to reconstitute the VFPMC and finalize its members. People turned up in large numbers, representing almost every household from the various habitations. However, no sooner had the meeting begun than a major fight took place between the habitations. As soon as the people of Richwara, Kyara Khet, and Sakria found out that the old VFPMC was to be revived, with Chitravas as the only *haqdar* (owner of the forests), they protested this initiative and demanded their inclusion in the VFPMC. They explained to the FES and FD representatives that Richwara, Kyara Khet, and Sakria were both dependent on the Chitravas forest and responsible for its protection, as evidenced by their repeated participation in voluntary activities (*shramdaan*) on the forestland. These included participating in repairing the fence, in patrolling the forest as a vigilance measure, and in village meetings on forest related issues.

For these habitations, JFM was an attack on their "rights," because JFM would transform their "open-access" forest to an exclusive property of Chitravas. Thus they threatened to destroy the forest and disrupt JFM activities if they were not included in the VFPMC. Mansaram Garasia, a villager from Kyara Khet and an ardent community leader, summarized the issue:

> Forest Department and NGOs [in particular FES] have come now; but we have protected this forest for years. . . . Now if the Forest Department and the people of Chitravas decide to keep us out, do you think we will listen to them? Moreover, who do you think can best protect the forest from outsiders? It is us, the people of Richwara, Kyara ka Khet, and Sakria, who live next to the forest and keep a close watch on illegal felling or grazing or fire in the forest. Chitravas is too far, and they don't even use this forest since they have alternate resources closer by.

For the next few months, the FES team conducted a series of meetings in all the habitations that claimed rights over the forest, cross-verified some of those claims with the FD records, and consulted the Gram Panchayat. Finally, a new VFPMC was constituted with the inclusion of all 485 households from Richwara, Kyara Khet, Sakria, and Chitravas and with a fairly large executive committee representing all the habitations.

Thus, in defining the forest boundaries and its *haqdars*, the communities at Chitravas wove together traditional practices and knowledge, JFM rules, expertise of external agencies (e.g., the FES and FD), and the livelihood concerns of local communities. As far as CPR theories go, both Chitravas and Karech VFPMCs defied the argument about the negative relationship between the size of a group and collective action. Despite the large and diverse membership, both these VFPMCs governed their forests successfully, thereby creating grounds for more robust theorization of the governance of the commons.

Table 10.3

Summary of VFPMC Meetings, 2002–2009

		Key agendas and corresponding number of meetings				
Name of VFPMC	Protection of the forests	Management issues (e.g., planning, payments, sanctions, forest use, and monitoring)	Biophysical interventions (e.g., fencing, plantation, and soil and water conservation measures)	Conflict resolution	Capacity building: training programs and exposure visits	Total number of meetings
Chitravas	23	70	31	14	9	147
Karech	13	60	36	4	7	120

Source: Meeting minutes of Chitravas and Karech VFPMCs.

Governing the Forests

Not only were the Chitravas and Karech VFPMCs innovative in defining forest boundaries and membership, but also they were creative in developing an array of institutional practices compatible with both local contexts and JFM rules. Discussed below are some of the important elements of their institutional practices.

Meetings

Meetings were the most important space where communities discussed and debated various issues concerning forest governance and developed a larger "community vision" for effective natural resource management. Rajasthan State JFM guidelines mandate six meetings a year in a VFPMC: two general assemblies and four executive committee meetings. While many VFPMCs, especially the ones supported directly by the FD, failed to meet a target as low as this (Baruah 2010), Chitravas and Karech VFPMCs far exceeded these minimums. Although both VFPMCs had specific dates for their monthly village assemblies, on many occasions more than one meeting a month was conducted. More importantly, in lieu of the "exclusive" executive committee meetings, the two VFPMCs conducted village assemblies, which were more inclusive and participatory. A range of issues, from protection and regeneration of the forest to conflict resolution and capacity building of different sections of the community, were discussed (Table 10.3).

Although more meetings do not necessarily correspond to a strong institution, more meetings do mean increased opportunities for interactions among community members, thus creating greater potential for public participation in decision making. With an average attendance of above fifty people per meeting, the village assemblies in these two VFPMCs were attended by men and women, and by young and old, from all the habitations. The meetings were held in places convenient to most of the households,

A village assembly at the Chitravas Village Forest Protection Management Committee. *(Photo by Mitul Baruah)*

thereby enabling larger participation. Moreover, detailed meeting minutes were maintained and regularly reviewed, which helped in monitoring the actions taken against meeting decisions.

The FES team made special efforts to enhance women's participation in the meetings. Despite the largely patriarchal nature of Rajasthan, women played a significant role in these two VFPMCs, as they do in most tribal societies in India. Thus women were generally present in the meetings, and some of them were active participants. Additionally, "women groups" were organized by FES to work more directly with women, which led to increased female participation in the VFPMCs.

Despite FES's important role in the meetings, the village community was at the center of most of the processes. The village communities played the following irreplaceable roles: informing all the habitations about meeting dates and venues; attending the meetings, sometimes even at the cost of a day's wage; organizing internal meetings in a habitation before the village assembly, if required; maintaining detailed meeting minutes; discussing and debating issues for hours, and sometimes for days, if issues were not settled in one meeting; and resolving conflicts. Perhaps most important is that all of these activities continued consistently for years.

Protection Measures

Open grazing is the dominant livestock-rearing practice in the area. Thus one of the first measures to restore degraded common land in and around the Udaipur area was

The fencing around the JFM site of the Karech Village Forest Protection Management Committee shows the obvious effect of the boundary. *(Photo by Mitul Baruah)*

to erect stone fencing around it. Stone fencing generally works as an efficient protection measure: it is cost-effective, since stones are readily available inside or near the degraded sites; fencing generates local employment; and stone fencing allows fast regeneration of rootstocks by preventing open grazing. Communities in the area also mix stone fencing with "live fencing," or the planting of local shrub species along the stone fencing, which has the benefits of being more permanent and providing additional livelihood benefits.

 Patrolling complements the stone and live fencing and is viewed as an essential measure in the area, given the scarcity of resources and the fear of illegal tree felling or grazing. In VFPMCs directly assisted by the Forest Department, patrolling is done either by forest guards, also called "cattle guards" (the lowest rank in the FD hierarchy), or by a village member in receipt of a nominal payment from the FD. The VFPMCs of Chitravas and Karech developed what they called a *"lathi* system." *Lathi* literally means a "stick"; thus this system involves patrolling the forest with a stick in hand. The lathi here serves two purposes: it works as a weapon that can be used in case of a fight with an infractor or an attack by wild animals, and it works symbolically as an assertion of community rights over the forests. The lathi system works rotationally: each day two persons from different habitations patrol the forest (as shramdaan, or free labor), and at the end of the day they hand over the sticks to the next household in their respective habitations to perform the same task the following day. Thus the lathi keeps rotating within the village, involving every household in protecting the forest. Shankar Garasia from Chitravas explained the benefits of the lathi system:

The Karech JFM site in 2002 *(top)* and in 2006 *(bottom)*. *(Photos by Mitul Baruah)*

> In our *lathi* system, today's guard can tell if yesterday's guard had performed his duty well by looking at the condition of the forest. Suppose I am on duty today, and I notice evidences of illegal activities, such as tree felling or grazing. I will immediately bring those to the attention of the VFPMC. But we can also tell from the evidences whether the damages are old or fresh; hence there is a way to find out if the previous guards have done their duties well. It's a very strong system. Also, it is not too much work, since every household gets its turn only about twice a year, or maybe less.

Several factors made the lathi system an effective protection measure: (1) it is self-monitoring, as evident from Shankar's statement above; (2) it strengthens the sense of community ownership of the forest, given the amount of time and effort the community spends on it; and (3) it saves money for the community since it runs on shramdaan. Even though soil and moisture conservation activities and replanting were undertaken, the lathi system and the fencing were fundamental to the successful regeneration of forests in both VFPMCs.

Planning

The state JFM rules require every VFPMC to prepare a "microplan," a document with detailed activity plans for the restoration of the forestland. These then require FD approval. For FD approval, the microplan needs to be "technically sound," meaning that it should adequately integrate concerns of "scientific forestry." Given the general divide between indigenous knowledge and scientific knowledge—and a perceived inferiority of the former, especially within the government departments in India—microplanning in FD-assisted VFPMCs is often a top-down process. However, the microplans at Chitravas and Karech were developed through participatory processes that involved the following factors: a series of meetings in different habitations; use of participatory rural appraisal techniques, such as participatory resource mapping, walking examinations, called "transact-walks," in the forest to understand the microenvironments, and participatory planning; documenting oral histories of the forestland and its relationships with the communities; discussing the proposed plan at the village assembly; and, finally, submitting the microplan to FD for approval. Once the microplan was approved by the Forest Department, the VFPMCs then implemented the various biophysical measures with financial support from FES.

In addition to the microplans, which were solely forestland-focused, the two VFPMCs also prepared "perspective plans," or village development plans. The perspective plan focused on the development of the commons, agricultural developments, livestock improvement, livelihood enhancement activities, infrastructure developments, and institutional mechanisms for each of these. These plans were prepared through public participation from different sections of the community and different habitations, generating public awareness on developmental issues and contributing to building a common vision, or "perspective," of the community.

More significantly, by focusing on the overall development of the village and the governance of natural resources in their entirety, the perspective plan strengthened the VFPMC's relationship with other institutions, especially the Gram Panchayat, different government departments, and the ongoing livelihood and watershed projects. For example, after the perspective plans of Chitravas and Karech were presented at the general assembly of the Chitravas Gram Panchayat, natural resource management (NRM) became an agenda at the Gram Panchayat, leading to its consensus on constituting an NRM subcommittee.

Monitoring

Intricate monitoring mechanisms were developed in both VFPMCs to actively audit the conditions of the forest and the activities of the *haqdars*. The rotational lathi system enabled daily observation of any unlawful activities in the forest. Besides the daily patrolling, the VFPMCs often held their meetings inside the forestland, which further allowed the communities to monitor forest conditions.

The two VFPMCs also devised monitoring mechanisms for equitable benefit sharing from the forests. For example, the following systems were witnessed in fodder sharing:

1. Each household was charged a nominal fee, which was then deposited in the VFPMC account.
2. Harvesting was permitted only within a specific period in a season to prevent overexploitation.
3. Only one person from each household was allowed to harvest.
4. At the end of each harvest, the VFPMC reviewed, and modified if necessary, its postharvest activity plan for the forests.

Another precondition for an effective monitoring system is to have a strong and realistic *sanction* mechanism. Usually, the sanctions in CPR institutions are modest—a token fee, for example—since the appropriator-monitor might be in a similar situation in the future. Moreover, the main idea behind the sanction is to remind the infractor about the importance of compliance, as noted by Ostrom in *Governing the Commons* (1990). The two VFPMCs devised a detailed system of sanctions for different types of potential violations, with varying fines imposed on grazing by different animals. For example, the fine for a camel grazing was much higher than the fine for a goat, which was higher than the fine for a cow. Similarly, specific systems of penalties were worked out for various infractions or for levels of participation in the VFPMC process, such as for someone found with an axe in the forest, someone not participating in shramdaan, or someone who did not attend three consecutive village assemblies.

Monitoring systems were also in place to ensure the efficient implementation of biophysical measures (e.g., plantation development, or soil and water conservation measures), equitable employment generation in the communities, and transparent payments for activities implemented by the VFPMC. Not all of these monitoring mechanisms worked perfectly, however. In fact, some failed repeatedly and had to be constantly renegotiated. More important is the fact that the VFPMCs developed and redeveloped these systems through democratic processes, documented those in the form of bylaws, and worked constantly toward their best execution.

Conflict Resolution Mechanisms

Conflicts are inevitable in any VFPMC due to a variety of factors, such as competing interests of stakeholders, lack of efficient leadership, mismatch between short-term livelihood needs and long-term ecological considerations, preexisting socioeconomic inequalities, and conflicting interests between the Forest Department and communities. The two VFPMCs, however, effectively applied low-cost, locally devised conflict resolution mechanisms, thereby keeping the community together. These VFPMCs first attempted to resolve conflicts internally, failing which the Gram Panchayat was involved, and the last resort was to involve the NGO (the Foundation for Ecological Security), the Forest Department, and other concerned government departments. The following example from Chitravas illustrates the conflict resolution mechanisms in the two VFPMCs:

> Lala Bhuji, a member of the Chitravas VFPMC, "encroached" a small portion of the forest in 2003 and cultivated maize. Furious at his action, the community called for a village assembly and notified Lala to be present, but Lala did not show up. The VFPMC then sent him a message urging him to come to the next meeting and present his case, failing which the VFPMC would penalize him. But again Lala did not show up. The third time, VFPMC members gathered outside Lala's home and asked him to come out. This time they further threatened to burn his crop and chase him away from the village if he did not comply. As defiant as before, Lala never stepped out of his home, even though the VFPMC members waited there for hours. After these repeated failed attempts, the VFPMC then approached the Gram Panchayat and FES for assistance. A small group of villagers, along with the *sarpanch* (Gram Panchayat president) and an FES staff member, went to Lala's home one last time. Involving the panchayat perhaps put an additional pressure on Lala, since he might have feared losing various benefits from the panchayat. This time he met with the group and agreed to remove his encroachment. However, he appealed to the VFPMC to allow him that crop, since he had already invested money and labor in it. The VFPMC agreed on the condition that after the harvest he would repair the fencing and that such activities would never be repeated. Lala complied with the VFPMC judgment. In fact, he later started actively participating in VFPMC activities.

Lala Bhuji's case, especially the way the VFPMC resolved the crisis, strengthened the VFPMC. Ever since this incident, there have been no other cases of encroachment in Chitravas, and the monitoring systems of the institution have been further strengthened.

Lessons Learned

My objective in this section is not to discuss the causalities of the successes of the two cases (see Baruah 2010 for a detailed discussion of them); instead, the purpose is to tease out some of the more generalizable lessons from the two cases on the governance of common-pool resources (CPRs) and on forests in particular. The issues discussed in this section are thus broader in nature, keeping in focus the theoretical relevance of this case study.

First, the two cases demonstrate the centrality of the role of local communities in the governance of CPRs. Despite the important part played by the FES, it was the village community—the *haqdars*—who carried out most of the institutional processes of governing the forest. Further, the communities did not just implement the JFM rules; rather, they devised what can be called hybrid JFM practices by blending traditional approaches with JFM rules, as evident in their protection mechanisms, meetings, monitoring measures, and conflict resolution systems. What was most fundamental to the institutional processes at both VFPMCs was the key role of the village assemblies, which provided the space for transparent and participatory decision making, thereby enabling successful governance of the forest.

Second, the case study illustrates the significance of interagency coordination. At the heart of the successes of Chitravas and Karech was the FD-FES-VFPMC coordination. If the village community was responsible for designing and leading the institutional processes on the ground, it was FES that initiated joint forest management in both villages and worked as a bridge between the community and the Forest Department. Similarly, the FD's role was critical on the following grounds: (1) its openness to the hybridity in the VFPMCs' management practices enabled practical conservation measures; (2) by remaining largely noninterfering, the FD facilitated local innovations and greater public participation in JFM; and (3) the FD's trust in the FES helped bring different expertise and resources together, ultimately strengthening the VFPMCs. While some of these details may be unique to the two VFPMCs, there are still lessons to learn about how to build such interagency coordination, which can be then replicated elsewhere.

Finally, the two cases demonstrate that CPRs are part of broader socioecological systems; hence, successful management of CPRs is contingent upon good governance of these overall socioecological processes. The forest was critical for the communities at Chitravas and Karech, but the forest alone could not meet the full range of social, economic, and political needs of these communities. The FES, therefore, intervened in multiple areas, including forests, pasturelands, farmlands, drinking water, irrigation, livelihoods development, and capacity building. Similarly, FES worked with a network of institutions, including VFPMCs, women's groups, self-help groups, pastureland committees, and the panchayats. Thus, CPR governance is a process that is contingent upon and part of overall governance of natural resources, livelihoods development, and political empowerment of local communities.

Conclusions: From Joint Forest "Management" to Forest "Rights"

In 2006, the government of India passed the landmark Scheduled Tribes and Other Traditional Forest Dwellers (Recognition of Forest Rights) Act, also called the Forest Rights Act (FRA). This act sought the restitution of deprived forest rights for tribal and other forest dwellers across India—both "individual rights" to live and cultivate, and "community rights" to protect and regenerate community forest resources. Such an explicit focus on "rights" makes the FRA far more progressive than JFM. Is JFM, therefore, passé now, or can it complement the FRA? The case study presented here supports the latter position.

Fundamental to the FRA are rights "claims"; that is, an individual or a community must "claim" its forest rights through the Gram Panchayat. This requires that rural com-

munities possess a certain level of awareness about their forest rights and that they have
the skills and confidence to appropriately articulate these rights. Moreover, communities
with prior experiences of natural resources governance are better equipped for successful implementation of the FRA. Thus, a strong VFPMC can facilitate rights claims and
other implementation processes at both community and panchayat levels. Similarly, as
the two cases demonstrate, a successful VFPMC works closely with the concerned Gram
Panchayat, thereby strengthening the relations between village communities and the
panchayat as well as centering natural resources governance in the panchayat's agenda.
Furthermore, a VFPMC can be used as the basis for claiming "community rights" over
forestland under the FRA provisions. Thus, a well-implemented JFM program can advance FRA implementation by facilitating rights claims at both the individual and the
community levels.

JFM is not as progressive as the Forest Rights Act, and it is not implemented everywhere as efficiently as in Chitravas and Karech. Nonetheless, JFM marked the first radical
departure in the erstwhile centralized, bureaucratic, and revenue-oriented forest policies
of India. Besides, JFM remains the only participatory forest management system in India
covering the length and breadth of the country. JFM is not enough, but it has significant
potentials, especially in areas like southern Rajasthan, where alternative institutional
arrangements are lacking but effective collaboration exists among local communities,
NGOs, and the Forest Department. Therefore, this case study suggests the benefits of
widespread implementation of JFM, wherever feasible, with necessary modifications as
demanded by local situations. However, JFM must not be an end; rather, it is a means to
secure people's forest rights and to maintain ecological sustainability. Finally, this case
study has wider global relevance. It is instructive not only for the implementation of JFM
in India, but also for the participatory governance of CPR globally.

References and Further Research

Baruah, Mitul. 2010. "Joint Forest Management (JFM) and Role of NGOs: Cases from Raj-
    asthan, India." Master's thesis, SUNY College of Environmental Science and Forestry.
Foundation for Ecological Security. 2006. "Mapping the Development Context of Rajast-
    han: A Rajasthan State Atlas." Internal Report. Udaipur, Rajasthan, India: Foundation for
    Ecological Security.
Gadgil, Madhav, and Ramachandra Guha. 1992. *The Fissured Land: An Ecological History
    of India*. Berkeley: University of California Press.
Government of India. 2006. The Scheduled Tribes and Other Traditional Forest Dwellers
    (Recognition of Forest Rights) Act, 2006. DL-(N) 04/0007/2006-08. New Delhi: Ministry
    of Law and Justice (Legislative Department). http://forestrightsact.com/the-act.
———. 2011. *Report to the People on Environment and Forest, 2010–11*. New Delhi: Ministry
    of Environment and Forests. http://envfor.nic.in/downloads/public-information/Report-To-
    The-People-on-Environment-And-Forests%20-2010-11.pdf.
Government of Rajasthan. 2002. *Joint Forest Management: Operational Guidelines*. Jaipur,
    Rajasthan: Office of the Principal Chief Conservator of Forest.

Lele, Sharachchandra. 2000. "Godsend, Sleight of Hand, or Just Muddling Through: Joint Water and Forest Management in India." *Natural Resources Perspectives* 53: 1–6. http://www.odi.org.uk/sites/odi.org.uk/files/odi-assets/publications-opinion-files/2857.pdf.

Nayak, Prateep K., and Fikret Berkes. 2008 "Politics of Co-Optation: Community Forest Management versus Joint Forest Management in Orissa, India." *Environmental Management* 41, no. 5: 707–718.

Ostrom, Elinor. 1990. *Governing the Commons: The Evolution of Institutions for Collective Action.* Cambridge and New York: Cambridge University Press.

———. February 1999. *Self-Governance and Forest Resources.* IFOR Occasional Paper, no. 20. Bogor, Indonesia: Center for International Forestry Research. http://www.cifor.org/publications/pdf_files/OccPapers/OP-20.pdf.

Saigal, Sushil. 2006. "Beyond Experimentation: Emerging Issues in the Institutionalization of Joint Forest Management in India." *Environmental Mangement* 26, no. 3: 269–291.

Sundar, Nandini. 2000. "Unpacking the 'Joint' in Joint Forest Management." *Development and Change* 31, no. 1: 255–279.

11

Khwaja Sira
Transgender Activism and Transnationality in Pakistan

FARIS A. KHAN

In 2009, the transgender people of Pakistan, known as *khwaja siras*, were granted rights by the Pakistani government after decades without any legal recognition or protection. This action coincided with attempts by transgender activists, nongovernmental organizations (NGOs), and the government to organize and empower khwaja siras. NGOs involved in HIV intervention have been financially supported by the Pakistani government and foreign donor agencies since the early years of the twenty-first century. In addition to the surveillance and control of the disease, these funds are meant to support and empower vulnerable groups, including khwaja siras. NGO-led sexual health programs have created opportunities for khwaja siras to learn about advocacy, rights, and organization management, which in turn have helped to propel transgender activism in the country. Khwaja sira activism has been not only encouraged but also influenced by the intervention of NGOs and their international benefactors. However, even as they play a key role in defining and representing transgender people, these transnational forces are met with varying degrees of acceptance and resistance from khwaja sira activists.

Khwaja siras, commonly known as *hijras* in many parts of South Asia, are male-to-female transgender individuals, and they are among Pakistan's most marginalized citizens. They are viewed with ambivalence not only due to their ambiguous physical features, but also because they are believed to possess the power to bless and curse. Invoking a sense of fear, disgust, and curiosity in the general public, they have been excluded from mainstream society. Faced with ridicule from family and friends, many leave their homes at an early age to find refuge among other transgender people. Most khwaja siras receive very little formal education, and employers are typically unwilling to hire them due to their gender difference. The few who manage to find employment emphasize the difficulty in retaining jobs because of routine harassment by coworkers. Consequently, a large majority of transgender people end up joining khwaja sira social networks in order to access the traditional sources of hijra livelihood, including begging, singing and dancing, and blessing newborns and newly married couples. Most khwaja siras also engage in sex work, which increases their susceptibility to sexually transmitted diseases. Moreover, their inferior social status makes them vulnerable to physical violence and to emotional and sexual abuse.

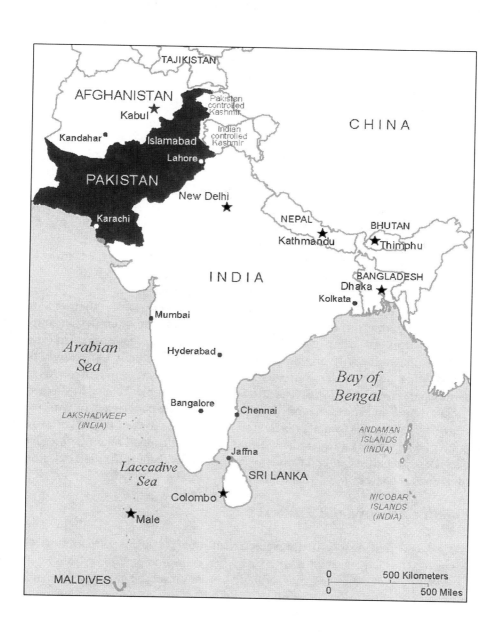

"Transgender Life in Pakistan," a photo essay by Guy Calaf, was posted on CNN World in 2012 (http://cnnphotos.blogs.cnn.com/2012/06/01/transgender-life-in-pakistan/).

In light of this situation, the Pakistani Supreme Court's 2009 decision to grant rights to khwaja siras was hailed by civil society groups as a crucial step to rehabilitate the transgender population. Though unexpected, the court's decision coincided with similar developments in other South Asian countries. India allowed transgender citizens to register for passports in 2005, added a third gender category to the country's voter registration process in 2009, and included transgender people in the country's census and citizen identification system in 2011; Nepal created a third gender category in 2007 and included transgender people in its census in 2011; and Bangladesh allowed transgender citizens to register to vote in 2008. Improvement in their legal status has created a public discourse around transgender rights in Pakistan and provided certain protections to khwaja siras, particularly with respect to their treatment by law enforcement personnel. However, it has done little to positively impact other aspects of the everyday lives of ordinary khwaja siras, thus explaining the involvement of transgender rights groups and NGOs in the rights activism and social development of this minority population.

The efforts of established NGOs are influenced by the decisions of their elite leaders and by the funding trends of their international donors, who are interested in supporting a diversity of causes across the globe. The foreign sponsors of these organizations often dictate which sexual minority groups are most vulnerable and how they should be supported. In keeping with project requirements, NGOs regularly recruit indigenous khwaja sira activists and provide them with educational training on topics related to gender, sexuality, human rights, and sexual health. This training and the experience of working with NGOs have taught many khwaja siras how to run organizations of their own. However, despite their best efforts, khwaja sira organizations, handicapped by a lack of education and basic skills, are still heavily dependent on established NGOs for material, financial, and educational resources.

Khwaja Sira: History and Context

South Asia has a rich history of transgenderism, one that the anthropologist Gayatri Reddy—in the 2005 work *With Respect to Sex: Negotiating Hijra Identity in South India*—broadly divides into four chronological time periods: ancient, medieval, colonial, and contemporary. Evidence of hijras appears foremost in ancient Indian texts from the Hindu, Buddhist, and Jain traditions. The historical record of the medieval period focuses on eunuchs, or castrated men, of the royal Mughal courts, who were known as *khwaja siras*. These individuals served as army generals, harem guards, and advisers to the emperors. Khwaja siras were considered ideal for the protection of the women of the harem due to their inability to reproduce. Later colonial accounts of Indian history

---

Box 11.1

Notes on Methodology

When studying activism, collaborating with relevant organizations can be mutually beneficial to the researcher and to the groups involved. Research results can help the organization better understand both the constraints on and the potential of their activism, while ensuring that the data collection process goes unhindered for the researcher. Moreover, institutional constraints can often affect the conduct of research. For instance, researchers often encounter "gatekeeping," a process whereby outsiders, including researchers, are prevented from gaining access to information, people, and events. Understanding the workings of such institutional constraints, therefore, is useful in finding solutions to the problems they pose.

Box 11.2

Notes on Terminology

In this chapter, the term *queer* is not used as an identity label but to describe those whose gender role or sexual behavior does not conform to dominant social norms. Khwaja siras do not use the word as a self-descriptor. The term transgender is used in the broadest sense to refer to those whose gender identity differs from their assigned sex. For instance, a person who is born physically male but does not identify as a man is considered transgender.

---

indicate that British rulers identified hijras as a criminal caste, a classification under which they could be subjected to surveillance and arrest. Following the partition of the Indian subcontinent and the formation of Pakistan, hijra activities were banned in the early 1960s during the presidency of Ayub Khan. However, as discussed by Nauman Naqvi and Hasan Mujtaba in "Two Baluchi Buggas, a Sindhi Zenana, and the Status of Hijras in Contemporary Pakistan" (1997), the ban was lifted after hijras staged a sit-in in front of Khan's residence.

Pakistan is an Islamic republic with a majority Muslim population. Homosexual acts are illegal under Section 377 of the country's penal code, an injunction that was inherited from British colonial rulers. Through rarely invoked, same-sex sexual behavior is punishable by up to ten years in prison. With Section 377 intact, the Supreme Court granted rights to khwaja siras in a series of historic rulings in 2009, and it ordered the government to issue them national identity cards indicating their transgender status. Pakistan now recognizes "khwaja sira" as a distinct sex in addition to male and female. In subsequent hearings, the court ordered the provision of security, inheritance, and voting rights, educational and job opportunities, and access to government-sponsored welfare programs for khwaja siras.

See the BBC article published online in April 2011, "Pakistan's Transgenders Pin Hopes on New Rights" (http://www.bbc.co.uk/news/world-south-asia-13186958).

Khwaja siras have a centuries-old system of social organization through which they forge alliances with other transgender people. This social structure is based on the master-disciple (*guru-chela*) relationship in which a mentor, typically an experienced khwaja sira, takes on a student, a novice khwaja sira, through ritual initiation. By forging relationships, transgender people are enmeshed in a vast network consisting of khwaja sira households, classes, and lineages. Initiation into this system allows transgender people to earn a living through begging, dancing, and blessing.

While there is no firm consensus about who should be enumerated under the broad khwaja sira category, transgender people generally acknowledge that *khunsa, zennana,* and *hijra* are the three main khwaja sira subcategories. The word *khunsa* refers to those who are intersex, meaning those born with a mixture of both male and female hormonal, chromosomal, and/or genital features. However, intersexual khwaja siras are few in number, and they rarely if ever join khwaja sira social networks.

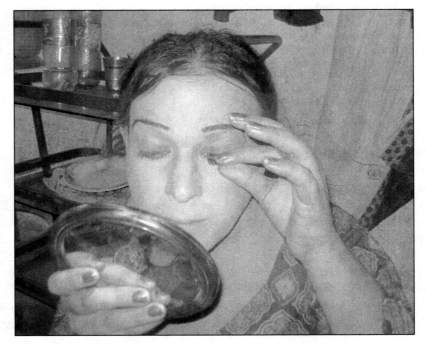

Naila beautifies herself for work. She is regularly hired to dance at weddings. *(Photo by Faris A. Khan)*

Naila kneads dough while Saima cooks chapati bread for lunch. *(Photo by Faris A. Khan)*

The majority of khwaja siras are zennanas. A zennana is someone born physically male; that is, with male sexual organs, but who is believed to have a feminine spirit. Zennanas situationally adopt the appearance of men or women—they may wear men's clothes, keep their hair short, and sport beards and mustaches, or they may dress in women's clothes, wear makeup, and grow out their hair or use wigs. Zennanas tend to transition back and forth between looking and behaving like men and like khwaja siras, since many of them are married to women and have children. Their fluid and situated identities allow them to manage the split between their familial and khwaja sira lives.

A relatively small number of zennanas decide to undergo emasculation surgery, which involves the removal of the penis and testicles. Emasculation is desirable not only because it enhances femininity, but also because it improves one's status among khwaja siras. Yet very few transgender people choose to undergo the procedure because it is irreversible—not only does it close the option to marry and reproduce, but physical emasculation is also believed to be prohibited in Islam. The identity of an individual changes from zennana to hijra after the removal of the genitals. Hijras dress in women's clothes almost full-time and permanently grow out their hair.

What unifies zennanas and hijras, who come from lower-class backgrounds, is their defining characteristic: a feminine spirit, which all khwaja siras are believed to possess from the time of birth. Khwaja siras claim that this spirit makes them effeminate and drives them to be feminine in appearance and gender role; not only does it produce in them the desire to dress like women, but also to engage in women's work, such as cooking and cleaning.

The feminine spirit is also believed to shape the sexual preferences of khwaja siras. Zennanas and hijras engage in a variety of sexual relationships with men. The majority of these men are heterosexual, but some maintain that they are exclusively attracted to transgender people. Khwaja siras refer to their male lovers as *giryas*, with whom many maintain both long- and short-term relationships. In addition to their partners, khwaja siras who are involved in prostitution regularly engage in sexual activity with their clients. Zennanas are typically passive sexual partners or recipients in sexual encounters with men. However, their sexual behavior does not always conform to a strict top-bottom or active-passive oppositional binary, according to Shivananda Khan and Tahir Khilji, the authors of the 2002 World Bank report *Pakistan Enhanced HIV/AIDS Program*, because role reversals occur often. In contrast, hijras can only assume the receptive role in sexual encounters with men, since they are physically emasculated. The idea of a khwaja sira engaging in sexual activity with another khwaja sira, be it a zennana or a hijra, is considered anathema.

Transgender Activism in Pakistan

Khwaja sira activism started around 2005, when several transgender groups began to mobilize and publicly challenge the status quo. Several factors facilitated the development of transgender organizing in Pakistan. First, the economic liberalization of the early 1990s introduced changes in trade policies, strengthened the private sector, and increased the transnational traffic of people and ideas. Second, the sexual health and advocacy programs that were set up to contain HIV/AIDS created opportunities for sexual minorities to organize and learn about rights activism. Third, the Supreme Court's ruling in favor of khwaja siras further encouraged transgender activism in the country.

A variety of stories have been published online, many by the Euro-American press and LGBT advocacy publications, reporting on how transgender individuals have been speaking out politically during Pakistan's 2013 national election campaigns. Here are two:

- "Transgender Candidates Stake Claim in Pakistan Vote" (http://www.rawstory. com/rs/2013/04/18/transgender-candidates-stake-claim-in-pakistan-vote/)
- "Pakistan's Hajiras: Transgender Seeks Election" (http://www.thedailyactivist. com/lgbt-pakistans-hijras/)

The term *khwaja sira* has regained currency since the early years of the twenty-first century owing partly to the efforts of transgender activists who have appropriated the title as a politically correct identity label to replace *hijra*, which they believe carries negative connotations among the general public. However, the term *hijra* is still used within khwaja sira communities. In addition, some khwaja sira activists have started calling themselves

Khwaja siras protest the delay in the processing of their new identity cards at the Karachi Press Club. They also demand that authorities take action against terrorist activities in the city. *(Photo by Faris A. Khan)*

transgender, an identity label they have acquired through their participation in HIV/AIDS intervention programs.

Pakistan is home to a host of NGOs that are engaged in the surveillance and control of HIV/AIDS. Many of these organizations work on the health issues of vulnerable "males who have sex with males" (MSM), a broad framework that includes transgender populations. Along with disease prevention and control, a few NGOs even work on the issue of rights and on the social development of khwaja siras, but up until 2011 little progress had been made in this area.

A strong yet complex link exists between health and activism, in that issues of public health invite social reform when they become life threatening, according to Vincanne Adams and Stacey Leigh Pigg, the authors of *Sex in Development* (2005). Consequently, political organizing often occurs in and through public health domains. This has certainly been the case for HIV/AIDS intervention in India and now increasingly in Pakistan, where programs to control the spread of the virus have mushroomed across the country in the last decade or so. Sexual health organizations have created spaces for khwaja sira activists to convene and share experiences. These NGOs are entangled in webs of structured interactions with each other and with local, national, and transnational entities. The hierarchal relationships of dependency among them are based on the distribution of material, financial, and educational resources. For instance, NGOs obtain funding from a combination of sources, including the Pakistani government, United Nations agencies, and other local and foreign foundations and charities. These funds are meant primarily for projects focused on HIV intervention, but also they are allocated for the capacity-building efforts of smaller organizations that provide services to sexual minorities. Capacity building involves a host of activities, including the provision of material and financial support, educational training and skill enhancement, leadership development, alliance formation, fund-raising, research and assessment, media advocacy, strategic planning, and so on. The educational training of these NGOs covers topics related to gender, sexuality, and human rights along with the issues of sexual and reproductive health.

In recent years, donor agencies have become increasingly interested in funding community-based organizations (CBOs) in developing countries. CBOs are either independently run or are nonprofit subsidiaries of large NGOs. Individual CBOs are run by and for specific local or indigenous communities, and they are either self-funded or operate on a voluntary basis. Some CBOs receive support through their parent NGOs during their initial years until they become self-sustaining. Their recent popularity among donors is based on the notion that small local groups are more effective than large organizations in addressing the needs of target populations.

In addition to established NGOs, several small transgender activist groups are run independently by khwaja siras. In 2011, there were about ten such indigenous organizations in Pakistan, but less than half of them were registered with the government. As mentioned earlier, development programs play a key role in transforming target populations by educating them about sexuality, identity, and rights. Similarly, these small groups occasionally receive instructional support from larger organizations, and they are impacted by flows of information that have the potential to shift local understandings, including the ways in which sexual minorities view their own behavior. To date, NGOs in Pakistan have done little in terms of supporting and transforming transgender groups. However, this may change with the arrival of new players in the NGO sector.

In this chapter, I have used pseudonyms for organizations and the people affiliated with them in order to protect their identities. Gender Solidarity Society (GSS) is one of the few registered entities run by and for khwaja siras. It has been in operation in the southern port city of Karachi since 2009, and it functions primarily as an advocacy group that speaks on behalf of khwaja siras. Since its inception, GSS has organized and participated in various activist events, such as World AIDS Day festivities, national and provincial consultation workshops, press conferences, training programs, and public protests.

GSS's Origins: Local and Transnational Influences

The transnational context of khwaja sira activism can be better understood by tracing the origins of GSS. Payal Choudhery, the president of GSS, is an illiterate khwaja sira who comes from a poor family. She started her journey as a social worker in 2006, and around the same time she met Hira, a student of gender and sexuality at a liberal arts college in the United States, and her mother, Aaliya, a veteran activist of the women's movement in Pakistan. Hira wanted to make a documentary on khwaja siras for her senior thesis, and her project connected her with Payal. Payal was suffering from a sense of disillusionment about her dream to make a difference, but her outlook changed when she met Hira. She credits Hira for inspiring her and instilling confidence in her to begin working for her community.

In fact, it was Hira who suggested that Payal set up her own organization, and she even coined the name Gender Solidarity Society. According to Aaliya, the title of the organization reflects Hira's personal philosophy as an activist and her desire for greater collaboration between different genders and sexual identities:

> When she was thinking about what she should do, we played off ideas and were a sounding board for her. I think Hira was interested in gender interaction herself. She believes there should be alliances between all the groups of the spectrum, [in order to] . . . build a strong community. Hira was keen on that happening because it was part of her philosophy . . . . But Payal had the tendency of putting people into boxes because that is the life she had led. In that sense, I think Hira's explanation of identities made a difference. She asked Payal, "So what's wrong with somebody who wants to be a cross dresser or somebody who is gay or identifies differently? What is it to you? . . . Should we be breaking people up into smaller and smaller minorities or should we be collecting them if we want to move forward?" (Author's transcript)

Payal was receptive to Hira's ideas, which Aaliya attributes to Payal's intrinsic acceptance of difference, a quality that sets her apart from most other khwaja siras. When GSS was eventually formed, Aaliya contributed to the online content of the organization's new website. Aaliya also introduced Payal to women activists and took her to various meetings. This gave Payal the opportunity to learn how other activist organizations function. The transnational links in GSS's creation are evident in Payal's relationship with Hira and Aaliya. The intervention of this mother-daughter duo was instrumental not only in establishing GSS, but also in influencing Payal's thinking and in shaping her into the activist leader she is today.

GSS has had a tenuous existence since its formation, and it almost shut down in late 2010 due to a lack of resources, including funding, education, and the skills required to keep it afloat. In early 2012, GSS's existence was yet again threatened when many of its core members were offered high-paying jobs by a transnational NGO. As part of their employment contract, they were required to step down from their posts at GSS, which they did. By early 2013, GSS's dwindling leadership was struggling to run the organization in the absence of experienced khwaja siras to replace its executive committee. In the event that GSS is forced to close its doors, transnational influences will have played a role not only in establishing the organization, but also in bringing about its demise.

Creating Activists: Change and Resistance

Dominant beliefs against same-sex sexuality in Pakistan stem from a combination of religious and cultural beliefs. The notion of sin, the fear of God and an afterlife, and views on morality and propriety shape the ways in which both the general public and khwaja siras view sexual behaviors and lifestyles. In addition, negative attitudes toward alternative sexualities are rooted in patriarchy, marriage and familial obligations, the importance of maintaining ancestral bloodlines through reproduction, and the concept of respect.

Religious and cultural notions of morality and decency play a role in shaping the legal and activist discourse around transgender rights in Pakistan. The discourse about the emancipation of transgender individuals in the Supreme Court rulings and in Pakistani media aimed at making them "decent citizens." This reasoning emphasizes the need to create job opportunities for khwaja siras in order to prevent them from leading an immoral life of begging, dancing, and prostitution. Similarly, the approach of most NGOs involved in HIV intervention in Pakistan has been consistent with this discourse. Previous efforts to promote safe-sex practices through various media failed in large measure because HIV/ AIDS-related messages did not clearly explain how the infection spreads. For example, posters attempted to communicate ideas about virus transmission through the idiom of morality. Instead of stating explicitly how the infection circulates, posters warned against leading an "immoral and unnatural lifestyle" and encouraged people to "use caution," "observe the Islamic lifestyle," and "protect our country from this shame" (Khan and Khilji 2002, 15). Informed by the failures of earlier HIV programs, some NGOs are attempting to expunge moralistic views from their intervention efforts. The following case provides an in-depth look into the ways in which social norms pertaining to sexual propriety continue to influence transgender politics despite efforts to separate morality from activism.

In late 2011, Payal and I, along with two other GSS representatives, attended a workshop hosted by an NGO called Male Health Society in Islamabad. Various NGO and CBO partners from across the country were invited to the event to share their knowledge and experience of working with marginalized communities. The training was designed to enhance the ability of the partners to work collectively. This was a sizable gathering consisting of khwaja sira, zennana, gay, and HIV/AIDS activists, along with NGO workers. Many of the participants were non-queer identifying.

One of the sessions focused on the impact of social conditioning on the well-being of MSM and transgender populations. A close analysis of this session provides useful insights into both the effects of transnationalization and the identity politics of khwaja siras. The moderator of the session, Saif, a tall and lanky man, was dressed in skinny jeans and a fitted top paired with leather boots. He stood before the participants with one hand on his hip. He held a marker in his other hand, which was supported by a limp wrist. With a slight lisp, Saif asked, "What is normal?" Met with silence, he rephrased his question: "What does the general public consider normal? A girlish boy or one who is completely like a boy?" Finally, a khwaja sira responded by saying that a person who is physically and behaviorally a man or a woman is considered normal, according to Islam and Pakistani culture. In agreement, Saif stated that society determines what is and is not normal, even though in reality all individuals are normal in and of themselves. Next, Aisha, a woman doctor wearing a *hijab* (headscarf), stated that it is the job of medical professionals to determine whether or not a person is normal or sick. In response, Saif emphasized the role of science in determining normality and abnormality, noting that scientific knowledge differs across time and space:

> Back in the day, psychology manuals used to say that homosexuality and transsexuality were abnormal, but then scientists realized that they were wrong. Today, transgender people are not considered abnormal in the US. . . . But here, even now our medical books say that it is abnormal. Perhaps people in the West are more broadminded. . . . Who a person sleeps with in their bedroom should not concern us. That is between them. (Author's transcript)

An NGO worker reacted strongly to Saif's comment by asserting that sexual encounters between men are abnormal. Surprisingly, the khwaja sira participants applauded the man's remark. Aisha echoed the NGO worker's response by declaring same-sex sexual behavior to be immoral. Again, the khwaja sira attendees applauded enthusiastically.

Saif's objective was to challenge the participants' preconceived ideas about normal and abnormal, to highlight that each society defines normalcy differently, and to make clear that those who are deemed "abnormal" have fewer rights. He emphasized that every person is normal and has equal human rights, including the right to health, regardless of their sexuality. Saif's agenda was to transform his audience into critical thinkers who are capable of emancipation from sociocultural restrictions. This form of capacity building is a vital component of HIV intervention through which individuals from marginalized groups are transformed into community leaders and avid activists.

Unfortunately, the exercise was a failure, and heated arguments broke out between the moderator and the participants who perceived Saif's radical statements as an affront to religious and social norms. To them, Saif encompassed unbridled modernity with his radical views, effeminacy, and "Western" clothes. For instance, in describing cross-cultural and temporal differences in medical information, Saif privileged knowledge originating from the West. Moreover, he advocated beliefs and practices that are considered immoral and sinful, or the antithesis of what it means to be Muslim and Pakistani. Consequently, the participants openly resisted what they were being taught because they felt their views were under attack by a "sellout."

It is both interesting and important that the khwaja sira trainees reacted to the discussion by expressing support for those who spoke against same-sex sexual behavior. By applauding their remarks, the khwaja sira activists distanced themselves from men who have sex with men, a view enhanced by their new legal status as a third sex distinct from male and female. By this logic, their sexual encounters with men would not fall under the category of same-sex sexual behavior.

Later in the session, Beena, a khwaja sira activist, reacted strongly when Saif started explaining the sexual practices of khwaja sira sex workers. When she urged him to stop focusing on the "vices" of khwaja siras, Saif suggested that she change her perception of sex work as a vice:

Beena: Please stop talking about our vices!
Saif: Beena, we cannot call it a vice.
Beena: *You* don't have to call it a sin if you don't want to, but *I* think it is a sin. Even though some khwaja siras engage in sex work, we ourselves are against it and we declare that this is wrong! Wrong! Wrong! (Author's transcript)

The audience clapped in support of Beena, and the fervor of the participants grew as Aisha went over to embrace her:

Saif: Beena considers sex work to be a bad thing, but not everyone thinks that way.
Beena: I was talking about us khwaja siras—*we* think it is bad!
Aisha: Beena is right! A vice is a vice no matter what! (Author's transcript)

In the above conversation, the moderator attempted to change Beena's negative perception about sex work by separating it from the notion of vice. Saif wanted to use this opportunity to underscore his argument that culture and society determine propriety and impropriety, and that sex work should not be considered a vice merely because people are conditioned to believe that it is wrong. Nonetheless, Beena upheld her views by defiantly declaring sex work to be a sin.

Beena's strong statement against sex work came as a surprise to me, because earlier that day I had overheard her telling a group of her khwaja sira friends that one of her students—also a workshop attendee—had been covertly engaging in sex work with a male participant at the training. Beena was excitedly giving her listeners a graphic description of her student's sexual encounter with the client. I wondered why someone whose own students participate in sex work and who takes great pleasure in talking about sex would vehemently oppose both during the training.

Beena's aggressive stance against the moderator's remarks makes sense given the presence of non-queer individuals at the workshop, some of whom had already expressed their condemnation of non-heteronormative sexual behavior. That the discussion kept focusing on the sexual behavior of khwaja siras agitated a number of transgender activists, who were uncomfortable that these issues were being discussed in the presence of people who were not khwaja siras. They were afraid that the moderator would damage the reputation of khwaja siras by exposing the particulars of their lives. Beena's strong reaction speaks to the identity politics of khwaja siras, which hinges on maintaining a public image of respectability.

This situation is further complicated by the fact that the majority of my khwaja sira interlocutors consider themselves to be sinners and view their lifestyle to be in conflict with Islam. In other words, Beena's proclamation about sex work being a sin does not merely reflect her attempt to portray khwaja siras as respectable people. Many khwaja siras believe that they are indeed sinners due to their involvement in socially and religiously prohibited behavior. However, they also believe that they are helpless due to their feminine spirit, which allows them to be attracted only to men. Moreover, many are unable to earn a "respectable" livelihood and resort to sex work due to workplace harassment or the reluctance of prospective employers to hire nonconforming individuals. That the khwaja sira trainees resisted the moderator's acceptance of their sexualized lifestyle reveals the paradox of their lives, highlighting their internal conflict between their desire for a lover and their involvement in sex work, on the one hand, and their conviction that having a lover and engaging in sex work are immoral and prohibited in Islam, on the other.

Khwaja siras neither resist behavior that is considered socially unacceptable nor advocate for it to be legally and socially sanctioned. Instead, they conceal their involvement in such activities and engage in a public representation of khwaja siras as good Muslims and responsible Pakistani citizens. For instance, during the training, Beena felt compelled to represent khwaja siras as decent members of society when Saif began discussing the sexual behavior of transgender people. Beena reacted strongly when Saif highlighted that not all khwaja siras are recipients in male-male sexual encounters:

Please don't think that we khwaja siras want that someone should have sex with us. There are so many hijras who have never done it with men. You shouldn't talk about something you don't know. Our big households where our elders live are locked up at dusk . . . and no stranger can enter their home. Many of them have been to Mecca for holy pilgrimage, and Allah's grace is upon us since we can bless people. Some of our khwaja siras even veil their faces and go out in burqas. My point is that if one woman is a character that doesn't mean everyone is like that. (Author's transcript)

Beena's response demonstrates the tendency of khwaja sira activists to represent themselves and their communities in a socially acceptable manner as respectable and religious people. She emphasized the conservatism and asexuality of khwaja sira elders and urged the moderator not to misrepresent khwaja siras by focusing exclusively on those transgender people who engage in "sin."

This representational strategy is most prominent in the media advocacy of khwaja sira activists. At the workshop, this maneuver was exercised in response to the negative remarks of the non-queer participants against same-sex sexual behavior. The transgender trainees aligned themselves with these "respectable" people and spoke out against the moderator, who was clearly in favor of the sexualized lifestyle of khwaja siras. They thought that the moderator was doing them a disservice by exposing their clandestine sexual life. They countered his claims by depicting khwaja siras as religious and moral, even though they engage in socially objectionable behavior in their private lives.

The above analysis of the workshop demonstrates the inclination of transnational NGOs to challenge the beliefs of local sexual minorities in an attempt to transform them into rights-conscious individuals. Such attempts are characteristic of organizations that receive large sums of money from international sponsors to educate vulnerable populations. Moreover, the workshop reveals the resilience of local beliefs among khwaja sira activists. Their resistance to external—and purportedly foreign—influences reveals not only their conviction involving certain religious tenets but also their propensity to maintain a positive image of their communities in an effort to gain social respectability.

Looking Ahead

Transnational forces influence the direction of khwaja sira activism when elite leaders and the invisible hand of foreign donors attempt to transform sexual minorities through capacity building. However, ethnographic research reveals the complex realities on the ground, where khwaja sira leaders encounter and address transnationalizing forces by negotiating and resisting ideas that do not resonate with them, while also accepting those ideas that hold the promise of individual and communal gain. Khwaja siras are not passive beings who unquestioningly adhere to the views that are imposed on them by NGOs. Instead, they openly contest ideas that either conflict with their long-standing beliefs or could lead to a loss of respect. Moreover, transgender activists are heavily vested in representing khwaja siras in a manner that is culturally and religiously appropriate. That khwaja sira activists are allured by globalizing influences speaks to the power of money, but the fact that they also resist these influences reveals the resilience of culture in the face of change.

Since about 2000, resistance from local activists has coincided with an increasing emphasis on indigenism in the NGO sector in South Asia and elsewhere. For instance, in neighboring India, queer organizing was largely motivated by the interests of elite leaders who, for a long time, played a central role in defining the contours of indigeneity. Today, however, foreign donors are increasingly interested in supporting indigenous sexual minorities by funding both new and existing CBOs. As a result, the constitution of queer groups has started to change as a host of new social actors take up leadership positions and vie for a share of the funding pool. In terms of organizing, these developments, while giving rise to a moderately equitable power structure, also create conflict within and between queer groups in India. How will the surge in importance of CBOs and indigenous leadership affect khwaja sira activism in Pakistan? Will disagreements between elite and indigenous leaders escalate, and what form will they take as various stakeholders continue to contend over who should represent transgender people? What unanticipated outcomes will arise from evolving donor interests and their changing funding patterns, and how will they continue to shape khwaja sira activism?

References and Further Research

Adams, Vincanne, and Stacey Leigh Pigg. 2005. "Introduction: The Moral Object of Sex." In *Sex in Development: Science, Sexuality, and Morality in Global Perspective*, edited by Vincanne Adams and Stacey Leigh Pigg, 1–38. Durham, NC: Duke University Press.

Awan, Muhammad Safeer, and Muhammad Sheeraz. 2011. "Queer but Language: A Sociolinguistic Study of *Farsi*." *International Journal of Humanities and Social Science* 1, no. 10: 127–135.

Bochenek, Michael, and Kyle Knight. 2012. "Nepal's Third Gender and the Recognition of Gender Identity." Jurist, April 23. http://jurist.org/hotline/2012/04/bochenek-knight-gender.php.

Dave, Naisargi. 2008. "Between Queer Ethics and Sexual Morality." In *Frontiers*, edited by Monica Narula, Shuddhabrata Sengupta, Jeebesh Bagchi, and Ravi Sundaram, 387–395. Sarai Reader 7. New Delhi: Centre for Studies in Developing Societies.

Junejo, Tanvir. 1994. "Eunuchs: The Cultural Heritage of Sindh." *Sindh University Arts Research Journal* 29: 32–46.

Khan, Shivananda, and Tahir Khilji. 2002. *Pakistan Enhanced HIV/AIDS Program: Social Assessment and Mapping of Men Who Have Sex with Men (MSM) in Lahore*. Report for the World Bank, Pakistan. Naz Foundation International. http://www.nfi.net/NFI%20Publications/Assessments/LahoreFullAssessRp.pdf.

Naqvi, Nauman, and Hasan Mujtaba. 1997. "Two Baluchi Buggas, a Sindhi Zenana, and the Status of Hijras in Contemporary Pakistan." In *Islamic Homosexualities: Culture, History, and Literature*, edited by Stephen O. Murray and Will Roscoe, 262–266. New York: New York University Press.

Pamment, Claire. 2010. "Hijraism: Jostling for a Third Space in Pakistani Politics." *TDR: The Drama Review* 54, no. 2: 29–50.

Reddy, Gayatri. 2005. *With Respect to Sex: Negotiating Hijra Identity in South India*. Chicago: University of Chicago Press.

Toor, Saadia. 2011. "Gender, Sexuality, and Islam under the Shadow of Empire." *The Scholar and Feminist Online* 9, no. 3. http://sfonline.barnard.edu/religion/toor_01.htm.

12

Establishing a Traditional Medicine Industry in Bangladesh

KAREN MCNAMARA

Across the globe, the last several decades have seen an increased recognition of and demand for traditional medicines and herbal products. The cures used in traditional medical systems are now considered part of the array of drugs called pharmaceuticals, and more and more they are being produced on a large scale and sold across the globe by pharmaceutical companies. Bangladesh, where several traditional medical systems have been practiced for centuries, has had its traditional medicine and pharmaceutical industry transformed as a result of these global shifts. Both internal and export demand have reconfigured the pharmaceutical industry, leading to the rewriting of laws and conflicts about appropriate policies. Always in the background are the strictures of the World Health Organization (WHO) and other international monitoring bodies, because partaking in the global market means adhering to policies set by global regulatory organizations. This case study examines changes in the pharmaceutical industry in Bangladesh and the goals of the Bangladeshi state to increase its footprint in the global marketplace, especially as it relates to traditional medical systems.

In Bangladesh and elsewhere, various forms and types of medicine are used in a pluralistic health-care system. Some of these medical treatments are allopathic (called biomedicine in the West), using practices and technologies based in the biological sciences to diagnose and treat diseases. Allopathic or biomedical approaches view bodies as universally the same, despite differences in outer appearances and in social and economic contexts. Other treatments, including Ayurveda and Unani, are considered traditional or indigenous medicines, which rely primarily on herbs and other natural components. Both systems understand health and illness to be connected to social and natural environments. Ayurveda, often translated as the "knowledge of longevity," is associated with Hinduism. Unani is the South Asian form of Greco-Islamic medicine. Nowadays, traditional medicines are often commoditized and manufactured using modern, large-scale production methods, so that traditional medicines are sold both in prepackaged capsules and bottles and also as unprocessed herbs.

Patients seeking cures from traditional medicines can find and buy these medicines in multiple forms and places. Patients can directly approach a practitioner of traditional medicine, either in his or her home, medical office, clinic, or even on the street. Sometimes the practitioner makes the specific medicines needed to treat the patient, but often

186

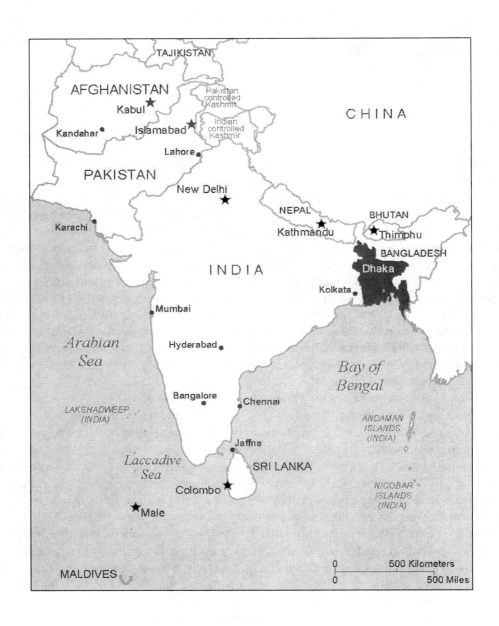

Box 12.1

What Is the World Health Organization (WHO)?

Part of the United Nations, the WHO has its headquarters in Geneva, Switzerland. Employing more than 7,000 individuals in 150 countries, it provides leadership on global health issues, monitors global health trends, and helps to set policies, such as those related to drugs discussed here (http://www.who.int/en/).

Shohidul Islam Kobiraj, an herbal medicine practitioner, sits on the street with his assortment of herbs, ready to compound them as necessary for his patients. *(Photo by Karen McNamara)*

the practitioner will sell premade manufactured varieties of traditional remedies. It is also common for a patient to buy packaged forms of traditional medicines from retail stores of different manufacturing companies, directly from company representatives, from pharmacies, or even from allopathic practitioners.

In Bangladesh, the national and international focus on pharmaceuticals influenced the production and regulation of traditional herbal medicines used in Ayurvedic and Unani medical systems. Encouragement from WHO and the increasing critiques of the pharmaceutical industry within Bangladesh led the government to create the Drugs (Control) Ordinance in 1982. This measure resulted in numerous controversies about who was on the

---

Box 12.2

Examining the "Social Lives" of Medicines

A useful methodology for analyzing the role of medicines in contemporary South Asia is to follow their social lives. This means following medicines from their pharmaceutical production to testing, marketing, distribution, prescription, and consumption. Each phase of a medicine's life reveals the multiple actors, policies, transactions, ideas, and values associated with the process. Here I focus mainly on the production phase of traditional medicines. To do this research in Bangladesh, it is essential to know and speak Bengali, which makes it possible to read government documents, company reports, and advertisements, as well as to interview and talk with local people, whether government officials, company owners, or shopkeepers of "drug" stores.

Expert Committee, about a ban on importing foreign-made medicines, and about which allopathic and traditional medicines were considered essential or banned as nonessential. The Bangladeshi government appointed academics, allopathic doctors, and health activists to the first eight-member Expert Committee, formed on April 27, 1982, to review drug manufacture and sales in the country and to make recommendations for a National Drug Policy. The 1982 ordinance also officially recognized Unani and Ayurvedic medicines as drugs for the first time.

This case study examines the production of traditional medicines in Bangladesh as it has been transformed by these broader forces, policies, and institutions. As detailed in the study, the issues involved in these changes are complex, involving not just economic and policy implications but the social and cultural meanings of medical practices. A renewed interest in traditional medicines is related to both the success of the local allopathic pharmaceutical industry and the market potential of producing and exporting herbal medicines globally. Traditional manufacturers are contesting the meaning of herbal medicine in Bangladesh because some allopathic companies have recently started to manufacture a new category of "modern" herbal medicine. In response, the Bangladeshi government issued a new herbal drug-manufacturing license in addition to the existing manufacturing licenses for the manufacture of allopathic medicines and the predominantly herbal Unani and Ayurvedic medicines.

History and Overview of Traditional Medicine in South Asia

Historically, traditional medical practices developed alongside allopathic ones, and what is considered traditional medicine has changed across time. Many traditional medical practices, including Ayurveda and Unani, which are healing practices indigenous to South Asia, were professionalized and institutionalized in South Asia during British colonial rule. Unani and Ayurveda both have a highly developed pharmacopoeia of primarily herbal and natural medicines, which they have shared and traded over the centuries. By the nineteenth and twentieth centuries, the practice of Ayurveda was radically different from the classical texts it was based on, and it was deeply influenced by Unani medicine. Unani and Ayurveda have a shared history and medical foundation, in that both understand the body as composed of humors. Because of this similarity, Unani and Ayurveda are often lumped together or band together for political clout, since they receive less state support than allopathy does.

Ayurveda

Ayurveda literally means "the science of longevity," and important texts written about Ayurveda (from about 2500 BCE to 1000 BCE) present the practice as a unitary body of classical medical knowledge. The two main texts of Ayurveda are the *Caraka-Samhita* and the *Susruta-Samhita*, composed well before 500 CE and written respectively by Caraka (also spelled Charaka) and Susruta (also Sushruta). The former text deals primarily with pharmacology, and the latter with surgical procedures. These texts describe three humors: *vata* (gaseous element or wind), *pitta* (fiery element or bile), and *kapha* (liquid element or phlegm). These three humors make up the fundamental elements, or *dhatus*, of the human body, and they interact with seven basic constituents of the body—chyle (from the intestines), blood, flesh, fat, bone, marrow, and semen—as well as bodily wastes. Disease is often understood to occur when an imbalance of these *dhatus* arises, and this imbalance is treated through pharmacological or surgical intervention. Disease can also involve other factors, such as weather and season of the year, food and diet, inappropriate behavior, emotional agitation, or sins from a past life. Central to Ayurvedic pharmacology are the five properties inherent in all substances: *rasa* (taste), *guna* (quality), *virya* (potency), *vipaka* (assimilability), and *prabhava* (inherent nature or specific action). Drugs are divided into two categories, depending on whether they purify (*samsodhana*) or pacify (*samsamana*). Humans are envisioned as a small representation of the larger natural world outside themselves. As Ayurveda developed over time, its textual traditions and descriptions often differed from the multiple practices of Ayurveda, which sometimes led to new texts that incorporated new ideas and practices.

For a contemporary account of the history of Ayurveda by an Indian practitioner, see the video *Origin and History of Ayurveda*, presented by the National Library of Ayurveda Medicine and hosted by Sumit Kesarkar (http://www.youtube.com/watch?v=G1OOSP_PbNo).

Unani

As Ayurveda was practiced and patronized through the medieval period in India (sixteenth–seventeenth centuries), new medical documents associated with Averroes (or Ibn

Rushd, 1126–1198), Avicenna (or Ibn Sīnā, 980–1037), Galen (129–c. 199), and others led to the development of Unani practices of medicine. Accordingly, Unani is commonly described as Greco-Islamic, because of its roots in the Middle East and the influences of both Greek Galenic medicine and prophetic medicine. Unani medical practices spread to South Asia through the first Arab invasion in the eighth century and the establishment of Muslim regimes, including in Bengal in the thirteenth century. In the fourteenth century, Unani began developing strong roots in the Indian subcontinent, even though it had been practiced from the western Mediterranean to Southeast Asia over the previous thousand years. In the nineteenth century, the main texts used by Unani practitioners (*hakims*) in India were Arabic translations of the medical texts of Avicenna, Hippocrates, Aristotle, and Galen.

Unani's understanding of health is based mainly on the balance of four humors. The four humors (*akhlaat*) are blood, black bile, yellow bile, and phlegm, which combine with the four basic qualities (*quwaat*) of heat, cold, moisture, and dryness. Humoral balance is based on such external factors as climate, age, lifestyle, the environment, and the locale of the patient. The combination of the external elements and humors determines a person's temperament (*mizaj*). Today, Unani medicines are used not only to bring a person's humors back into harmony, but also to restore balance between a patient and nature. Patients are treated by adjusting their normal routines or through various regimental therapies, including cupping, purging, massage, surgery, or drug therapy. Products used in drugs come from various regions in the world and include herbs, spices, animal parts, and fruits. Natural medicines—including many drugs formulated to treat chronic sickness—are considered the most suitable for treatment because they provide few side effects.

Allopathy

In South Asia, the term *allopathy*, or *allopathic medicine*, commonly refers to medical treatments known as biomedicine in the United States. It comes from the Greek words *allos*, which means "different," and *pathos*, which refers to suffering or passion. The term was coined in Europe during the eighteenth century to distinguish it from homeopathy, which was a common form of medical treatment at the time. The word *homeopathy* derives from the Greek word *homoios*, meaning "similar." One of homeopathy's broad principles is the *principle of similars* or that "like cures like." Thus, homeopathic treatments are based on the idea of treating illnesses with substances that mirror the patient's symptoms. Allopathy, on the other hand, is based on treatments that are different from, or the opposite of, a patient's symptoms.

Colonialism and Medicine

The histories of medicine in South Asia reflect the development of British colonial rule and how it influenced medical policies and practices during the late nineteenth and early twentieth centuries. The British colonial state gave more support to allopathy than to indigenous practices like Unani and Ayurveda, which the British viewed as inferior.

Allopathy became a symbol of modernity and progress and marked the superiority of colonial rule. Therefore, the expansion and support of allopathy was one way that the colonial state sought to establish and expand its control of South Asian society. At the same time, there were many Indians in colonial India who were interested in learning and practicing allopathic medicine, which often gave them more power and influence. Some practitioners of traditional medicine also sought to modernize and revitalize their practices by incorporating modern medical techniques and ideas, establishing teaching institutions, creating professional organizations, and printing texts and journals.

The large-scale manufacture of indigenous medicines began during larger movements to revive Unani and Ayurveda in colonial India during the late nineteenth and early twentieth century. There were calls to revitalize medical knowledge and improve the poor quality of traditional practitioners and traditional medication. According to Claudia Liebeskind (2002), in the first half of the twentieth century, *hakims* (Unani practitioners) supported two revivalist strategies: either to integrate Unani with allopathy, and thus create a system that was superior to both, or to keep Unani pure and revive it from within. However, advocates of both strategies agreed that indigenous systems of medicine had declined, and they wanted to prove that Unani was a science. Two well-known revivalists were P.C. Ray (1861–1944) and Hakim Ajmal Khan (1863–1927). A chemist, Ray argued that Ayurvedic medicines needed to be reconfigured along modern lines by using up-to-date scientific methods to extract the active components. Khan, a well-known hakim affiliated with the Congress Party, sought to revitalize Unani by emulating medical pedagogy used in Europe and by incorporating modern anatomy and surgery.

Ray and Khan both thought that traditional systems of medicine were declining largely because of British colonial influence, and they saw the revival of Unani and Ayurvedic traditions as a part of the larger nationalist struggles to end British rule. They thought that the manufacture and distribution of Ayurvedic and Unani medicines could fill the gap left by foreign medicines, which were banned at the time. Indians were also encouraged to buy nationally manufactured medicines. Part of the "anticolonial nationalism" involved an attempt to be modern and economically developed without being Western. Through this nationalist politics, traditional medicines became associated with certain languages and religions. For example, some nationalists began to identify Unani as "Muslim" medicine and Ayurveda as "Hindu" medicine. After independence, when the Indian and Pakistani states officially promoted allopathy, Unani and Ayurvedic practitioners struggled to define their practices in relation to it.

Pluralism in Practice

There is much overlap among allopathic, Unani, Ayurvedic, and other healing practices, creating a pluralism that defines medicine in South Asia and exists to varying degrees throughout the region. In Bangladesh, in addition to allopathy, Unani, and Ayurveda, homeopathy and many local healing practices are used, including herbal remedies, spiritual and religious healing methods, bone-setting, and regional practices of Islamic or prophetic medicine.

These boxed herbal Unani medicines are sold on the street in Dhaka. *(Photo by Karen McNamara)*

Patients often take advantage of a plural medical environment by seeking out different types of medicines and medical practitioners depending on the availability of the treatment, the seriousness and type of illness, and the cost of the treatment. The commonality between most treatments is the use of some type of medicinal drug.

Manufacturing Medicines in Bangladesh

After independence in 1971, the new Bangladeshi state, much like the colonial state before it, gave more support to allopathic health ideologies, institutions, and practices than to indigenous ones like Unani and Ayurveda. The Bangladeshi state sets public health agendas. It also influences the size of pharmaceutical markets by establishing limits and policies about the manufacture of drugs, and it sets regulations for product approval and advertisements. However, the state is not the only force involved in these decisions and policies. International institutions like the World Health Organization and the World Trade Organization (WTO) also create, influence, and enforce regulations involving health policies and the pharmaceutical industry. Thus, allopathic and traditional pharmaceutical industries in Bangladesh are connected both to state and transnational institutions and to global regulations and trade. Some Bangladeshi manufacturers of traditional medicine are redefining their practices in order to gain political and market legitimacy in light of this global context.

In the early 1980s, eight Bangladeshi multinational drug companies manufactured 75 percent of all pharmaceuticals (by value). Also at this time, about $30 million of raw materials were imported, which created conflicts within the government due to a limited foreign exchange. Therefore, in 1982, the Drugs (Control) Ordinance, also called the National Drug Policy, was formulated with encouragement from WHO to respond to public criticism of the powerful multinational pharmaceutical industry. This policy adopted WHO's worldwide guidelines in *The Selection of Essential Drugs (1979)*, declaring 150 drugs essential to public health and banning drugs considered nonessential. (Later versions of the list from WHO retitled the document *The Selection of Essential Medicines*.) Controversies ensued about who was on the drugs committee established under the 1982 ordinance and about which medicines were banned as nonessential under WHO guidelines, including traditional medicines and imported and locally made allopathic medicines. The ordinance emphasized a reliance on the national production of medicines, which included measures to protect local manufacturers. No drug imports were allowed from multinational manufacturers if they were already being made locally.

Both local and international pharmaceutical firms directly opposed the new ordinance. In addition, foreign governments argued that the new policy would discourage private investors from investing in Bangladesh. The pressure from foreign governments was considerable, since, at the time, approximately 80 percent of the Bangladeshi government's development funds came from foreign aid. The Bangladeshi government gradually allowed some banned products to be manufactured locally again, and by 1986 the drug policy was supported by most local pharmaceutical companies. In 1981 the top five firms in sales of pharmaceuticals were all multinational corporations, but by 1991 the top three firms were all Bangladeshi-owned (Reich 1994).

The new policy was also significant because it was the first effort at official regulatory control over traditional medicine in the country. Created during British colonial rule, the Drugs Act of 1940 did not regulate traditional medicine. Therefore, Unani and Ayurvedic medicines were not officially recognized and regulated as drugs until the institution of the 1982 ordinance, which included many new regulations to monitor and register traditional drug manufacturers. Particularly important was the recommendation to create a National Drug Control Laboratory to develop and set appropriate standards and specifications for Unani and Ayurvedic drugs. This coincided with a rise during the 1980s in the number of local manufacturers of traditional medicines. According to Zafrullah Chowdhury, the author of *The Politics of Essential Drugs: The Makings of a Successful Health Strategy* (1996), some groups were alarmed by this development because they thought that there was not adequate control of traditional medicines, while others claimed that the stricter controls on allopathic medicines had contributed to the increase in sales of traditional drugs.

In 1992 these tensions in Bangladesh between the state, the Unani and Ayurvedic manufacturing companies, and the allopathic manufacturing companies culminated in a lawsuit. The Unani, Ayurvedic, and homeopathic manufacturing committees filed a lawsuit against the Bangladeshi government because the Ministry of Health and Family Welfare had not included them in a new committee formed in 1992 to amend the 1982 National Drug Policy, even though the Ministry of Health had assured Unani, Ayurved, and homeopathic manufacturers they would have representation on the committee. Not only were they left out of the Ministry of Health meeting, but during the meeting it was decided that "Unani, Ayurved, and Homeopathic medicines [were] not modern medicines and as such they did not feel it necessary to include their representatives in the said committee" (Writ Petition 1992, 4). In their lawsuit, the traditional drug manufacturers alleged that the new review committee was breaking the law under the 1982 ordinance, which had established the legitimacy of the medicines they manufactured, and that it was violating the constitution by not including them. The lawsuit included a reference to WHO's recognition of traditional medicine and its encouragement to develop traditional medicine in all countries, including Bangladesh. The lawsuit also alleged that "the Government [was] being influenced by the manufacturers of the allopathic medicine and to perpetuate their monopoly in the business of medicine and to shut out the petitioners [they] have most illegally and with malafide intentions constituted the present committee" (Writ Petition 1992, 5), excluding the homeopathic, Unani, and Ayurvedic manufacturers. Six years later, in 1998, the traditional medicinal manufacturing committees won their lawsuit against the government.

TRIPS and Manufacturing Pharmaceuticals

The success of allopathic pharmaceutical manufacturing in Bangladesh is due in part to the Agreement on Trade-Related Aspects of Intellectual Property Rights (TRIPS). The TRIPS Agreement is the basis for global agreements about intellectual property rights and trade. It was negotiated in 1994, has been signed by two-thirds of the world's nations, and is regulated by the World Trade Organization. Under the TRIPS Agreement, patents and processes are granted twenty years of protection from the date they are registered. Protection means that the creators of patents and processes have the right to prevent others from using them without appropriate payment. All members of WTO are required to introduce or upgrade to a standardized level of protection. The deadlines for conforming to these requirements varied, depending on a country's state of "development." Developed countries had until 1996, developing countries had until 2000 (some extended until 2005), and forty-nine countries considered "least developed" have until 2016 to pass legislation requiring patent protection for pharmaceuticals and agricultural chemicals (Foreman 2002).

Bangladesh falls under the category of a least developed country (LDC) and so was allowed to manufacture pharmaceuticals without purchasing patents until 2016. This meant that many allopathic medicines could be produced without paying the companies that had developed them in laboratories, often at great cost. However, developing and least developed countries felt that developed countries were pressuring them to conform to TRIPS rules before the 2016 deadline. In 2001, the Doha Declaration was adopted by WTO to reaffirm the flexibility of WTO members to access essential medicines. In this declaration, it was agreed that TRIPS "should be interpreted and implemented in a manner supportive of WTO Members' right to protect public health and, in particular, to promote access to medicines for all" (quoted in Foreman 2002, 20). Even with the Doha Declaration, many countries are still under pressure to adopt TRIPS more quickly and to make legislation for even stronger protection of patents than is required by TRIPS.

In Bangladesh, a new National Drug Policy was formulated in 2005, partially to take advantage of the TRIPS rule that allows least developed countries to produce pharmaceuticals with patent exemption until 2016. Of the forty-nine countries that are considered LDCs, Bangladesh is the only one to have a manufacturing base. Private industry is frustrated with the government delay in improving the Bangladesh Drugs Testing Laboratory, which is not recognized by some European nations, and hence denies Bangladesh export options. Therefore, the private sector market plans to open its own independent standardized testing laboratory. The new 2005 drug policy also repealed the price control mechanism for most drugs, which led to price increases, causing many drugs to be unaffordable at the local level, leading to widespread public criticism.

One significant growth area is the herbal medicine market, especially since many herbal medicines, including Ayurveda and Unani, are increasingly popular globally. The herbal pharmaceutical market in Bangladesh was estimated to be around Tk 100 crore (US$14.5 million) in 2004, while WHO reports that the global market is over US$60 billion annually and growing steadily. Herbal pharmaceutical companies in Bangladesh are eager to become bigger players in this global market. To encourage this growth, the Bangladeshi government set up a business promotion council for the herbal pharmaceutical sector in 2004. The Export Promotion Bureau lists exportable items, including 136 homeopathic medicines, 52 Unani medicines, 52 Ayurvedic medicines, and 48 herbal plants (Haque 2004). Part of the promotion of these medicines includes a call to increase the number of herbal plants that are grown in Bangladesh in order to become less dependent on imports of raw (usually plant) materials.

An indication of the global reach of the modern herbal medicine market in Bangladesh can be seen in the websites of two of the leading manufacturers, Hamdard Laboratories (WAQF) Bangladesh (http://www.hamdard.com.bd/) and Modern Herbal (http://www.modernherbal.com/).

Most herbal pharmaceuticals in Bangladesh are either Ayurvedic or Unani medicines. The highly developed pharmacopoeia of herbal/natural medicines is an important component of both Unani and Ayurveda treatment. Rather than being made by local practitioners themselves, most Unani and Ayurvedic medicines are now mass-produced, packaged, labeled, and sold as a commodity. In 2004, there were more than 300 pharmaceutical companies of traditional medicine in Bangladesh, often offering incentives, training, and employment for traditional practitioners (Osman 2004). According to government data, by 2008 this number had increased to more than 422 traditional medicine manufacturing companies. It is common for herbal pharmaceutical companies to provide free consultations with traditional practitioners at their retail stores. The government is promoting the development of these companies and sees them as a potential export industry. In another step to open up the trade in herbal medicines, the 2005 National Drug Policy also mentions herbal medicines for the first time in its description of registration criteria. The inclusion of a new category of "herbal" medicine in this policy is significant because it opens the door to all types of herbal medicines, not just Unani and Ayurveda. Not surprisingly, some Unani and Ayurvedic manufacturers are contesting the production of herbal medicines that are not Ayurvedic or Unani.

In 2006 the government also insisted Unani and Ayurvedic manufacturers improve quality controls in their production. All medicines are required to follow the guidelines for good manufacturing practices (GMP) as set by WHO. A GMP certificate is given to manufacturing facilities for a certain product if it meets standards for base materials, premises, equipment, processes, documentation, training, and staff hygiene. Although WHO sets the standards for GMP or "current good manufacturing practices," it does not actually carry out inspections. In Bangladesh the certificates are issued either by the government, through the Directorate of Drug Administration (DDA), or by international organizations, such as UNICEF. By 2007 the DDA had certified thirty facilities for export, and UNICEF had fully GMP-certified four companies and partially certified two (i.e., not all their facilities or products were certified). This certification gives Bangladeshi manufacturers a valued credential to help them expand the sale of their medicines globally.

In the summer of 2006, Hamdard Laboratories (WAQF) Bangladesh, a manufacturer of Unani medicines, received government praise for passing certification from the International Organization for Standardization, giving it valued credentials to compete in a global market. These standards and other classifications can be viewed as sites of power in which flows of knowledge, capital, and resources are channeled and organized in specific ways. In addition, the regulation of drug production and compliance with good manufacturing practices set by WHO encourages companies to comply and conform to standardization as a form of symbolic capital representing their eligibility to participate in a global marketplace.

The promotion and expansion of herbal medicines has caused tensions in Bangladesh, especially when the DDA created a new herbal manufacturing license in 2009. Allopathic pharmaceutical companies were the primary firms pushing the Bangladeshi government to issue this new herbal manufacturing license. These allopathic companies, perhaps not surprisingly, were those cited in the 1992 lawsuit brought by the Unani, Ayurved, and homeopathic manufacturing committees against the Ministry of Health. In the lawsuit, these allopathic companies were alleged to have influenced the government against traditional medicines. Although Unani and Ayurvedic medicines are predominantly herbal, most Unani and Ayurvedic companies were not interested in the new herbal manufacturing license because they operate under an Ayurvedic or Unani drug manufacturing license. Therefore, it was mostly allopathic companies that were interested in manufacturing under the new herbal medicine license. Their interest in herbal medicines arose not only because of the increasing global demand for green, natural, and herbal medicines, but also because of the coming expiration of the TRIPS agreement in 2016, under which allopathic companies may no longer produce many allopathic medicines without purchasing a patent. By moving into "herbal" medicines, which carry few patents, allopathic companies hope to supplement the uncertain allopathic market.

In August 2009, I met with an official from the Bangladesh Directorate of Drug Administration. When I mentioned that I had heard of a lawsuit involving the new herbal license, he did not seem very concerned about it or worried that it might change the issuance of herbal drug manufacturing licenses. He was quick to let me know the official version of the story: the government had decided to create a new herbal drug license in 2007 because "some herbs are not in Unani and Ayurvedic systems, but are useful and are used in the modern world." He told me that the herbal license had become official and that the board had agreed on a definition that defined herbal medicinals in multiple forms:

- *Herbal medicines* include herbs, herbal materials, herbal preparations, and finished herbal products.
- *Herbs* include crude materials that can be derived from lichen, algae, fungi, or higher plants such as leaves, flowers, fruit, fruiting bodies, seeds, stems, wood, bark, roots, rhizomes, or other parts, which may be entire, fragmented, or powdered.
- *Herbal materials* include, in addition to herbs, fresh juices, gums, fixed oils, essential oils, resins, and dry powders or herbs.
- *Herbal preparations* are the basis for finished herbal products and may include comminuted or cut herbal materials or extracts, tinctures, and fatty oils of herbal materials.
- *Finished herbal products* are medicinal products containing as active substances exclusively herbal drugs or herbal drug preparations. They may consist of herbal preparations made from one or more herbs. However, herbal medicines may contain natural organic or inorganic active ingredients, which are not of plant origin. They may also contain excipients in addition to the active ingredients.

With a definition, testing criteria, and a set of reference books for drug manufacturers to follow, herbal licenses can be granted. The DDA hopes that the finalization of these criteria will help the sector to grow in a disciplined manner. In 2009, only four companies had herbal licenses, but more than twenty companies were awaiting approval.

During our meeting, another man heard me asking about the new herbal license and commented that the new license should not be allowed and that "those" medicines had no "tradition." I found out later that he had his own small Unani drug company. In interviews with other Unani companies, I brought up the topic of the new herbal license. The owner of one of the first Unani companies in Bangladesh said that "there are no books or formulary for new herbal medicines and the pharmacopoeia are not the same because people get information from sources like the Internet." Indeed, such statements indicate that many Unani and Ayurvedic manufacturers do not consider new herbal medicines to be part of the history and tradition of herbal medicine in Bangladesh. Traditional manufacturers also fear that the new herbal license will create even more competition in the market for herbal medicines.

These proposed broad-based definitions of herbal medicine also show how Bangladesh's drug administration is drawing from a much wider range of sources to define what drugs can be produced under the new herbal drug license. When I talked with a government official in the Bangladesh Drug Administration in August 2009, he told me that the administration had compiled the following reference books and book series for herbal medicines:

Modern herbal medicines packaged according to international standards and ready for sale. *(Photo by Karen McNamara)*

- *The ABC Clinical Guide to Herbs* (from the American Botanical Council)
- American Herbal Pharmacopeia and Therapeutic Compendium (book series)
- *British Herbal Pharmacopeia*
- *The Complete German Commission E Monographs: Therapeutic Guide to Herbal Medicines*
- *E/S/C/O/P Monographs: The Scientific Foundation for Herbal Products*
- *Herbal Drugs and Phytopharmaceuticals*
- *Mosby's Drug Consultant*
- *PDR for Herbal Medicines*
- WHO Monographs on Selected Medicinal Plants (book series)

Before this list was developed, only a national pharmacopeia for Unani and Ayurvedic medicines was used as a reference for manufacturers. Therefore, how Unani and Ayurvedic manufacturing companies produce, brand, and market their medicines becomes more significant, as they are all using the same formulas to make their medicines. As one marketing manager at a Unani company told me, "It is like imagining a curry, where everyone who makes it uses the same ingredients, but it comes out differently for each person . . . it matters how it is cooked." However, the new herbal medicines do not necessarily follow the national formulas for making Unani and Ayurvedic medicines. Instead, they are developed (though not necessarily tested for results) on the basis of new knowledge from the global market of possible herbal cures.

Conclusion

In the first lawsuit about amending the National Drug Policy of 1982, WHO was mentioned as a de facto witness because of its authority as a global institution. The authority of WHO is called into play as a legitimate source of knowledge (and evidence), often for contradictory purposes, both by the state (in its policies) and by other local actors, such as the traditional manufacturers. WHO gives technical advice but does not establish institutions. In Bangladesh, this advice is used in a range of policy situations, such as creating the curriculum for the schools, as well as establishing good manufacturing practices, quality control, and guidelines for ensuring the efficacy of medicines.

The development of national drug policies in Bangladesh coincided with global priorities to use pharmaceuticals to treat health, as represented by international institutions like WHO and WTO. In addition, national drug-production companies expanded in the 1980s during the liberalization of the Bangladeshi economy. These economic and policy shifts led to national debates about the role and production of traditional medicine in Bangladesh. As herbal and traditional medicines gain in popularity and acceptance (the U.S. National Institutes of Health now has a center that includes traditional medicines), these examples and debates reveal the struggle to standardize and regulate these medicines on a global and national scale.

As a less developed country, yet with changing traditions of herbal medicines in Unani and Ayurveda, Bangladesh is well positioned to become part of this global trade. However, globalization also means following international guidelines and regulations. Therefore, the opening of the global market for pharmaceuticals also means a tightening of regulations. For Bangladeshi drug manufacturers, meeting these regulations will allow entry into the global marketplace, an opportunity that brings the possibility of growth as well as uncertainty for the future.

References and Further Research

Alam, Md. Jahangir. 2007. *Traditional Medicine in Bangladesh: Issues and Challenges.* Dhaka: Asiatic Society of Bangladesh.

Alavi, Seema. 2005. "Unani Medicine in the Nineteenth-Century Public Sphere: Urdu Texts and the Oudh Akhbar." *Indian Economic and Social History Review* 42, no. 1: 101–129.

Attewell, Guy N.A. 2007. *Refiguring Unani Tibb: Plural Healing in Late Colonial India.* Hyderabad, India: Orient Longman.

Baber, Zaheer. 1996. *The Science of Empire: Scientific Knowledge, Civilization, and Colonial Rule in India.* Albany: State University of New York Press.

Bode, Maarten. 2008. *Taking Traditional Knowledge to the Market: The Modern Image of the Ayurvedic and Unani Industry, 1980–2000.* Hyderabad, India: Orient Longman.

Chowdhury, Zafrullah. 1996. *The Politics of Essential Drugs: The Makings of a Successful Health Strategy: Lessons from Bangladesh.* Dhaka, Bangladesh: University Press.

Foreman, Martin. 2002. *Patents, Pills and Public Health: Can TRIPS Deliver?* London: Panos Institute.

Habib, S. Irfan, and Druv Raina. 2005. "Reinventing Traditional Medicine: Method, Institutional Change, and the Manufacture of Drugs and Medication in Late Colonial India." In *Asian Medicine and Globalization*, edited by Joseph S. Alter, 67–77. Philadelphia: University of Pennsylvania Press.

Haque, Zahidul. 2004. "Business Promotion Council for Herbal Medicine Sector on Cards." *Daily Star* (Dhaka), August 1.

Hardiman, David. 2009. "*Indian Medical* Indigeneity: From Nationalist Assertion to the Global Market." *Social History* 34, no. 3: 263–283.

Langford, Jean. 2002. *Fluent Bodies: Ayurvedic Remedies for Postcolonial Imbalance*. Durham, NC: Duke University Press.

Leslie, Charles. 1976. "The Ambiguities of Medical Revivalism in Modern India." In *Asian Medical Systems: A Comparative Study*, edited by Charles M. Leslie, 356–367. Berkeley: University of California Press.

Liebeskind, Claudia. 2002. "Arguing Science: Unani *Tibb*, Hakims and Biomedicine in India, 1900–50." In *Plural Medicine, Tradition and Modernity, 1800–2000*, edited by Waltraud Ernst, 58–75. New York: Routledge.

Osman, Ferdous Arfina. 2004. *Policy Making in Bangladesh: A Study of the Health Policy Process*. Dhaka, Bangladesh: A.H. Development Publishing House.

Petryna, Adriana, Andrew Lakoff, and Arthur Kleinman. 2006. *Global Pharmaceuticals: Ethics, Markets, Practices*. Durham, NC: Duke University Press.

Reich, Michael R. 1994. "Bangladesh Pharmaceutical Policy and Politics." *Health Policy and Planning* 9, no. 2: 130–143.

Ross, Anamaria Iosif. 2012. *The Anthropology of Alternative Medicine*. New York: Berg.

Sheehan, Helen E., and S.J. Hussain. 2002. "Unani Tibb: History, Theory, and Contemporary Practice in South Asia." *Annals of the American Academy of Political and Social Science* 583: 122–135.

World Bank. March 2008. *Public and Private Sector Approaches to Improving Pharmaceutical Quality in Bangladesh*. Bangladesh Development Series Paper no. 23. Dhaka, Bangladesh: World Bank Human Development Unit, South Asia Region. http://apps.who.int/medicinedocs/documents/s16761e/s16761e.pdf.

World Health Organization. December 2008. "Traditional Medicine." Fact Sheet no. 134. http://www.who.int/mediacentre/factsheets/fs134/en/.

Whyte, Susan Reynolds, Sjaak Van der Greest, and Anita Hardon. 2003. *Social Lives of Medicines*. Cambridge, UK: Cambridge University Press.

Writ Petition No. 3892. 1992. Supreme Court of Bangladesh.

Wujastyk, Dominik. 2001. *The Roots of Āyurveda*. Rev. ed. New Delhi: Penguin.

Zannat, Mahbuba. 2007. "Drug Policy Lacks Control Over Price." *Daily Star* (Dhaka), May 6.

13

Ethnic Conflict in Sri Lanka

Robert Oberst

The Sri Lankan civil war, which lasted from the 1980s until its end in 2009, was one of the bloodiest conflicts in the world. Sri Lanka society, like the rest of the South Asian subcontinent, is divided by ethnic groups and faces the constant challenge of mediating conflict between them. The Sri Lankan war offers many lessons about how ethnic wars begin and how difficult it is to end them. There are also lessons about how governments can and should respond to such conflicts.

The war was fought between the Sri Lankan government and a rebel group, the Liberation Tigers of Tamil Eelam (LTTE). The LTTE became the self-appointed representative of the Tamil ethnic minority in Sri Lanka, and the government side was dominated by the Sinhalese ethnic majority. The conflict began with sporadic attacks in the 1970s and escalated into a full-fledged war after 1983. For the next twenty-six years, until the military defeat of the rebel group in 2009, the war escalated in violence, causing more than 100,000 deaths by the end.

The war began with an ill-equipped and militarily untrained group of young fighters. As the fighting progressed, however, the LTTE emerged as one of the world's most feared and ferocious military organizations. In addition, foreign powers were drawn into the conflict, and by its end it had become internationalized, with the United Nations, the United States, and the European Union trying to mediate the conflict, and Iran, China, and Russia supporting the government with arms sales. After the LTTE was defeated in May 2009, the country embarked on what was expected to be a period of rebuilding and reconciliation. This process has progressed very slowly, and many of the wounds of the war continue to plague Sri Lankan society.

Overview of the Conflict

Despite its small size, Sri Lanka is a very densely populated country. More than 20 million people live in a land area the size of Kentucky. They are divided by language, religion, and ethnicity. The war disrupted the normal patterns of society, and the government of Sri Lanka was unable to carry out a complete national census until 2012. The results of that census have been disputed by some Tamil sources, which see it as an attempt to understate the Tamil population. (For full census results, see Sri Lanka Department of Census and Statistics 2012.) The majority of the population, or 74.9 percent, are members of the Sinhalese ethnic group. They speak the Sinhala language, and most are Buddhist.

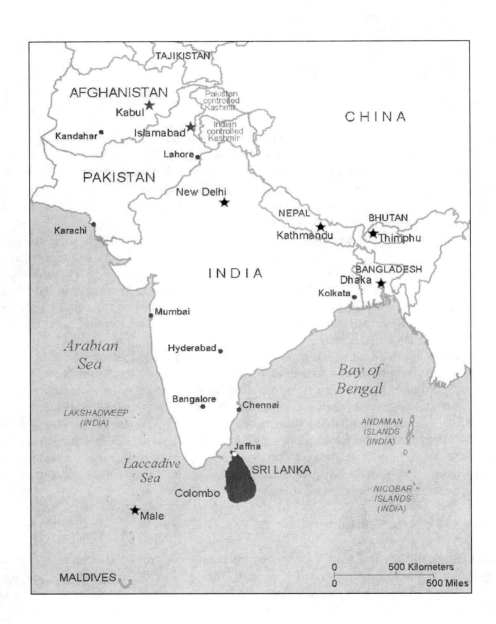

They claim to be the original civilized inhabitants of the island, and they believe that they have played a crucial historical role in the protection and propagation of the Buddhist religion.

The second largest group on the island is the Tamils. They are divided into two culturally distinct groups: Sri Lanka and Indian Tamils. The Sri Lanka Tamils, who can trace their history on the island to the original inhabitants, make up 11.2 percent of the population, down from 12.7 percent in 1981. They speak the Tamil language, and most are Hindus, although there are significant numbers of Christians among them. The Indian Tamils are the descendants of South Indian Tamils, who were brought to the island in the nineteenth and early twentieth centuries to work on its tea and coffee plantations. They make up 4.2 percent of the population, down from 5.5 percent in 1981. They also speak the Tamil language and are mostly Hindus, with significant numbers of Christians. Muslims make up a fourth significant group, with 9.2 percent of the population. They are the descendants of Muslim traders who arrived on the island several centuries before the arrival of the Europeans, who first arrived there in the sixteenth century.

Sri Lankan ethnic groups are geographically separated. The Sinhalese are found in the southern and western parts of the island, while the Indian Tamils are found in the central hill country. The Sri Lankan Tamils predominate in the north around the city of Jaffna and in much of the coastal areas of the east. The Muslims are concentrated along the east coast, especially in the Ampara district in the southeast. They are also found in pockets in the Sinhalese areas. The capital city, Colombo, in the heart of the Sinhalese area of the country, has large numbers of all ethnic groups.

The ethnic groups appeared to live in relative harmony until the arrival of the Europeans, beginning in the sixteenth century. As they did in India, the British, who began their rule in 1796, divided the local population by creating alliances with different ethnic groups and factions. The minority Tamil population was favored by the British, who rewarded them for their support. The result was a large number of Tamils in the government administration at the time of independence in 1948, as well as higher levels of education among them. The British favoritism toward the Tamils resulted in the Sinhalese assuming power after independence as a majority with a minority complex. They felt oppressed and sought to reestablish the Sinhalese Buddhist people to their "rightful" place in Sri Lankan society. This effort to restore Sinhalese Buddhism provoked Tamil demands for an independent state, Eelam, which is the Tamil word for "state."

The Tamil uprising was caused by a complex set of social forces that grew out of the domination of the country by the Sinhalese ethnic majority and the economic plight of the Sri Lankan people after independence (for a good description of the origins of the war, see Neil DeVotta's 2004 book, *Blowback: Linguistic Nationalism, Institutional Decay, and Ethnic Conflict in Sri Lanka*). The British-based political system adopted by independent Sri Lanka appeared to be democratic. However, it was a highly majoritarian system that allowed the Sinhalese majority to carry out whatever policies it wanted with little or no input from the ethnic minority groups. The Tamils and Muslims had no safeguards to prevent the Sinhalization of the society. One of the first acts of the newly independent government in 1948 was to deny citizenship to the Indian Tamils, then around 11 percent

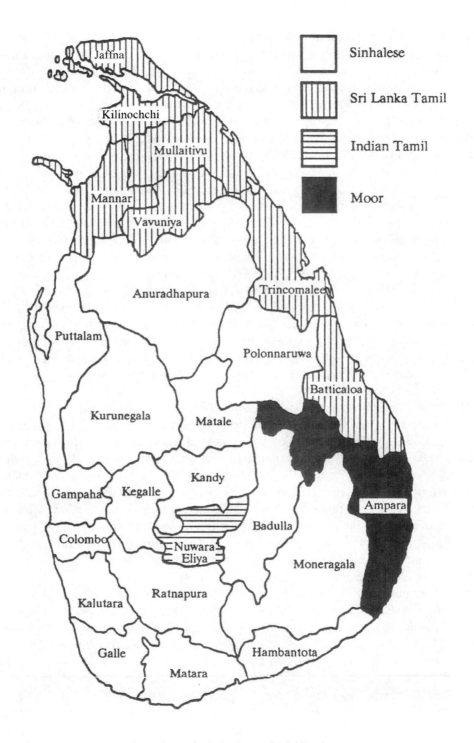

Locations of ethnic groups in Sri Lanka.

of the population. Efforts were made to deport them to India, but India refused to accept them, and many of the Indian Tamils remained stateless from 1948 until the 1990s. Gradually, about half of the Indian Tamil population would leave the country for India, and the rest would receive citizenship.

In 1956, the government enacted a "Sinhala Only" policy, making the Sinhala language the official language of the country. As a result, Tamil speakers were unable to compete for government jobs or to understand government forms and court proceedings. In the 1960s, the government took away the educational vehicle the Tamil people used to excel educationally by taking over Christian schools. The most inflammatory policy, however, was the creation of an "affirmative action" program to increase the number of Sinhalese students admitted to the university system. Prior to this program, Tamils scored higher on the university admission exams and had a higher success rate in university admissions. The policy, implemented in the 1970s, resulted in an immediate decline in the number of Tamil university admissions.

The Tamils and Muslims, constituting less than one-third of the population, were unable to stop these actions and were economically hurt by them. Sri Lanka had one of the best educational systems in Asia during the 1950s and 1960s, and the country produced highly qualified high school and university graduates. These graduates came from all the ethnic communities. The result was intense competition for university admissions—and for jobs. The "Sinhala Only" policy of 1956 denied Tamils access to government jobs, the main source of employment in the country. Thus the only outlet for Tamils was to obtain a university education and hopefully find employment in Colombo or with a foreign company. However, most high school and university graduates were unable to find jobs even before the affirmative action program. The effort to increase Sinhalese university enrollment focused the Tamil youths' frustration on the government and the Sinhalese majority, causing a deep sense of frustration among Tamil youths. It also created a pool of well-educated and angry unemployed young people.

The failure of the economy to provide jobs for the young increased unrest among young people across the board. Tamil youths would therefore become willing fighters in the Tamil uprising. At the same time, two uprisings by Sinhalese youth, one in 1972 and the other in 1988–1990, reflected the frustration felt by young people from all ethnic groups. The government ruthlessly suppressed the Sinhalese uprisings, but it would find the Tamil revolt harder to suppress. The actions by the government to promote Sinhalese Buddhism angered many Tamils and left them with the belief that the only way to protect their way of life was to create an autonomous state for the Tamils. The dominant Tamil political party in the country, the Federal Party (which became the Tamil United Liberation Front, or TULF), initially demanded a federal system such as that found in India or the United States, and then it reluctantly demanded an independent state in 1976.

While the TULF was trying to work with the Sinhalese leadership, a younger generation of Tamils became restless and angry. A young high school dropout, Velupillai Prabhakaran, harnessed the frustration and created the LTTE, commonly called the Tamil Tigers. The nickname came from the use of the tiger as the symbol of their movement. It had also been the symbol of the South Indian Tamil Empire, the Chola Empire, which united much

---

Box 13.1

Velupillai Prabhakaran, LTTE Leader

Profile   Velupillai Prabhakaran, Founder and Leader of Liberation
             Tigers of Tamil Eelam

Born   November 26, 1954, in Valvettithurai, Jaffna, Sri Lanka

Father   Thiruvenkadam Veluppillai, district lands officer for the
             government of Sri Lanka and the son of a wealthy and
             influential family in Valvettithurai

Died   May 18, 2009, in Nanthikadal Lagoon, Mullaitivu,
             Sri Lanka

Married   Mathivaihani Erambu, 1984

Children   Charles Anthony, Duwaraka, and Balachandran

Prabhakaran, his wife, and their children were all shot to death on May 18, 2009, as government forces captured the last stronghold of the LTTE.

---

of India and unsuccessfully invaded Sri Lanka in the tenth through thirteenth centuries. In 1973 Prabhakaran formed his first rebel organization, the Tamil New Tigers, which would become the core of the LTTE. At first he and his supporters carried out attacks with homemade weapons and bombs. As the movement grew, however, they eventually sent members to Lebanon for training, and in the 1980s they were sent to India, where the Indian government cooperated in the creation of training camps. Their weapons also improved as they built an international financial empire, which generated enough revenue to buy modern weapons. This financial growth was based on legal enterprises, such as shipping and a merchant marine, as well as illegal activities, such as drug smuggling.

In 1983 the LTTE ambushed an army patrol near Jaffna, killing thirteen soldiers. The attack ignited intense anger among the Sinhalese population, and mobs, often assisted by government politicians, attacked Tamils in the Sinhalese areas of the country. When the riots were over, more than 1,000 Tamils had been killed, and young Tamils flocked to the LTTE to join its rebellion. Many moderate Tamils viewed the riots as a sign of the government's unwillingness to treat Tamils as equal citizens, and many Tamils began supporting the Tigers or sympathizing with them even as they renounced their violent methods.

The rebellion, begun by a small group of angry fighters, evolved into a full-scale civil war. Between 1983 and 2009, more than 100,000 people would die. Sri Lankan society was transformed into a militarized state fighting to control violent crime and a rapidly eroding social structure. The atrocities committed by both sides immunized the population to levels of violence that the society had never previously experienced.

On May 17, 2009, the last of the LTTE fighters died and the country embarked on the postwar era with great hope for the future. However, reconciliation and peace building did not occur. The war's end left the Tamil people defeated and demoralized; militant

Tamils described the Sri Lankan government's policies as genocide. Thousands had tried to flee the war, and those who fled to the West or to India during the war refused to return. The government of Mahinda Rajapaksa, who presided over the end of the war, restricted both the media and opponents, while also taking over the judiciary and other independent offices of the government. Thus, while the military victory would become a textbook example of how to defeat a guerrilla uprising, the postwar era would become a model of how not to build peace after the end of a conflict.

Ethnic Conflict and War

The twenty-six-year war in Sri Lanka has become a case study in how not to manage ethnic tensions. It also exhibits how deep ethnic divisions in a society can become unmanageable and cause thousands of deaths and untold hardship. Before the conflict, few scholars or researchers understood or recognized the deep animosity that existed between the two groups. Sri Lanka seemed a model of Third World democracy. However, somewhere between the textbook and reality, both the government and the LTTE misread and failed to address the country's ethnic divisions, leading the country into a civil war. The war's history is a list of missed opportunities and mismanagement.

Lack of Meaningful Communications and Negotiations

Scholars argue that communication between competing groups reduces tensions and the likelihood of war. Over the course of the war in Sri Lanka, however, the two sides rarely communicated with each other, and when they did, they communicated through low-level surrogates. The few efforts at peace rarely involved high-level talks. In 1985, the two sides met in Bhutan, but after the government sent low-ranking officials to the talks, the LTTE reciprocated by sending representatives of low rank as well. In 1987, the Indian government attempted to negotiate an end to the conflict with the Sri Lankan government. In what became the Indo-Lankan Accord, the Indians did not consult with the LTTE before agreeing to a peace treaty. Instead, the Indian Peacekeeping Force arrived in the north and east to enforce the accord, only to end up fighting the LTTE from 1987 to 1990. The Indian forces left the island in 1990 after a humiliating defeat by the LTTE. In 1994, the sides would meet again, but once again both sides sent low-ranking officials to negotiate.

The most successful effort at peacekeeping was carried out by the Norwegian government, beginning in the late 1990s. The Norwegians tried to mediate between the two sides and ultimately obtained a ceasefire agreement, which went into effect in February 2002. The agreement stopped the fighting and allowed each side to control the areas of the country it held at the time of the agreement. The ceasefire was to be the first step to a formal peace agreement that aimed to transform the Sri Lankan government by protecting the rights of the minorities in the country.

For four years, peace returned to Sri Lanka. Foreign aid donors poured money into rebuilding the war-torn areas of the north and east. The LTTE established a de facto independent government without a declaration of independence. Both sides benefited from the ceasefire; however, both sides also avoided any serious effort to negotiate a final peace accord. The government refused to allow a change in the political system to accommodate minorities, and the LTTE found reasons not to cooperate with the government and mediators. The ceasefire slowly disintegrated as a new Sri Lanka government took power and committed to a military solution in 2004.

Cycles of Violence

Excessive actions by both sides resulted in overreactions from the other side; and both sides committed atrocities of horrific proportions. The LTTE perfected the use of suicide bombers and attacked both military and civilian targets with their human bombs. In 1993, a bomber killed the president of Sri Lanka, Ranasinghe Premadasa. In 1991, the former Indian prime minister Rajiv Gandhi was assassinated by a young woman who brought him a bouquet of flowers. The LTTE also attacked Sinhalese and Muslim villages, slaughtering the inhabitants. The government of Sri Lanka retaliated by slaughtering Tamil villagers and sexually abusing Tamil women. The use of sweep arrests, in which hundreds of thousands of Tamils were arrested and held until they could prove their innocence, inflamed Tamil civilians. The widespread use of torture by the government forces was meant to intimidate Tamils, as the bodies of detainees would be dropped by the side of the road or burned. The LTTE would justify bomb or village attacks against Sinhalese civilians after government soldiers slaughtered Tamil civilians, and the government used the LTTE attacks as a justification to carry out more attacks on Tamil civilians. The never-ending cycle of violence and retribution escalated and fueled the deep-seated anger felt by both sides, resulting in a total loss of trust between Tamils and Sinhalese.

International Factors

The LTTE became known as one of the most violent and ruthless guerrilla organizations in the world. The Tamil Tigers were brutal and unforgiving with their enemies. Their attacks against civilians and their use of suicide bombers prompted the U.S. State Department to place them on its list of terrorist organizations. This action prohibited U.S. citizens from openly supporting the LTTE or providing them with donations. Support by the U.S. government in its "war on terror" became a crucial part of the Sri Lankan government's ultimate success in the war. At different times in the war, the United States provided military training, armaments, and logistical support to the Sri Lankan government.

The LTTE, however, believed that history and the international community would judge them favorably. As a result, they avoided negotiations while trying to provide the government with opportunities to "prove" how ruthless and racist it was. This author's meetings with the LTTE leaders left him with the perception that they believed in what could be called a form of manifest destiny. They appeared to believe that the righteousness of the Tamil cause would result in their ultimate victory. Their approach to negotiations with the government—avoiding them—became a part of their strategy to win the conflict.

In the end, their lack of cooperation would result in the death of their leadership and the annihilation of their fighting forces.

> Both the government and the Tamils claim that the other side committed war crimes and atrocities against them. The government has created extensive websites highlighting LTTE atrocities:
>
> - "LTTE Atrocities," posted by Sri Lanka News Online (http://www.slnewsonline.net/ltteatro.htm).
> - "List of LTTE Terrorist Atrocities," posted by The Permanent Mission of Sri Lanka to the United Nations (http://www.slmission.com/news/17-other-news/583-list-of-ltte-terrorist-atrocities.html).
>
> Tamil groups have also created websites highlighting atrocities by government forces:
>
> - "Indictment against Sri Lanka—Ethnic Cleansing of Tamils," posted by Tamilnation.org (http://tamilnation.co/indictment/disappearances/index.htm).
> - "War Without Witness in Sri Lanka," which includes a list of atrocities in the last months of the war (http://warwithoutwitness.com/).

The brutality and violence committed by both sides during the war reflects a level of inhumanity rarely seen in South Asia. The LTTE killed thousands of innocent civilians in its bombings and village attacks. The security forces of the government of Sri Lanka matched the LTTE's death toll of civilians and treated Tamil civilians as enemies. Tamil civilians were frequently arrested with no cause, and Tamil women were raped and sexually assaulted. Critically, the level of violence against Tamil civilians exceeded the level of violence by the LTTE against Sinhalese and Muslim civilians.

The final assault against the LTTE may have resulted in the deaths of more than 40,000 civilians in the last six months of the war, during which the Tamil Tigers held more than 260,000 civilians as a human shield in the small strip of seaside land where they made their final stand. They erroneously believed that the government forces would not slaughter innocent Tamil hostages and that the international community would not allow such a massacre. They were wrong on both counts.

The Final Stand and Its Aftermath

The final stand of the LTTE, and its aftermath, illustrates the nature of the conflict. The LTTE, throughout its thirty-six-year history, was led by the charismatic Velupillai Prabhakaran who did not tolerate any dissent among his followers. He would battle against five Sri Lankan leaders, losing finally to President Mahinda Rajapaksa of the Sri Lankan Freedom Party.

Box 13.2

Mahinda Rajapaksa, Sri Lankan President

Profile	Mahinda Rajapaksa, President of Sri Lanka
Born	Percy Mahendra Rajapaksa on November 18, 1945, in Weeraketiya, Hambantota
Father	D.A. Rajapaka, member of Parliament and minister of agriculture
Married	Shiranthi Wickremesinghe, 1983
Children	Namal, Rohitha, and Yoshihta
Political career	Member of Parliament (first elected in 1970); prime minister (2004–2005); elected president of Sri Lanka (2005; reelected 2010)

Rajapaksa first won election in 2004, as prime minister. Unable to form a majority in Parliament, he made alliances with a broad array of factions and political parties. At the core of his coalition was the extreme Sinhalese Buddhist wing of his own party. The most extreme Sinhalese Buddhists believe that Sri Lanka belongs to Sinhalese Buddhists and that the Tamils are allowed to live in the country as guests. Rajapaksa's close advisers were comfortable with a military strategy that resulted in large numbers of civilian deaths. The strategy involved using the ceasefire to attack the LTTE in small areas, far away from their headquarters in the jungles south of the Jaffna peninsula.

Thus the government forces began their offensive in the southernmost areas of the Eastern Province, in the Ampara and Batticaloa districts. Before the final offensive, the government persuaded the most important and effective military general in the LTTE army to defect to the government side. The general, known by his nom de guerre, Karuna, brought his forces over to the government side in 2004. His knowledge of LTTE tactics and hideouts was critical. Colonel Karuna was one of the most successful military leaders of the LTTE. His battlefield successes won him the admiration and support of the LTTE leader, Prabhakaran. Karuna would also be associated with widespread wartime atrocities, including the execution of nearly 1,000 captured Sinhalese members of the army and police force in 1990. After his defection, he led his supporters from army bases in attacks on the LTTE. They targeted LTTE political officers operating in government-held territory. The ceasefire agreement allowed LTTE political officers to carry out political organizing in government areas as long as they were unarmed, which allowed Karuna's men to assassinate many LTTE political cadres. Many other civilians who criticized the Karuna group or were believed to be LTTE sympathizers were also murdered. Hundreds, perhaps thousands, were killed. The Sri Lankan security forces allowed Karuna to fund his actions by kidnapping Tamil civilians for ransom. The reign of terror would decimate the LTTE forces in the Eastern Province and allow the government to claim that its forces were not involved in the attacks.

The second stage of the strategy began in 2006 when government forces attacked the jungle areas held by the LTTE in the Eastern Province. By July 2007, most of the Eastern Province had been recaptured. The government began attacking LTTE strongholds in the southern Mannar district and overran the last LTTE stronghold there in December 2007. The territory controlled by the LTTE was reduced to half of its pre-ceasefire size. On January 2, 2008, the government formally withdrew from the ceasefire and began its assault on the last two districts held by the LTTE, Kilinochchi and Mullaitivu. Military divisions attacked the last LTTE forces from the north, west, and south.

The government forces incurred large losses in their victories. The actual number of deaths will never be known, however, because the government banned the reporting of government losses in 2008 and barred journalists from the war zone, eventually expelling aid workers as well. As the government forces progressed to the LTTE capital of Kilinochchi, tens of thousands of Tamil civilians fled the fighting, going deeper into LTTE-held territory. During the previous twenty-five years of the war, ebbs and flows in the fighting had occurred, during which the LTTE always recovered the land it lost. The Tamil civilians feared going over to the government side because they faced imprisonment or worse possible fates, including the disappearance of the youth among them and the sexual assault of Tamil women. Thus the civilians fled away from the fighting and into LTTE-held territory.

The number of displaced Tamil civilians would grow to more than 260,000 as the government captured Kilinochchi on January 2, 2009. The LTTE forces and civilians fled toward their last stand near Mullaitivu, on the western coast. From January to May 19, 2009, the government pushed the LTTE forces back until they reached a small strip of land, with a lagoon on one side and the sea on the other. Mullivaikal was a nearly uninhabited beach paradise before the war, but for those last months of the LTTE, the two-mile stretch of beach in Mullivaikal would become a killing field and home to more than one-quarter of a million civilians. They dug holes in the ground to protect themselves from the daily shelling, which went on for more than two months. Food was in short supply and civilians had nowhere to go. The LTTE prevented them from leaving, but if they did try to flee, they risked being shelled by the government forces or shot by snipers on the other side of the lagoon.

The full extent of the suffering of the Tamil refugees will never be known. The Sri Lanka government's ban on all reporters and aid workers in the war zone prevented any reporting of the events. There were no outside observers of the last days of the conflict, and controversy abounds. The government claims that only a few thousand civilians died in the final offensive. Independent observers place the death toll as high as 60,000, however.

The details surrounding the end of the war are also in dispute. Many Tamils believe that the LTTE leadership surrendered under white flags. The families of some of the leaders claim that they saw their husbands and fathers taken away by government security forces after surrendering. The official government statement is that all the leaders died while fighting to the end against the government forces. Among the dead were Prabhakaran and his family.

Since the war's end, the government has faced intense criticism from human rights groups, which have accused it of committing war crimes. The Sri Lankan government responded with strong denials and a refusal to allow independent observers into the war zone. In addition, the government has been forced to address a series of videos leaked by human rights groups showing atrocities against Tamils. Among them were photos of Prabhakaran's twelve-year-old son being shot five times. While the government claims that the videos are false, no evidence of falsification has been produced.

The aftermath of the war has also been controversial. Nearly 240,000 Tamil civilians "liberated" from Mullivaikal at the end of the war were locked into camps for six to eight months afterward. Large parts of northern Sri Lanka were taken over by the military, and the original inhabitants of the areas were prevented from returning to their homes. Gangs allied to the government patrolled the streets of the northern and eastern Tamil cities, intimidating Tamil civilians, and political intimidation was rampant. At one point, relatives of members of Parliament were kidnapped and threatened with death if their family member voted in Parliament. Tamils have claimed that Hindu temples have been looted and destroyed. Many critics of the government have claimed threats or assaults by gangs allied with the government. Meanwhile, outside observers are prevented or limited from visiting the area. Three years after the war's end, as more Tamils have been allowed to return to lands in Kilinochchi and Mullaitivu districts, resettled Tamils have reported finding fields filled with human bone fragments.

In addition to the unresolved human suffering of the internally displaced Tamils, there has been a lack of reconciliation, healing, and effort to address the problems that led to the conflict in the first place. Key issues surrounding power sharing remain unresolved. The Rajapaksa government has rejected a federal solution that would give the north and east limited autonomy, and it has also failed to follow through on promises to implement the thirteenth amendment to the constitution, created as part of the Indo-Lanka Accord in 1987, which established provincial councils. While the councils were created and some effort to devolve power occurred, the details of the amendment were never fully implemented. In addition, the plan contained serious weaknesses that prevented true decentralization of power, the most significant being a lack of funding for local governments. While President Rajapaksa has promised to consider some changes to the amendment, his government has made no effort to take action.

The government has also taken few actions to address the deep distrust and anger left by twenty-six years of war. In May 2010, President Rajapaksa created a commission to address the healing. The report of the Lessons Learnt and Reconciliation Commission was released to the public on December 15, 2011. However, very little action has been taken to implement its recommendations.

Another serious threat to reconciliation is the Rajapaksa government's postwar efforts to consolidate power by intimidating opponents and the media. While intimidation has been common in the Tamil areas, Sinhalese have also been intimidated, and the Rajapaksa government hopes to hold on to power for as long as it can. The government has removed term limits on the presidency, allowing Rajapaksa to be reelected an unlimited number of times. Opposition media outlets have been attacked and journalists arrested or beaten.

Tamils in Sri Lanka have faced an uncertain future since the war's end. Northern Sri

Box 13.3

Postwar LTTE

Profile	Transitional Government of Tamil Eelam
Formed	May 17, 2010
Prime Minister	Visvanathan Rudrakumaran
Legislature	Transnational Constituent Assembly of Tamil Eelam, 135 members from more than 20 countries

Source: http://www.tgte-us.org/index.asp.

Lanka remains economically depressed. The plight of the Tamils is reflected in the flight of Tamils seeking asylum in other countries. In the first nine months of 2012, over 5,000 Tamils arrived by boat in Australia, prompting that country to consider closing its doors to refugees. Untold others have died during the boat voyage across the Indian Ocean, and thousands more were arrested by Sri Lankan and Indian authorities as they prepared to leave by boat for Australia. In addition, Sri Lankan refugees in India have chosen to remain there rather than face the uncertainties of returning to their homeland.

The Return of the LTTE

All of the LTTE's leaders were killed in May 2009, and the organization was destroyed by the triumphant government forces. However, the Sri Lankan government has kept most of its wartime emergency powers, allowing unrestricted and unmonitored arrests of Tamils. Large tracts of land in the north and east are still held by the security forces, and the owners of the land remain unable to access their property. The government has justified the continued restrictions by arguing that the LTTE has been regrouping and reorganizing. Tamils returning to Sri Lanka are routinely interrogated and monitored. It has been reported that Tamils deported from other countries have been arrested and tortured by the government authorities, who believe that Tamils in India and the West have been gathering arms and money for a new war. There is no doubt that many in the Tamil diaspora in Western countries still hope for an independent Tamil state in Sri Lanka, and many of them have financial resources to support a new independence movement. However, there is very limited evidence that the LTTE has rebuilt its organization to the extent that it could pose a threat to the Sri Lankan government.

After the LTTE was defeated in 2009, two factions of the LTTE emerged. The Transnational Government of Tamil Eelam, led by the U.S. attorney Visvanathan Rudrakumaran, disavows violence and has created a democratically elected government in exile. The Nediyavan faction, led by Norway-based Perinbanayagam Sivaparan, is considered more likely to reorganize a violent uprising in Sri Lanka. At this time, neither group appears to have the organizational or financial strength to pose a military threat to the government. Nevertheless, the government continues to warn of a LTTE resurgence, and it uses the possibility of one to continue the militarization of northern Sri Lanka and the unlimited detention of terrorist suspects.

The Sri Lankan government has focused most of its international attention on blocking efforts by the Tamil diaspora to create a war crimes tribunal or to use courts in Western countries to address war crime charges. In the United States, efforts to charge President Rajapaksa and his brother Gotabaya with war crimes have been unsuccessful. Gotabaya is the secretary to the Ministry of Defense and is considered the architect of the final offensive of the war and the siege of Mullivaikal. He could be vulnerable to charges because he is a U.S. citizen and owns a house in Los Angeles. Human rights groups in European countries have also tried to bring charges in their countries and to persuade the United Nations to address the charges. Thus far, no serious war crime tribunals have been established. However, the secretary-general of the United Nations appointed a "panel of experts" to examine allegations of war crimes. Its 2011 report has been widely condemned by the Sri Lankan government.

References and Further Research

DeVotta, Neil. 2004. *Blowback: Linguistic Nationalism, Institutional Decay, and Ethnic Conflict in Sri Lanka*. Stanford, CA: Stanford University Press.

Oberst, Robert C. 2012. "Sri Lanka." In *Countries at the Crossroads*. Washington, DC: Freedom House. http://www.freedomhouse.org/report/countries-crossroads/2012/sri-lanka.

Oberst, Robert C., Yogendra Malik, Charles Kennedy, Ashok Kapur, Mahendra Lawoti, Syedur Rahman, and Ahrar Ahmad. 2013. *Government and Politics of South Asia*. 7th ed. Boulder, CO: Westview Press.

Sri Lanka Commission of Inquiry. November 2011. *Report of the Commission of Inquiry on Lessons Learnt and Reconciliation*. http://www.priu.gov.lk/news_update/Current_Affairs/ca201112/FINAL%20LLRC%20REPORT.pdf.

Sri Lanka Department of Census and Statistics. 2012. "Population & Housing Data 2012." http://www.statistics.gov.lk/PopHouSat/CPH2011/index.php?fileName=Activities/TentativelistofPublications.

United Nations. March 31, 2011. Report of the Secretary General's Panel of Experts on Accountability in Sri Lanka. www.un.org/News/dh/infocus/Sri_Lanka/POE_Report_Full.pdf.

14

The Federally and Provincially Administered Tribal Areas of Pakistan
The Most Dangerous Places in the World?

SUBHO BASU AND SUSAN SNOW WADLEY

One of the most contested regions of the world in 2013 is the part of Pakistan comprising the seven tribal agencies and six frontier regions of the Federally Administered Tribal Areas (FATAs) and the Provincially Administered Tribal Areas (PATAs), made up of the five districts of the adjacent province of Khyber Pakhtunkhwa. For several years, this region has been the primary site of U.S. drone attacks in South Asia, as it is thought to be home to both Taliban from Afghanistan and regional Pakistani militants working with both the Taliban and al-Qaeda, as well as to other foreigners seeking to maintain a state of instability and conflict in Pakistan and Afghanistan. In the first half of January 2013 alone, forty-seven residents of the region were killed in drone attacks, according to the South Asia Terrorism Portal website.

In addition to drone attacks, the Pakistani military has repeatedly conducted operations into these two regions, with thousands killed and millions forced from their homes. On February 2, 2013, the Pakistan Tehreek-e-Insaf (PTI), one of three parties competing in the country's 2013 elections, staged a protest demanding an immediate end to military incursions in the region. The protest was supported by Imran Khan, a former cricket star and the leader of the PTI. Speaking to the group of thousands, Juma Ihan Afridi, who had family members killed by the Pakistani military in January 2013, said, "The military operations have brought lives of the eight million population in FATA to a standstill. The seven tribal agencies have remained under curfew and the population has become completely idle" (Yusufzai 2013).

FATA is governed by political agents and the president of Pakistan, while the five PATA districts of the province of Khyber Pakhtunkhwa are governed by the provincial governor, who reports to the president of Pakistan. Hence PATA is considered to be administered provisionally, as opposed the federal administration of FATA. Regular access to courts and legal redress through channels laid down by the constitution of Pakistan are absent in FATA but available in PATA. Much of the information and analysis that follows is applicable to both regions, although the primary focus is on FATA.

216

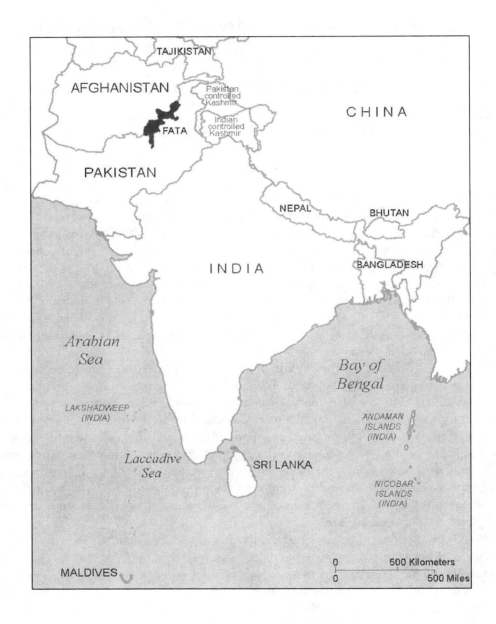

The South Asia Terrorism Portal website (http://www.satp.org/) publishes analysis and data on drone attacks, terrorist incidents, and other violence in FATA and PATA. See in particular the website's "FATA Assessment, 2013" (http://www.satp.org/satporgtp/countries/pakistan/Waziristan/index.html).

Understanding the current tensions in this vital region requires knowledge of its history, which has its roots in the "Great Game" for territorial control played out between England and Russia in the nineteenth century, as well as an understanding of its more recent history as the borderland between Afghanistan and Pakistan. The use of drones here is not accidental: drone warfare is mostly used in those regions of the world that are true borderlands, only vaguely controlled by states. Such buffer zones essentially belong to no one, and they have special "geo-legalities" that make drone warfare more politically acceptable than elsewhere. Much of the conflict in the region can be tied to the region's special legal status, which is indeed tied to its geographic position as a buffer zone. This position reemerged as vital after the terrorist attacks in the United States on September 11, 2001, and the subsequent U.S. invasion of Afghanistan.

The backdrop of Rudyard Kipling's famous book *Kim* is the geopolitical rivalry between the Russian and British empires in Central Asia, referred to as the "Great Game." *Kim* was originally published in serial installments in magazines in Great Britain and the United States in 1900 and 1901. The novel can be accessed today on the Project Gutenberg website (http://www.gutenberg.org/ebooks/2226).

The Great Game and the Making of the Anglo-Afghan Border

In the nineteenth century, the British Empire in South Asia was expanding, reaching to the borders of what is now Afghanistan. At the same time, the Russian Empire was moving south, and British and Russian territorial aspirations collided in Afghanistan. This collision played out in two Anglo-Afghan wars—one from 1839 to 1842, and the second from 1878 to 1880—in which Britain sought a secure northern boundary against the Russians. One goal in 1839 was to restore the Afghan throne to Shuja Shah Durrani, a presumed ally of the British East India Company. The invasion proved to be a failure, and it was costly to the East India Company's army, which recognized the outermost periphery of Britain's newly growing empire in the Indian subcontinent as a result of the war.

In 1849 the British East India Company acquired the Sikh Kingdom, stretching from the Sutlej River, which runs through present-day northern India and Pakistan, to the border of Afghanistan, including the territory that later came to be known as the North-West Frontier Province. The British felt the need to establish an effective government over the region and to develop an adequate border security force. The region's importance to the British Empire in India was primarily strategic, since Britain sought a stable state to buffer its territory against the expanding Russian Empire. Between 1863 and 1870, the Russian Empire moved into Central Asia and aroused fears among the British rulers of India that the Russians would advance further through Afghanistan to the frontiers of India in an attempt to gain access to a warm-water port. In 1878, when the Afghan emir (king) was visited by an uninvited Russian envoy from the north, the British also expressed their desire to send an envoy. When the emir sought to prevent this intrusion into his kingdom by his imperial neighbors, the British declared war against Afghanistan and came to occupy much of the country. Under the resulting treaty, the Afghani government accepted British control over Afghan foreign policy and agreed that the Pashtun-speaking borderland east of the Khyber Pass would be part of British Indian territory.

In 1893, under the leadership of the British foreign secretary in India, Mortimer Durand, the British also imposed a new border, the Durand Line (also known as the Great Game Buffer Line), separating Afghani and British territories. The Durand Line would have two long-term repercussions: (1) it split the Pashtun population into two, and (2) it created, with British help, a true buffer zone between Afghanistan and Pakistan.

The Pashtuns

While the Durand Line marked a border geographically, it split the native Pashtun population between British India and Afghanistan. Made up of several hundred distinct tribal groups, the Pashtun population has never been a coherent whole. But Pashtuns have ruled in Afghanistan for more than 200 years, and they dominate the world's views on Afghanistan, despite being only 40 percent of the Afghani population. In contrast, in Pakistan the Pashtuns are a minority population, geographically located in FATA and PATA.

Defining what is meant by Pashtun (also spelled Pakhtun and Pathan) is not easy. Pashtuns share a common language, Pashto, though with much regional variation. They are primarily subsistence farmers, though some are pastoral migrants, moving their livestock as the seasons demand. Culturally, they claim to share a Pashtunwali code, a set of ethics and rules for social behavior, the most fundamental of which is maintaining honor and reputation. Another component of Pashtunwali is the offering of hospitality and asylum to all who seek it. Nominally, they are egalitarian, though disputes between relatives, especially patrilineal cousins (*tarbur*), are frequent. Pashtun men are famous for claiming to fight for three things: *zar*, *zan*, and *zamin* (gold, women, and land). Many official writings have created the stereotype of Pashtun males as individualistic, entrepreneurial, and egalitarian in outlook but compromised by qualities such as fanaticism and treachery. In many ways, the idea of a Pashtun egalitarian spirit is manifested in the *jirga,* or council of elders, where decisions are arrived at through discussion without jeopardizing an individual's honor. For women, Pashtunwali focuses on maintaining family honor and not bringing shame to it, especially through behaviors that impinge on men's honor.

Significant differences exist among Pashtuns. Those from the western regions of Afghanistan, whose lineages, especially the Durrani, have provided the Afghani rulers for generations (including Hamid Karzai, the current president of Afghanistan), are used to working in collectivities and being ruled by the state. Those in the FATA region and the other eastern regions of Afghanistan that produced the Taliban were often of Ghilzai lineages and are intensely egalitarian but thrive in periods of chaos and war. Mullah Omar and other Taliban leaders of the last two decades came from this group. In these regions, too, poverty and inability to move beyond minimal subsistence contributed to egalitarianism, for without resources, it was difficult to build enduring leadership.

See Thomas Barfield's *Afghanistan: A Political and Cultural History* (2010) for more on the various implications of this history for Afghanistan and the FATA region.

FATA as a Buffer

The Pashtun residents of FATA form one half of the equation that makes the region important. Equally important is the geography of the FATA region—10,500 square miles of very wild and rugged land, with high hills and narrow, nearly inaccessible valleys, located on the border of what is now Pakistan and Afghanistan. This landscape has made it difficult for any government to control the region. In 2000, the population was estimated at about 3,300,000, with only 3 percent of the people living in established towns. In 1998, literacy was less than 18 percent, with female literacy at 3 percent and male literacy at 29.5 percent. FATA's long unmarked border with Afghanistan makes it a prime area for smuggling and undocumented cross-border traffic. In 2001, it became the haven for the many Taliban and al-Qaeda members, as well as Arabs and others, who escaped the U.S. bombardment following the September 11 terrorist attacks.

Using Google Earth, fly to Peshawar in the PATA region and then scroll north and south to get a sense of this terrain. It is lightly inhabited, with often dense forest. Not surprisingly, there are minimal signs of agriculture.

FATA today consists of seven tribal agencies and six frontier regions. The British first sought to control the area in the 1840s, and by 1848 they were compelled to institute the Frontier Crimes Regulation (FCR), which remains in effect under independent Pakistan today. Under these regulations, the tribal areas were the exclusive preserve of British officials. They often negotiated with the local community elders and paid allowances for good behavior. They selected wealthy landlords, known as *maliks*, to whom they offered a hereditary stipend over and above what they earned as members of the local *jirga*.

The British had a three-part vision of the governance of the northwestern regions of their Indian empire. In order to contain the Russians, the first line of defense was Afghanistan, an independent state that they sought to control through friendship and trade. The second line of defense was a buffer, the FATA region, which the British also ruled indirectly, through tribal leaders. Its status was exceptional: it was—and still is—only loosely part of a more traditionally governed state. As a frontier region, a hinterland, it was barely a part of the British Empire. Today it is barely a part of the Pakistani state (Shaw and Akhter 2012). The third line of defense was the British Empire in India, which ruled up to Peshawar in the PATA region with strong state control.

After independence in 1947, the Pakistani government continued the special treatment of the FATA and PATA regions. The regulations in force continue to deny residents of both areas the rights normally given to Pakistani citizens. Article 247.3 of the Constitution of Pakistan states, "No Act of Parliament shall apply to any Federally Administered Tribal Area or to any part thereof, unless the President so directs." The constitution goes on to say, in Article 247.6, "Neither the Supreme Court nor a High Court shall exercise any jurisdiction under the Constitution in relation to a Tribal Area, unless Parliament by law otherwise provides" (http://www.pakistani.org/pakistan/constitution/part12.ch3.html). In PATA, the provincial governor as well as the president of Pakistan has these powers. The districts are each governed in turn by a political agent who has the powers to act on behalf of the president and governor.

The Constitution of Pakistan thus effectively denies all residents of FATA any legal rights. Among the rights denied are the right to appeal detention, the right to legal representation, and the right to present a reasoned defense. In addition, the FCR allows the collective punishment of a family for the crimes of one individual family member. Since 1996, elections have been held, but no political parties are allowed, so that those elected are religious leaders who use their mosques and schools as sites for political rallies. The secular landowners (*maliks*), who might normally provide leadership, are thus excluded from the political process.

The official FATA government website (http://fata.gov.pk) is a good source for information on the region.

The Khidmatgar and the End of Colonial Rule

During the latter part of British rule, an unusual (for a Muslim-dominated territory) Gandhian movement for independence, called the Khudai Khidmatgar ("servants of god"), emerged in this area. Abdul Ghaffar Khan led a nonviolent uprising against the British government—and against the separatism advocated by Mohammed Ali Jinnah and the All-India Muslim League—in alliance with Mahatma Gandhi and the Indian National Congress. The Khudai Khidmatgar was able to cultivate a following among poor peasants and marginalized small landlords through a program of land reforms and a sharing of resources. It emphasized Pashtun identity in Pakistan, according to Mukulika Banerjee in *The Pathan Unarmed* (2000), and demanded a separate homeland within Pakistan for Pashtun speakers.

Despite winning the 1936 election in the North-West Frontier Province, the party ultimately bowed to the power of the Muslim League and the demand for a Muslim state. In the election of 1947, the region voted to join the Pakistan state by a bare majority of 50.1 percent, with the Khidmatgar boycotting the election. The legacy of the independence movement had wider repercussions on life in the FATA and PATA areas. In the North-West Frontier Province (later Khyber Pakhtunkhwa), the leaders of the Pashtun nationalist movement emphasized Pashtun identity and sought to win over the local population to their cause through secular left-wing politics, advocating the federalization of the Pakistan polity, land reforms, and the rights of smaller nationalities.

The events that worried the British in the 1840s, during the Great Game with Russia, finally materialized in 1979 when the Soviets entered Afghanistan, ostensibly to assist their allies in the People's Democratic Party–controlled Afghan government. Eventually, the Afghani insurgency known as the mujahideen ousted the Russians in 1989. In 2001, the Americans went into Afghanistan to flush out the foreign fighters who had filled spaces left by the Soviet exodus and who had been enabled by the U.S. arming of the mujahideen in the 1980s. Throughout this period, the Durand Line remained at the center of political military conflicts and insurgency. To this day, the Afghanistan government does not recognize the Durand Line as an international border.

The Pakistani Postcolonial Nation-State and FATA/PATA

After independence in 1947, the Pakistan government sought to control FATA/PATA by installing heavily supported landlords in the two regions, empowering them to distribute government contracts for construction projects and to grant permission for migration outside FATA and Pakistan. Such moves often proved to be counterproductive, however, since most members of tribal *jirga* came to regard such *maliks* as corrupt and nepotistic.

The urbanized areas of FATA and PATA gradually became integrated into Pakistan's mainstream economy and society: Pashtuns served in the army, worked in road construction projects, and increasingly established control over the transportation trade. Contrary to the colonial stereotype of Pashtun society, the mullahs (religious leaders) did not have an individual support base. Instead, they were dependent on the landlords who controlled large tracts of land. But the Soviet invasion and the U.S. reaction changed this. First, the mullahs received massive aid from Saudi Arabia to open religious seminaries, called madrassas, to train "holy warriors." The United States also provided aid to religious leaders in order to ideologically train refugees to fight the Soviets and the Communist Afghan regime. FATA/PATA became one center of such activities.

U.S. president Jimmy Carter responded quickly to the 1979 Soviet invasion, and the first U.S. arms arrived in Pakistan only ten days after the Soviet takeover. Throughout the following years, U.S. support was controlled in country by Pakistan's secretive military intelligence agency, the Directorate for Inter-Services Intelligence (ISI). By 1986, the American antiaircraft Stinger missile was deployed in Afghanistan through Pakistan. By the time the Soviets withdrew in 1989, U.S. aid had reached the $2 billion mark, mostly through Pakistan, and much of it through FATA/PATA (Cogan 1993).

FATA/PATA received close to 3 million refugees fleeing from Soviet military operations. Pashtunwali demanded that those who opposed the government could seek refuge in the area as guests. This Pashtun custom was further reinforced by the announcement by President Muhammad Zia-ul-Haq that Pakistan had been carved out of the Indian subcontinent as a home for Muslims and that Muslims persecuted in other lands were thus welcomed. The cross-border ties among Pashtuns further reinforced the tradition of hospitality offered to the refugees, most of whom were Pashtuns. The flow of international resources went directly to Pashtun society, which was regarded as the center of resistance against the Communist regime in Afghanistan.

American and Saudi aid also provided mullahs in Pashtun villages with a new status. They became independent actors who were often involved with the madrassas, which were run with Saudi aid, and thus gained enormous support bases in Pashtun society. More importantly, different mujahideen groups, primarily Afghani refugees, gained access to arms, which changed the local political culture. In addition, the flourishing cross-border heroin trade helped finance the activities of some mujahideen groups. In 1989, with the withdrawal of Soviet forces, local mujahideen groups gained control over Afghanistan and became involved in a civil war. As Afghanistan was parceled out among locally influential warlords, crime and lawlessness reached new heights, reinforcing the culture of guns and the heroin trade in FATA/PATA.

The New Great Game and the Collapse of the Government's Strategy

One goal of the Pakistani military leaders over recent decades has been to gain access to the rich mineral deposits of Afghanistan and the former Soviet Central Asian republics. The government of Pakistan coordinated support to the various mujahideen militias through the ISI. It was this support that helped refugee students from conservative Muslim madrassas in Pakistan to form the Taliban (literally "students"). In 1996, with massive support provided by the Pakistan military, the Taliban assumed political power in Kabul and sought to extend its control over most parts of Afghanistan. It followed a policy of persecution of Shia minorities and curtailed all forms of public presence of women in Afghanistan.

The government of Pakistan also encouraged the formation of ties between the Afghan Taliban and various Sunni extremist groups with young Pashtun political activists in FATA with the aim was of reducing the influence of the left-wing Pashtun nationalists. In FATA this translated into the growing influence of various types of extremist groups who aimed to introduce radical Islamic politics into local regions. One example is Maulana Sufi Mohammad, who formed the now defunct Tehreek-e-Nifaze Shariate Mohammadi (Movement for the Enforcement of Islamic Law, or TNSM) in 1994 in an area known as the Bajaur Agency. His movement soon took the form of a rebellion seeking to replace Pakistani secular law with the enforcement of Sharia law. In this instance, the TNSM was filling a vacuum created by the ineffective control of the political agent who ruled the area on behalf of Pakistan. Given the absence of any legal redress created by the area's constitutional status, the TNSM gained support as the populace sought a means of legal justice. The demand for justice and equal citizenship is behind much of the discontent in the FATA and PATA. In a grand tribal *jirga* in 2007, representatives sought a series of changes in the governance of the area, including good governance, education, employment opportunities, Islamic financial assistance, utility stores, and more (see Gul 2009).

For additional details on more recent conflicts in FATA, see Imtiaz Gul's *The Most Dangerous Place: Pakistan's Lawless Frontier* (2009).

Pakistan has responded to the increased insurgencies and demands with military force. Initially, the Pakistan government concentrated on expelling foreign Islamist groups. But by 2009, the government had deployed nearly 100,000 troops in the tribal regions in five major, and many minor, operations. The Frontier Corps, created to maintain stability in the border areas during colonial times, worked with the army, but the collateral damage was enormous. Schools and homes were destroyed by the invasions, aided by insurgents who focused on educational institutions, with 120 girls' schools demolished during the May 2009 operations in the Swat Valley. The internal dislocation resulting from the military operations has been massive, with more than 3 million people becoming internal refugees during the 2009 operations in FATA and PATA, especially in the Swat Valley.

The long-term psychological damage is also extreme. Many residents in communities under constant military control, such as the FATA region, Indian-occupied Kashmir, areas of northeastern India (especially Assam), and the Tamil regions of Sri Lanka face exposure to violence and threat suffer from post-traumatic stress disorder. Nightmares, loss of appetite, depression, and threats of suicide are common. In refugee camps, normal family relationships are disrupted. Without employment or farming, men lose their roles as heads of households, often forcing women to become the primary caretakers. Women, living without the protection of both their household enclosures and sometimes their menfolk, are also subject to various forms of violence, ranging from harassment to rape. Not surprisingly, the residents of FATA/PATA see these military operations as a threat to their culture and ethnicity, and they have demonstrated for the operations to end; one such protest, in February 2013, was supported by the cricket star and PTI leader Imran Khan, mentioned above.

During his time in office (2001–2008), President Pervez Musharraf of Pakistan also sponsored peace deals, aiming to secure a temporary halt to the war and also to discourage FATA leaders from harboring Afghan Taliban and organizing cross-border raids. He also promised, in 2008, to consider revising the constitution to remove the articles that deny legal rights to the residents of FATA/PATA. Such deals provided only temporary solutions, however. The government also promised to enforce Sharia laws if the Taliban and its allies

Box 14.1

Malala Yousafzai and the Education of Girls

The tragic shooting of the young Swat Valley resident Malala Yousafzai on October 9, 2012, by insurgents who are against the education of girls represents the current difficulties facing girls who seek education in this region. Malala's efforts, following her recovery, to fight for the education of girls in her region, and indeed worldwide, moved forward in April 2013 with the establishment of the Malala Fund by the Vital Voices Global Partnership (www.vitalvoices.org/global-initiatives/support-malala-fund).

laid down their arms. Winning against the insurgency was all but impossible, however. Indeed, in 2008 the Taliban leader Baitullah Mehsud was named one of *Time* magazine's 100 most influential people. Carrying a $5 million bounty, Mehsud was the founder of the Tehreek-e-Taliban (TTP), an organization that united several smaller Taliban groups. By the time of his death in a drone attack in 2009, he supposedly controlled some 25,000 men. In May 2007, the TTP embarrassed the Pakistan security forces when it took 250 officers and soldiers hostage, before releasing them after extensive talks. Although his death left the Taliban without effective leadership, the Taliban retaliated by organizing suicide bombing in the settled areas of Khyber Pakhtunkawa.

For more on Baitullah Mehsud, see the *Foreign Policy* article "Commander of the Faithful" (http://www.foreignpolicy.com/articles/2009/07/09/pakistans_bin_laden) and Al Jazeera's report on Mehsud's death on YouTube (http://www.youtube.com/watch?v=TFfFwjg7oq8).

The Introduction of Drone Attacks

Mehsud's death sheds a sharp light on the use of drones in FATA and PATA. Since 2004, the United States has used unmanned Predator drones to target insurgents in the region. Operated by the Central Intelligence Agency's Special Activities Division, the drone attacks cause high levels of collateral damage. While uncertainty surrounds the number of civilian deaths resulting from drone attacks, Daniel Byman (2009) at the Brookings Institution argues that some ten civilians are killed for every mid- or high-level insurgent killed. Other reports suggest fewer civilian casualties, but it is certain that drone attacks are not as surgically precise as the CIA claims.

Currently, American drone strikes undermine and weaken the Pakistani military's effort to counter the militants. Public outcry against them from all over Pakistan is enormous. In order for the country to truly combat the Pakistani Taliban, both Pakistan and the United States need to rethink their strategies.

Table 14.1

Fatalities in FATA, 2009–2013

Year	Civilians	Security forces	Militants	Total
2009	636	350	4252	5238
2010	540	262	4519	5321
2011	488	233	2313	3034
2012	549	306	2046	2901
2013	12	0	72	84
Total	2,225	1,151	13,202	16,578

Source: South Asia Terrorism Portal, "FATA Assessment, 2013," http://www.satp.org/satporgtp/countries/pakistan/Waziristan/index.html.
Note: Data through January 6, 2013.

For data, research, and analysis on drone operations in FATA and PATA, see these organizations:

- The Brookings Institution (http://www.brookings.edu/research/topics/drones)
- The Bureau of Investigative Journalists (http://www.thebureauinvestigates.com/category/projects/drones/)
- New American Foundation (http://counterterrorism.newamerica.net/drones)
- South Asia Terrorism Portal (http://satp.org)

Rethinking the Region's Needs

Writing about the status of the FATA/PATA region, Ian Shaw and Majed Akhter state, "At least since British engagement with the region, . . . the legal and constitutional status of the region in relation to state power has been co-determined with its geopolitical role" (2012, 7). The current situation in these areas is indeed the product of long-standing failures of the established state to address the colonial wrongs imposed on the local people by powers outside the region. Since the Sikh empire extended into the region, military solutions have been the preferred way to deal with the local residents, who still have little to aspire to and no legal protections. The British and Russians artificially imposed a border that completely divided local ethnicities and groups. Soviet and U.S. involvement in the region's activities further politicized it. U.S. and Saudi support to the erstwhile marginalized village mullah, along with the influx of refugees, eroded earlier tribal social organization and created conditions for a new politics of Islamization. The result has been the creation of a militant movement that the state is unable to control.

Attempts to control the militancy through military interventions and drone attacks have only further angered a population that already feels disadvantaged due to its legal status and the lack of any significant efforts to develop the region. Pashtun nationalists are speaking the truth when they claim that other people's wars have been imposed on their land and have brought enormous negative consequences to their people. Instead of repressive security measures, many, both within the region and outside of it, argue that what is needed is integration of FATA and PATA into the political economy of Pakistan, along with the implementation of land reforms, mass education, and cultural assurance of observance of the Pashtun code of honor. The involvement of the Pashtun people in various occupations, as well as Pashtun workers in the far-off Persian Gulf region, indicates that the century-old notions of fierce warriors who need to be isolated in their ancestral homeland have no cultural or political validity in the twenty-first century. It is only through such integration that solutions to the Islamic insurgency can be achieved. The current situation demands humanitarian consideration of a people devastated by wars imposed on them by outside powers for their own ideological and security concerns. Military interventions and drone attacks are not the answer. Massive development aid, education, and a rewriting of Article 247 are more viable alternatives.

References and Further Research

Banerjee, Mukulika. 2000. *The Pathan Unarmed*. Oxford: Oxford University Press.

Barfield, Thomas. 2010. *Afghanistan: A Political and Cultural History*. Princeton, NJ: Princeton University Press.

Byman, Daniel L. 2009. "Do Targeted Killings Work?" Brookings Institution. http://www.brookings.edu/research/opinions/2009/07/14-targeted-killings-byman.

Cogan, Charles G. 1993. "Partners in Time: The CIA and Afghanistan since 1979." *World Policy Journal* 10, no. 2: 73–82.

Edwards, David B. 2002. *Before Taliban: Genealogies of the Afghan Jihad*. Berkeley: University of California Press.

Gul, Imtiaz. 2009. *The Most Dangerous Place: Pakistan's Lawless Frontier*. New York: Viking.

Hollings Center for International Dialogue, and American Institute of Afghanistan Studies. July 2007. *The Durand Line: History, Consequences, and Future*. Conference Report. http://www.hollingscenter.org/wp-content/uploads/2010/03/07–2007_Durand_Line.pdf.

Khan, Zahid Ali. "Military Operations in FATA and PATA: Implications for Pakistan." *Strategic Studies* 11, no. 4; 12, no. 1: 129–146. http://www.issi.org.pk/publication-files/1339999992_58398784.pdf.

Orakzi, Ali Mohmmad Jan, et al. 2009. *Situation in FATA: Causes, Consequences and the Way Forward*. Policy Perspectives 6, no. 1. http://www.ips.org.pk/global-issues-and-politics/1057-situation-in-fata-causes-consequences-and-the-way-forward.html.

Shaw, Ian Graham Ronald, and Majed Akhter. 2012. "The Unbearable Humanness of Drone Warfare in FATA, Pakistan." *Antipode* 44, no. 4: 1490–1509 (originally published online in 2011).

Yusufzai, Ashfaq. 2013. "Pakistan Tribes Turn against Army." Inter Press Service News Agency, February 2. http://www.ipsnews.net/2013/02/pakistan-tribes-turn-against-army/.

Film

Khudai Khidmatgar. 1937. Directed by V. Panchotia. Kolkata: Bharat Lakshmi Pictures. This old film captures the essence of this all but forgotten movement. Information on the film is available online (http://www.gomolo.com/khudai-khidmatgar-movie/605).

15

Sex Trafficking in Nepal

MARY CRAWFORD

Jyoti had just turned thirteen, and she was worried. Her parents had already taken her out of school—they could not pay the fees, and there was plenty of work for her to do at home. Every day, Jyoti walked several miles to collect fodder for the family's water buffalo, carrying the heavy load home in a basket strapped to her head. After that, she worked around the house, sweeping and mending, and took care of her younger brother and two sisters while their parents worked the fields. But lately she had overheard her parents talking about arranging a marriage for her with Lal, a man in his forties who already had a wife.

Jyoti did not know exactly what marriage entailed, but she did know that daughters are not worth as much as sons. Often, she had heard the adults in her village repeat the old proverbs: *Choriko janma, hareko karma* (To be born a daughter is a lost destiny) and, regarding mothers of girls, "It's better early than late, but even if it's late, let it be a son." She also knew that she did not like Lal and did not want to go live in his village, where she would have to obey his mother and his other wife. Her parents were poor, but they did care for her, and she loved her little brother and sisters. If only they had enough food and enough money to fix their leaking roof and let her go back to school, Jyoti knew she would be satisfied.

When a strange woman turned up in Jyoti's Nepali village, everyone listened to what she had to say. The woman wore gold jewelry and a beautiful silk sari. She was the same caste as Jyoti and her family, she said, and she came from a village just a few days' walk away. The woman had come home to visit her family and give them money for a new tin roof and a pair of goats. And she was willing to help others to become equally wealthy. She would take girls to Delhi, India, and set them up with jobs as maids and dishwashers in hotels. Soon they, too, would be sending money home and helping their families live more comfortably.

Her parents' decision to send her to Delhi—and Jyoti's eager agreement—was a tragic mistake. The woman took Jyoti and several other girls across the open border to India and handed them over to an agent for a brothel in Mumbai. Held by force in a foreign country where she did not speak the language, with no one to turn to, Jyoti was beaten and raped into submission. She had gone from the poverty and deprivation of village life to the horror of sex trafficking.

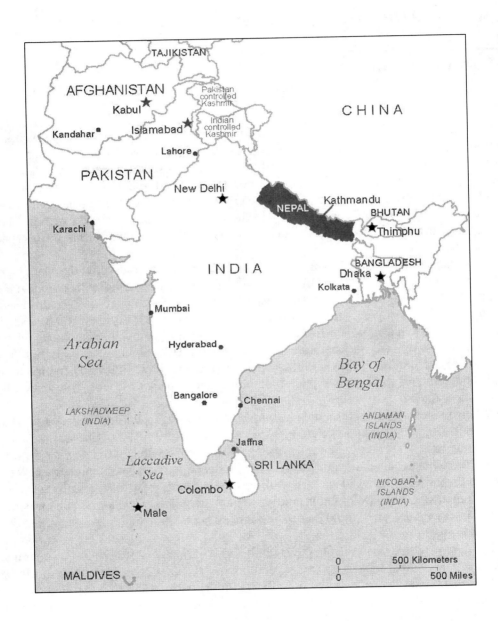

Definitions and Statistics

What is sex trafficking? A 2000 United Nations (UN) Protocol signed by more than eighty nations specifies that human trafficking, whether it is for forced labor or for sexual exploitation, involves deception or fraud, coercion, and working or living under slavery-like conditions. Anyone who recruits, abducts, or deceives another person into forced labor is guilty of the crime of trafficking. If the victim is a child under the age of eighteen, he or she cannot consent under any circumstances. Sex trafficking occurs when the victim—female or male, adult or child—is not just coerced or deceived into forced labor but is enslaved into sexual exploitation, such as forced prostitution or work in the pornography industry.

How prevalent is sex trafficking? As one might imagine, it is difficult to find out. Human trafficking is illegal and almost always occurs outside the gaze of law enforcement. Worldwide, the International Labor Organization estimates that 20 million people have been trafficked or are in forced labor in 2012 with 4.5 million being in sexual slavery. Other estimates give figures of 700,000 to 900,000 trafficked persons per year (U.S. Department of State, Trafficking in Persons Report 2007).

People are trafficked for two main purposes: forced labor and sexual exploitation. Some 1 million children are thought to be sexually exploited every year in the global commercial sex trade (U.S. Department of State, The Facts About Child Sex Tourism 2005). The U.S. Department of State estimates that 70 percent of those who are trafficked for sexual exploitation are female, and half are under the age of eighteen.

> See the ILO report (http://www.ilo.org/global/about-the-ilo/newsroom/news/WCMS_182109/lang--en/index.htm).

Each year, the Department of State issues a federally mandated Trafficking in Persons (TIP) Report, which ranks countries into three tiers. Tier 1 countries are those that meet minimum standards for the "3 Ps": preventing trafficking, protecting its survivors, and prosecuting traffickers. Tier 2 countries do not meet minimum standards but are making significant efforts to do so; and Tier 3 countries are doing little or nothing in the way of prevention, protection, or prosecution. There is also a category termed "Tier 2 Watch List," which includes countries that are in danger of slipping into Tier 3 because of their inadequate response to trafficking.

> Trafficking in Persons (TIP) Reports for the past decade are available on the U.S. State Department website (http://www.state.gov/j/tip/rls/tiprpt/).

The TIP Report is not a perfect indicator of the scope of human trafficking. Its biggest limitation is that it relies on each country's government to report its own data, and these reports may be biased, incomplete, or based on guesswork. Moreover, the accuracy of a country's report may be lowest when that country has a trafficking problem that it is unwilling or unable to address. Nevertheless, the annual TIP Report is an important effort to document human trafficking worldwide. In the 2012 report, which ranked 185 countries, only thirty-three achieved Tier 1 status. The ninety-three countries in Tier 2 included Pakistan, Bangladesh, Sri Lanka, and India. Afghanistan, Burma, and China were among the forty-two nations on the Tier 2 Watch List; and the seventeen Tier 3 nations, those with intractable problems and no evidence of efforts to change, included North Korea, Iran, and Saudi Arabia. When sex trafficking is assessed separately from labor trafficking, it is clear that Asian countries, and particularly South Asian countries, generate the largest number of cases.

Jyoti grew up in Nepal, one of the world's poorest countries. Nepal is ranked 157th out of 187 countries on the UN's Human Development Index (United Nations Development Programme 2011), and it is consistently ranked as a Tier 2 country in the TIP Reports. Relative poverty and wealth are important factors in trafficking. In general, more victims are trafficked from poor countries than wealthy ones. These *source countries* include underdeveloped nations like Nepal, as well as industrialized countries where there is high unemployment, economic inequity, or political instability. Wealthier nations serve as *destination countries*, where trafficked girls and women are forced into prostitution, or *hubs*, where multinational traffickers buy, sell, and move women. Hub countries often have powerful organized crime syndicates (Nigeria, Albania) and large commercial sex industries (Thailand, India). But poverty alone cannot explain why girls and women are sold into brothels and forced to endure grim lives of sexual slavery.

The root causes of trafficking are complex, and they differ from one society to another. It may seem paradoxical, but human trafficking is a *global* problem that demands *local* analysis. To understand why sex trafficking is a problem in Nepal in particular; one must situate it in the context of Nepali history and culture.

Nepal in the Modern World

Sandwiched between India to the south and Chinese-occupied Tibet to the north, Nepal is home to eight of the ten highest peaks in the world, including Mount Everest. Unlike India and China, Nepal is not a major player in international politics. Indeed, many Westerners know it only as a legendary, remote land, the site of mountaineering exploits or hippie escapism, an exoticized Shangri-La. Nepal was indeed remote as late as the 1960s, because its autocratic ruling families had closed the borders and restricted entry for generations after its feudal kingdoms were united into a nation. It was not until 1951, after a long-delayed democratic revolution, that Nepal established a constitutional monarchy and began to open the country to foreign visitors. Wealthy tourists with a taste for exotic South Asia began to arrive, followed by large numbers of young people looking for adventure, spiritual enlightenment, and drugs. By the 1960s, Kathmandu had become a haven of hippiedom. At the same time, Peace Corps volunteers began helping the people of Nepal improve agriculture, nutrition, health, and education. The first Peace Corps volunteers arrived in Nepal in 1962, and as of 2013, after a gap from 2004 to 2012, the Peace Corps continues to work in remote regions of the country.

As a new democracy, Nepal struggled for decades to establish a multiparty system, to control corruption, and to achieve coherence as a national entity. However, its religious, ethnic, and linguistic diversity, along with the hierarchies of caste, made unity an elusive goal. Hinduism is Nepal's predominant religion, with about 80 percent of the population as adherents, but Buddhism, Islam, Christianity, and indigenous animistic religions are also represented. There are many ethnic and caste groups, dispersed among three distinct geographical zones: the Terai, or lowland plains bordering northern India; the Kathmandu Valley; and the hill regions. The ethnic/caste groups are aggregated into four subgroups: the Hindu caste elite (Brahmin and Chhettri); the indigenous ethnic groups (Sherpa, Magar, Gurung, and about sixty others); the regional groups of the Terai; and the Dalit, traditionally the "untouchables" of the Hindu caste system. More than 100 different languages are spoken by the indigenous people of Nepal. The very terrain of the country—formidably rugged, with extremes of altitude and weather—makes travel, communication, and coalition-building difficult.

Inequality and Insurgency

Diversity in Nepal is not just a matter of difference; it is a matter of inequality and discrimination. Although the caste system was officially abolished fifty years ago, caste-linked inequities in material resources and social status are still pervasive. The elites who govern and control the country are almost all upper-caste Hindus; although they are only about 30 percent of the population, they occupy 70 percent of the choice positions in political parties, the national parliament, the judicial system, local and regional government, universities, and the media. Meanwhile four out of five Dalits, the former untouchables, live below the poverty line. About half of all Nepali children are underweight or malnourished. In the capital city, Kathmandu, upper-caste children attend elite private schools, while others scavenge for food in garbage-filled dumpsters and sleep in the gutters.

The inequitable distribution of wealth and the pervasive corruption among police, government officials, and the judicial system fueled a Maoist insurgency that began in 1996 and, for the next decade, caused incalculable suffering and hardship for many Nepalese people, particularly those who were poor and rural. Tourism and foreign aid—crucial sources of capital in Nepal—dwindled. Urban Nepalis, caught between the Royal Army and the Maoists, learned to live stoically with shortages (of cooking fuel, foodstuffs, etc.), power outages (i.e., electricity blackouts), strikes, and demonstrations that sometimes turned violent. Rural schools closed as teachers were murdered by the Maoists or fled to Kathmandu. Agriculture, the major source of sustenance for the rural majority, was disrupted. Often, the Maoists would occupy a rural village, taking food, burning houses, and terrifying the villagers. They also demanded that each household provide a recruit for the Maoist cadres. After the Maoists left, the Royal Army would arrive, accuse villagers of collaborating with the enemy, and commit its own atrocities. Large numbers of Nepali people—no one knows exactly how many—fled their homes, abandoned their family land, and headed for Kathmandu or across the border to India.

As the social fabric shredded, Nepal became notorious for human rights violations by

Box 15.1

How Researchers Study Sex Trafficking in Nepal

Researchers studying the topic of sex trafficking usually employ methods and theories from the traditional social sciences (social psychology, sociology, anthropology), as well as development studies, political science, and public health approaches. They use both quantitative and qualitative methods. For example, a large-scale quantitative survey can document the kinds of work that women and men do in a rural economy, whereas a qualitative observational study can provide insight into beliefs about women's and men's proper roles. By integrating in-depth qualitative studies and large-scale quantitative ones, researchers can learn how gender is enacted in its social context. The interdisciplinary field of gender studies is crucial to research and development endeavors. Because gender is a universal in human societies, development projects that are planned without an awareness of gender relations in a given society are likely to fail, and they may even do more harm than good.

both sides in the conflict. Both the Royal Army and the Maoists engaged in torture, rape, and murders of civilians. Disappearances were common; the government used "preventive detention" and the Maoists used forced recruitment. When my colleagues and I interviewed Nepali citizens in Kathmandu in 2004, almost everyone had a heartbreaking story to tell of how the insurgency had brought suffering, hardship, and physical and psychological trauma to their families; but even the trauma of war was not evenly distributed. Many high-caste, wealthy Nepalis in Kathmandu carefully remained loyal to the monarchy and the army (and relatively safe), while rural villagers, who may or may not have sympathized with the Maoists' methods for achieving an egalitarian, Communist society, bore the brunt of the destruction of homes, crops, and schools and the forced displacement of families.

A Slow Transition to Democracy

The insurgency came to a close in 2006, after a decade of war. The leader of the Maoist rebels became the world's first democratically elected Maoist prime minister, the monarchy was abolished, and a constitutional assembly was set up to draft a new constitution. Unfortunately, that process has not gone well, and, as of this writing, in early 2013, Nepal still has no constitution. As competing factions jockey for power, Nepal's pressing problems remain largely unresolved. In addition to creating a constitution that mandates inclusion for people of different caste, gender, ethnicity, and geographical region, those in power need to focus on establishing a responsible and ethical justice system, improving the war-devastated economy, and undoing the other damages caused by the war. Rural villagers who were displaced need to be able to reclaim their land, and military personnel (both Maoist and Royal Army) need to be reintegrated into society. On all these fronts, progress has been slow and uneven.

Poverty, civil war, and political instability all help create a climate where human trafficking is likely to take place. However, the most important causal factor in sex trafficking in Nepal is as old as the country itself: the low status of girls and women. Understanding why Nepali girls and women are vulnerable to trafficking requires an understanding of what it means to be born female in Nepal.

The Gender System in Nepal

Every known society uses gender as a classification system. In other words, every society uses the social categories "male" and "female," and these categories are linked to an individual's power, status, and access to resources. Some societies are relatively egalitarian; others subordinate girls and women through systematic devaluation and discrimination.

Gender inequality is a global reality; men have more status, power, and control than do women in most societies, to a greater or lesser degree. The United Nations Development Programme provides a measure, the Gender Inequality Index (GII), which is a composite of statistical information on three key aspects of gender inequality: women's reproductive health, their empowerment, and their participation in the labor force. As of 2011, the most recent data, Nepal's rank on the GII is 113 out of 144 countries. (For comparison purposes, the top-ranked country is Sweden, followed by the Netherlands; the United States ranks forty-seventh.) As an example of the measures used to compile the GII, let us look at one of the statistics in the empowerment category: the percentage of members of the national parliament who are women. Because women are about half the population, gender equity would be reflected in parliaments or congresses that are 50 percent female. No country has achieved that goal, but some are very close. In Sweden, it is 45 percent; in the Netherlands, 38 percent; in Nepal, it is a respectable 33 percent, due to the inclusion of diverse groups after the Maoists took control of the country; and in the United States, it is just 17 percent. In other areas, such as women's literacy and maternal health, Nepal's statistics are extremely low compared to more developed nations. In sum, Nepal is neither the best nor the worst country on measures of gender inequality, but it remains a nation where the lives of girls and women are deeply shaped and constrained by gender.

The United Nations Human Development Index and Gender Inequality Index, based on population measures, provide useful tools for assessing overall development and women's equality. The data are available on the United Nations Development Programme website (http://hdr.undp.org/en/statistics/indices/). A table shows the most recent (2011) GII data for 144 countries (http://hdr.undp.org/en/media/HDR_2011_EN_Table4.pdf). The UN 2013 Human Development report is also available (http://hdr.undp.org/en/reports/).

Global gender inequality is created and maintained by three broad forms of gender devaluation and discrimination: (1) overt violence against girls and women, (2) denying them access to resources, and (3) promulgating beliefs that justify their subordination. These general aspects of gender systems have been observed in many societies, but their specific forms vary widely. For this reason, I will briefly describe how each is enacted in Nepal.

Violence Against Girls and Women

Many researchers have noted that gender-linked violence is pervasive in Nepal. Wife-beating is a normal feature of village life, according to anthropologists, and something that a man does not have to explain or apologize for. There are no reliable statistics on rape rates, but Nepali women who work for women's rights in rural areas report that rape is common, that the victim is rarely believed, and that the standard remedy for an alleged rape is to arrange a marriage between rapist and victim. Marital rape is a virtually unknown concept. One of my female informants told me with a shrug, "He's married, it's his right." A study of married women in Kathmandu reported a 49 percent rate of marital rape—that is, virtually half of the women had been forced to have sex against their will.

Resource Control

When the men in a society control more than a fair share of its valued resources, women are disadvantaged and have less access to power. The resources can be anything—land, cattle, education, high-paying jobs, positions of power in government and academe, ownership of the media—depending on the particular society and historical era. In Nepal, women have little control of resources and little power in the public sphere. Virtually all political leaders are high-caste men. In addition, girls are denied equal access to even basic education, making it harder for them to become persons of power and influence. There is a nationwide gender gap in school enrollment, and it is larger in rural areas. The government schools are poorly equipped and maintained, and wealthier families send their children to private schools. Half of all first graders in government schools either repeat first grade or drop out, and only 8 percent of Dalit children get as far as fifth grade. Among Nepali adults, the literacy rate for women is significantly lower than for men. As a valuable resource, access to education depends on interlinked hierarchies of social class, caste, and gender.

Gendered Beliefs

Every known society has beliefs about the fundamental natures of women and men, beliefs that justify its particular system of gender discrimination. For example, in U.S. society, it was widely believed for generations that women were unsuited to be president because their female hormones would make them emotionally unstable, placing the country in danger. Although fewer people today would profess that belief publicly, the United States still, after more than 230 years of democracy, has never elected a female president, and some people still believe that women are inherently less suited to positions of power and leadership than are men. Beliefs about gender constitute what social psychologists call *consensual ideologies*—shared beliefs that justify the status quo.

In Nepal, the preference for sons is a consensual ideology, justified both by religious dogma and everyday patterns of living. In the Hindu religion, sons are expected to care for their parents in old age, and only sons can perform death rites for their parents. Having at least one son is therefore a practical necessity and a significant religious duty. Having a daughter, on the other hand, is less of a blessing and more of a liability. Upon marriage, virtually all Nepali girls move to the house of their husband's parents, and they work in the household or in a paid job that benefits their husband's family. It is not surprising, then, that in a country where many people struggle to get enough to eat, Nepalis say that educating a daughter is like watering someone else's garden. Many families adopt a practical strategy of marrying their daughters off soon after puberty, to minimize their investment. For the girls themselves, early marriage is a disaster. It ends their schooling, separates them from their network of family and neighbors, puts them at risk for pregnancy and childbirth in their early teens, leaves them vulnerable to beatings and marital rape, and increases their risk of being trafficked.

Another aspect of the consensual ideology of gender in Nepal is the belief, based in Hinduism, that women's sexuality is dangerous and disruptive to men's spirituality. Traditional religious rites enact the beliefs that women should be subordinate to their husbands and that women's bodies are a source of dangerous pollution for men. For example, high-caste Hindu wives were traditionally expected to wash their husbands' feet daily and then drink the washing-water, symbolizing that husbands are so far above wives that even a man's impurities are good for his wife. Hinduism also prescribes that menstruating women must be secluded—which, in a rural village, may mean sleeping in the cowshed for five days—in order to prevent their touch from polluting the boys and men in their families. Although these customs are loosening with modernization, Nepali women who come from urban, educated families still report that they are expected to observe rituals to control the supposed pollution of the female body and that these restrictions create dilemmas in their busy lives of work and family responsibilities. When negative beliefs about female sexuality are deeply rooted in culture, it is easier to blame a victim of sexual exploitation for her own misfortune.

The three major components of the gender system—coercive control, inequitable allocation of resources, and consensual ideologies—are linked and mutually reinforcing. They work together to maintain the higher status and power of boys and men and to limit the options for girls and women. For example, we have already seen that the literacy rate for women in Nepal is substantially lower than for men, curtailing women's opportunities. Why is this so? Families are less willing to invest in educating a daughter because of the belief that she is less worthy than a son (a consensual ideology). They know that the fruits of her labor will go to her husband's, not her natal, family (resource allocation). If a girl resists, demanding to stay in school or refusing a child marriage, her family can arrange a marriage, perhaps to a much older man, and send her to live in his village, where she may be beaten or abused if she does not submit to her husband's and in-laws' demands (coercive power). Gender is a pervasive and effective system of social control that works to disadvantage girls and women.

Many rural Nepali girls do want to escape the life that awaits them. They have seen fashion magazines and Bollywood DVDs brought to their villages, and they yearn for a "love marriage," not one arranged by their parents. They want to contribute cash earnings to help their families buy a goat or send a little one to school. The hope of escaping from poverty and subordination motivates them to take risks. Studies of trafficking survivors show that the main methods used by traffickers are the promise of a job (as in Jyoti's case) or a fake marriage.

The life of a girl who is trafficked is one of sexual slavery. She is taken from her home and family, transported to a country where she does not know the language, and held as a prisoner. She is beaten, raped, and sold for prostitution until she is "broken" into compliance. Several studies have shown that the average age for being trafficked is between fourteen and sixteen. There is a constant demand in Indian brothels for new, young girls. Despite the odds against them, many girls try repeatedly to escape, only to be returned to the brothel by corrupt police and beaten for their attempts to gain freedom. In a major report on girls and women working in the brothels of Mumbai and Kolkata by the organization Terre des Hommes, virtually *all* the Nepali women working as prostitutes were there because they had been trafficked. Typically, trafficked girls and women work for several years, until they become sick with tuberculosis, HIV/AIDS, or other diseases. Very few ever return to Nepal, because of the stigma associated with their past and because they have no way to earn income there. It is impossible to know how many Nepali girls have been lost over the years—vanished into the underworld of the sex industry, with their lives, sufferings, and deaths unrecorded and unacknowledged.

Interventions: What Is Being Done About Sex Trafficking?

Attacking the problem of sex trafficking requires three distinct kinds of interventions, characterized as the "3 Ps" in the U.S. State Department's TIP Reports: preventing trafficking, protecting its survivors, and prosecuting the perpetrators. Ideally, the design and implementation of interventions should be locally derived and focused. What works in Libya, Croatia, or Thailand might not work in Nepal, because the root causes and the specifics of trafficking differ in each locale. Moreover, the ability and willingness of central governments to intervene also differ from one nation to another. In Nepal, the central government remains weakened by the ten-year civil war, factional infighting, corruption, and the lack of a functioning constitution. Therefore, although there are some governmental initiatives, the bulk of the antitrafficking work is done by nonprofit charitable organizations. These nongovernmental organizations (NGOs) may be local, national, or international. They raise money from private and institutional donors and use it to implement intervention projects.

Empowering Women

In Nepal, several NGOs have focused on preventing trafficking by attacking its most deeply rooted cause, the low status and power of girls and women. They have designed and implemented programs to teach rural, low-caste, and impoverished women about their human rights and to encourage families to keep their daughters in school. They have also sought to increase women's economic power by creating village cooperatives and microlending plans. They have sponsored educational programs that teach villagers about trafficking and how to know when it is safe to take a job elsewhere. In 2012, one of the largest international NGOs, the Asia Foundation, began a five-year program of interventions to promote safe migration. Programs aimed at empowering girls and women are vital forms of intervention. By helping girls and women increase their options and have more voice in their futures, such interventions reduce the risk of their being trafficked.

Many international organizations work to promote safe migration, an end to labor trafficking and sex trafficking, the empowerment of girls and women, and human rights for all, including the following:

- Asia Foundation (http://www.asiafoundation.org)
- Human Rights Watch (http://www.hrw.org)
- International Labor Organization (http://www.ilo.org)
- Terre des Hommes International Federation (http://www.terredeshommes.org); see also the TDH Nepal Delegation Office (http://tdhnepal.org/)

Protecting Survivors

The task of protecting and caring for survivors of sex trafficking is equally important. When a girl or woman manages to escape the brothel life, she is in need of many things, including a safe place to stay, trauma counseling, medical care, education or vocational training, and legal support. She is likely to be depressed and to blame herself for what happened to her. She is also very much alone in the world, cut off from family and stigmatized by others. She may want to be reunited with her family but need help contacting family members. Ultimately, she wants to return to society as a respected person, but it may be months or years before she can achieve that goal.

Several NGOs founded and run by Nepali women provide services for survivors. The largest and best known is Maiti Nepal, which funds rescue operations, preventive interceptions at the Nepal-India border, and a variety of helping resources for rescued girls and women. Another woman-founded organization, ABC Nepal, was the first NGO to take on the issue of trafficking. It operates shelters in Kathmandu and five regional towns, where girls and women can stay as long as they need, get basic medical care and psychological counseling, and learn skills for employment. This NGO helps girls reunite with their families by approaching family members and assessing whether they can be encouraged to accept the girl after knowing her past. Reducing stigma and discrimination against trafficking survivors is an important part of their rehabilitation. ABC Nepal also coordinates more than 200 microcredit cooperatives in rural districts, and it sponsors human rights education for disadvantaged women.

> These three Nepal-based organizations lead the way in helping survivors, em-powering girls and women, and educating the public about sex trafficking in Nepal:
>
> - ABC Nepal (http://abcnepal.org.np/)
> - Maiti Nepal (http://www.maitinepal.org/)
> - Shakti Samuha (http://www.shaktisamuha.org.np/)

Shakti Samuha, an organization founded by trafficking survivors themselves, has conducted systematic research on trafficking and trafficking survivors, including those trafficked within Nepal (e.g., to the massage parlors of Kathmandu). This NGO has also sponsored a series of regional conferences for trafficking survivors, in which hundreds of women come together to tell their stories and develop strategies for raising awareness about trafficking. Other antitrafficking NGOs are also working on behalf of survivors, and most antitrafficking NGOs also offer services for rape victims and women who have experienced domestic violence. Space does not permit describing them all, but it is useful to note that many of these groups have participated in establishing a national consortium of NGOs, the National Network Against Girl Trafficking.

Prosecution

Eliminating sex trafficking requires attention not just to its victims, but to its perpetrators. Who are the brokers who go to villages and deceive girls into leaving home? Who are the brothel operators that buy and sell girls? Who are the clients who pay for sex with enslaved underage girls? And what is being done to bring the perpetrators to justice?

There has been very little research on the perpetrator side of sex trafficking. Studies suggest that, in Nepal, brokers are often "small businessmen." The typical trafficker is a Nepali man in his twenties or thirties who is experienced in crossing the border and has a network of contacts in Indian brothels. He can make a great deal more money by selling girls than he can by farming. Female brokers and brothel owners are often former victims of trafficking who become hardened to violence and pain, both their own and that of others. As they move up in the brothel system and gain more power, they perpetuate the cycle. After a trafficked girl is sold to a brothel owner, organized crime becomes part of the equation. Prostitution in India's cities is controlled by powerful syndicates that play a role in every part of the sex industry, from controlling the enslaved girls, to paying off the police and politicians, to money laundering. Meanwhile, the clients who buy sex with young Nepali girls in the brothels of Delhi, Mumbai, or Kolkata are most often local men who claim that they did not know the girls were underage or held captive.

Nepal has enacted antitrafficking legislation and has sought to reduce trafficking by establishing the Ministry of Women, Children and Social Welfare. The government has also sponsored trafficking awareness training for police and border officials. However, governmental resources in Nepal are limited, and law enforcement on this issue remains less than ideal. Perhaps for this reason, few trafficking survivors file a legal case against their traffickers. Many are uneducated and illiterate, and they do not expect the legal system to help them. They also fear revenge from the traffickers if they go public. According to Shakti Samuha, the NGO founded by survivors, only 9 percent of the formerly trafficked women they surveyed had filed a criminal complaint. If a trafficked woman remains in India, the odds are also against her in bringing her trafficker to justice. One of the reasons that India is classified as a Tier 2 country in the annual TIP Reports is its very low rate of prosecution and conviction of brokers, brothel owners, pimps, and corrupt police and public officials.

Are efforts to end sex trafficking making a difference? The efforts of Nepal's NGOs are certainly heroic. They have saved many lives by offering shelter; medical, psychological, and legal services; and education, training, and rehabilitation. As one survivor told me, "I'll never forget what ABC Nepal did for me when I didn't want to live. I wanted to end my life . . . [but it] helped me all the way." But NGOs may not be able to provide all the medical and psychological services that survivors need. Some NGOs have also been criticized for questionable practices that violate survivors' rights to privacy and autonomy. In attempts to prevent trafficking, some have advocated restrictions that violate adult women's right to travel or migrate freely. In order to end the horror of sex trafficking, it is necessary to prevent it from happening by fostering the education of communities and the empowerment of women, not by restricting women's rights. Plus it is necessary to bring to justice the traffickers and those who enable their crimes.

Jyoti was rescued when Indian police raided Mumbai brothels and found more than 200 underage Nepali girls who had been trafficked. The girls were taken to a temporary shelter, where they stayed for months because the Nepali government was reluctant to help them. Finally, Jyoti was among the 124 girls allowed to return to Kathmandu and placed in the custody of antitrafficking NGOs. There, she began the slow process of returning to normal life. Jyoti suffered from depression and feelings of hopelessness. Although she had physical problems—a skin disease, stomach pain—she had not contracted HIV during her two years in the brothel. (According to best estimates, however, over half of the female sex workers in Indian brothels are HIV positive.) The NGO provided her with shelter, schooling, basic medical care, rudimentary psychological counseling, and a community of other rescued girls and women. Fifteen years after her rescue, Jyoti is a healthy, poised woman who works in the offices of Shakti Samuha, alongside other survivors of trafficking. She has established contact with her family but does not feel that she could go back to live in her village. She has not married. Jyoti still cannot talk about her ordeal in the brothel without breaking into tears. Her traffickers have not been brought to justice.

References and Further Research

Bennett, Lynn. 1983. *Dangerous Wives and Sacred Sisters: Social and Symbolic Roles of High-Caste Women in Nepal.* New York: Columbia University Press.

Cameron, Mary. 1998. *On the Edge of the Auspicious: Gender and Caste in Nepal.* Urbana: University of Illinois Press.

Crawford, Mary. 2010. *Sex Trafficking in South Asia: Telling Maya's Story.* London: Routledge.

Crawford, Mary, and Michelle R. Kaufman. 2008. "Sex Trafficking in Nepal: Survivor Characteristics and Long Term Outcomes." *Violence Against Women* 14, no. 8: 905–916.

Crawford, Mary, Michelle R. Kaufman, and Alka Gurung. 2007. "Women and Children Last: The Effects of the Maoist Insurgency on Gender-Based Violence." In *Contentious Politics and Democratization in Nepal*, edited by Mahendra Lawoti, 95–119. New Delhi and Thousand Oaks, CA: SAGE.

Farr, Kathyrn. 2005. *Sex Trafficking: The Global Market in Women and Children.* New York: Worth.

International Labor Organization. 2012. "21 Million People Are Now Victims of Forced Labour, ILO Says." http://www.ilo.org/global/about-the-ilo/newsroom/news/WCMS_181961/lang--n/index.htm.

Kaufman, Michelle R., and Mary Crawford. 2011. "Sex Trafficking in Nepal: A Review of Intervention and Prevention Programs." *Violence Against Women* 17, no. 5: 651–665.

Lawoti, Mahendra, ed. 2007. *Contentious Politics and Democratization in Nepal.* Thousand Oaks, CA: SAGE.

McCabe, Kimberley A., and Sabita Manian, eds. 2010. *Sex Trafficking: A Global Perspective.* New York: Lexington.

Østergaard, Lise, ed. 1992. *Gender and Development: A Practical Guide.* London: Routledge.

Puri, Mahesh, Jyotsna Tamang, and Iqbal Shah. 2011. "Suffering in Silence: Consequences of Sexual Violence within Marriage Among Young Women in Nepal." *BMC Public Health* 11: 29. http://www.biomedcentral.com/1471–2458/11/29.

Silverman, Jay G., Michelle R. Decker, Jhumka Gupta, Ayonija Masheshwari, Brian M. Willis, and Anita Raj. 2007. "HIV Prevalence and Predictors of Infection in Sex-Trafficked Nepalese Girls and Women." *Journal of the American Medical Association* 298, no. 5: 536–542.

Terre des Hommes. 2005. *A Study of Trafficked Nepalese Girls and Women in Mumbai and Kolkata, India.* Kathmandu, Nepal: Terre des Hommes Foundation. http://cfsc.trunky.net/_uploads/Publications/A_Study_of_Trafficked_Nepalese_Girls.pdf.

United Nations Development Programme. 2011. *International Human Development Indicators: Nepal.* http://hdrstats.undp.org/en/countries/profiles/npl.html.

16

Likhiyā
Painting Women's Lives in Rural Northern India

SUSAN SNOW WADLEY

For generations, women in the Mithila region of the northern Indian state of Bihar have been painting auspicious images on the inner walls of their courtyards and houses. They use the word *likhiyā*, which means "write," to describe what they do as painting a story. The images they use to tell stories often represent their gods and goddesses, or fertility symbols, and some provide social commentary on the women's daily lives. Once outsiders discovered the paintings in the 1930s, they became subject to new influences, eventually resulting in a series of changes related to commodification, style, and content. As folk art moves into the modern marketplace, instead of being something created for family or community use, it becomes commodified; that is, it comes to be seen as having economic value beyond its household use. Fundamental to commodification are buyers (in this case, middle-class Indians and tourists), intermediaries (government organizations, nongovernmental organizations, and individuals or commercial entities), and the artists' experiences that define content. Ultimately, the success of folk art in the marketplace is dependent upon artists producing content, often with the advice and guidance of intermediaries, which buyers desire and hence acquire (see Adams 2005 for a discussion of these processes).

Intermediaries are vital to the now transnational fame of Mithila painting. In the late 1960s, Indian government officials encouraged female painters to transfer their paintings to paper and sell them in markets around the world. The use of paper in turn encouraged the development of new artistic styles. As the paintings reach wider and wider audiences, the painters, still mostly girls and women, began to transform their art to capture new messages that would attract new audiences, including addressing issues of social justice for women. The current popularity of Mithila art in both India and the world is a story of globalization. More specifically, it is a story of the interactions of one remote rural community with the wider world.

Additional paintings illustrating the ideas and styles discussed here and providing additional depth to these case studies are available on the Global South Asia website of the South Asia Center at Syracuse University (http://globalsouthasia. syr.edu/). This chapter refers to the website with "see SU's website" in specific sections of the text.

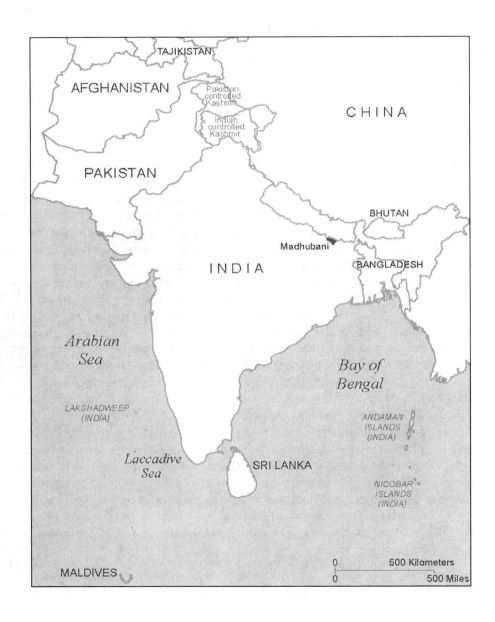

This painting of the god Krishna by the Brahmin artist Sita Devi, made in 1981, is typical of the bhārnī style that was most popular in the early marketing of Mithila painting. Krishna is portrayed playing his flute and standing by his vehicle, the peacock. *(Photo by David Szanton/Ethnic Arts Foundation. Used by permission.)*

Folk arts (artistic creations made for local family and community consumption) are found throughout the world, and in every region of South Asia, though the exact styles and contents shift depending on local contexts, including the local environment, social groupings, and rituals. Not surprisingly, the folk arts of any region relate to its local ecology. Hence the folk arts of Mithila contain many images of fish and ponds, bamboo groves, and rice fields. They also often contain images of deities and rituals not found in other parts of South Asia. In contrast, the ritual scrolls found in arid Rajasthan in western India are filled with camels, barren deserts, and large sandstone forts. Other variations across India concern the caste and gender of those making the art, which is sometimes done only by the lowest castes in a given region and sometimes by the highest. In Bihar, Mithila art was originally made almost solely by high-caste women, though now a group of former untouchables, both male and female, known as Dusadhs or Dalits, are prominent producers of the art. Moreover, a few high-caste men have become renowned Mithila painters. Three hundred miles to the east, in the Bengali region near Kolkata, the painters of the scrolls known as *pat* are of a very low-caste group and originally were all

---

Box 16.1

Notes on Studying the Imagery in Mithila Art

The earliest known Mithila paintings depict gods and goddesses, as well as auspicious symbols attached to weddings and other rituals. In fact, the most important paintings were those that adorned the walls of the bridal chamber, creating a promising beginning to the married life of the newlywed couple. To understand the meaning and significance of this imagery, scholars of art history and religion have to decode the images of the deities and the stories contained in each image and then relate them to various textual traditions in Sanskrit, vernacular texts, and oral stories.

---

male, though now women also paint the scrolls. In Rajasthan, scroll painters are solely higher-caste males.

Folk paintings from Rajasthan, Bengal, and Mithila share one common feature: a considerable change in the content portrayed in recent years due to commercialization. Throughout most of the twentieth century, the paintings depicted the gods, goddesses, saints, and mythological stories that have long captured the imaginations of those living in South Asia. Now these folk artists, of whatever region, are affected by new global trends and events, as well as new economic situations, and they paint images that speak to a broader constituency, including potential purchasers in a global market.

In many instances, Indian folk arts have barely survived into the twenty-first century. Like other folks artists, however, those in Mithila are adapting their art to new markets: using new painting styles; often focusing on new themes, including social justice; and employing new media, including different paints and painting surfaces. These changes have evolved within the context of new and expanding audiences for their work, including tourists at markets in Delhi and middle-class housewives in Kolkata, who seek art for their homes as reminders of the "traditional" India of their imaginations or the modern India in which social justice is often a focus of middle-class and foreign interest. With folk art now a commodity to be sold, painters are increasingly aware of the desires of potential buyers—of their likes and dislikes concerning style and content.

A Brief History of Mithila Painting

Mithila art—also referred to as Madhubani after the district of the same name, though Mithila is preferred because its geographic spread is wider, even extending thirty miles into neighboring Nepal—is thought to be hundreds of years old. The earliest documentation of the style, however, was by the British administrator William Archer. In 1934, after the region was hit by a massive earthquake, Archer, a British subdivisional officer, set out on horseback to examine the destruction. Many of the village's mud houses were heavily damaged, but he was astonished to find colorful paintings still visible on the inner

---

Box 16.2

Tara Books: Commodification in Action

In a vibrant form of commodification of folk arts, Tara Books, a publisher from Chennai, produces high-quality books based on India's folk arts, but with modern themes—such as a Bengali scroll telling of the life of Martin Luther King Jr. or a set of Mithila paintings of "water life," including forms not known in the Mithila region, by the young male painter Rambharos Jha. Some artists now paint on cloth, decorating saris and scarves with Mithila designs for the increasingly large numbers of Indian upper-middle-class consumers.

To view the products featuring Mithila styles published by Tara Books, go to its website (http://www.tarabooks.com) and search for "Mithila."

---

walls of some of the homes. Painted by the households' women to celebrate rituals such as marriage or to honor various gods and goddesses, this artistic tradition had been hidden from outsiders and ignored by local male elites. Several years later, Archer returned to the Mithila region to photograph this tradition, and in 1949 he published an article on Mithila painting that expanded the awareness of the paintings beyond India.

The Ethnic Arts Foundation (EFA), which has been working with Mithila artists since the 1980s, runs a school for young women, the Mithila Art Institute. The EFA sponsors a web page titled "Mithila Painting: The Evolution of an Art Form" (http://www.mithilapaintings-eaf.org), which describes an exhibition of Mithila paintings and gives a visual history of the tradition of Mithila art, as well as numerous examples. See also the blog on recent Mithila work (peterzirnis.com).

The wall paintings were part of a tradition that also included ritual designs on the cow-dunged floors of village houses, as well as designs drawn on paper in which to wrap the *sindur*, a ritual gift given to a bride as she departed for the home of her in-laws. *Sindur* is the red powder used in the hair parting of an auspiciously married woman in Hindu communities. The gift of *sindur* was a key part of the bride's trousseau, and decorating the paper wrapper with images of gods and goddesses denoted its auspiciousness. Nowadays it is the old gods and goddesses reimagined on paper—or many topics unheard-of prior to 1968—that make paintings from the Mithila region famous (see SU's website).

Caste and Style in Mithila Painting

Caste plays an important role in Mithila painting, as social interactions across caste boundaries, especially for women, were rare in rural India until recently. (Even now, most

Painting of Ganesh by an unknown artist, early twenty-first century. *(Photo by Susan Wadley)*

women socialize only with those of their own caste group.) The two highest castes of the region—the Brahmin, or priestly, caste, and the slightly lower-ranking Kayastha, or accountant/scribe, caste—were the only ones whose paintings Archer wrote about. Both castes were landowners, and most of their members were comparatively well-off. For most, food was not an issue, and by the 1950s some high-caste girls, as well as most boys, received a primary education, although the overall literacy rate for females in Bihar was barely 8 percent in 1961 and barely 53 percent in 2011. All of Archer's photographs were taken in high-caste—Brahmin or Kayastha—houses; however, it is not known whether this was due to his limited access to the homes of the region or to the possibility that the painting was exclusively done in households of these castes.

Notably, the two groups painted in distinct styles: the Brahmin in a style known as *bhārnī*, meaning "filled" (i.e., filled with color), and the Kayastha in a style known as *kachnī*, meaning "linear" (i.e., drawings primarily in black and red hues).

The *bhārnī* style, as represented by the Brahmin artist Sita Devi, became the most popular in the Delhi markets, while the Kayastha painters were best known abroad. The colorful gods and goddesses of the *bhārnī* style captured the imaginations of the urban and tourist audiences who were easily able to appreciate the imagery through their personal

The Sun Deity by a Dusadh painter, 2003. *(Photo by Susan Wadley)*

knowledge of Hindu deities and religious epics known across India. The most popular paintings in the Mithila region—the complicated *kohbar* that adorned the bridal chamber with line drawings of a lotus pond, bamboo, Shiva and Parvati, fish, birds, and the bride and groom—seldom made it to the Delhi markets because deciphering the imagery and meanings of these complex drawings required an intimate knowledge of the symbols used in the Mithila region in contrast to the images of well-known pan-Indian gods and goddesses (see SU's website).

In 1972, the German folklorist Erica Moser worked with the Dusadh community in the village of Jitwarpur, a few miles from Madhubani town, to create a style of Mithila art based on their traditional tattoos. The Dusadhs are a formerly untouchable caste of landless laborers who have been painting on paper over the past forty years. Lower castes and untouchables were not previously known for their painting, although they often made clay reliefs on their walls. Around the time Moser began her work with the caste, a Dusadh woman began using cow dung as a wash on the paper before painting.

Box 16.3

Commerce, Family Production, and Mithila Art

In a telling example of the commercial links forged between rural Indian communities and the broader global market, fourteen members of one Dusadh family paint more or less full-time in order to sell inexpensive paintings, costing between US$1 and $25, in the Delhi markets. They often supplement their own productions with pieces bought from other families in their neighborhood (see SU's website).

Nowadays, upper-caste differences in painting style have all but disappeared, with the linear style of the Kayastha community dominating the commercial market. As painters have become more skilled, this style allows a refinement that is increasingly popular with both painters and buyers. Further, the Dusadh low-caste painters are now painting in high-caste styles in order to meet market demands, although almost no high-caste painters have borrowed from the Dusadh styles.

In the late 1960s, Bihar was hit by a severe drought, resulting in a famine. Knowing of the women's wall paintings in the Mithila region, Pupul Jayakar, then head of the All India Handicrafts Board and committed to the commercializing of Indian crafts, conceived of a plan to help the women of the region earn a small income. She commissioned a Bombay-based artist, Bhaskar Kulkarni, to go to Madhubani to help women learn to paint on paper. Few women were willing to work with him, because he was an elite urban male and this was a very conservative area. However, several high-caste (Brahmin or Kayastha) women, mostly widows, were apparently more willing to step outside the bounds of female propriety to earn a living, and they began to paint on paper. Working with other government agencies seeking to commercialize Indian folk arts, Kulkarni provided paper and helped the women find markets through the new government-sponsored folk crafts and arts emporia in Delhi. Working to popularize Mithila painting, the railways minister also commissioned Mithila art in rail stations across India, including in Madhubani (see SU's website), while the then-renowned Akbar Hotel in Delhi decorated its coffee house with paintings in the Mithila style.

In a move that shifted the marketing of Mithila paintings directly to the United States, the American anthropologist Raymond Owens visited the region in the late 1970s and worked with the artists to develop alternative markets. Helping to form a cooperative, he bought paintings and sold them in the United States for significantly more than the Indian government outlets and local vendors were paying, returning the income to the artists. He also made a film featuring five Mithila painters that was distributed across the United States. Owens founded the Ethnic Arts Foundation, through which he sought to encourage young artists. Following his death in 2003, his estate funded the small Mithila Art Institute (MAI) in Madhubani, where young women—and an occasional male—began to train in the Mithila tradition. Many of the institute's former students are among the very best of the new generation of Mithila painters (see SU's website).

Box 16.4

Two Styles, Both Contemporary

Despite the major transformation in style, the aesthetic at the heart of Mithila art has been maintained. This is readily apparent in the work of its best young artists. Painted by Shalinee Kumari, this vision of the sun goddess heating the earth is in marked contrast to the depiction of Krishna with his flute.

Painting of the earth goddess entreating the sun god to cease heating the earth by Shalinee Kumari, 2009. *(Photo by David Szanton/Ethnic Arts Foundation. Used by permission.)*

Another young woman, Amrita Jha, has taken the style in yet a different direction, as found in her painting of two snails (see photo on SU's website). Using techniques developed for Mithila art, she has transformed it in ways that almost deny its roots. These two young women, along with other Mithila artists, are moving Mithila art away from its place in the folk tradition, blurring the boundaries between folk and contemporary art.

Box 16.5

A Sign of Commodification

In yet another mark of the commodification of Mithila art, in 2010 the chain Crate and Barrel hired a low-caste woman and her family to produce 400 copies of one painting at $10 each, which the store then framed and sold for $199 in the United States. The difference between what is paid to the artist and the cost to the U.S. buyer suggests exploitation of the "illiterate folk artist" by commercial interests. The ad on the Crate and Barrel web page described the painting:

The naïve art form of Madhubani paintings has been passed down from mother to daughter, generation to generation in a remote region of northern India. Today, income from the paintings helps provide food, clothing, and education for their children. Artist Lalita Devi is paralyzed, but continues to paint with the help of family members who steady her hand. Her vision is that of a jungle where predator and prey live together in harmony. Paper handpainted with brilliant colors made from natural spices, leaves, flowers and soot; framed in a sustainable solid shesham wood frame covered by glass.

- Depicts a jungle where prey and predator live in harmony
- Handcrafted paper with natural dyes from spices, flowers, and soot
- Sustainable solid shesham wood frame
- Each is signed and numbered with the story on the back of the frame

Since the founding of the Mithila Art Institute (MAI) in 2003, about twenty-five young women and a few men have been trained each year. Still funded by the estate of Raymond Owens and now by donations from the United States, the MAI holds a yearly competition for class seats. Some 200 to 300 eager artists in their late teens compete for the twenty-five seats. Those who excel are offered a second year of training, and some go on to gain worldwide recognition, including Rambharos Jha, whose book *Waterlife* was published by Tara Books, and Shalinee Kumari, whose work was exhibited in San Francisco. The MAI has thus succeeded in both teaching the tradition and graduating artists who lead the way in transforming the art, both in quality and in content.

Two museums, one in Delhi and one in Japan, have enormously influenced Mithila art. In Delhi, the National Crafts Museum was an early supporter, especially under its director Jyotindra Jain in the 1980s. Dr. Jain was the patron of one of the most renowned of the early painters, Ganga Devi of the Kayastha caste. Disowned by her husband when he took a second wife (Ganga Devi had not given him an heir), she began painting in the late 1960s, and she made many important innovations in Mithila art. She represented India at the 1985 Festival of India in Washington, DC, and also traveled to Japan and the Soviet Union. Her paintings depicting her travels abroad, as well as her treatment for cancer, broke through the barrier of religious art and made paintings about current events acceptable.

The Mithila Museum in Niigata Prefecture, Japan, opened in the early 1980s. Its founder

Dulari Devi painting the Ramayana Clock Tower, Madhubani, 2010. *(Photo by Susan Snow Wadley)*

and director, Tokio Hasegawa, had discovered Mithila art in the mid-1970s through a friend. Starting with works collected in Madhubani, Hasegawa eventually brought various painters to Japan for residencies of two to six months, including Ganga Devi in 1988. Ganga Devi's Kayastha *kachnī* style of painting dominates the collection, since almost all those invited were of the Kayastha caste.

In the early twenty-first century, Mithila painting is readily available in crafts markets across India and especially in Delhi, where several stalls selling inexpensive Mithila art are usually found at Dilli Haat, the folk arts market in South Delhi. Mithila painters also regularly have stalls at the National Crafts Museum, where different folk artists are featured each month. Some of these artists have remained in Delhi, operating what are best termed "factories" for producing paintings, often by relatives, mimicking the family style.

The Mithila style has garnered admiration beyond that usually reserved for folk art. Four older Mithila painters have won the Padma Shri (also spelled Padmashree), the Indian government's highest award for artists and other cultural and social luminaries. Although most Mithila paintings in India cost less than $25, a few now sell for thousands, including those of the twenty-five-year-old painter Shalinee Kumari, who had a solo exhibition at a San Francisco gallery in 2009, with paintings priced at $3,500.

One of the most prominent new painters is a middle-aged woman, Dulari Devi, of the Mala, or fishing, community. Working as a maidservant in the house of a famous Kayastha painter, she slowly began to learn to paint. Her life story is found in her book, *Following My Paintbrush* (2010). Dulari was recently commissioned by the Madhubani town government to paint the clock tower near the town's center with a series illustrating the epic story of the Ramayana. The town's goal is to prominently display Mithila art in order to attract tourists to a small, remote town—five hours by car from Patna, Bihar—with no attractions for outsiders beyond its art.

Painting Women's Stories

Beginning with Ganga Devi in the 1980s, many Mithila painters have illustrated women's lives and the issues that women face. As one prominent Delhi-based Mithila painter put it, "We write (*likhiyā*) women's stories through our paintings." The lives of the rural women of the Mithila region revolve around their families (especially arranging happy marriages for their offspring) and the worship of many deities, all ideas captured in their wall paintings. The artists seek, even today, to bring good luck and blessings to bride and groom by decorating the bridal chamber with images of fertility symbols and deities—especially the happily married god and goddess, Shiva and Parvati. Yet the stories now told move far beyond marriage and the worship of these divinities.

Mithila women, like those in most of rural India, seldom make major life decisions, for their lives are defined first by their parents and then by their in-laws. One recent painting by Jyoti Kumari, a second-year student at the MAI, captures these restrictions on women through metaphorical imagery. The painting features three female puppets with male puppeteers (see SU's website). The first puppet is a young girl, with the strings held by her controlling father. The second is a young woman, controlled by her husband. The third is an old woman, with her son as the puppeteer. Reinforcing the dictates of a centuries-old Hindu tradition that men control women in every phase of their lives, Jyoti's painting suggests that even today women lack choices and must bow to the dictates of the men in their families.

Opportunities for girls and women in the Mithila region were limited in the past, and they continue to be so now. Girls are expected to contribute to housework and child care, in part because their mothers might have five or more children. Many girls never receive an education, and if they do, they attend school only through the primary level (although almost all of the middle- and upper-class students in the MAI are in high school or college). In addition, major caste and rural-urban disparities exist: women of low castes receive significantly less education than those in high castes, and education for those living in rural areas is below that of those in urban areas.

Higher-caste women painters belong to landowning groups, so their time is taken up with processing harvests, grinding grain into flour, and cooking for large families over stoves fueled with dried cow dung. Many families are "joint families," which means that several married couples and their children share the house and labor. Often these households are headed by grandparents, with their married sons, their sons' wives, and

Painting concerning lack of schooling for girls by Vinita Jha, circa 2005. *(Photo by David Szanton/ Ethnic Arts Foundation. Used by permission.)*

their grandchildren sharing a mud-walled house (though richer landlords now have large cement-block compounds). Many Brahmin families hire laborers who do much of the field work, while the men conduct religious rituals and chat with their friends. Women's work never stops, however, for there are always meals to be prepared, pots to wash, and children to care for. For lower-caste women who also work as field laborers, the burdens are even greater. Modern painters often capture this aspect of women's lives, focusing on women's work while men perform rituals or chat or go to school. One such work, painted by Vinita Jha around 2002, portrays a working mother with her daughters helping her at her grinding stone, while the boys attend school (see SU's website).

Older women tell of learning to paint as children from their mothers and grandmothers. Relatives invited those who became skilled to paint their bridal chambers, so that painting became a way to earn some local recognition. Young girls would keep bits of paper with designs on them that they could carry to their husbands' houses when they became brides. While those in the older generation, now in their seventies and eighties, would have been forty or older when painting on paper began, painters now in their forties and fifties often learned to paint directly onto paper. Vinita Jha, now about fifty years old, tells of foreigners becoming fascinated by her aunt's painting and floor designs. She herself began to paint and by age thirteen she seldom did her schoolwork, focusing instead on her drawings. She had to give up her craft, however, when she was a young housewife and mother of four, returning to it only when her children were older. It now provides crucial support to her family.

Most of the younger painters learned basic designs from mothers or grandmothers. Those attending the Mithila Art Institute have to display basic skills to pass the initial screening, which requires them to create a painting in a four-hour period. Admittance to MAI is so sought-after that some graduates of the school now teach girls in their communities how to draw so that they can pass the test. But the goal of students at MAI and in the villages of the region is to make paintings that will sell. It is this commercial goal—coupled with a desire to capture the issues in the world around them, a desire also influenced by the various intermediaries that find urban consumers—that determines the subjects of paintings today. Indeed, as many of the artists have discovered, paintings about social justice are popular with foreign, as well as some Indian, audiences.

Detailed Social Commentary

While women paint about being under the control of men in their daily lives, they also portray broader themes, such as social and economic inequities, women's seclusion, and discrimination against women more generally. Much of their work focuses on marriage, including dowry and dowry deaths, childbirth, the preference for sons, and the discrimination against female children and fetuses. Although outlawed nationally in 1961, dowry payments are still demanded throughout India, and they are the source of much discrimination against Indian women.

The lower-caste servant Dulari Devi has produced two paintings with explicit imagery illuminating the problems of economic discrimination against poor families. One painting shows women taking their children to a health clinic, where the babies inside the building receive polio immunizations and care from the nurses. But a nurse stands at the entrance barring the remaining poor women from the clinic. One mother, tears flowing down her cheeks, holds her sick baby. Unable to pay the bribes demanded, the poor are often barred from clinics such as this one. In another painting, titled *The Rich Flee from the Flood While the Poor Collect and Mourn the Dead*, rich people dressed in lavish garb flee rising floodwaters in a boat, while the poor, shown without jewelry and often bare-chested, use nets to recover bodies and care for corpses (see SU's website).

Dulari's personal circumstances, despite her success as a painter, might well be the subject of one of her paintings. She lives in a three-room mud hut with her brother and his family, whose children she helps to raise, while also working as a servant for her high-caste neighbor (and one-time teacher) in the neighbor's large, cement, multiroom house, surrounding a huge courtyard. She sometimes works with the daughter of her employers, who often claims credit for Dulari's work. Indeed, Dulari has firsthand experience with economic discrimination.

Another example of explicit social criticism is a painting titled *Corruption*, made in 2011 by a young Brahmin student, Supriya Jha. At a time when Indian politics are focused on issues of corruption, she provides specific everyday examples (see SU's website). Within a border of snakes (representing evil), she shows four scenes where corruption flourishes. In the first, a trucker pays a guard to get onto a road that is marked "no entry." In the second, a teacher sits reading her newspaper while a student talks on a

Painting of mothers and children at a child health clinic by Dulari Devi, circa 2004. *(Photo by David Szanton/Ethnic Arts Foundation. Used by permission.)*

cell phone, so no teaching or learning takes place. In the third, a line of men wait at the ticket counter in the train station where a sign says "Open 9 am to 12," although, as the clock on the walls indicates, it is 11:30 and the window is closed. In the fourth scene, a man pays a bribe to the medical attendant to ensure his wife's abortion, despite a sign on the wall banning the procedure. Related to Supriya's painting of corruption is one by Bharti Kumari, titled *The Fire Brigade* (see SU's website). Using a palette of colors of oranges, rusts, and reds that is atypical in Mithila art, Bharti's painting depicts a village on fire and the residents working hard to put it out, while the fire brigade takes its time in arriving, providing almost no help to the besieged community.

Rani Jha, a Brahmin woman and teacher at the MAI who recently received her PhD from nearby Dharbhanga University, with a dissertation in the local Maithili dialect on the songs and folk arts of the region, has painted two works that deal directly with women's ability to speak and communicate. While veiling one's face with a sari is not as prevalent in this region as in other parts of northern India, women, especially as young brides, are seldom allowed to leave the house without an escort. Instead, they are secluded in their homes and allowed little mobility. In a painting from 2003, Rani Jha shows the transformation of a woman from a student into a bride, with the loss of freedom that accompanies this change in status. In the lower panel are young unmarried college students, while the recent bride, locked inside, peers out at them from the barred window of her husband's home. While bars on windows are actually the norm in rural India, where screens are rare and window glass is expensive, the effect shown—not just keeping out unwanted intruders, but keeping the new bride in—is powerful (see SU's website). In 2010, Jha made an even stronger statement in a painting titled *Before We Could Only Peek through the Curtain, Now Together We Are Breaking through the Curtain*. This painting shows the eyes of women secluded behind a curtain, while in the center a group of four women are fully visible as their hands rip the curtain open, forcing their way into the world.

Discrimination Against Women

Two major forms of discrimination against females in India directly challenge women's lives: the disfavor of girl children and the mistreatment of brides. In South Asia (as in China and other parts of eastern Asia), sons are desired because they carry on the lineage, serve important ritual functions, and also mark the possibility of bringing economic prosperity to their families. Sons can begin contributing to family income at an early age, if only by herding cattle or helping in the fields. Before demands for schooling were high, raising a son cost relatively little, although the new aspirations for college and postgraduate degrees for both sons and daughters have significantly raised the costs of child rearing. Daughters, in contrast to sons, have always been seen as expensive in most parts of South Asia, primarily due to the costs of providing dowries for their marriages. A dowry comprises cash and gifts that are given to the groom and his family by the bride's family. Today, noncash gifts might include a sofa set, a refrigerator, and possibly a motor scooter or car. Dowries for a bride with an MA degree can exceed $4,000, a price almost impossible for lower-middle-class families, even if they are landowners. Even the poor are expected to pay $500 or more for a marriage, at a time when the average income of a landless family is $2 or $3 a day. Further, while a bride is thought to represent Lakshmi, the goddess of prosperity, she is also blamed for any misfortune that befalls her new husband's family. This disfavor of females leads to three practices that are increasing in modern India: the neglect of young female children, sex-selective abortion (female feticide), and bride burning (also known as dowry death).

Over the past centuries, the neglect of female children, especially from birth to five years, was common, and baby girls often died from this lack of care. Comments like "It's only a girl" might be heard if a baby girl started to topple off a cot. Girl children were more likely to suffer from malnutrition and were less commonly admitted to hospitals or taken to doctors' offices than were boy children. The Mithila artist Rani Jha recalled, "My brothers, they would all eat. Only then would I get food. This wasn't my mother's fault . . . it was the norm of that period. That first the boys should be given good food, and the girls would get whatever is left over" (personal communication, December 2011).

According to the 2011 Census of India, the all-India sex ratio for the general population was 940 females per 1,000 males; however, for those aged six and under, it was 914 females per 1,000 males, meaning that for every 1,000 boys, 86 girl children died after birth or were aborted. Bihar, in which the Mithila region is located, had one of the lowest ratios of all states in India: 916 females per 1,000 males for all ages. Given these trends, ads for sex-selective abortions from the 1990s, which might read, "Invest only Rs. 500 now and save your precious Rs. 50,000 later," resonated with many families, despite a 1994 law outlawing sex-selective abortion. Hence modern technology has changed

Painting of an abortion clinic by Rani Jha, 2004. *(Photo by David Szanton/Ethnic Arts Foundation. Used by permission.)*

family decision making. Instead of a women bearing an unwanted girl child and then not providing it with the sustenance and medical care needed for survival, families are choosing to determine the sex of an unborn child and then abort it if it is female. In most instances, the mother has no choice in the matter, for the decision to abort is made by the husband and the mother-in-law.

This practice of female feticide is frequently condemned in Mithila women's paintings. A 2004 painting by Rani Jha portrays the abortion clinic. A woman is on the table, attached to an ultrasound machine. Jha shows the female doctor as a snake, capturing the female fetuses. Nurses stand by, while female relatives weep. A younger student, Ganjeshwaran, has also created paintings about abortions, using only black and white. A 2010 painting depicts a tree filled with unborn females, with a woman thinking that it is better to be a tree than a woman (see SU's website).

For women who survive childhood, marriage brings another round of discrimination. Initial dowry payments are made at the time of marriage, but for hundreds of years brides' families have been liable for additional gifts at other times, such as the birth of a child, a child's marriage, or even a family visit. Some men refuse to visit their sisters regularly, because every visit requires gifts, which over time can exceed the brothers' means. In addition, as India has become more urban, the traditional guidelines for what is an appropriate dowry have become blurred. Formerly, the community knew how to gauge a bride's family's ability to give, as well as what was appropriate to offer a groom

---

Box 16.6

Vinita Jha's *The Girl and the Calf*

Vinita Jha is more likely to paint images relating to mythology than social commentary; however, she does address discrimination against women in one painting, *The Girl and the Calf*, which she claims reflects a true story in her caste community (see SU's website). The story is broken into nine panels in the black-and-white linear style:

There was an old woman who had no grandson, so her neighbors told her to take her daughter-in-law to the river to bathe. Through the mercy of the river god, the daughter-in-law became pregnant. She gave birth to a beautiful daughter named Radhiya. When Radhiya was older, they arranged a marriage for her with a competent young man. When she went to her groom's house, she took a female calf with her. Sometime later, both Radhiya and the calf were pregnant. Her husband was away in a foreign land, but her in-laws cared for both her and the cow. Both Radhiya and the cow gave birth to females. Her mother-in-law was very sad at the birth of a girl child. When the neighbors came, her mother-in-law cursed her granddaughter. But Radhiya's in-laws loved the female calf and tied an auspicious black amulet around its neck. The husband returned and played with and loved his daughter. But his mother stood with her back to the happy family. One day the daughter became ill, and no one helped Radhiya. She could only give her daughter herbal medicines. Both mother and child cried. The female calf was also ill, and the in-laws called a veterinarian to cure it. He gave the calf an injection. Thus, it is better to be a cow than a human.

---

who worked as a farmer (e.g., they could evaluate his wealth by a given amount of land, a house, two bullocks, a tube well). Today, however, a groom might be a clerk in a city, or he might own a small business with his father. Likewise, the bride's father might be a labor contractor or a lower-level government employee. Knowing what an appropriate dowry is under these new circumstances is not easy. At the same time, the groom and his family may desire more and more consumer goods, leading to escalating demands on the bride's family after the marriage. When these demands are not met, the bride may be abused. Far too often, she is murdered, a practice known as dowry death or bride burning. It is estimated that more than 8,000 dowry deaths occurred yearly in India in both 2007 and 2008. That equals one death every 65 to 70 minutes, despite the passage in 2005 of the Protection of Women from Domestic Violence Act.

Not surprisingly, marriage and dowry are frequent themes of the young painters who face these issues themselves. Roopan Kumari, the daughter of Vinita Jha, made a six-part painting in 2005 of marriage and its aftermath, titled *From Marriage to Bride Burning*. In the first scene, the bride is dressed for her wedding by her friends, while in the second the groom is adorned with the distinctive Mithila groom's headgear. The third scene shows the marriage ceremony itself, with the priest performing sacred rituals, including the fire sacrifice to the gods. In the fourth scene, the bride is carried to her husband's house in a

From Marriage to Bride Burning by Roopan Kumari, circa 2005. *(Photo by David Szanton/Ethnic Arts Foundation. Used by permission.)*

palanquin, and in the fifth she is shown doing all the housework while her mother-in-law shakes a scolding finger at her. In the final scene, the husband is shown pouring kerosene over her while her mother-in-law strikes a match.

Roopan's painting is only one of many made by the young artists of the Mithila region that focuses on dowry and marriage, issues all too present in these young women's lives. It is not surprising that they have put their new skills to work illustrating new stories of women's lives.

Changing Mithila Art

As with most "traditional" cultural activities in contemporary contexts, Mithila art changes continually. And the tradition itself, stretching back hundreds of years, has only been known to the outside world for a generation or two. Evidence of the influence of globalization on Mithila art is already seen in a 1930s photograph by William Archer, showing a train running across the top of a painting. The painter has juxtaposed traditional imagery, including the god Vishnu, with the train, updating the effect and indicating that Mithila women in the 1930s responded to their changing environment, including early twentieth-century forms of globalization.

Indeed, folk arts are no more static than agricultural practices, types of governance, or new products and machines. And folk arts, in the Mithila region and across the globe, are increasingly responding to facets of globalization involving consumerism, commodification, changing patterns of education, and new roles for women. As Mithila art continues to evolve, it will raise questions that go to the heart of what the tradition is and what it means to the people who make it, use it, and purchase it: How much more transformation can Mathila painting accommodate before it is no longer coherent as a tradition? Will the current shifts in content from ritual art to art about social issues—as well as future shifts—signal a fundamental change in Mithila art, resulting in work that is no longer meaningful under the umbrella of Mithila art? Will stylistic changes, such as those by Amrita Jha, mark a similar shift away from the tradition of Mithila painting?

Still other questions concern whether this painting tradition, now taught in schools and made primarily for commercial profit, can be considered folk art. Some scholars would claim that a shift from an anonymous painting on a wall in a relative's house to the recording of the artist's name on a painting on paper sold thousands of miles away from where the painter lives marks a movement away from the folk art tradition, where the group, not the individual, is valued. It is in fact this anonymity that gives folk art, as well as folklore, its power, as folk forms belong to and represent the group, not the individual artist. Are artists such as Shalinee Kumari and Amrita Jha part of a rich folk art tradition, or are they contemporary artists working in a modern world characterized by the commerce of ideas and products? Answers to these questions await the further evolution of Mithila art. Meanwhile, we can celebrate what it has been and is today, and appreciate the ways in which modern artists are invoking the new worlds in which they live.

References and Further Research

Adams, Jacqueline. 2005. "When Art Loses Its Sting: The Evolution of Protest Art in Authoritarian Contexts." *Sociological Perspectives* 48, no. 4: 531–558.

Archer, William G. 1949. "Maithil Painting." *Marg* 3, no. 3: 24–33.

Census of India. 2011. "Sex Ratios of India, 1901–2011." Delhi: Ministry of Home Affairs, Government of India. http://www.imaginmor.com/census-of-india-2011.html#Statement%20 12%20%20Sex%20ratio,%20India:%201901-2011.

Devi, Dulari. 2010. *Following My Paint Brush*. With text by Gita Wolf. Chennai: Tara Books.

Jain, Jyotindra. 1997. *Ganga Devi: Tradition and Expression in Mithila Painting*. Ahmedabad: Mapin Publishing.

Janakpur Women's Development Center. July 25, 1999. "Maithal Paintings, an Exhibition." http://www.asianart.com/exhibitions/jwdc/index.html.

Jha, Rambharos. 2011. *Waterlife*. Chennai: Tara Books.

Korom, Frank J. 2006. *Village of Painters: Narrative Scrolls from West Bengal*. Santa Fe: Museum of New Mexico Press.

———, ed. 2013. *The Anthropology of Performance: A Reader*. Chichester, UK, and Malden, MA: Wiley-Blackwell.

Sen, Amartya. 1990. "More Than 100 Million Women Are Missing." *New York Review of Books*, December 20. http://www.nybooks.com/articles/archives/1990/dec/20/more-than-100-million-women-are-missing/?pagination=false.

Szanton, David L., and Malini Bakshi. 2007. *Mithila Painting: The Evolution of an Art Form*. San Francisco: Pink Mango.

Yéquand, Yves. 1977. *Women Painters of Mithila*. London: Thames and Hudson.

17

From Hindi Cinema to Bollywood

TULA GOENKA

The term *Bollywood* means different things to different people. To the uninitiated, it is a new phenomenon, any film from India, the largest film industry in the world, or a frivolous spectacle filled with songs in dream locations, dances, lavish sets, superstars, and frothy romance. To its fans, it is an addiction far more satisfying than any drug, a constant source of amusement and entertainment, an extended family to belong to no matter which corner of the world they are in, the jukebox of their lives, and what memories are made of. Bollywood may not be the largest film industry in the world, but it is definitely the largest film segment within India, and it dominates music, broadcast news channels, newspapers, magazines, and social media. Its sheer size, its financial strength, and the glitz of its movie stars outshine any other, and its form and content are a treasure trove of cultural riches going back 100 years.

In the popular press across most of the globe, Indian film equals Bollywood, a term commonly used only since around 2000. In fact, much of the Indian film industry occurs outside of Bollywood. Not a place on any map, Bollywood refers only to the popular or mainstream cinema produced in Hindi (India's national language) in the bustling metropolis of Bombay, now known as Mumbai. Many of India's twenty-eight states and seven union territories have their own distinct languages and movie industries, with each state or region boasting of both mainstream cinema (with songs and dance) and more reality-based art-house films. In fact, many Hindi filmmakers object to the brand name "Bollywood," which was included in the *Oxford English Dictionary* in 2003. One of India's leading directors, Subhash Ghai, spoke of this issue:

> I think it is embarrassing to any Bombay filmmaker. It is somebody's idea of a joke on Indian cinema, particularly on cinema from Bombay because it implies that we are copying Hollywood, no? But I do have to agree that it has helped the marketing people because it has given the rest of the world a brand name to wrap their brains around. It is now easier for people to understand that Bollywood refers to the song and dance, mainstream Hindi cinema coming out of Bombay. The brand name is now used by everyone—by the government authorities, by the media, by the people.

This chapter is extracted from Tula Goenka's *Not Just Bollywood: Indian Directors Speak* (New Delhi: Om Books International, 2013).

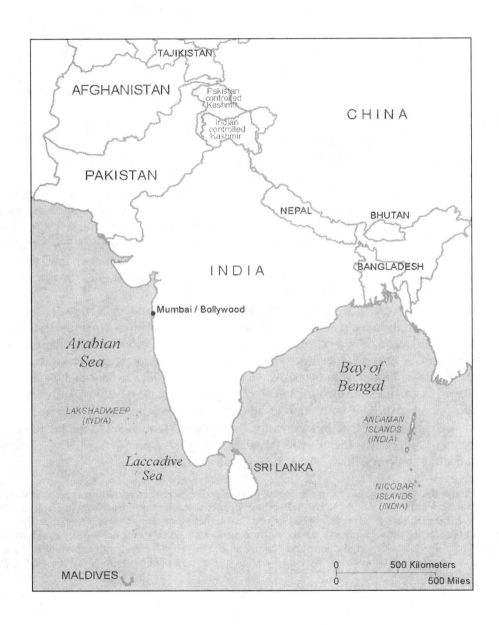

TAJIKISTAN

AFGHANISTAN

Pakistan
controlled
Kashmir

CHINA

Indian
controlled
Kashmir

PAKISTAN

NEPAL

BHUTAN

INDIA

BANGLADESH

Mumbai / Bollywood

*Arabian
Sea*

*Bay of
Bengal*

*LAKSHADWEEP
(INDIA)*

*ANDAMAN
ISLANDS
(INDIA)*

*Laccadive
Sea*

SRI LANKA

*NICOBAR
ISLANDS
(INDIA)*

0   500 Kilometers

0   500 Miles

MALDIVES

Box 17.1

Information About the Author and the Case Study

The author of this case study, Tula Goenka, is a filmmaker and professor of television, radio, and film at the Newhouse School, Syracuse University. She started her career in Indian media and has worked extensively in the United States. She was born and raised in India and routinely takes her filmmaking students for month-long internships in Bollywood. The quotes in the case study are excerpted from her book *Not Just Bollywood: Indian Directors Speak.*

The Early History of Hindi Cinema

Hindi cinema has enjoyed a large fan base across the world, especially in Asia, the United Kingdom, Russia, the Middle East, parts of Africa, and the South Asian diaspora, though mainstream audiences in the United States have discovered it only recently. The Indian film industry has a long history, with "100 years of cinema" being celebrated across India in 2013. Filmmaking came to India soon after the Lumière brothers—Auguste and Louis—recorded their first moving image using the cinématographe in Lyon, France, in 1895. Fully committed to the dream of an independent India free from the British Raj, early Indian filmmakers chose to use this Western technology to further their nationalistic goals and ideals by telling stories based on a rich tapestry of Indian stories, philosophies, and religions. India's first "feature" film, *Raja Harishchandra*, produced and directed by D.G. Phalke, was released in 1913—two years before D.W. Griffith's *Birth of a Nation*, considered to be Hollywood's first feature film.

In Phalke's film, a king sacrifices his kingdom, his wife, and his children to honor the demands of the sage Vishvamitra, who ultimately accepts Harishchandra's devotion and faith and restores his kingdom and family. Indian cinematic narratives, such as this one, have their own form and are often inspired by the two ancient Indian epics, the Ramayana and the Mahabharata. Even today, many plotlines in popular cinema continue to be morality tales of one form or another, dealing with issues of *dharma*, or duty, and personal *karma*, or action in the larger world.

The Introduction of Sound

Music is as inseparable from daily life as are family celebrations, religious worship, or entertainment, and it shapes much of the Indian psyche by evoking primal emotions of love, longing, and belonging. India also has a strong tradition of both classical music and dance, as well as deeply rooted folk traditions. Given the importance of music in Indian life, the introduction of sound redirected Indian cinema into new and exciting channels. The advent of the "talkies" ensured that India's multilingual society produced a wide array of movies in different local languages while also preserving diverse cultural beliefs and forms.

Brought up with traditions of theater like *nautanki* and *jātrā*, with frequent stops for songs, early filmmakers began to use elements of music and dance as soon as sound was introduced in 1931 with Ardeshir Irani's *Alam Ara*. Bombay Talkies, one of the first studios to be established (in 1934), looked for singers who could also act, and K.L. Saigal fit the bill perfectly. A handsome man with a mellifluous voice, he could be called Hindi/Urdu cinema's first film star. As the audience's tastes for more nuanced acting and attractive actors increased, the practical choice became lip-syncing to songs sung by a playback singer, some of whom, like the sisters Lata Mangeshkar and Asha Bhonsle, became stars in their own right, alongside their male counterparts Mohammad Rafi and Kishore Kumar.

To learn more about Indian cinema, both historically and today, see these websites:

- Wiki on Indian Cinema (https://cinemaofindia.org/)
- Business of Cinema (http://businessofcinema.com/)
- Anupama Chopra (http://www.anupamachopra.com/)
- Upperstall.com (http://www.upperstall.com/)

The Early Years of Independence

In 1947, independence from the British Raj and the simultaneous partition of India and Pakistan into separate countries, with the latter being an Islamic country, created fresh challenges for Indian cinema. Many of the early filmmakers were Urdu writers, as Urdu was the primary language used in the Bombay film industry. (Hindi and Urdu are mutually intelligible, and many consider them the same language with different writing systems.) Many Muslims working in Bombay left for Pakistan, while others remained in India. In addition, a large influx of displaced people from what is now Pakistan came to make a new life in the fledgling film business, where one's ethnicity or religion did not matter as much as one's talent and ability to work.

Even with the civic and religious strife between Hindus and Muslims in the 1940s, the Hindi cinema industry was a safe and integrated space. However, to be more readily accepted by a majority Hindu audience, many Muslim actors were compelled to adopt Hindu names, including the superstars Dilip Kumar and Meena Kumari. This practice has now ceased, however, and several leading male superstars in today's Bollywood are Muslim actors who usually portray Hindu characters on screen, such as Shah Rukh Khan, Salman Khan, Saif Ali Khan, and Aamir Khan. (Despite their common last name, these actors are not related by blood.) Indeed, Bollywood can today be considered the epitome of secularism and national integration, with people from different religions, communities, and ethnic backgrounds working together to visualize the collective dreams of the everyday man. The director Jabbar Patel spoke about this secularism:

Baiju Bawra, made in 1952, had a song on Krishna, "Hari Om," written by Shakeel Badayuni, a Muslim. Sung by Mohammed Rafi, a Muslim. And composed by Naushad, who is a Muslim. Where else can this be possible? Another example would be Dilip Kumar. He decided to change his Muslim name, Yusuf Khan, to a Hindu name because he felt it would be better at that time. In fact, two days ago, Dilip Kumar and Saira Banu, his Muslim wife, sent a Diwali card to me. To me! Muslims sending a Diwali card to me, a Muslim! [Diwali is a Hindu festival.] I think this country is truly amazing.

Filmmakers in the 1950s were idealistic and wanted to tell stories with social significance that made a difference. Hence, socially conscious films, such as Mehboob Khan's Oscar-nominated *Mother India* (1957), portrayed the struggles and triumphs of the average person in a newly independent India, and they moved fans and critics alike in doing so. *Mother India*, a metaphorical reference to the nation of India, tells the story of a poverty-ridden single mother who raises her children through endless trials and tribulations but never gives in or compromises her moral code.

In the mid-1950s, a new kind of cinema emerged in Calcutta. Satyajit Ray, undoubtedly the most internationally well-known and influential filmmaker from India, single-handedly gave birth to the parallel, neorealist cinema movement in India in his *Pather Panchali* (1955), which tells the story of a poor family struggling to survive in rural Bengal. The film set the standards for what an Indian "art" film could be, and Ray continues to inspire and inform Indian filmmakers today, years after his death in 1992. Another seminal influence was the Bengali filmmaker Ritwik Ghatak, who directed *Meghe Dhaka Tara* (1960). Ghatak died young (in 1976, at fifty), but he taught at the Film Institute in Pune for several years, leaving behind a lasting legacy. Until recently, such filmmakers were the only ones whose work was lauded at international film festivals, because their realistic sensibilities hewed most closely to those of Western filmmakers and audiences. Shyam Benegal, India's legendary film director of socially conscious cinema, put it this way:

> The West also never took popular Indian cinema seriously because they thought that it was just a diluted and totally distorted version of Hollywood cinema in some kind of a native way. So when Ray made *Pather Panchali*, everybody sat up and said, "Oh, my goodness! Here is someone who seems to be speaking our language."

Socialist Economic Policies and Film

After 1947, India's socialist government understood the power of the cinematic medium and began to develop its state institutions to support it. The Ministry of Information and Broadcasting, under India's first prime minister, Jawaharlal Nehru, took a multipronged approach to harness the powerful medium. The Cinematograph Act that codified the rules of film production and distribution was passed in 1952, and both the International Film Festival of India and the Central Board of Film Certification (more commonly known as the Censor Board) were immediately established. Two years later, in 1954, the National Film Awards were also established. In 1960 the Film Institute of India started in Pune—on the lot of the pioneering Prabhat Studios—and in 1964 the National Film Archives of India opened across the street.

Trade restrictions on imported goods, instituted to encourage the development of local industries and businesses, were also extended to cinema. These protectionist policies helped the Indian film industry thrive, especially in the face of competitive pressure from Hollywood cinema, with its slicker production values and more worldly plots. By the time the government lifted these trade restrictions in 1991 with the neoliberalization of the Indian economy, they had had their intended effect on film, particularly on popular cinema. By then, most Indians wanted *paisa vasool*, or their full money's worth of entertainment, preferring to watch popular Indian films with song and dance rather than the more realistic ones with serious story lines.

Just as Western content (i.e., the films themselves) could not be imported, the protectionist policy also prohibited the import of equipment and film stock, so the production values of Indian cinema did not progress with international standards. In an unexpected consequence, because of poor quality microphones and loud, unsilenced cameras, dialogue in nearly all Indian films was dubbed or rerecorded later. Even today, given difficult production conditions, a pilot track is recorded on set, and the actors and actresses come in to rerecord their lines only after an edit has been done. This contributes to the often stilted or theatrical feeling of popular Indian cinema. As the talented young film director Farhan Akhtarput put it,

> Most studios here, equipment, tracks, trolleys, cameras, lights, everything is set up to deal with dubbing. Cameras are noisy, cranes creak, dollies creak, studios aren't quiet, lights buzz, and air conditioning makes sounds. Nothing's equipped to go ahead and do a film in sync sound. It's difficult shooting in Bombay when you're doing sync sound even in the studio, because we don't have anything [like] a true sound stage. It's even more difficult because we have so many birds. Before takes you have to throw firecrackers up in the air! And then you take a shot. And then they come back two to three takes later, and you throw another cracker. It's like a little war going on set, with nature anyway, or Diwali! [a fall festival where lights are strung to welcome Lakshmi, the goddess of prosperity. Most families also sent off often elaborate fireworks to further guide her way.]

The 1960s to 1980s

As democracy came of age in India in the 1960s, a certain disillusionment with the socialist ideals seeped in, and a more youthful entertainment with light romances evolved. Films were no longer in black and white but in sumptuous color. Heroines were dressed in fashionable outfits, heroes were suave, parents fierce, and the villains Machiavellian—all set against exotic locations as a backdrop. Movie plot lines revolved around young people falling in love and living happily ever after, despite fierce resistance from disapproving (but eventually forgiving) parents. Happy endings were de rigueur, but kisses were not, and sex was completely off limits.

To counter this trend toward superficial storytelling, in 1969 the Indian government set up the Film Finance Corporation, which provided federal funding for alternative or "new wave" cinema in India. This support encouraged the growth of the art house, or "parallel," cinema movement. Indeed, the 1970s and 1980s were the golden age of Hindi art films. Several filmmakers, such as Shyam Benegal and Govind Nihalani, flourished as their films found a ready audience in the country's growing urban centers. The increased political awareness of average middle-class Indians, their rising levels of education, and the ever-growing feminist movement also contributed to the growth of interest in art films. Many of the stories told in this type of cinema were set in rural India or among the disenfranchised in urban India, and they focused on women's rights, police corruption, social decay, caste, and class politics.

The 1970s were also marked by political turbulence. In 1975 Prime Minister Indira Gandhi declared a state of emergency, which suppressed democratic processes and imposed a dictatorship for twenty-one months. In cinema, this period was marked by the writing partnership of Salim Khan and Javed Akhtar (popularly known as Salim-Javed), who changed Hindi movie storytelling. They tackled more complex and realistic kinds of stories and helped create the antihero persona of the actor Amitabh Bachchan, whose "angry young man" avatar appealed to the masses, reflecting anger and frustration against the dictatorial political regime. The 1970s also found India still to be an avowedly secular nation, where religions coexisted with minimal conflict. In film, this was portrayed in Manmohan Desai's blockbuster *Amar Akbar Anthony* (1977), which portrays the comedic reunion of three brothers separated at birth and raised in different faiths (Hindu, Muslim, and Christian).

Broadcast television was introduced in the next decade, resulting in a declining cinema-going audience in the 1980s. With the introduction of video recorders came cable television, and people would get a VHS player and transmit signals to different houses in their neighborhoods via jerry-rigged cable. Movie theaters physically deteriorated, as middle-class audiences declined drastically by the end of the decade. Hindi cinema audiences reached all-time lows through the early 1990s. Then, in 1994, Sooraj Barjatya released a traditional wedding saga with fourteen songs, *Hum Aapke Hain Koun . . . !!* The film brought audiences back to the theater in droves. Seeing such success, other filmmakers redoubled their efforts for the rest of the decade, often unsuccessfully, trying to rediscover and rejuvenate their splintered audiences—both at home and abroad.

Economic Liberalization and the Growth of the Middle Class

The tectonic shift for Indian cinema occurred in 2001, when the Indian government finally recognized the moviemaking business as an "industry." This official declaration made filmmaking a part of the organized industrial sector, and producers now had formal access to bank loans and were able to raise money from legitimate sources for cash-strapped projects. Historically, popular cinema had been heavily taxed, and movies were not seen as a viable economic resource by the Indian state, despite the fact that Raj Kapoor's films had gained popularity in Russia in the 1950s. Said to be funded by "black" or not declared money, most popular films used to be produced under "banners," or individual production houses. Even today, India does not have an organized middle-management system of studios and talent agencies, as is the case in Hollywood, and filmmaking is largely an ad hoc process. But with the establishment of a new area for growth and investment, big industrial houses, commonly known as "corporates," became involved in the film and television business, thereby influencing both the process and the content of popular cinema. As a result, most Hollywood studios now have a presence in India, for both television and cinema, and coproductions are more common.

More secure financing also meant access to previously unavailable equipment, and Hindi film directors were able use a more sophisticated style of shooting, with better cameras and lenses. In fact, many directors continue to import their cinematographers and stunt coordinators from the West or Australia. Inspired by a ubiquitous MTV style of production, editing became more cutting-edge, with digital technology replacing celluloid splicing and taping. Visual effects (VFX) have become a booming industry, and much of Hollywood's VFX work is now outsourced to India. Experiments with 3-D cinema are also now common. In addition, a more contemporary storytelling style has been adopted, and the traditional *filmi* (melodramatic) dialogue, with its origins in Urdu and Parsi theater, has been replaced with a more colloquial style of speaking. "Hinglish," a mixture of Hindi and English, is now used liberally. Hindi cinema has thus transformed itself and emerged as the slick, sexy, and sophisticated "Bollywood" of the twenty-first century that people around the world have come to associate with the term.

Mark Bennington has created an excellent photo essay on Bollywood (http://www.vqronline.org/articles/2013/winter/bennington-bollywood/).

The Multiplex Theater

With economic liberalization came the rapid expansion of India's middle class, including an influx of high-tech jobs in software development, call centers, and other support sectors. A burgeoning middle class—now numbering 250 million or more in a total population of 1.3 billion—has affected everything from food consumption to shopping. For the film industry, a key shift was the building of indoor shopping malls with multiplex movie theatres, first in the major cities and then in smaller cities and towns.

Traditionally, movie theaters in India, like those in the rest of the world, were single-screen movie palaces, some of which seated nearly 1,000 people at a time. Since national television was not introduced in India until 1982, cinema was the primary source of entertainment for millions of people. Movie going was often a family event—grandparents, parents, children, uncles, and aunts all attended together—with the downstairs "stalls" largely reserved for men, while the balconies were set aside for ladies and families. Films were presold as territories which gave those distributors access to theaters in that area: the distributor paid a fixed sum regardless of how much money was generated. Hence no accurate accounting of box-office returns was possible. Producers resorted to pan-Indian films that appealed to all demographics to ensure that their investment paid off. In this mass-market environment, the so-called *masala* film, named for the blending of spices typical in Indian cuisine, was the best bet, because it had it all: drama, comedy, romance, action, and suspense. Much of popular mainstream cinema in India, whatever its language, continues to be of this variety.

Today, multiplex theaters, modeled after those in the United States, seat a smaller audience—in the range of 300 to 400 viewers—and have computerized accounting systems to track ticket sales. Several big distribution companies, such as Eros International, Reliance Big Cinemas, UTV, and Yash Raj Films, have sprung up to handle these functions, representing a final and crucial step in the development of the film industry. They undertake all publicity and niche marketing, relying heavily on the Internet and social media to generate excitement. Now, thanks to satellite distribution, Bollywood films open in movie theaters across the world on the same day.

These developments have allowed filmmakers to make movies for targeted groups. A new cinema independent in both content and financing and aimed at the hip, young population of urban India is now known as "indie," or multiplex, cinema. These films are individualistic and gritty, and they portray more violence. The language is also coarser, and *gālis*, or abusive slang, abounds. The Censor Board (all films in India have to be approved by the Censor Board) has become more permissive in its rulings, allowing things it once would have banned. However, indie cinema has a hard time competing in a market ruled by box-office returns. The indie director Onir outlined the issue this way:

> Honestly, I don't think that multiplexes support independent cinema. First of all, the ticket pricing, because when you to go your multiplexes and see your [multistar] big screen films offered to you at a certain price, and if an indie film is offered to you at the same price, it doesn't quite work. . . . Independent films work on word of mouth. It really grows on the masses. Multiplexes solely operate from the first few days of the film's collection, and if you don't have that kind of a collection then your films won't work on the big screens. The problem is that most of the theaters expect you to screen them for free. That doesn't work. People very often forget that independent cinema also costs to produce. The colleges invite you, festivals invite you, but no one pays you. So how are you going to make your film?

Critics and traditionalists are quick to point out that multiplex cinemas are too expensive for the average moviegoer at 250 rupees a ticket (US fifty cents, the equivalent of several days' wages for the poor). PVR Gold tickets (a more exclusive viewing experience, with its own special entrance and lobby) often cost double that amount. Often, a person who does not look "respectable" or middle-class is not even allowed to enter shopping malls. Going to the movies, therefore, has become a limited option for many in India, as the closing of single-screen theaters has accompanied the rise of the multiplex.

Shifting Locales and Values

Current Bollywood films are more global than in the past, both in terms of production and market share. Filming is as likely to take place in Switzerland or Sydney as in Mumbai or Mysore. Because of the educated urban population as well as the ever-growing nonresident Indian diaspora across the globe, there is a demand for high-quality, sophisticated films. Younger filmmakers are now creating films that are often *zara hat ke* (a tad removed from the norm). They have a younger, hipper sensibility while employing modes of filmmaking and storytelling that have been tried and tested by Hindi cinema over decades, including the ever-popular romantic comedy and action film. One of the most profitable businesses for Bollywood has become song-and-dance tours abroad. Movie stars travel with a troupe of dancers, singers, and musicians and perform in one city after another to a stadium filled with screaming fans. In 2000, the International Indian Film Academy Awards were instituted by an Indian public relations and event management firm, Wizcraft International, to build a global fan base for Bollywood.

Like any business in which the stakes are high, it is extremely difficult to get a foot in the door, whether in front of or behind the camera. Bollywood is fast becoming even more of a family occupation, and it increasingly seems that one has to have a family connection to get a break. Younger generations are routinely "launched" by their parents or relatives in films created especially for them. One Bollywood insider, the director Zoya Akhtar, who is the daughter of the famous 1970s script writer Javed Akhtar and the sister of Farhan Akhtar (an actor, director, producer, screenwriter, and television host), made her first film, *Luck By Chance* (2009), about this very narrative.

While urban India grows increasingly cosmopolitan, public displays of affection remain controversial in real—and reel—life. In India's patriarchal society, a family's honor is tied up with the sexual purity of its women, especially the virginity of its unmarried daughters. To suggest any sexual impropriety on screen, therefore, is not allowed. To get around the lack of intimate contact on screen, film directors of popular cinema perfected the art of suggestion to titillate the imagination. While a couple might be shown engaged in sexual intercourse to consummate a relationship in Western cinema, in Indian films they are likely to burst into highly erotic and suggestive song. This is changing quickly in the new millennium, however, and younger movie stars more readily engage in intimate contact on screen.

Another dramatic change can be found in the fanfare that accompanies the movies. Until recently, intellectuals and critics looked down on popular Hindi cinema, considering it populist or low-art, but many have now given way to the Bollywood juggernaut. Fueled by the 24/7 news cycle and an infinite number of entertainment web portals on the Internet, film news and information has exploded, especially on social media. Bollywood is now fashionable, and celebrity information (usually paid for) has proliferated to the extent that it is commonly referred to as "Page 3" culture, since it is typically published on page 3 of leading daily Indian newspapers. Products are launched, movies premiered, and events celebrated by special invitation to anybody even vaguely attached to the film industry. Movie superstars now make more money from product endorsements and advertising than from their day jobs. Much like celebrities worldwide, they sell makeup, chocolates, cars, watches, mobile phones, underwear, and even cement with equal conviction, both at home and internationally. The director Madhur Bhandarkar has made a trilogy showcasing this moral slippery slope: *Page 3* (2005), *Fashion* (2008), and *Heroine* (2012). The director Nagesh Kukunoor describes the paparazzi mentality as follows:

> It's horrible and it's invasive. I just cannot believe what is happening with the paparazzi now. A few months back, I went to watch a random film in a theater, and suddenly what I'd seen only on TMZ in the U.S.—cameramen and photographers chasing someone—happened to me! It was just insane! I was just there to watch a movie, but they were there to cover a premiere. They said to me, "Can you give us a sound bite?" I said, "No, I'm here to watch

another film." And they said, "Just give us a bite." This is at 11:30 at night, mind you. I said, "No, I just came to watch a film with a friend." They insisted, "That's okay, just give us a bite." Then I firmly said "no," and I started walking away and they all started following me, and I said, "This is ludicrous." So I put up my hand to cover my face, and they chased me up the escalators taking pictures!

As celebrity has become so important, so too has body image and visual appeal. With "size zero" becoming the rage, women are encouraged to look unnaturally thin, and superstars like Aishwarya Rai Bachchan have been criticized for not shedding their postpregnancy pounds. For their part, men have begun to look startlingly buff, which suggests the increasing connections between a globalized India and cultural trends in the rest of the world.

Music in Bollywood Cinema

One of the most visible influences worldwide is Hindi film music. The Australian director Baz Luhrman was one of the first filmmakers to pay homage to Bollywood, in his film *Moulin Rouge* (2001). Since then, television dance competitions worldwide and movies like the Oscar winner *Slumdog Millionaire* (2008), directed by Danny Boyle, display the requisite Bollywood dance numbers. In the United States, college campuses regularly have dance troupes made up of *desi* (first- and second-generation Indian youth) and non-*desi* alike, and many youngsters want to have Bollywood-themed weddings, even if they are marrying a non-South Asian. Celebrity hosts such as Oprah Winfrey in the United States and David Frost in the United Kingdom have had Bollywood stars on their talk shows, and many actors and singers have regularly begun to collaborate with their Indian counterparts. One of the most famous examples is American R&B and hip hop artist Akon singing the song *Chammak Chalo* for Shah Rukh Khan's science fiction film *Ra.One*.

For more on the global reach of Bollywood, see the blog post "Bollywood and Africa: A Love Story" by Sylviane A. Diouf, curator of digital collections at the Schomburg Center for Research in Black Culture in New York City (http://www. nypl.org/blog/2011/12/06/bollywood-and-africa-love-story).

In the new millennium, Bollywood has become one of India's chief exports, and its glitz and glamor light up the red carpets of international film festivals, including Cannes in France, and world premieres. In a reverse globalization, many Westerners now want to share in its glory, including superstars like the British-born Katrina Kaif and eastern European dancers who appear in Bollywood chorus lines.

Songs are the *masala* (spice) of Hindi cinema, and their changing flavors can be traced easily to the changing sensibilities and times. Modern-day movie soundtracks are a unique amalgamation of Indian and Western music styles, and they easily incorporate genres like disco, hip-hop, and salsa, among others. With the launch of the entertainment radio program *Vividh Bharati* in 1957, film songs became constant companions in people's lives, and they have even been incorporated into ceremonies and rituals. With the new practice of identifying a song with a particular movie, the roles of the playback singer, composer, and lyricist became more important, and films were presold for distribution based on their musical potential. One of India's first TV game shows was based on a popular game, Antakshari, in which opposing teams had to identify and sing film songs.

In the twenty-first century, movie soundtracks continue to shape the most powerful sector of the music industry, and a new film is introduced to the world one song at a time through radio, television, and the Internet. This is followed by a mini-premiere for the soundtrack—the music launch—a few weeks before the actual movie hits theater screens. The mega-industry of reality TV competitions—including *Jhalak Dikhla Jaa, Dance India Dance, Sa Re Ga Ma Pa, Nach Baliye, Indian Idol, India's Got Talent*, among others—is based wholly on song and dance. As a delightful and unexpected side effect, film composers, playback singers, dance choreographers, and movie stars from yesteryear have suddenly found fame and fortune as judges of these shows. Bollywood can now rightfully be called India's opera for the masses, a cultural phenomenon that influences society well beyond the screen, and even beyond India.

Today's actors do not need to sing, but they do need to know how to dance—and dance well. Inserting a sexy song and dance—referred to as an "item number"—in the middle of a movie adds spice that is now expected, and it is a growing trend for aspiring female actors and big-time movie queens alike to shake their body parts with equal abandon, often bordering on the vulgar. These heart-thumping songs have given rise to a new craze: Bollywood dance and exercise classes all over the world, fueled by *Jai Ho!*, the Oscar-winning song by composer A.R. Rahman (which was first created for the 2008 film *Yuvraaj*, directed by Subhash Ghai).

Conclusion

With more cost-effective digital subtitling, satellite distribution, and online availability through sites such as Netflix, YouTube, and Pandora, Bollywood is now truly globalized, with its influence felt across India and far beyond. It is not the only popular film tradition in India, as active regional film industries exist in various Indian languages, but Bollywood's effects are evident in all of them, seen even in the nicknames applied to these regional developments: Tamil popular cinema is often referred to as "Kollywood," Malayalam cinema (based in Kerala) is referred to as "Mollywood," and, inexplicably, "Tollywood" refers to cinema from both West Bengal and Andhra Pradesh. Indeed, India's filmmaking industry is vast and complex, but it is Bollywood that is the most well-known and has the most extensive and complex reach in the globalizing cultural landscape that Hindi film has helped create.

References and Further Research

Bennington, Mark. 2013. "Inside Bollywood." *Virginia Quarterly Review* 89, no. 1: 28–45, http://www.vqronline.org/articles/2013/winter/bennington-bollywood/.

Bose, Derek. 2006. *Brand Bollywood: A New Global Entertainment Order*. Thousand Oaks, CA: SAGE.

Chopra, Anupama. 2007. *King of Bollywood: Shah Rukh Khan and the Seductive World of Indian Cinema*. New York: Warner Books.

Dechamma, Sowmya, and Elevarthi Sathya Prakash, eds. *Cinemas of South India: Culture, Resistance, Ideology*. New Delhi: Oxford University Press, 2010.

Dwyer, Rachel, and Jerry Pinto, eds. 2011. *Beyond the Boundaries of Bollywood: The Many Forms of Hindi Cinema*. New Delhi: Oxford University Press.

Derné, Steve. 2000. *Movies, Masculinity, and Modernity: An Ethnography of Men's Filmgoing in India*. Westport, CT: Greenwood.

Dickey, Sara. 2007. *Cinema and the Urban Poor in South India*. Cambridge: Cambridge University Press.

Ernst and Young, and the LA India Film Council. *Film Industry in India: New Horizons*. Kolkata, India: Ernst and Young. http://www.ey.com/Publication/vwLUAssets/New_Horizons_Final/$FILE/New_Horizons_Final.pdf.

Ganti, Tejaswini. 2012. *Producing Bollywood: Inside the Contemporary Hindi Film Industry*. Durham, NC: Duke University Press.

Goenka, Tula. 2013. *Not Just Bollywood: Indian Directors Speak*. Delhi: Om Books International.

Gokulsing, K. Moti, and Wimal Dissanayeke, eds. 2009. *Popular Culture in a Globalised India*. New York: Routledge.

Kavoori, Anandam P., and Aswin Punathambekar, eds. 2009. *Global Bollywood*. New Delhi: Oxford University Press.

Larkin, Brian. 1997. "Indian Films and Nigerian Lovers: Media and the Creation of Parallel Modernities." *Africa: Journal of the International African Institute* 67, no. 3: 406–440.

Morcom, Anna. 2007. *Hindi Film Songs and the Cinema*. Burlington, VT: Ashgate.

Rai, Amit S. 2009. *Untimely Bollywood: Globalization and India's New Media Assemblage*. Durham, NC: Duke University Press.

Films

Deewaar. 1975. Directed by Yash Chopra. Mumbai: Yash Raj Films. Two brothers are divided by the death of their father.

Dilwale Dulhania Le Jayenge. 1995. Directed by Aditya Chopra. Mumbai: Yash Raj Films. True love unites lovers across national borders.

Gangs of Wasseypur. 2012. Directed by Anurag Kashyap. Mumbai: Viacom 18. Three generations cannot escape their destiny of revenge and violence.

Om Shanti Om. 2007. Directed by Farah Khan. Mumbai: Red Chillies Entertainment. All is finally well, even after lifetimes.

Pyaasa. 1957. Directed by Guru Dutt. Guru Dutt Films. A poet searches for his muse.

18

Globalizing Bangalore
Urban Transformation in the High-Tech City

Sanjukta Mukherjee

You may have heard of Bangalore while paying your credit card bill by phone, booking a flight for travel, or fixing your computer. Capital of the southern state of Karnataka, Bangalore is one of India's fastest-growing cities, with a booming information technology (IT) industry. Fairly recently, however, it was considered a small town, popularly referred to as a "pensioner's paradise" in the postindependence era. Its pleasant climate, bungalow-style architecture in the cantonment areas, parks and green spaces, and minimal traffic congestion made Bangalore an attractive destination for retired folks from the large public-sector companies and research laboratories that were set up in the city.

Then, starting in the late 1990s, Bangalore's urban landscape underwent a complete change. The city saw a proliferation of "new economy" jobs, particularly in export-oriented IT and biotechnology industries, under the aegis of large-scale urban reforms. Bangalore now symbolizes India's ties to the global market. It has become the focus of multinational investment from both Indian and foreign corporations, attaining the unique distinction of becoming a verb in business circles. Anti-outsourcing lobbyists in the United States, who lament the local implications of jobs being "Bangalored" (Rajghatta 2004), have put this Indian city on the global map in new ways.

The new Bangalore faces many contradictions, however, despite the IT-led development. On the one hand, Bangalore's path to development and the success of the IT industry have been celebrated by policymakers, business owners, and IT professionals, who argue that it has created new jobs and social mobility, increasing India's visibility as a modern, high-tech nation in the global economy. On the other hand, critics have cautioned about the uneven growth of the IT industry, labeling the IT professionals providing low-end services as "cyber-coolies" dependent on the demand of foreign clients (Bidwai 2003), thus highlighting the increasing social and economic inequalities in India since it opened up its economy. Although the rapid growth of the IT industry since the early 1990s has created new job opportunities, it is only the highly skilled middle classes who have benefited from them. The central government and the states have prioritized this sector by drawing investment away from the agrarian and rural sector on which most of India's population still depends for its livelihood. The increasing agrarian crisis and mass-scale farmer suicides across the country bear testimony to this. In Bangalore, public funds have been syphoned into the private sector, and new private-public partnerships have been

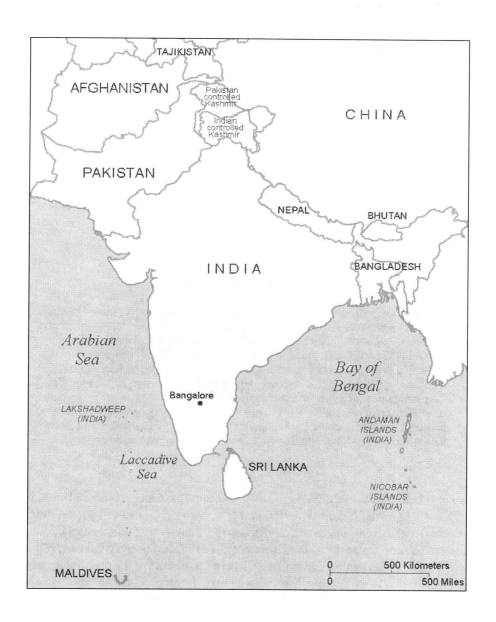

Table 18.1

Uneven Geographic Distribution of the Software Industry in India (based on top 600 software companies)

City	Number of company headquarters	Percent share
Mumbai	131	21.83
Bangalore	122	20.33
Delhi and suburbs	111	18.50
Hyderabad	64	10.67
Chennai	55	9.16
Kolkata	25	4.16
Pune	23	3.83
Thiruvananthapuram	14	2.33
Others	55	9.16

Source: Adapted from *The IT Software and Services Industry in India: Strategic Review 2000* (New Delhi: National Association of Software and Service Companies, 2000).

Box 18.1

The Lens of Geography

The tools of geography are used to explore city-spaces as a complex nexus of social and spatial relationships. Space is thus not merely a Cartesian territorial construct, a "container-like" backdrop, within which people are located and events take place. Instead, spaces are created through political and social processes, which are often imbued with underlying inequalities and constantly struggled over. This case study of Bangalore brings into sharp relief the manner in which gender and class differences interact with the processes of globalization, including the growth of the IT industry, giving the city its unique character in contemporary India. It is based on qualitative research, particularly interviews, focus groups, policy analysis, and archival data.

forged to build infrastructure, create special economic zones, and provide other incentives for the IT industry. Finally, although women have gained immensely as they enter this industry, challenges continue, especially involving issues of personal safety.

Moreover, the uneven regional development of IT in select urban centers of India, such as Bangalore, Delhi, Hyderabad, Pune, and Chennai, has generated increasing levels of social anxiety and income inequality. Struggles against the construction of special economic zones and the attendant displacement and dispossession of the poor have culminated in violent struggles in many places, such as Nandigram and Jagatsinghpur. Despite growing inequality and persistent poverty, high-tech professionals and the IT industry to which they belong continue to represent the new face of a modern and globalized India.

This case study examines Bangalore's transformation into India's Silicon Valley, focusing on the changing urban landscapes. I explore the visible markers of this shift on the city spaces, especially its built environment, and on the lives of people who live in the city. In the process, I reflect upon the implications of IT-led development in Bangalore and India, especially in light of the fact that this sector mostly employs young, English-speaking, middle-class men and women.

The first section provides a brief economic history of the city of Bangalore, highlighting its past as a divided city with colonial and precolonial roots. The second section looks at the emergence of Bangalore as the hub of the IT industry in India. The third section highlights the specific transformation of the city spaces of Bangalore due to the influence of the IT sector, looking especially at new spaces of urban production and consumption. Finally, the fourth section explores the gender- and class-based implications of IT-led growth in Bangalore. The high-tech sector has provided new opportunities for middle-class women, but it continues to perpetuate gender-based inequalities, and indeed it has resulted in increased violence in Indian cities.

Bangalore: A Brief Economic History

Bangalore, argues Janaki Nair in *The Promise of the Metropolis: Bangalore's Twentieth Century* (2005), has always been a divided city. The old city in the western part, built around a fort, is about five centuries old, while the cantonment (an area for military offices, a training camp, and accommodations) in the eastern part is more recent, dating back about two centuries. Until the sixteenth century, Bangalore was predominantly agrarian; the city's socioeconomic landscape was structured by the prominence of temple complexes (under the control of the Brahmins and the ruling classes) and the construction of tanks or reservoirs that were not only the main source of water for the region, but also a meeting place for its residents.

Textile production flourished in different parts of the old city, and Bangalore is still important for silk production. During the Mughal era, Bangalore was the manufacturing and commercial capital of the princely state of Mysore. Textile production, particularly the well-established weaving industry, declined drastically with the advent of the British in the last decade of the eighteenth century. Cheaply priced machine-made cloth from England began flooding the Indian market, and the indigenous weavers could not compete. Indeed, colonial economic transactions, according to Nair, converted Bangalore into an entrepôt for British goods. In the 1700s, the British established the cantonment area in the eastern part of the city, and the marked distinction from the older, western part of the city persists to this day. The trade, manufacturing, and services that predominated in the cantonment were limited to what was needed to support the military. Colonial zoning regulations and modern town planning in the early part of the twentieth century reproduced existing class and caste hierarchies by creating purely residential areas. Compulsory building codes, fitness certificates for older buildings, outright demolition, and the creation of small parks or squares led to new upscale residential neighborhoods or gentrified older areas that were either mixed or predominantly working-class. Many areas that were previously inhabited by communities, such as those of the leather workers and potters, were razed following the plague epidemic of 1898. When rebuilt under rubrics of town planning after 1923, these areas were stripped of their working-class character. Migrant workers who started moving to the city in the 1930s to work in the mills and workshops, according to Nair, were crowded into the older areas of the city or the low-lying lands belonging to the municipality.

In the postindependence period of state-led industrialization in the late 1940s and 1950s, Bangalore became a hub for public-sector investment, led by the establishment of Hindustan Aircraft (now Hindustan Aeronautics Limited) in 1940, Indian Telephone Industries Limited in 1948, Hindustan Machine Tools Limited in 1955, and Bharat Electronics Limited in 1956. According to Nair, these were all located in the northern and eastern outskirts, separated from the city by agricultural lands. By the 1970s, other state-run units had been established, including national research and defense-based laboratories such as the National Aeronautical Laboratory, established in 1959 (now National Aerospace Laboratories). Large private-sector companies followed suit, but the state remained the main player in industrial production.

Since the mid-1980s, with the first phase of liberalization in India and the arrival of Texas Instruments, the focus began to shift away from public-sector enterprises to private-sector-led growth, dominated by computer software and hardware development. The skilled labor already existing in the public-sector establishments, the large numbers of engineering graduates from local and regional institutes of higher education, and proactive policies of the state governments fueled this transition. These new economy industries have been set up in the southeastern part of the city. The map of Bangalore today reflects the different economic and social histories of this divided city, differentiating the older, western parts from the newer cantonment areas of the colonial era and the more recent, high-tech corridor that stretches along the south-southeastern fringes of the city.

Globalization of the IT Industry: The Role of Bangalore

Advancements in the field of IT, especially software development and the expansion of Internet use, created some of the conditions for the global integration of markets. For example, it is now possible for corporations based in Bangalore to write software codes that can be digitally transmitted through the Internet, installed in a Microsoft software program in the United States or in hardware made in Taiwan, and sold in computer stores worldwide. Thus, without technological advancements in the IT industry, globalization in its current form would not be possible.

India's Software Industry

Since the late 1970s and early 1980s, a number of political and economic transformations have resulted in significant restructuring of the IT industry. Increasingly, countries of the Global South are emerging as major producers of IT goods and services and gaining recognition as new markets. Firms seeking cheaper skilled labor, new markets, and quick turnaround time have relocated software and IT-enabled services, comprising back-office operations such as data entry, call centers, and business process outsourcing (BPO), offshore to countries of the Global South. As a result, the inflow of direct foreign investment to these regions has increased.

Although the IT industry is very unevenly distributed in South Asia, India has emerged as an important player and has received global attention for attracting an increasingly significant proportion of these offshore service investments. There are various reasons why India became a popular destination for IT companies. First, India has a geographical advantage, in that it has almost a twelve-hour time difference with the United States. This means that companies in the United States can run twenty-four-hour operations, because when they close for the day, their Indian counterparts and service providers are just beginning their day. Second, India has a large pool of skilled labor from engineering and management schools. Third, given the country's colonial roots, English has been adopted as one of its official languages and is taught widely in schools. Finally, and most importantly, the Indian government has been proactively promoting the growth of the IT industry, with special incentives like tax exemptions, easy access to infrastructure, and deregulation of some labor laws. In fact, the computer industry was the first sector that got liberalized in the mid-1980s, even before India officially opened its economy to the global market in 1991.

Although India does not figure significantly in global manufacturing of IT products (computer hardware), it is a leader in the export of software services (coding, testing, and customizing software for particular sectors such as retail, airlines, and banking), especially when the total number of employees in the software industry is taken into account. The National Association of Software and Service Companies estimated that in 2011–2012, India's IT and IT-enabled services industry generated revenue worth US$87.6 billion and that the IT sector employed 2.8 million people directly and another 8.9 million people indirectly. One of the most significant aspects of employment generation is that this sector employs large numbers of women. According to estimates of the Ministry of Information and Communication Technology, in 2007 the proportion of women in high-skilled software production was more than 35 percent. However, in the lower-skilled call centers and BPOs, this proportion is much higher, reaching 69 percent according to official estimates. The incorporation of young, middle-class, English-speaking graduates, both women and men, into the country's fastest-growing, highly paid, and most globally integrated economic sector has wrought remarkable transformations in urban lifestyle and landscapes, in spaces of work and home.

In India the IT industry is unevenly distributed, concentrating mainly in the urban metropolitan regions. While the industry has its roots in Mumbai, it has shifted over the years toward the south, especially to Bangalore, which is historically referred to as a "Science City." Bangalore's laboratories nurtured research of national and strategic importance in the realms of science, technology, and defense. The southern region also has the highest number of engineering colleges, both private and state-sponsored, and the highest sanctioned capacity (that is, the number of seats allowed by the government for students in that college or university) of students. Two of the most prestigious engineering and management schools, Indian Institute of Technology in Chennai and Indian Institute of Management Bangalore, are located in this region. Thus, already existing institutional infrastructures and a potential supply of skilled labor made Bangalore an attractive location for software firms. As of early 2013, the city housed 125 multinational corporations and 1,150 software companies, accounting for more than 35 percent of India's software exports. In addition to Bangalore, other regional clusters of the software industry have sprung up, often due to concerted efforts by regional states.

Bangalore: India's "Silicon Valley"

There are two main clusters of high-tech firms in Bangalore: Electronics City in the southeast and International Technology Park Limited (ITPL) in the east. Apart from these two regions, software firms have also set up shop in various pockets in the city, including Koramangala, Jayanagar, HAL 2nd Stage, Airport Road, Lavelle Road, Whitefield Road, and Hosur Road. The concept of IT-led growth captured the imagination of Bangalore's political and technocratic elite, and it was particularly evident under the Congress Party leadership of S.M. Krishna, the chief minister of the state of Karnataka (of which Bangalore is the capital) from 1999 to 2004. Under his patronage, many public announcements and policy interventions established Bangalore as the "IT Capital of India."

As part of this process, Karnataka gave special incentives to the software industry, such as exemption from entry tax on computers and similar equipment and other capital investments up to five years from a project's commencement. The Karnataka State Pollution Control Board made it easier for this sector to get clearances under the Air Act and Water Act. In addition, it provided subsidized power, simplified labor laws, and investment in infrastructure, such as the construction of IT parks specifically for the needs of this industry. Indeed, Karnataka's IT-focused interventions have generated more investment for megadevelopment projects jointly financed by the government of India and international financial institutions like the World Bank. These include the new international airport, several new flyovers (overpasses), a major ring road, and a spectacular chrome-and-glass corporate center of information technology, the International Technology Park Limited in Whitefield. The International Tech Park is a joint venture between Tata Industries (the investment arm of the Tata Group), a Singapore consortium led by a company called Ascendas, and the Karnataka state government through the Karnataka Industrial Area Development Board.

For more on the International Tech Park, see the development's website (http://www.itpbangalore.com/).

The best-known example of the public-private partnership characteristic of the current form of globalization was the establishment in 1999 of the Bangalore Agenda

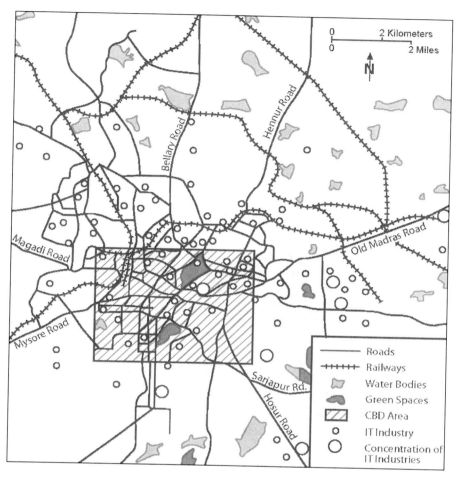

Map of Bangalore, showing IT-oriented areas and development.
(Adapted from IT Corridor Structure Plan—Final Report, in Nair 2005: 342)

Task Force (BATF), headed by Nandan Nilekani, CEO of Infosys, one of India's largest software companies. Most of BATF's leadership is made up of nominated senior leaders from the IT industry. Their agenda to streamline and improve the city's infrastructure for its efficient management was thus prioritized in urban planning. The BATF worked closely with other local government bodies. It has been lauded by both the World Bank and the central government as a successful model for emulation by other cities in India and abroad. At the same time, critics have exposed the middle-class and corporate bias in the urban reform programs of BATF, which, while converting Bangalore into a "world class" city, have completely sidelined the needs of the large number of urban poor by failing to address social welfare issues such as public health and education (Ghosh 2005).

It should be noted that "nominated" here refers to non-elected members. These people are not democratically elected by the people but nominated by the corporate/ IT sector. As a result, often urban reforms and initiatives taken in the name of "public interest" are really in the interest of the IT industry and the middle class people who work in it.

Several examples clearly reflect BATF's privileging of the interests of the corporate-led IT sector and the emerging new middle class in Bangalore. First, BATF proposed the IT corridor in 2003. The intention was to connect the two regional hubs of IT and software companies in the city—the ITPL in the east and Electronics City in the southeast. This continuous stretch of high-tech production also aims to link Bangalore to its neighboring state, Tamil Nadu. In line with the technocratic vision of converting Bangalore into a mirror image of Singapore, a Singapore-based company called Jurong Consultants was hired to prepare initial plans for building this 15.5-mile (25-kilometer) privatized enclave, which would provide a self-contained environment with world-class, state-of-the-art infrastructure, including residential, commercial, and recreational facilities for IT professionals to "live, work, play and strike business deals" in comfort. The construction of this spectacular private enclave for the exclusive benefit of the IT industry and its middle-class knowledge professionals not only reflects the inherent corporate bias in urban planning, but also necessitates the dispossession of poor farmers who would be divested of their land in the process.

The contentious issue of the Karnataka Industrial Area Development Board's land acquisition on behalf of IT firms is exacerbated by the sheer lack of consideration for proper compensation and relocation of poor landowners. Public debate over claims on the city by these indigent groups is exemplified by the case of Bellandur village on the outskirts of Bangalore, where local landowners have been resisting the offer of very poor compensation for the acquisition of prime land. During my visits to software companies in Electronics City, local auto-rickshaw drivers often told me how these land acquisition schemes provided some farmers with ready money for the short term, but deprived them of long-term security, turning many of them into daily wage laborers, as gardeners, food vendors, construction workers, and the like. The stark contrast between "world-class" office complexes and high-rise apartments in one area of the city and the increasing poverty and expansion of slums in another highlights the increasing gap between the prosperity of highly paid managerial and professional "knowledge workers" and the rest of the working classes. While IT companies are building the best infrastructural facilities and services on their campuses, the urban poor continue to have limited access to basic amenities such as water, toilet facilities, primary education, and basic health care. Despite the privileges already enjoyed by the IT sector, it continues to lobby for even more infrastructural facilities; in fact, senior executives often argue that if Bangalore is not able to provide better infrastructure for IT companies, it will lose its competitive edge to other cities.

Urban Transformation: New Spaces of Production and Consumption

The everyday activities of those who live and work in the city shape the urban landscape. This section demonstrates how specific spaces of urban production and consumption, directly or indirectly related to the IT industry, have emerged in Bangalore to cater to the rising demands of those who work in this sector.

Most of the big Indian software firms and foreign multinationals have located in large, self-sufficient, campus-like establishments, characterized by clean, air-conditioned office spaces and heavily guarded by private security. Entry and exit is strictly monitored. Software companies require workers to swipe punch cards to enter the premises, and to wear these cards strung around their necks. These access cards have become a key bodily marker that clearly distinguishes those who work in the IT sector in the city, although other sectors are readily adopting similar practices.

The luxurious corporate offices of the software firms, with their shiny glass facades, manicured lawns, and sophisticated telecommunication and power lines, are built on huge tracts of land acquired with government subsidies. These private enclaves strive to make India part of global business networks. "Infosys City," the headquarters of the Indian software giant Infosys, is a stellar example of how IT-led growth has become prioritized in Bangalore. Modeled on Western corporate standards, Infosys City boasts a swimming pool, a billiards and exercise room, a basketball court, a food court, retail outlets (including a grocery store that operates around the clock), and an open-air theater. These facilities project the image of a workplace that is safe and secure, where the boundaries between work and leisure are often blurred under the popular high-tech corporate slogan "Work is fun."

For more on Infosys City, see the web page "What a city!" (http://www.kora-mangala.com/korasoft/infosys.htm).

These spectacular corporate campuses are also adorned with replications of global icons like the Sydney Opera House and the Louvre Pyramid. When I was given the tour of the Infosys campus, I was told that these buildings were constructed to make foreign clients "feel at home" and to give Indian software professionals a glimpse of the "global." These global icons are supposed to instill a sense of pride and privilege (of working for a global technology firm) and to nurture the aspiration of foreign travel among the employees, as software work sometimes requires workers to travel abroad.

Software professionals, whose salaries are relatively higher than those in many other sectors in the country, are among the main consumers of Bangalore's swanky new cafés, malls, retail outlets featuring foreign brands, high-rise apartments, clubs, and bars. Those who frequent these meccas of urban India have played an important role in imbuing them

Global icons inside Infosys City: the Louvre Pyramid *(top)* and the Sydney Opera House *(bottom)*. *(Photos by Sanjukta Mukherjee)*

Box 18.2

Lifestyle Apartments: Homes for the IT Moguls

Many of these complexes are being built and marketed for nonresident Indians who live abroad but visit India regularly for business or to see family, and seek modern accommodations for their stays. Some may also intend to relocate to India at a later date.

with new meanings, as these spaces of consumption have become iconic of cosmopolitan, technomodern cities with a "global" outlook in contemporary India. By extension, visits to these spaces of consumption have become markers of a new social status. City governments and entrepreneurs acknowledge the importance of these icons in attracting and retaining "creative, high-tech talent" from within the country and in luring expatriates from abroad. A senior executive from one of Bangalore's largest software firm explained this perspective in a 2005 interview:

> Our employees are the best and the brightest creative talent India has to offer, most of them are graduates from premier engineering and management schools, . . . they deserve the best, . . . they have high standards and are not hesitant to ask for what they want. Many of them are roaming around with two to three job offers in hand, . . . all of them want to work in this city, we recruit from all over the country. . . . Bangalore is an exciting place for the youngsters [with] its great pubs and nightlife, cosmopolitan culture, multiethnic restaurants, and the well-reputed world-class workspaces.

In another mark of modern consumption, "lifestyle apartments" have taken Bangalore by storm. High real-estate prices notwithstanding, the propensity toward fancy, high-rise apartments modeled on international standards of the "IT moguls," often aided by housing loans from their companies, is spearheading a tremendous transformation of the city skyline. These multistory, gated communities boast such amenities as twenty-four-hour security, children's play areas, clubhouses with indoor games, and swimming pools. Realtors specifically target those who work in the IT sector, as shown in a 2004 real-estate listing in the "Housing Rentals" section of the *Deccan Herald* and *Times of India*: "Very conveniently and centrally located for people working in and around Koramangala, Inner Ring Road, Outer Ring Road, Electronic City and M.G. Road." The ad notes that these rentals are "most suitable" for nonresident Indians, employees of multinational corporations, and "Expats."

Bangalore has also seen a rapid mushrooming of shopping malls. Upscale stores and international brands are striving to transform middle- and upper-class consumption culture with the seductive lure of transforming shopping into an "experience" in sanitized, air-conditioned spaces. Multiplex theaters, food courts, and expansive car parks devoid of the dust, grime, and stark poverty of busy streets are changing the face of urban India.

The Acropolis, luxury homes in Koramangala by the Prestige Group. *(Photo by Sanjukta Mukherjee)*

For information on one of the largest malls in Bangalore, the Forum, visit the mall's website (http://www.theforumexperience.com/forumbangalore.htm).

Certain services have arisen specifically to meet the needs of the IT sector, such as food catering within the premises of software and IT companies, as well as immediately outside these twenty-four-hour office complexes. The food retail industry has also experienced a boom, with more supermarket-style establishments and the proliferation of ready-made processed food items. For those who work long and demanding hours, particularly women, but also young unmarried men, this is an asset. Companies such as Infosys actually have a Foodworld, one of the city's largest grocery chains, on campus. Another business venture directly related to the growth of the software and IT industry is private car pooling, providing safe and secure transport for employees and targeting mainly women during late hours of the night. However, these private car pools and other transport facilities that women use at night have become a source of critical debate in the aftermath of the increasing sexual violence against women in Indian cities.

Gender- and Class-Based Implications of IT-Led Development

The growth of the IT industry has had significant social and cultural impacts, with particular gender- and class-based ramifications in Bangalore. The average software professional is expected to be smart and well-dressed, with a good command of the English language. There are increasing numbers of women in the software industry, especially at entry level, which has altered the gender division of labor in the workplace. The image of a male "techie" is fast disappearing as women enter technology domains that used to be exclusively male. In 2003, 79 percent of software professionals in Indian software companies were men and 21 percent were women. This ratio has been narrowing rapidly; by 2007, the most recent year for which data are available, 65 percent were men and 35 percent were women. The increasing presence of Indian women in software, particularly in lower- and mid-level management, can be attributed to the rising dependence of software services on communication skills and gendered constructions of women as good communicators and organizers.

Software work has been constructed to be ideal for women because it entails flexible working hours, a safe and secure environment, nonstrenuous labor, and good communication skills. These attributes have led to new forms of exploitation, but at the same time they have provided middle-class professional women with new opportunities. For example, flexible hours allow women who have family responsibilities to negotiate different office hours or work from home, but it is also a corporate strategy that allows companies to hire more part-time and temporary workers who do not get the same pay or benefits as full-time workers.

Additionally, because this kind of job does not necessarily challenge women's roles as homemakers and caregivers, women often feel doubly burdened, finding it hard to balance the increasing demands of home and work. Nevertheless, those women who have managed to negotiate these challenges with consistent support from family and domestic help have found working in the software industry particularly rewarding. The financial independence that many young, middle-class women have achieved has allowed them to support their families. Indeed, some have become the sole breadwinners and gained more respect and social status within their communities. In addition, financial independence has allowed some women to negotiate traditional gender norms linked to household chores and the age at which they are married. For example, in a 2004 interview, Usha, a thirty-year-old software professional who works in one of the software firms in Bangalore as a program manager, remarked, "I work long hours, often coming home late at night, but I love what I do. I am responsible for my whole team, and this gives me the opportunity to hone my leadership skills. At home I have a very supportive husband and parents-in-law . . . they don't expect me to cook or clean, the usual stuff women do, you know."

Many women in this industry are also able to delay their age of marriage, stay single, or marry outside their caste or community. The construction of the software industry as a modern, progressive sector that is nationally important and has global ties is instrumental in the new status of middle-class women as professionals, and it has increased their access to public spaces in Bangalore.

Feminist geographers have often argued that access to public spaces in the city is gendered in unique and multiple ways. For some groups, the city provides mobility, new opportunities, and freedom; for others, however, it is a source of fear and alienation. In Bangalore, specific class-, caste-, and gender-based differences influence how people

Table 18.2

Crimes Against Women in Select Indian Cities, 2012

City	Female population (in 100,000s)	Rape		Kidnapping and abduction		Dowry deaths		Cruelty by husband or his relatives	
		I	P	I	P	I	P	I	P
Bangalore	40.58	90	2.98	433	7.78	51	7.47	524	3.12
Chennai	43.07	94	3.11	65	1.17	12	1.76	237	1.41
Delhi	75.76	585	19.34	1787	32.12	100	14.64	1870	11.14
Hyderabad	37.64	74	2.45	31	0.56	23	3.37	1339	7.97
Kolkata	67.93	68	2.25	210	3.77	19	2.78	865	5.15
Mumbai	85.20	232	7.67	141	2.53	11	1.61	388	2.31
Pune	23.90	85	2.81	77	1.38	9	1.32	215	1.28

Source: Adapted from statistics released by National Crime Records Bureau of India, Table 5.2, 2012. ncrb.gov.in.

Note: I = Incidence; P = Percent share of all cities listed.

There are limitations to these figures because they are not differentiated by caste, income bracket, religion, or other criteria that may make particular women more vulnerable than others. Also these figures are based on reported and convicted cases. There are many cases that do not get reported and the conviction rates are abysmally low.

experience the city. For the vast majority of urban poor and Dalits (members of the traditionally untouchable lower caste), the private, high-tech enclaves are inaccessible except as workplaces for janitors, cleaners, maids, cooks, gardeners, and drivers. The middle-class women who have attained a degree of financial freedom working in the software industry are challenging traditional patriarchal social norms about gender roles, transgressing many hitherto "appropriate" behavioral patterns that used to separate the private and public spaces for middle class women, and making themselves more visible in the city's new spaces of urban production and consumption. However, class-based differences continue to mark the "new economy" jobs and associated spaces of urban production and consumption as middle-class niches.

The increasing socioeconomic gap and cultural anxieties associated with these new types of work, particularly night shifts, have exposed some women to scathing comments questioning their morals and often made them targets of violence and sexual abuse. Although software and IT firms in Bangalore arrange car pools and escorts for their female workers, women increasingly feel unsafe, especially while accessing ATMs or driving home at night. According to regular reports in the national dailies *Deccan*

Herald and *The Hindu*, crimes against single, working women in Bangalore are on the rise. There have been several cases of sexual abuse, abduction, and murder of women working in the IT sector. In response to increasing demand to make Bangalore safe for women, particularly those who work in high-paying IT and BPO sectors, the municipal government has increased police patrols in specific city neighborhoods. However, this has not stopped these crimes, and gender-based violence continues to be a serious threat in Indian cities, including Bangalore.

Examples of violence against women are numerous. In 2005, a woman employed in a BPO company in Bangalore was abducted, raped and murdered by the driver of the car she was traveling in on her way to night shift. Recently a senior officer at the Bangalore based IT service company iGate was sacked following sexual harassment charges against him. According to a recent report (May 21, 2013) in the national daily *Hindustan Times*, "88% of women in India's IT/BPO sector reported having witnessed some form of workplace sexual harassment, according to the Workplace Sexual Harassment Survey conducted by NGO Centre for Transforming India in 2010" (http://www.hindustantimes.com/India-news/NewDelhi/Other-high-profile-sexual-harassment-cases/Article1-1063317.aspx).

The transformation of labor laws so that women are now allowed to work in night shifts in the IT industry has thus become a contentious arena for gender-based struggles. The IT industry requires workers to work beyond their stipulated eight hours, including night shifts. In India, historically, the Factories Act (1948) has protected against the deployment of women working at night. The IT industry has been lobbying the state to amend the labor laws to accommodate late-night working for women and to provide flexibility on daily staffing norms within the boundary of a forty-eight-hour workweek. In response to demands from the industry, the Labor Ministry and Ministry of Commerce stipulated that women would be allowed to work three shifts, subject to provision of all ILO-specified conveniences, including transport from and to the doorsteps of employees, and the Contract Labor Act was repealed for the IT industry.

The particular implications for extending women's working hours require that companies identify and provide a list of women who are willing to work at night, make sure work is carried out on a rotation basis, provide crèche (day-care) facilities and sufficient restrooms, and take responsibility for safe and secure transportation for these women at night. However, the issue of labor law is far from resolved, especially in the aftermath of the rape and murder of a Bangalore-based BPO employee in December 2005, the IT industry has attempted to become more vigilant about the security of their female employees, especially regarding background checks of the drivers and transport vendors they use for ferrying workers to and from their homes. A number of similar incidents (see Table 18.2) have been reported in other cities, including Gurgaon, Pune, and Delhi, and frequently the drivers that IT firms subcontract to transport their workers have been found guilty of these crimes. The National Commission for Women, a statutory body of the Indian government, initiated a roundtable discussion attended by women activists, senior officers from the Ministry of IT, and the police. Representatives from the Call Centre Association of India, set up in 2005, were also in attendance, and they lamented that while their organization has formulated strategies for the safety of women workers, it lacks the regulatory powers to demand compliance. None of the attendees, however, questioned the actual nature of high-tech work (the long hours and night shifts) or suggested legislation that would be binding on the employers. Organizations like the Centre of Indian Trade Unions have expressed concern over the health and safety of both male and female workers, drawn attention to social and cultural norms that often lead to women's double burden in this sector, and noted an overall shift in labor laws, without any protective measures, to curtail the rights of working people in the process of globalization.

The narratives of sexual abuse and murder in this industry are uncannily similar to the murder of almost 200 women, most of who worked in the maquiladora industry, from 1994 to 1999 in Ciudad Juarez, Mexico. Feminist scholars have argued that these deaths were intricately linked to the devaluation of such workers as unskilled, untrainable, temporary, and disposable, and to the uneven social and economic impacts of globalization in Mexican borderlands (Valentine 1989; Wright 2001). Similar to the "bad girl" image of the *maquila* women, the women who work odd hours in the IT industry in India have been on the receiving end of suspicion; they are often held up as exemplifying the "cultural decline" of Indian values due to increasing contact with the West—an ironic contrast to the IT sector's attempt to valorize these women as exemplars of a new, modern, tech-savvy India.

Thus, it is clear that women's increasing visibility in public spaces does not necessarily represent an unequivocally empowering experience of the city, for while it has increased some women's mobility and access to public spaces, it has simultaneously exposed them to new forms of surveillance, fear, and violence.

Conclusion: Uneven Development of IT-Led Growth

IT-led development has clearly created complex and contentious urban transformations in India. While the city of Bangalore has evolved into a "global city" with new and spectacular spaces of urban production and consumption linked to IT, such spaces have mostly benefited the middle classes. Income inequalities continue to rise, as this sector pays its employees more than any other formal sector in India, awarding those who work in it with new social status. The national and state governments continue to create special monetary and fiscal incentives, infrastructures, new special economic zones, and public-private partnerships for the IT industry at the expense of the agrarian sector, which in effect still employs the majority of India's working population. This is particularly problematic given that IT firms continue to be located in select urban centers, mostly metropolitan cities, resulting in uneven urban development in the country. Apart from the economic impacts, there has been significant social and cultural transformation in cities like Bangalore due to the emergence of the IT industry. In particular, the incorporation of large numbers of middle-class women in the new high-tech workplaces has somewhat altered the gender division of labor. Financial independence has provided some women with new social and cultural status at home (sometimes as the main breadwinner); enhanced their ability to play a role in decision making, delay marriage, and buy their own property; and given them increased mobility in the new spaces of urban consumption. However, this does not mean gender-based inequalities have been obliterated. In fact, women have been increasingly finding work in this sector based on the gendered stereotype that they are better communicators. The IT industry is still dominated by men who have more access to engineering degrees. Most of the women are found in entry-level positions and lower and middle management, and a gendered glass ceiling continues to thrive. In addition, employment in the IT sector, particularly working in night shifts, has exposed women to an increased threat of sexual violence.

Without doubt, the globalization of the IT sector in Bangalore has materially altered the everyday spaces of the city and is embodied in the lives of women and men who are part of it in complex and complicated ways. India is not alone in this development. For example, Singapore and Jakarta, Indonesia, have seen somewhat similar transformations. Of course, in the United States, Silicon Valley has a comparably transformed landscape, where the Google and Facebook campuses have replaced apricot orchards and farmlands and the poor are no longer visible, having been pushed out of the area. Here, too, are gated communities, fancy malls, private schools, and high housing costs. While the Internet has transformed the lives of many people around the globe as it reaches into homes, schools, and workplaces, it has also significantly transformed the spaces and communities of the companies that power it. Each of these transformed locales has a unique character, but common to all is a drastic transformation of space accompanied by social and economic exclusion for large segments of its poor and working classes.

References and Further Research

Benjamin, Soloman. 2000. "Governance, Economic Setting, and Poverty in Bangalore." *Environment and Urbanization.* 12, no. 1: 35–56.

Bidwai, Praful. 2003. "The Rise of the Cyber-Coolies." *New Statesman*, November 10. http://www.newstatesman.com/node/146674.

Ghosh, Asha. 2005. "Public-Private or a Private Public? Promised Partnership of the Bangalore Agenda Task Force." EPW Special Articles. *Economic and Political Weekly*, November 19–25, 4914–4922. http://www.sarai.net/research/urbanism/publications/asha01.pdf.

Mukherjee, Sanjukta. 2008. "Producing the Knowledge Professional: Gendered Geographies of Alienation in India's New High-Tech Workplace." In *In an Outpost of the Global Economy: Work and Workers in India's Information Technology Industry*, edited by Carol Upadhya and A.R. Vasavi, 50–75. New Delhi: Routledge.

Nair, Janaki. 2005. *The Promise of the Metropolis: Bangalore's Twentieth Century*. New Delhi: Oxford University Press.

Rajghatta, Chidanand. 2004. "Bangalore! BPO Bashers' War Cry." *Times of India*, July 21. http://portal.bsnl.in/bsnl/asp/content%20mgmt/html%20content/hotnews/hotnews38347.html.

Saith, Ashwani, and M. Vijayabaskar, eds. 2005. *ICTs and Indian Economic Development: Economy, Work, Regulation*. New Delhi: SAGE.

Srinivas, Smriti. 2001. *Landscapes of Urban Memory: The Sacred and the Civic in India's High-Tech City*. Minneapolis: University of Minnesota Press.

Upadhya, Carol, and A.R. Vasavi. 2008. *In an Outpost of the Global Economy: Work and Workers in India's Information Technology Industry*. New Delhi: Routledge.

Valentine, Gill. 1989. "The Geography of Women's Fear." *Area* 21, no. 4: 385–390.

Wilson, Elizabeth. 1991. *The Sphinx in the City: Urban Life, the Control of Disorder, and Women*. Berkeley: University of California Press.

Wright, Melissa W. 2001. "Feminine Villains, Masculine Heroes and the Reproduction of Ciudad Juarez." *Social Text* 19, no. 4: 93–113.

About the Editor and the Contributors

Susan Snow Wadley is the Ford Maxwell Professor of South Asian Studies at Syracuse University. She first went to India as an undergraduate in the 1960s, before studying anthropology at the University of Chicago. She is the author of numerous articles on gender, rural social change, and folklore and folk arts.

Sandeep Banerjee received his PhD in English and textual studies from Syracuse University in 2013 and is an assistant professor of English at McGill University, with a specialization in world Anglophone literatures. His primary work focuses on the varying landscapes presented in writings on South Asia in colonial and anticolonial writing.

Mitul Baruah is a doctoral student in geography at Syracuse University, where he is currently studying conflicts over water rights in the northeast regions of India. Previously he worked for the Foundation for Ecological Security in Rajasthan, India, before receiving an MA from the State University of New York College of Environmental Science and Forestry.

Subho Basu received his PhD in history from the University of Cambridge in 1994 and currently is associate professor of history at McGill University. He has written on work and labor politics in India, on politics and the state in Nepal, and on South Asian politics more generally.

Stephen Christopher is a doctoral candidate in anthropology at Syracuse University. In 2013, with support from a Fulbright grant, he will be conducting research on the ethnic interactions between the Tibetans and the traditional landholders of Dharamsala, India.

Mary Crawford is a professor emeritus of social psychology at the University of Connecticut. She specializes in feminist methodology, gender and communication, and, most recently, sex trafficking, especially in Nepal. Her book *Sex Trafficking in South Asia: Telling Maya's Story* was published by Routledge in 2010.

Tula Goenka is a filmmaker and social activist who received her MS in television, radio, and film at Syracuse University in 1986, where she now teaches filmmaking and Indian cinema at the S.I. Newhouse School of Public Communications. She regularly takes students to do internships in Bollywood.

Faris A. Khan is a doctoral student in anthropology at Syracuse University, where he is completing a dissertation on transgender identity politics in Pakistan. His research was funded in part by the American Institute of Pakistan Studies.

Karen McNamara studies medical anthropology at Syracuse University, where she is completing her dissertation on herbal remedies, pharmaceuticals, and the politics of health in Bangladesh. Her research was funded by a Fulbright-Hays Doctoral Dissertation Research Abroad fellowship and a junior research fellowship from the American Institute of Bangladesh Studies.

Sanjukta Mukherjee received her doctorate in geography from Syracuse University. Currently she teaches women and gender studies at DePaul University. Her work focuses on the changing dynamics of labor and gender linked to globalization in various Indian cities.

Robert Oberst received his PhD in political science from Syracuse University in 1981. Currently teaching at Nebraska Wesleyan University, he is one of the leading experts in the United States on Sri Lankan politics.

Nicole A. Wilson is completing a dissertation at Syracuse University, focusing on middle-class women residing in the southern Indian city of Madurai. A student of anthropology, her research was funded by a Fulbright-Hays Doctoral Dissertation Research Abroad grant.

Index

Note: Page numbers in *italics* indicate illustrations.